Climate Change in the Mediterranean

THE FONDAZIONE ENI ENRICO MATTEI (FEEM) SERIES ON ECONOMICS AND THE ENVIRONMENT

Series Editor: Carlo Carraro, *University of Venice, Venice and Research Director, Fondazione Eni Enrico Mattei (FEEM), Milan, Italy*

Editorial Board

The Fondazione Eni Enrico Mattei (FEEM) was established in 1989 as a non-profit, non-partisan research institution. It carries out high-profile research in the fields of economic development, energy and the environment, thanks to an international network of researchers who contribute to disseminate knowledge through seminars, congresses and publications. The main objective of the Fondazione is to foster interactions among academic, industrial and public policy spheres in an effort to find solutions to environmental problems. Over the years it has thus become a major European institution for research on sustainable development and the privileged interlocutor of a number of leading national and international policy institutions.

The Fondazione Eni Enrico Mattei (FEEM) Series on Economics and the Environment publishes leading-edge research findings providing an authoritative and up-to-date source of information in all aspects of sustainable development. FEEM research outputs are the results of a sound and acknowledged cooperation between its internal staff and a worldwide network of outstanding researchers and practitioners. A Scientific Advisory Board of distinguished academics ensures the quality of the publications.

This series serves as an outlet for the main results of FEEM's research programmes in the areas of economics, energy and the environment.

Titles in the series include:

The Endogenous Formation of Economic Coalitions
Edited by Carlo Carraro

Climate Change in the Mediterranean
Socio-economic Perspectives of Impacts, Vulnerability and Adaptation
Edited by Carlo Giupponi and Mordechai Shechter

Climate Change in the Mediterranean

Socio-economic Perspectives of Impacts, Vulnerability and Adaptation

Edited by

Carlo Giupponi

Professor of Agricultural Ecology and Agronomy, University of Milan, Italy and Coordinator of the National Resources Management Research Programme, Fondazione Eni Enrico Mattei (FEEM)

Mordechai Shechter

Professor of Economics and Director, Natural Resource & Environmental Research Center, University of Haifa, Israel

THE FONDAZIONE ENI ENRICO MATTEI (FEEM) SERIES ON ECONOMICS AND THE ENVIRONMENT

Edward Elgar
Cheltenham, UK • Northampton, MA, USA

Published by
Edward Elgar Publishing Limited
Glensanda House
Montpellier Parade
Cheltenham
Glos GL50 1UA
UK

Edward Elgar Publishing, Inc.
136 West Street
Suite 202
Northampton
Massachusetts 01060
USA

A catalogue record for this book
is available from the British Library

ISBN 1 84376 154 8

Printed and bound in Great Britain by MPG Books Ltd, Bodmin, Cornwall

Contents

Figures

Tables and boxes

TABLES

BOX

Contributors

Y. Avnimelech, Professor Emeritus, Water and Soil Sciences, Faculty of Civil and Environmental Engineering, Technion, Israel Institute of Technology, Haifa, Israel

O. Ayalon, Dr, Natural Resource and Environmental Research Center, University of Haifa and S. Neaman Institute, Technion, Israel Institute of Technology, Haifa, Israel

Gérard Begni, Director of MEDIAS-France

E. Bou-Zeid, Graduate Student, Department of Geography and Environmental Engineering, Johns Hopkins University, Baltimore, MD, USA

Carlo Carraro, Professor of Econometrics and Environmental Economics, University of Venice, Italy; Research Director, Fondazione Eni Enrico Mattei (FEEM), Milan, Italy

Alberto Garrido Colmenero, Associate Professor, Department of Agricultural Economics, Universidad Politécnica de Madrid, Spain

Mutasem El-Fadel, Department of Civil and Environmental Engineering, Faculty of Engineering and Architecture, American University of Beruit, Lebanon

Guy Engelen, Research Institute for Knowledge Systems b.v., Maastricht, The Netherlands

Samuel Fankhauser, European Bank for Reconstruction and Development, London, UK

Dimitris G. Georgas, Marine Geologist, United Nations Environmental Programme/Mediterranean Action Plan Consultant on Impacts of Climatic Change, Athens, Greece

Carlo Giupponi, Professor of Agricultural Ecology and Agronomy at the University of Milan, Italy and Coordinator of the Natural Resources Management Research Programme, Fondazione Eni Enrico Mattei (FEEM)

Ana Iglesias, Research Scholar at the Universidad Politecnica de Madrid, Spain and collaborator with the Goddard Institute for Space Studies at Columbia University, New York, USA

Mohamad R. Khawlie, Director and Chief Researcher at the National Center for Remote Sensing, Beirut, Lebanon

Richard J.T. Klein, Potsdam Institute for Climate Impact Research (PIK), Germany

Onno J. Kuik, Institute for Environmental Studies, Vrije Universiteit, Amsterdam, The Netherlands

Wietze Lise, Economic Researcher, Institute for Environmental Studies, Vrije Universiteit, Amsterdam, The Netherlands

Eva Iglesias Martínez, Department of Agricultural Economics, Universidad Politécnica de Madrid, Spain

Manuel Menendez, Spanish Ministry of Public Works, Spain

Allen Perry, Senior Lecturer, Department of Geography, University of Wales, Swansea, UK

Almudena Gómez Ramos, Department of Agricultural Economics, Universidad Politécnica de Madrid, Spain

S. Reese, Research and Technology Centre West Coast, University of Kiel, Germany

Paolo Rosato, Department of Civil Engineering, University of Trieste and Fondazione Eni Enrico Mattei (FEEM), Italy

Cynthia Rosenzweig, NASA Goddard Institute for Space Studies, USA

Mordechai Shechter, Professor of Economics and Director, Natural Resource & Environmental Research Center, University of Haifa, Israel

Joel B. Smith, Stratus Consulting Inc., Boulder, CO, USA

Horst Sterr, Professor, Department of Geography and Coastal Research Institute FTZ, University of Kiel, Germany

Richard S.J. Tol is the Michael Otto Professor of Sustainability and Global Change at the Centre for Marine and Climate Research, Hamburg University, Germany; Principal Researcher at the Institute for Environmental Studies, Vrije Universiteit, Amsterdam, The Netherlands and Adjunct Professor at the Center for Integrated Study of the Human Dimensions of Global Change, Carnegie Mellon University, Pittsburgh, PA, USA

M. Neil Ward, International Research Institute for Climate Protection, Columbia University, New York, USA

Nahum Yehoshua, Graduate Student at the Department of Natural Resource and Environmental Management and Research Assistant at the Natural Resource & Environmental Research Center at the University of Haifa, Israel

Preface

The co-operation between the network RICAMARE (Research in Global Change in the Mediterranean: a Regional Network) and the Fondazione Eni Enrico Mattei (FEEM) has been very fruitful. In the last years, not only have several workshops on the economic impacts of climate changes in the Mediterranean been organised, but also new research efforts have been undertaken and the related research reports have been disseminated through the FEEM working paper series. This book is an effort to provide a synthesis of those workshops, researches and publications. Here, some of the best papers presented at the FEEM workshop on 'Impacts of Climate Change in the Mediterranean Area' – held in Venice and attended by several researchers belonging to RICAMARE – and at the FEEM-RICA-MARE workshop on 'Socio-economic Assessments of Climate Change in the Mediterranean', held in Milan, are collected and re-organised. The goal of this collection is to provide an overview of recent knowledge on the economic impacts of climate change on Mediterranean industries, coastal zones and ecosystems. The studies contained in this book cover both methodological and empirical issues, provide interdisciplinary analyses of climate change impacts, discuss recent empirical results and observations, and explore the policy implications of those analyses and results. I am very grateful, also on behalf of FEEM, for the work provided by Carlo Giupponi and Mordechai Shechter, editors of this book, who organised the workshops, gathered the papers, co-ordinated a careful refereeing process and helped all authors to improve their papers. The final output is very good. This book is both informative and stimulating. New researches are likely to be based on the results and analyses contained in this volume, which therefore constitutes a first step towards a better understanding of the economic consequences of climate change in the Mediterranean. I am also grateful to FEEM staff, and particularly to Monica Eberle and Rita Murelli, for the excellent organisation of the workshops, to Roberta Ranzini for editorial assistance, and to Gérard Begni and the network RICAMARE for their support and co-operation.

Carlo Carraro
Research Director and Series Editor
Fondazione Eni E. Mattei

Foreword: Bridging physical and socio-economic research in the Mediterranean basin

Gérard Begni

Political, industrial and commercial specific interests, as well as public opinions balanced within extreme sensitivities, most often obscure the debates about global change issues, consciously or not. There is a wide range of viewpoints on these issues, two extreme being to consider them as an abstract intellectual speculation without any day-to-day interest, or as a major threat to mankind, more or less related to metaphysical fears of a mythological final apocalypse. On other opposite sides, people feel either strongly motivated to act against adverse events, or consider them as a manifestation of an everlasting destiny. In addition, *bona fide* people tend to analyse such phenomena according to how much they remind them of a few years period change, a time scale in which significant long-term changes are quite obscured by natural interannual variability. Facing such rational or irrational debates, scientists have a major and unavoidable responsibility. Addressing global change issues over the longest possible period, including paleoclimates, and at least using the very detailed information collected in past decades from an authentic scientific point of view, is mandatory. According to basic ethical rules, it is absolutely necessary to analyse and underline basic hypotheses, qualify and, whenever possible, quantify uncertainties sources. This is a complex task, especially when regional levels such as the Mediterranean basin are taken into consideration.

The Mediterranean region is a transition area covering the Mediterranean Sea as such and land encompassing it, limited by deserts to the south and temperate areas to the north. It is characterised by contrasting variations in temperature and precipitation between winter and summer. Winters are cool and relatively wet, while summers are warm and dry. The climate is very variable on interannual to secular time frames, and prone to extremes. The ocean and land ecosystems are undergoing rapid change with a strong impact on the well-being of people living in lands surrounding its shores. The region is very varied and is one of the richest in the world in terms of biodiversity. Water is a limiting resource, not only for plants and animals, but also for humans. The geographic complexity of the region deeply impacted the cultural, social, economic and political history of Mediterranean populations, which in turn have left a strong imprint on its environment. Ecosystems and landscapes are mainly the product of ancient human use. Cultural features are strongly embedded in the landscape, and there is a sharp contrast in socio-economic features, particularly along the north–south gradient. It is very densely populated along the shores of the Mediterranean Sea. The south is experiencing considerable population growth, and imbalances are likely to increase in coming decades, making pressures on scarce water resources more and more acute.

So the Mediterranean basin is indeed a highly heterogeneous region. Natural phenomena interact in a very complex way. Human activity has strong feedback on climate at both local and regional scales. In socio-economic terms there is a wide spectrum of interactions with natural impacts, from local to regional scales. They in turn impact on land use and land cover practices, and more generally on economic and social factors, such closing the loop.

The Mediterranean basin climate is also very sensitive to interactions with other parts of the world, for instance influences of the North Atlantic Oscillation (NAO), of the Indian Monsoon, and of dust transported from the Sahara to the Atlantic Ocean through the Mediterranean basin. This is also obviously true in socio-economic terms since the various Mediterranean nations are integrated in different international political and socio-economic structures, while 'globalisation' is strongly impacting the agriculture, industry and trading balances of most countries in the region.

While such complex interactions exist under 'stationary' climatic conditions it has been established that 'there are stronger evidences that most of the warming observed over the last 50 years is attributable to human activities' (IPCC, 2001 – see http://www.ipcc.ch). Such a climate tendency must have some impacts on the Mediterranean basin and neighbouring regions, such as sea level rise and modified rainfall patterns. It should be emphasised that, during the past 50 years, there has been evidence of global change and projected signatures onto the Mediterranean Sea. In this context and without careful planning, no long-term sustainable development can reasonably be envisioned in the Mediterranean basin. This is true at local, national, sub-regional and basin-wide levels.

Assessing the environmental status of the Mediterranean becomes a prerequisite – at least for the sake of knowledge and future implementation. This can be done following a nested methodological approach, going from simple to complex issues:

- Assuming that no natural or human-induced changes are occurring, what is the environmental status of the region at large?
- Assuming no global change is occurring, what are the relative influences of both natural and anthropic pressures? Can we identify relevant indicators to monitor environmental and sustainable environment evolutions? Subsequently can we apply regulatory actions? What scenarios have to be used in running numerical models in order to predict future changes and anthropic action feedback?
- Assuming global change impacts on regional scales, what happens to the picture? Do we need additional scenarios? How can numerical models tackle physical mechanisms on a regional scale? What are the resulting uncertainties? Which major impacts are likely to be expected? Are there any additional and/or modified proactive solutions to apply?

Considerable efforts have been made to improve predictions about climate change. Nevertheless, the results still remain somehow uncertain, particularly at regional level in such a complex area. The fourth report of the ECLAT-2 concerted action[1] presents some key results in that regard. Nevertheless, the climate change features in the Mediterranean region remain poorly studied and documented so far, as it may appear when looking for results the 2001 IPCC reports. It is generally acknowledged that the region could be severely impacted by changes in climate, most notably by changes in the precipitation regime. Current model projections into the 21st 'greenhouse gas' century tend to show quite a contrasting evolution between the northern and southern sides: intense warming and drying in the south; moderate warming and little variations, or even an increase of the precipitation in the north. Most likely, small alterations in water availability could have critical consequences at all natural and human levels in the region. Understanding such potential consequences of regional climate change therefore appears to be a critical issue. So, during the past years, a number of planning initiatives of Mediterranean regional significance have taken place aiming at evaluating its sensitivity to these impending threats of global change and promoting a regional research agenda.

Under the joint impetus of START[2] and the ENRICH[3] programme of the European Commission, a workshop was held in Toledo, Spain, from 25 to 28 September, 1996. Its objective was to set up a regional scientific agenda pinpointing the priorities to be refined by regional scientists in conjunction with the representatives of the international global change research programmes. A major conclusion was that a system approach was necessary to understand the many interactions in the region between the various intervening global change factors. Severe gaps appeared in such a regional integrated approach.

Taking such gaps into due consideration, some core actors of the Toledo workshop set up the RICAMARE project,[4] which was endorsed at the end of 1998 by the European Commission as a concerted action and carried out from 1999 to 2001. RICAMARE was sponsored by two EC programmes (ENRICH and INCO-DC[5]), by START and to a less extent by some other national and international sources (such as, for instance ICTP[6], CIHEAM[7], FEEM, CNES[8], UCLM[9], IBERDROLA[10]). It focused on a few multidisciplinary, intersecting issues that deserve additional attention before they shape up into collaborative projects of regional importance. RICAMARE purposely linked natural and social scientists from the countries around the Mediterranean who are interested in tackling the inter-relationships between the natural and human environment in order to develop strategies for sustainable development in the region.

RICAMARE was organised into three 'activities': building a regional research agenda, setting up capacity building actions and leading outreach activities. These three activities focused on four major synergistic issues, two related to some key physical aspects, one to data collection, validation and assimilation, and one, held in Milan in 2001, to socio-economic aspects.

'Global change' usually refers to human-induced climate changes at the planetary level and associated impacts. In the Mediterranean basin, integrated impacts are due to anthropic 'local' activities which are superimposed on (or coupled to) the global change. Those impacts might then be amplified or accelerated. In any case a serious environmental assessment must take into account these two combined sources. Sorting out their individual actions, if possible, may be vital for local or regional decision-making processes. Indeed, different policies to mitigate adverse impacts have to be set up and adopted for 'local', 'regional' and 'global' change issues. The ambition of the authors of the present volume is to bring a modest contribution of their own to that highly challenging objective.

NOTES

1. ECLAT-2 – Applying climate scenarios for regional studies with particular references to the Mediterranean, Toulouse workshop report No. 4, Toulouse, France, 25–27 October 2000, edited by Serge Planton, Clair Hanson, David Viner and Michel Hoepffner.
2. START (global change system for analysis, research and training; http ://www.start.org) is a joint initiative of the three major international programmes addressing global change issues: IGBP, IHDP and WCRP.
3. European Network Research in Global Change, an initiative of the European Commission.

4. The RICAMARE project was co-ordinated by Dr Gérard Begni and Pr J.M. Moreno, UCLM.
5. International Co-operation with Developing Countries, a programme of the DG Research of the European Commission.
6. International Centre for Theoretical Physics (Trieste, Italy).
7. French acronym of international centre for high agronomic studies.
8. CNES is the French space agency.
9. University of Castilla-la Mancha, located in Toledo, Spain.
10. IBERDROLA is a major Spanish private company.

PART I

Introduction

Introduction

Carlo Giupponi and Mordechai Shechter

There is rather wide concensus in the scientific community regarding the climatic consequences of doubling CO_2 concentrations, and the potential negative impacts of climate change on natural and human-made systems, as well as human communities. These impacts, aggravated by socio-economic driving forces, such as population growth, deserve careful investigation by social scientists, especially in regions which are already under development and population stresses, such as the Mediterranean, especially along its southern and eastern perimeters. It is expected that climate change will exacerbate many of the area's existing problems, including desertification, water scarcity and limits to food production. Changes in weather patterns and average temperatures are also likely to introduce new threats to human health and natural ecosystems. Such predictions, therefore, should provide a strong motivation for the scientific community to work on developing more accurate and integrated analyses of future scenarios for the area and its sub-regions, to increase our knowledge base and our ability to formulate strategies for adapting to new climatic conditions.

Thus observational records suggest marked changes in the climate of the Mediterranean region over recent years. Models developed by the most advanced institutes coincide in projecting temperature rise and decline in rainfall in the Mediterranean basin. Furthermore, there are some indications that the rainfall pattern could also see an increase in its intra- and inter-annual variability, with greater probability in the basin areas that flow into the Mediterranean. While it is impossible at the moment to be certain whether those changes represent significant trends or depend on short- and medium-term variability, it is also clear that significant proof of changes will be available only after remarkable impacts have started to occur. It is therefore necessary to be prepared for the future evolution of climate, to identify potential impacts and the most vulnerable situations, and to define adequate strategies for the adaptation to and mitigation of those impacts.

More specifically, a number of possible environmental and socio-economic impacts of climate change in the Mediterranean have frequently been mentioned in the literature: coastal flooding, erosion, sea water intrusion in aquifers, which could cause unacceptable hardship for particularly

3

vulnerable populations (e.g. those living on small island states), or threats to economic activity (e.g. tourism) in coastal zones; an increased probability of large-scale climate instabilities (e.g. a shutdown of the Gulf Stream), with very costly impacts on economies through floods and storms; an increase in the extent and severity of desertification, with possible consequent migration pressures due to changes in land use; increased frequency of water shortages and decline in water quality; food security threatened by a fall in production and world price rises; widespread risks to public health; and losses of valuable ecosystems and biodiversity, with potential threat to certain unique and valuable systems.

The present volume is one such attempt to address, in some greater depth, a number of key issues regarding socio-economic aspects of climate change impacts on various regions around the Mediterranean, their vulnerability to possible impacts, and the potential for adaptation. It brings together selected contributions from two recent international workshops which have focused on these very issues, and thus provides us with a close look at some of the scientific work carried out in these areas in recent years.

The first workshop, 'The Impacts of Climate Change on the Mediterranean Area: Regional Scenarios and Vulnerability Assessment', was held in Venice in December, 1999 and organised by FEEM (with the financial support of the European Commission, DG-Environment) and the Venetian Institute of Arts and Sciences. The objective of that meeting was twofold: (1) To assess the state of knowledge about regional climate scenarios and the potential impacts of climate change on the Mediterranean area, and (2) to identify effective strategies and measures in response to climate change.

The second workshop, 'Socio-economic Assessments of Climate Change in the Mediterranean: Impacts, Adaptation, and Mitigation Co-benefits', held in Milan in February 2001 and hosted by FEEM, was one of the activities of a European Commission Concerted Action project, titled RICA-MARE (*R*esearch *I*n global *Ch*A*nge in the *M*editerranean: *A RE*gional network), and funded by ENRICH, INCO-DC) and START. The overall objectives of RICAMARE were: (1) to define a medium-term regional research agenda on major global issues in the Mediterranean, in order to allow scientists to define research projects in line with major societal concerns, and policy-makers to set up the appropriate structures to lead such projects; (2) seeking to enlarge the circle of researchers who may lead such works, by encouraging networking efforts, spreading information and results, and organising courses in order to give young scientists the relevant means and knowledge to address these research domains in their professional plans. The Milan workshop aimed to (1) present ongoing or planned research projects on the impacts of global climate change on social and economic systems in the Mediterranean basin, in relation to such areas as water resources, agriculture and forestry, desertification, biodiversity, extreme weather events, sea-level rise and coastal areas, human health, tourism, and others; and (2) to set a research agenda for and create a network of social scientists from the Mediterranean basin, whose scope was intended to be interdisciplinary, with a primary focus on social science and related research.

Selected papers from the two conferences, revised and updated following a refereeing process, have been included as chapters in this volume and grouped into four sections.

The two chapters in Part II, by Tol *et al.* and Klein, set the general stage by addressing the principal issues of this volume – the social and economic aspects of climate change impacts, vulnerability and adaptation – from a broad, global perspective.

In shaping policies to control climate change, decision-makers invariably focus on the aggregate, in addition to the sectoral, or resource-specific impacts of climate change. Emissions reduction is costly and abatement costs should therefore be balanced against the avoided costs of climate change. Tol and his co-authors particularly address the issue of aggregate costs of climate change, and their distribution over world regions or individual countries. A key challenge for social scientists in this endeavour is the need to reduce the complex pattern of local and individual impacts to a more tractable set of indicators that can effectively summarise and make comparable the impacts in different regions, sectors or systems in a meaningful way. The authors argue that physical metrics suffer from being inadequately linked to human welfare. Instead, if the aim is to integrate the impacts of climate change with standard national accounts, it is necessary to express the costs of climate change in the same metric, that is money. Money is a particularly well suited metric to measure market impacts – that is, impacts that are linked to market transactions and directly affect GDP. It is less successful, however, to assess non-market impacts, such as effects on ecosystems or human health, in money terms. Nonetheless, the chapter presents an overview of various economic studies which have attempted to assess aggregate future damage from current emissions of greenhouse gases.

Klein's chapter underlines the crucial role of adaptation capacity-building in helping societies face future climate change impacts. It asserts that adaptation is intricately linked with non-climatic developments and takes place in a dynamic societal context. The identification of optimal and appropriate adaptation strategies is therefore fraught with difficulties. The chapter explores these caveats and discusses their implications for policy and funding. It concludes that the quantitative assessment of future adaptation costs and benefits should play a less significant part in determining the optimality or appropriateness of adaptation options. Instead, we should attempt to assess the economic value of an adaptation project to today's society and identify no-regret adaptation options, which would help to reduce vulnerability to both contemporary climate variability and anticipated climate change. Strengthening adaptive capacity and raising awareness should serve to create an enabling environment for adaptation.

Part III presents four chapters which focus on what is probably the most widely studied problem related to climate change in the Mediterranean: water resources. The first contribution by El-Fadel and Bou-Zeid deals in particular with the Middle East area. This chapter looks at the main water resources issues in several Middle Eastern countries and considers regional climate predictions by general circulation models for various scenarios. Adaptation measures are assessed with a focus on no-regret actions in the context of local socio-economic and environmental frameworks. Several potential socio-economic impacts are considered, such as a reduction of GDP, and population redistribution, as a consequence of altered water balances and resource stocks, which in turn may determine negative consequences like increased agricultural water demand, deriving from an expected average temperature rise of between 0.6 and 2.1°C.

Ana Iglesias *et al.* examine the possible adaptation strategies for agriculture under climate change in the Mediterranean. The food security issue is evaluated in face of the social impacts of increasing water scarcity in the Mediterranean. Sources of conflicts for water resources could come from concurrent increasing population and urbanisation, and expanding irrigation needs, in the case of Southern Mediterranean countries, presenting inadequate controls of water use, lack of political will, and cultural impediments. In-depth discussions about agriculture in various Mediterranean countries are presented, starting from the consideration that irrigation is the major consumer of water in the area, using more than two-thirds of the water withdrawn from the rivers, lakes and aquifers. Considerations about the risk management in agricultural production, as related to the ability to understand and respond to climate variability and change are derived in view of more effective decision-making processes for improving resource-use efficiencies that may lead to a reduction of current and future emergency actions.

Khawlie, in Chapter 5, discusses the impacts of climate change on water resources, focusing in particular on Lebanon and the Eastern Mediterranean. Contrary to current notions about water abundance in Lebanon, the author presents the current serious problems of water scarcity and water quality and their relations with social and economic origins; that is, management, low finance, non-integration and a lack of relevant awareness on water use. Once more the chapter presents the risks of further exacerbation of such problems expected as a consequence of climate change.

A relevant issue discussed by Khawlie is the availability of adequate data sets for interpreting correctly the trends of change: precipitation records, in fact, reflect a decreasing pattern over the last century. The need for adequate adaptation measures by both the public and private sectors is evidenced with different opportunities from short- to medium- to long-term phases.

Eva Iglesias *et al.* consider the economic impact of climate change in irrigated farming. Once more agricultural use of water is presented as a crucial aspect of water resource management in the Mediterranean in the future. The chapter focuses in particular on the Spanish situation and presents an approach based on a dynamic stochastic model that integrates climatic, hydrological, institutional and economic components, and evaluates economic losses resulting from plausible scenarios of climate change. The results from two irrigated areas in the Guadalquivir basin reveal that the economic impacts of climate projections may translate into a significant reduction of farmers' profits that could reach 24 per cent. Also, as drought episodes are expected to be more severe and frequent, as a consequence the economic losses will be more persistent and the return to average economic conditions after a drought shock will be significantly slowed down.

Part IV is devoted to Mediterranean lands, with one chapter on desertification and land degradation in general, two focusing in particular on agricultural land use, and one dealing with waste management. Rosato and Giupponi propose a methodology to integrate socio-economics in climate change scenarios, a relevant issue in current research in climate change, which attempts to provide always more integrated approaches in which interrelated cause–effects relationships of environmental and human drivers are simultaneously considered. The chapter presents first the main traits and prospects for Mediterranean agricultural systems, the possible direct and indirect consequences of climate change and the main adaptation options. Some concepts and definitions of the theory of scenario development are then presented to introduce the methodological proposal for building locally consistent agricultural scenarios. Some numerical examples are presented to clarify the procedure and conclusions are drawn about the potential of the proposed approach.

In Chapter 8 Engelen presents the results of European projects in which a decision support system tool was developed – MODULUS-DSS, for integrated environmental policy-making at the regional level. Details of the integration of various dynamic models at different spatial and temporal scales are presented, together with their implementation in a computerised context. Two applications in pilot case studies in Greece and Spain are reported and lessons drawn from those experiences are highlighted, in particular regarding the relationships between science and policy-making on a regional scale. In particular the difficulties in setting up effective relationships between scientists and local stakeholders during the time frame of a research project are discussed.

Yehoshua and Shechter present an exploratory economic assessment of climate change impacts on Israeli agriculture, in monetary terms. In attempting a preliminary estimate of expected future damage to agriculture in Israel resulting from climate change, the authors investigate the effects of uncertainty about the effects of farmers' adaptation options, the nature of demand for water, and the role of agriculture in the national economy. These sources of u ncertainty are added to the inherent uncertainty in forecasting climate change impacts. Also in this case the lack of adequate regional and local data is reported as a main problem for accurate estimations. Contrasting with other less developed countries of the Mediterranean, Israeli agriculture is an example of a highly technological and sophisticated sector, which has provided, during the past 50 years, increased yields of 16-fold, introducing also a variety of new crops. In more recent times, the economic role of agriculture has followed a similar path to the more developed countries, contributing only 2.4 per cent of GDP, with the proportion of labour employed in agriculture at around 3.4 per cent, and agricultural exports amounting to 4 per cent of total exports. Notwithstanding the peculiarity of the Israeli situation, the main issues are seen to be quite similar to the rest of the Mediterranean. The results of this exercise pointed out the importance of adaptation and correct proactive planning in counteracting the adverse effects of climate change. In addition to providing a range of quantitative economic estimates of costs, this is probably the major lesson of the study.

Ayalon *et al.* present an assessment of the ancillary socio-economic benefits of mitigating greenhouse gases from municipal solid waste management. In the sustainable management of the organic fraction of the waste, the ultimate goal is to minimise the amount of methane (CH_4), produced by biological processes of the organic content, by converting it to carbon dioxide (CO_2). The most cost-effective means to treat the degradable organic components is by aerobic composting which provides ancillary socio-economic benefits such as increasing the fertility of arid soils.

The authors propose that such an approach could be implemented, especially in developing countries, in order to reduce significantly the amount of greenhouse gases (GHG) for relatively low costs and in a short time. The chapter points out at this point that the development of a national policy for proper waste treatment could be a significant means to abate GHG emissions in the short term, enabling them to gain time and to develop other means for the long run. In addition, the use of CO_2 quotas will credit the waste sector and will promote a profitable proper waste management.

Part V of this volume deals with the assessment of impacts on coastal zone areas around the Mediterranean, and their vulnerability, a topic which has probably received a relatively large amount of attention, especially in light of development pressures on coastal environments and communities.

Georgas's chapter (Chapter 11) is a comprehensive review of 14 completed first-, second- and third-generation site-specific case studies in the Mediterranean region, carried out in the past 15 years. Today, the Mediterranean coastal zone is home to 70 per cent of the population, and responsible for 80 per cent of industrial activity and 90 per cent of tourism income. Although in the near future the vulnerability from climatic changes is expected to be one of the major consequences of coastal planning, sound central policy options are almost lacking. Consequently, he concludes that early preparation of Mediterranean climate impact studies could be considered as a very cost-effective and successful exercise through which countries and their interdisciplinary experts should be enlisted to study the potential threat that climate change may pose on their environment and socio-economic development.

The chapter by Sterr *et al.* deals in a more generic fashion with the socio-economics of climate change impacts on coastal zones, with a brief review of lessons drawn from German studies. Knowledge of vulnerability enables coastal scientists and policy-makers to anticipate impacts that could emerge as a result of sea-level rise, helping to prioritise management efforts that need to be undertaken to minimise risks or to mitigate possible consequences. One very important lesson – not confined, of course, to this area – is that data collection and information development are essential prerequisites for vulnerability assessment as well as for coastal adaptation. Coastal adaptation requires data and information on coastal characteristics and dynamics, and patterns of human behaviour, as well as an understanding of the potential consequences of climate change. In addition, there must exist awareness among the public and coastal planners and managers of these consequences and of the possible need to act.

The last two chapters in this part focus on tourism. Tourism, being volatile and situation-specific, is responsive to climate change. As Perry points out in Chapter 13, it is a major economic activity as the Mediterranean, especially in coastal zone areas, is currently the world's most popular and successful tourist destination, with 120 million visitors every year. Climate constitutes an important part of the environmental context in which recreation and tourism take place. Since tourism is a voluntary and discretionary activity, participation depends on favourable climatic conditions. The tourist industry is by its very nature fragile and susceptible to political, economic and social changes; the probability of climate change would add a significant element of uncertainty to planning future developments. Not unexpectedly, he argues that more research is needed to quantify the tourists' well-being, which can in turn be calibrated to include the effects of climate change, because the primary resources of sun, sea and beaches are likely to be re-evaluated in the light of climate change.

Lise and Tol have indeed conducted an empirical investigation from which one could draw some quantitative implications regarding tourist welfare in this context. Their chapter provides a cross-section analysis on destinations of OECD tourists and a factor and regression analysis on holiday activities of Dutch tourists, in an attempt to identify optimal temperatures at travel destination for different tourists and different tourist activities. Globally, OECD tourists prefer a temperature of 21°C (average of the hottest month of the year) at their choice of holiday destination. This indicates that, under a scenario of gradual warming, tourists would spend their holidays in different places than they currently do. The factor and regression analysis suggests that preferences for climates at tourist destinations differ among age and income groups. More work is of course needed in order to explicitly address the question of how predicted changes in climatic conditions would affect Mediterranean tourism. A very tentative conclusion, which should be greatly qualified given the nature of their work, is that the impact would probably be negative overall.

Many open methodological and research issues have been discussed in this book and indications for a future research agenda are also touched on, as they were also in the two events that gave rise to the present book. First of all is the need to launch research initiatives aimed at supporting integrated multidisciplinary work on the Mediterranean as a whole. A crucial starting point, mentioned by various authors, will be data collection and distribution of knowledge, which should be facilitated and targeted to comprehensive studies on both the northern and the southern shores of the sea.

A model or structure should be developed specifically for scenario development and for the analysis of vulnerability, and the potentials for mitigation and adaptation at the local level. These analyses should be conducted while maintaining an overall figure at the regional level and also maintaining consistency with larger-scale scenarios (continental to global). Several different categories of changes should be assessed: that is, population, economy, natural resources, etc.

The common aim of analyses should be the provision of results, which could have a significance for policy orientation, through better understanding of phenomena and more efficient implementation strategies.

Communication will play a fundamental role in future climate change research in the Mediterranean, both in terms of enhanced networks of scientists working in the various fields, but also in terms of the involvement of policy-makers and stakeholders at the various levels and from the various societal sectors.

It is the hope of the editors that this book could give a contribution in these directions.

ACKNOWLEDGEMENTS

The editors wish to extend a special word of appreciation to Ms Roberta Ranzini and Ms Luisa Rovetta of FEEM, for their highly efficacious editorial assistance. We are indebted to FEEM, and particularly its Scientific Director, Professor Carlo Carraro, for providing a most congenial and supportive environment for carrying out this work. Dr Gérard Bengi and Professor Jose Moreno, co-directors of the RICAMARE project, albeit natural scientists, have all along made great efforts to advance the role of socio-economic research in the study of global change in the Mediterranean area.

PART II

The issues: socio-economic impacts, vulnerability and adaptation

1. Recent economic insights into the impacts of climate change

Richard S.J. Tol, Samuel Fankhauser, Onno J. Kuik and Joel B. Smith

INTRODUCTION

Climate change continues to figure prominently as one of the major environmental concerns for the future. Some people argue climate change is a problem because it could cause unacceptable hardship for particularly vulnerable populations (e.g. those living on small island states). Others are concerned about the potential threat to certain unique and valuable systems (such as coral reefs). Still others worry that climate change will increase the probability of large-scale climate instabilities (e.g. a shutdown of the Gulf Stream), and will have costly impacts on economies through floods and storms. A fourth group wonders about the total (or aggregate) impacts of climate change. They argue that emission reduction is costly too, and that abatement costs should be balanced against the avoided costs of climate change (see Smith *et al.*, 2001). This chapter particularly addresses the aggregate costs of climate change, and their distribution over the world.

A key challenge when assessing the impacts of climate change is synthesis; that is, the need to reduce the complex pattern of local and individual impacts to a more tractable set of indicators. The challenge is to identify indicators that can summarise and make comparable the impacts in different regions, sectors or systems in a meaningful way. Various 'physical' indicators have been advanced, such as number of people affected (e.g. Hoozemans *et al.*, 1993), change in total plant growth (White *et al.*, 1998), runoff (Arnell, 1999), and number of systems undergoing change (e.g. Alcamo *et al.*, 1995). Such physical metrics suffer from being inadequately linked to human welfare.

If the aim is to integrate the impacts of climate change with standard national accounts, it is necessary to express the costs of climate change in the same metric, that is money (for estimates, see Ayres and Walter, 1991; Cline, 1992; Downing *et al.*, 1995, 1996; Hohmeyer and Gaertner, 1992; Fankhauser, 1995; Nordhaus, 1991, 1994; Mendelsohn and Neumann,

1999; Titus, 1992; Tol, 1995). This also allows one to compare the costs of greenhouse gas emission reduction with the impacts of climate change. Money is a particularly well suited metric to measure market impacts – that is, impacts that are linked to market transactions and directly affect GDP (i.e. a country's national accounts). The costs of sea-level rise can be expressed as the capital cost of protection plus the economic value of land and structures at loss or at risk; and agricultural impact can be expressed as costs or benefits to producers and consumers.

Using a monetary metric to express non-market impacts, such as effects on ecosystems or human health, is more difficult and even controversial. There is a broad and established literature on valuation theory and its application, including studies (mostly in a non-climate change context) on the monetary value of lower mortality risk, ecosystems, quality of life, and so on (e.g. Freeman, 1993). But proper economic valuation requires sophisticated analysis that is still mostly lacking in a climate change context (e.g. Pearce *et al.*, 1996). Monetary valuation introduces considerable uncertainties, further enhanced by benefit transfer, a procedure on which climate change impact analyses rely heavily. Monetary valuation is also better suited for small changes than for large changes such as climate change.

This chapter presents a brief overview of assessments of global warming damages and assessments of the *present value* of future damages of current emissions of greenhouse gases. It draws heavily on the review of literature that was carried out for the Intergovernmental Panel on Climate Change's (IPCC) Second and Third Assessment Reports (Pearce *et al.*, 1996; Smith *et al.*, 2001), the EU-DG Research ExternE and GARP projects (European Commission, 1998; Eyre *et al.*, 1999a, b; Tol and Downing, 2000), and related publications (Tol, 1999a; Tol *et al.*, 2000, 2001).

The assessment of monetary damages of emissions of greenhouse gases is usually carried out in three steps. First, it is assessed what impacts a specific level of climate change would have on the *present* economy. Usually the climate damages assessed are those that are due to a doubling of the concentration of greenhouse gases in the atmosphere relative to their pre-industrial level. The scenario that describes the impacts of a doubling of greenhouse gas concentrations on the present economy is called the $2 \times CO_2$ scenario. In the second step it is assessed how developments in population, economy, technology, and socio-political factors affect future climate change damages. The third step assesses the contribution of the present emission of one unit of greenhouse gas to the flow of future damages. The discounted sum of these marginal future damages measures the external damage costs of the present emission of one unit of greenhouse gas. The chapter presents these three steps in the next three sections, respectively, while the fifth section draws some conclusions.

EQUILIBRIUM $2 \times CO_2$ IMPACTS

The first step in the damage assessment is the assessment of global warming damage under the $2 \times CO_2$ scenario – the hypothetical scenario that imposes the impacts of a doubling of the concentration of greenhouse gases in the atmosphere on the present economy. Impacts of this scenario are both on market goods and on non-market goods, such as human health, biodiversity and ecosystems. Most of the research on the assessment of these impacts is carried out in and for the United States, see Table 1.1.

Table 1.1   Assessments of global warming damage in the United States, $2 \times CO_2$ scenario, billion US$, various studies

	Fankhauser (2.5°C)	Cline (2.5°C)	Nordhaus (3.0°C)	Titus (4.0°C)	Tol (2.5°C)
Coastal defence	0.2	1.0	7.5	–	0.2
Dry land	2.1	1.5	3.2	–	1.4
Wetland	5.6	3.6	–	5.0	12.4
Species	7.4	3.5	–	–	20.8
Agriculture	0.6	15.2	1.0	1.0	10.6
Forestry	1.0	2.9	–	38.0	–
Energy	6.9	9.0	–	7.1	–
Water	13.7	6.1	–	9.9	–
Other sectors	–	1.5	38.1	–	–
Mortality/morbidity	10.0	>5.0	–	8.2	8.6
Air pollution	6.4	>3.0	–	23.7	–
Water pollution	–	–	–	28.4	–
Migration	0.5	0.4	–	–	0.6
Natural hazards	0.2	0.7	–	–	0.6
Total USA	60.2	>53.3	50.3	121.3	68.4
(% GDP)	(1.2)	(>1.1)	(1.0)	(2.5)	(1.3)

Source: Pearce *et al.* (1996).

The selected studies in Table 1.1 report aggregate damage figures that are in a relatively close range (1.0 per cent to 2.5 per cent of GDP). This can be explained from the fact that the studies often use the same sources with respect to the assessment of physical impacts and that they make use of each other's results. Note that the figures in Table 1.1 are central estimates or 'best guesses'; below we will also consider the probability distributions around these central estimates. Table 1.1 presents damage estimates for 14 different impact categories. A detailed description of each can be found in Pearce *et al.* (1996).

A number of studies have estimated the total impact of climate change (disaggregated across sectors) in different regions of the world. Table 1.2 shows aggregate, monetised impact estimates for a doubling of atmospheric carbon dioxide on the current economy and population from the three main studies undertaken since the IPCC Second Assessment Report (Pearce *et al.*, 1996), and summarises the 'first generation' of studies already reviewed in the Second Assessment Report for comparison. The numerical results remain speculative, but they can provide insights on signs, orders of magnitude, and patterns of vulnerability. Results are difficult to compare because different studies assume different climate scenarios, make different assumptions about adaptation, use different regional disaggregation and include different impacts. The Nordhaus and Boyer (2000) estimates, for example, are more negative than others, partly because they factor in the possibility of catastrophic impact. The Mendelsohn *et al.* (1996) and Tol (forthcoming, a) estimates, on the other hand, are driven by optimistic assumptions about adaptive capacity and baseline development trends, which result in mostly beneficial impacts.

Standard deviations are rarely reported, but probably amount to several times the 'best guess'. They are larger for developing countries, where results are generally derived through extrapolation rather than direct estimation. This is illustrated by the standard deviations estimated by Tol (forthcoming, a), reproduced in Table 1.2. The Tol figures probably still underestimate the true uncertainty, for example because they exclude omitted impacts and severe climate change scenarios. Downing *et al.* (1996) provide a much higher range of uncertainty, from nearly 0 impact to almost 40 per cent of world GDP, reflecting a much wider range of assumptions than are commonly included.

Overall, the current generation of aggregate estimates may understate the true cost of climate change because they tend to ignore extreme weather events; underestimate the compounding effect of multiple stresses; and ignore the costs of transition and learning. However, studies may also have overlooked positive impacts of climate change and not adequately accounted for how development could reduce impacts of climate change. Our current understanding of (future) adaptive capacity, particularly in developing countries, is too limited, and the inclusion of adaptation in current studies too varied to allow a firm conclusion about the direction of the estimation bias.

While our understanding of aggregate impacts remains limited, it is constantly improving. Some sectors and impacts have gained more analytical attention than others, and as a result are better understood. Agricultural

Table 1.2   Estimates of the regional impacts of climate change[a]

	'First generation' 2.5°C	Mendelsohn et al. 1.5°C	Mendelsohn et al. 2.5°C	Nordhaus/ Boyer 2.5°C	Tol[b] 1.0°C
North America	−1.5				3.4 (1.2)
USA	−1.0 to −1.5		0.3	−0.5	
OECD Europe	−1.3				3.7 (2.2)
EU	−1.4			−2.8	
OECD Pacific	−1.4 to −2.8				1.0 (1.1)
Japan			−0.1	−0.5	
Eastern Europe & fUSSR	0.3				2.0 (3.8)
Eastern Europe				−0.7	
fUSSR	−0.7				
Russia			11.1	0.7	
Middle East	−4.1			−2.0[c]	1.1 (2.2)
Latin America	−4.3				−0.1 (0.6)
Brazil			−1.4		
South & Southeast Asia	−8.6				−1.7 (1.1)
India			−2.0	−4.9	
China	−4.7 to −5.2		1.8	−0.2	2.1 (5.0)[d]
Africa	−8.7			−3.9	−4.1 (2.2)
DCs		0.12	0.03		
LDCs		0.05	−0.17		
World					
Output weighted[e]	−1.5 to −2.0		0.1	−1.5	2.3 (1.0)
Population weighted[f]				−1.9	
At world average prices[g]					−2.7 (0.8)
Equity weighted[h]					0.2 (1.3)

Notes:
[a] Figures are expressed as impacts on a society with today's economic structure, population, laws, etc. Mendelsohn et al.'s estimates denote impact on a future economy. Estimates are expressed as percentage of gross domestic product. Positive numbers denote benefits, negative numbers denote costs.
[b] Figures in brackets denote standard deviations. They denote a lower bound to the real uncertainty.
[c] High-income OPEC.
[d] China, Laos, North Korea, Vietnam.
[e] Regional monetary impact estimates are aggregated to world impacts without weighting.
[f] Regional monetary impact estimates are aggregated to world impacts using weights that reflect differences in population sizes.
[g] Regional impacts are evaluated at world average values and then aggregated, without weighting, to world impacts.
[h] Regional monetary impact estimates are aggregated to world impacts using 'equity weights' that equal the ratio of global average per capita income to region average per capita income.

Sources: Pearce et al. (1996); Mendelsohn et al. (1996); Nordhaus and Boyer (2000); Tol (forthcoming, a).

and coastal impacts in particular are now well studied. Knowledge about the health impacts of climate change is also growing. Several attempts have been made to identify other non-market impacts, such as changes in aquatic and terrestrial ecological systems, and ecosystem services, but a clear and compatible quantification has not yet emerged. A few generic patterns and trends are nevertheless appearing.

Market impacts are low, and may be positive in some countries and sectors – at least in developed regions. This is largely due to adaptation. Efficient adaptation reduces the net costs of climate change because the cost of such measures is lower than the concomitant reduction in impacts. However, impact uncertainty and lack of capacity may make efficient and error-free adaptation difficult. Even so, market impacts could be significant in some conditions, such as a rapid increase in extreme events, which might lead to large losses and/or costly over-adaptation (if random fluctuations are mistaken for a trend) (see Downing *et al.*, 1998).

Developing countries are more vulnerable to climate change than developed countries because their economies rely more heavily on climate-sensitive activities (in particular agriculture), and many already operate close to environmental and climatic tolerance levels (e.g. with respect to coastal and water resources). Developing countries are poorly prepared to deal with the climate variability and natural hazards they already face today (World Bank, 2000). If current development trends continue, few of them will have the financial, technical, and institutional capacity and knowledge base to deal with the additional stress of climate change.

Differences in vulnerability will not only be observed between regions, but also within them. Some individuals, sectors, and systems will be less affected, or may even benefit, while other individuals, sectors, and systems may suffer significant losses. There are indications that poor people in general, wherever they live, may be more vulnerable to climate change than the better off. Differences in adaptive capacity are again a key reason for this pattern.

Estimates of global impact are sensitive to the way figures are aggregated. Because the most severe impacts are expected in developing countries, the more weight that is assigned to developing countries, the more severe are aggregate impacts (see the next section). Using a simple adding of impacts, some studies estimate small net positive impacts at a few degrees of warming, while others estimate small net negative impacts. Net aggregate benefits do not preclude the possibility of a majority of people being negatively affected, and some population groups severely so. This is due to the fact that developed economies, many of which could have positive impacts, contribute the majority of global production but account for a smaller fraction of world population. However, there are no studies so far that have consistently estimated the total number of people that could be negatively affected by climate change.

The need for synthesis and aggregation poses challenges with respect to the spatial and temporal comparison of impacts. Aggregating impacts requires an understanding of (or assumptions about) the relative importance of impacts in different sectors, in different regions and at different times. Developing this understanding implicitly involves value judgements. The task is simplified if impacts can be expressed in a common metric, but even then aggregation is not possible without value judgements. Aggregation across time, and the issue of discounting, is discussed by Arrow *et al.* (1996) and Portney and Weyant (1999). Discounting is particularly important for estimating the marginal costs of greenhouse gas emissions, an issue we return to in the fourth section. The value judgements underlying regional aggregation are discussed and made explicit in Azar (1999), Azar and Sterner (1996) and Fankhauser *et al.* (1997, 1998). We underline the importance of aggregation by using four alternative ways of computing world total impacts from regional impact estimates in Table 1.2.

Nevertheless, aggregation necessarily hides differences. For instance, Western Europe is commonly aggregated to one region, even though there are probably large differences between Scandinavia and Mediterranean Europe. Downing *et al.* (1999) find that Southern Europe may well get drier whereas Northern Europe would get wetter. Agriculture may thus expand in the north, but would get into trouble in the already drought-prone south. In the aggregate, these differences roughly cancel each other out. Unfortunately, economic impact studies have not yet sufficient regional detail to further disaggregate Table 1.2.

The impact estimates of Tables 1.1 and 1.2 are very uncertain, and the studies on which they are based suffer from many shortcomings. We list the most important.

A major difficulty in impact assessment is our still incomplete understanding of climate change itself, in particular the regional details of climate change (Mahlman, 1997). Impacts are local, and impacts are related to weather variability and extremes. Current climate change scenarios and current climate change impact studies use crude spatial and temporal resolutions, too crude to capture a number of essential details that determine the impacts.

Knowledge gaps continue at the level of impact analysis. Despite a growing number of country-level case studies (e.g. US Country Studies Program, 1999), our knowledge of local impacts is still too uneven and incomplete for a careful, detailed comparison across regions. Furthermore, differences in assumptions often make it difficult to compare case studies across countries. Only a few studies try to provide a coherent global picture, based on a uniform set of assumptions. The basis of many such global impact assessments tends to be case studies with a more limited scope, often undertaken in the United States, which are then extrapolated to other regions. Such extrapolation is difficult and will be successful only if regional circumstances are carefully taken into account, including differences in geography, level of development, value systems and adaptive capacity. Not all analyses are equally careful in undertaking this task. While our understanding of the vulnerability of developed countries is improving – at least with respect to market impacts – good information about developing countries remains scarce.

Non-market damages, indirect effects (e.g. the effect of changed agricultural output on the food processing industry), horizontal interlinkages (e.g. the interplay between water supply and agriculture; or how the loss of ecosystem functions will affect GDP), and the socio-political implications of change are also still poorly understood. Uncertainty, transient effects (the impact of a changing rather than a changed and static climate), and the influence of change in climate variability are other factors deserving more attention.

Another key problem is adaptation. Adaptation will entail complex behavioural, technological and institutional adjustments at all levels of society, and not all population groups will be equally adept at adapting. Adaptation is treated differently in different studies, but all approaches either underestimate or overestimate its effectiveness and costs. Impact studies are largely confined to autonomous adaptation; that is, adaptations that occur without explicit policy intervention from the government. But in many cases governments too will embark on adaptation policies to avoid certain impacts of climate change, and may start those policies well before critical climatic change occurs – for example, by linking climate change adaptation to other development and global change actions, such as on drought and desertification or biodiversity.

The analysis is further complicated by the strong link between adaptation and other socio-economic trends. The world will substantially change in the future, and this will affect vulnerability to climate change. For example, a successful effort to roll back malaria could reduce a climate change-induced spread of malaria risks. A less successful effort could introduce antibiotic-resistant parasites or pesticide-resistant mosquitoes, so increasing vulnerability to climate change. The growing pressure on natural resources from unsustainable economic development is likely to exacerbate the impacts of climate change. However, if this pressure leads to improved management (e.g. water markets), vulnerability might decrease. Even without explicit adaptation, impact assessments therefore vary depending on the 'type' of socio-economic development expected in the future. The sensitivity of estimates to such baseline trends can in some cases be strong enough to reverse the sign – that is, a potentially negative impact can become positive under a suitable development path or vice versa (Mendelsohn and Neumann, 1999).

FUTURE DEVELOPMENTS

Global warming damages under the $2 \times CO_2$ scenario are hypothetical damages on the *present* society. The real damages of global warming will occur in the future, and society will have changed in terms of population numbers, economic size and structure, technology and in terms of socio-cultural and political factors. These changes may affect the vulnerability of society to global warming. If we are interested in the absolute size of damages (for example per tonne of CO_2 emissions) it is necessary to establish the future size of the population and stock at risk. The timeframe of global warming damages is too long, however, to predict such future developments with any measure of precision. Hence, scenarios are used that describe *possible* futures but do not claim to describe the *most likely* future. Because of the use of these scenarios, global warming damage assessments have a contingent nature: they are contingent on the scenario assumptions used.

One of the main challenges of impact assessments is to move from this static analysis to a dynamic representation of impacts as a function of shifting climate characteristics, adaptation measures and exogenous trends like economic and population growth. Our understanding of the time path aggregate impacts will follow under different warming and development scenarios is still extremely limited. Among the few explicitly dynamic analyses are those by Sohngen and Mendelsohn (1999), Tol (forthcoming, b), Tol and Dowlatabadi (2001) and Yohe *et al.* (1996). These studies are highly speculative, as the underlying models only provide a very rough reflection of real-world complexities. Figure 1.1 shows examples from three studies. While some analysts still work with relatively smooth impact functions (e.g. Nordhaus and Boyer, 2000), there is growing recognition (e.g. Tol, 1996, forthcoming, b; Mendelsohn and Schlesinger, 1999) that the climate impact dynamics – the conjunction of climate change, societal change, impact, and adaptation – is certainly not linear, and might be quite complex.

Impacts in different sectors may unfold along fundamentally different paths. Coastal impacts, for example, are expected to grow continuously over time, more or less in proportion to the rise in sea level. The prospects for agriculture, in contrast, are more diverse. While some models predict aggregate damages even for moderate warming, many studies suggest that under some (but not all) scenarios the impact curve might be hump-shaped,

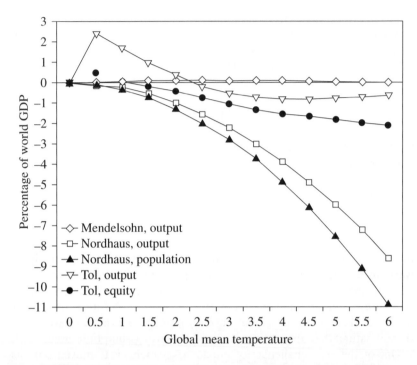

Note: These are impacts according to Mendelsohn *et al.* (1996), Nordhaus and Boyer (2000), and Tol (forthcoming, a). Mendelsohn *et al.* aggregate impacts across different regions weighted by regional output. Nordhaus and Boyer aggregate either weighted by regional output or weighted by regional population. Tol aggregates either by regional output or by equity; that is, by the ratio of world per capita income to regional per capita income.

Figure 1.1   The impact of climate change as a function of global mean temperature

with short-term (aggregate) benefits under modest climate change turning into losses under more substantial change (e.g. Mendelsohn and Schlesinger, 1999).

ASSESSMENT OF MARGINAL DAMAGES

The marginal damages caused by a metric tonne of carbon dioxide emissions in the near future were estimated by a number of studies, reproduced in Table 1.3. Most estimates are in the range $5–20/tC, but higher estimates cannot be excluded. The uncertainty about the marginal damage costs is right-skewed, so the mean is higher than the best guess, and nasty surprises

Table 1.3   *Estimates of the marginal damage costs of carbon dioxide*
emissions (in $/tC)

Study\PRTP[a]	0%	1%	3%
Nordhaus (1994)			
Best guess			5
Expected value			12
Peck and Teisberg (1992)			10–12
Fankhauser (1995)[b]		20 (6-45)	
Cline (1992, 1993)		6–124	
Plambeck and Hope (1996)[c]	440	46	21
	(390−980)	(20−94)	(10−48)
Tol and Downing (2000)[d]	20	4	−7
	75	46	16
Tol (1999a)[e]			
Best guess	73	23	9
Equity weighted	171	60	26

Notes:
[a] Pure rate of time preference, or utility discount rate. The more conventional
   consumption, or money discount rate equals the utility discount rate plus the growth rate
   of per capita income.
[b] Expected value, uncertainty about the discount rate included.
[c] Plambeck and Hope (1996) use pure rates of time preference of 0, 2% and 3%. The range
   is the 95% confidence interval (parametric uncertainty only).
[d] Tol and Downing (2000) report estimates from Tol's FUND model (top line) and from
   Downing's Open Framework model (bottom line).
[e] Tol uses consumption discount rates of 1%, 3% and 5%; the assumed per capita income
   growth is roughly 2%.

are more likely than pleasant surprises. Several studies confirm that the marginal costs are extremely sensitive to the discount rate.

The alternative estimate of Tol (1999a) uses equity weighting – an aggregation procedure that takes into account that a dollar is worth more to a poor person than to a rich one (see Fankhauser *et al.*, 1997, 1998). Equity weighting puts more emphasis on the impacts in developing countries, so the marginal damage cost estimate is considerably higher.

All the studies in Table 1.3 are based on what we above called the 'first generation' of impact studies, except the Tol estimate in Tol and Downing (2000). This last study uses more optimistic estimates of the impact of climate change (see Table 1.2). Consequently, the marginal damage costs are low and, for a high discount rate, may even be negative (i.e. marginal benefits).

Uncertainties abound in climate change. The uncertainties about the impact of climate change are estimated in Tol (forthcoming, a). These are confounded by uncertainties about the scenarios (which expand through time) and about the workings of the climate system. All these uncertainties need to be combined in a Monte Carlo analysis of the models used to estimate the marginal costs. Here, we show results of the FUND model (Tol, 1997, 1999a–e). The exact specification of the Monte Carlo analysis can be found in Tol and Downing (2000). The uncertainty analysis is restricted to parametric uncertainty. The uncertainties reflect the ranges found in the literature, thus the uncertainty calculated here is a lower bound to the 'true' uncertainty. This particularly holds for the uncertainties about the impacts of climate change. The literature on that is thin (excepting for agriculture), and ranges are therefore narrow.

Figure 1.2 depicts the uncertainty about the marginal costs of carbon dioxide emissions, based on a Monte Carlo analysis with 1000 runs. The best guess is $9/tC.[1] The uncertainty is large and right-skewed. The probability density can be reasonably approximated with a lognormal distribution (the line in Figure 1.2).

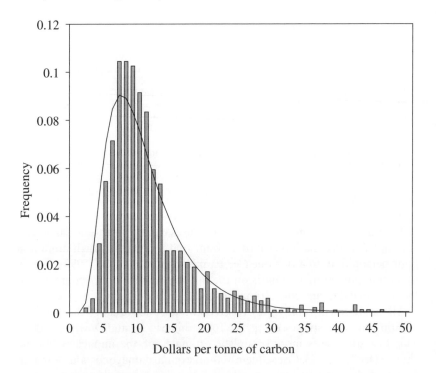

Source: Tol and Downing (2000).

Figure 1.2   Uncertainty about the marginal costs of carbon dioxide emissions for a 1 per cent PRTP and world average values

CONCLUSIONS

The economic impact of climate change is a hard subject to study. Current methodologies are weak, and uncertainties remain large. Nonetheless, four conclusions can be drawn with some confidence:

1. Vulnerabilities differ considerably between regions. Poorer countries would face proportionally higher negative impacts than richer countries.
2. (Sustainable) development may reduce overall vulnerability to climate change, as richer societies tend to be better able to adapt and their economies are less dependent on climate. But it is not known whether development will be fast enough to reduce poorer countries' vulnerability in time. Delays in reducing climate impacts could affect achievement of sustainable development targets.
3. The impacts of moderate global warming (say, up to 2–3°C in 2100) are mixed. Poorer countries are likely to be net losers, richer countries (especially in mid- to northern latitudes) may gain from moderate warming. The global picture depends on how one aggregates. If aggregation is on a dollar basis, the world as a whole may win a bit. If aggregation is based on people, the world as a whole may lose. In addition, impacts to natural ecosystems could be negative even at these levels of warming.
4. The impacts of more substantial global warming (more than 2–3°C or sooner than 2100) are probably negative, and increasingly so for higher or faster warming. This holds for the majority of countries. Note that, because of the slow rate of change in the energy sector, the atmosphere and the oceans, we are probably already committed to at least 2°C of warming.

It may be helpful to relate emerging relative confidence in climate change to our sense of progress in valuing climate change damage. Some climatic changes can be predicted with relatively high confidence – global and regional warming, sea-level rise and rising CO_2 concentrations. These changes will affect, among other things, agroclimatic suitability, heat stress and demand for water. Less confidence is ascribed to changes in storm- and water-related effects: precipitation, precipitation intensity, wind speeds, sunshine, and so on. However, the range of scenarios generally fall within defined limits, leading to modest confidence in expected impacts on crop production, water systems and other resources. Low confidence is likely to continue for some time in our ability to project changes in the risk of extreme events (prolonged drought, intense cyclones, etc.) and large-scale changes such as the collapse of major ice sheets. We have indicated earlier that confidence is higher in the valuation of market impacts than non-market impacts, and equity and welfare effects are especially contentious. What can we then conclude about the conjunction of confidence in climate change and the valuation of impacts (not ignoring uncertainties in GHG emissions and impacts science as well)? It does not take too much imagination to reach very significant damage, but this requires incorporating relatively uncertain climate changes and impacts, and the kinds of valuations of ecological and human systems that are not customary in present assessment models – that is the lower and right-hand cells in the table. On the other hand, we have relatively high confidence that the market impacts of some trends in the climate system will have benefits in some regions and sectors (e.g. northern agriculture) and costs in others (e.g. coastal habitation in vulnerable deltas). The area in between these two poles, where climate futures are at best uncertain and risks and valuation of non-market impacts are poorly understood, remains a fruitful research frontier.

NOTES

This chapter draws heavily on the IPCC Third Assessment Report of Working Group II, Chapter 19 (Smith *et al.*, 2001). We are grateful to all the authors, reviewers and review editors of that chapter. The EU Directorate General Research (JOS3-CT95-0002, JOS3-CT97-0015), the US National Science Foundation through the Center for Integrated Study of the Human Dimensions of Global Change (SBR-9521914) and the Michael Otto Foundation provided welcome financial support. Tom Downing, David Pearce, Ari Rabl and Richard Richels provided helpful comments on an earlier version. The interpretations and any errors in this chapter are, however, our own and do not necessarily reflect the views of any of the institutions with which we are affiliated.
1. This is the best guess based on FUND2.0, using a 1 per cent pure rate of time preference, a 'years of life lost' valuation methodology for health risks and world average values for regional aggregation.

REFERENCES

Alcamo, J., Krol, M. and Leemans, R. (1995) *Stabilizing Greenhouse Gases: Global and Regional Consequences – Results from the IMAGE 2.0 Model*, pp. 1–10. Bilthoven: RIVM.
Arnell, N.W. (1999) 'Climate Change and Global Water Resources', *Global Environmental Change*, **9**, S31–S50.
Arrow, K.J., Cline, W.R., Maeler, K.-G., Munasinghe, M., Squitieri, R. and Stiglitz, J.E. (1996) 'Intertemporal Equity, Discounting, and Economic Efficiency'. In: Bruce, J.P., Lee, H. and Haites, E.F. (eds) *Climate Change 1995: Economic and Social Dimensions – Contribution of Working Group III to the Second Assessment Report of the Intergovernmental Panel on Climate Change*, pp. 125–144. Cambridge: Cambridge University Press.

Ayres, R.U. and Walter, J. (1991) 'The Greenhouse Effect: Damages, Costs and Abatement', *Environmental and Resource Economics*, **1**, 237–270.

Azar, C. (1999) 'Weight Factors in Cost–Benefit Analysis of Climate Change', *Environmental and Resource Economics*, **13**, 249–268.

Azar, C. and Sterner, T. (1996) 'Discounting and Distributional Considerations in the Context of Global Warming', *Ecological Economics*, **19**, 169–184.

Cline, W.R. (1992) *The Economics of Global Warming*. Washington, DC: Institute for International Economics.

Cline, W.R. (1993) 'A Note on the Impact of Global Warming on Air Conditioning and Heating Costs', Mimeo, Institute for International Economics, Washington, DC.

Downing, T.E., Eyre, N., Greener, R. and Blackwell, D. (1996) *Projected Costs of Climate Change for Two Reference Scenarios and Fossil Fuel Cycles*. Oxford: Environmental Change Unit.

Downing, T.E., Greener, R.A. and Eyre, N. (1995) *The Economic Impacts of Climate Change: Assessment of Fossil Fuel Cycles for the ExternE Project*, pp. 1–48. Oxford and Lonsdale: Environmental Change Unit and Eyre Energy Environment.

Downing, T.E., Olsthoorn, A.A. and Tol, R.S.J. (eds) (1998) *Climate, Change and Risk*. London: Routledge.

European Commission (1998) 'Global Warming Damages', Chapter 2.8 of Final Report of Green Account Research Project II (GARP II), Contract ENV4-CT96-0285, Brussels, pp. 352–368.

Eyre, N., Downing, T.E., Hoekstra, R. and Rennings, K. (1999a) *Externalities of Energy, Vol. 8: Global Warming*, pp. 1–50. Luxembourg: Office for Official Publications of the European Communities.

Eyre, N., Downing, T.E., Rennings, K. and Tol, R.S.J. (1999b) 'Assessment of Global Warming Damages'. In: Holland, M.R., Berry, J. and Forster, D. (eds) *Externalities of Energy, Vol. 7: Metholodogy and 1998 Update*, pp. 101–112. Luxembourg: Office for Official Publications of the European Communities.

Fankhauser, S. (1995) *Valuing Climate Change – The Economics of the Greenhouse*. London: EarthScan.

Fankhauser, S., Tol, R.S.J. and Pearce, D.W. (1997) 'The Aggregation of Climate Change Damages: A Welfare Theoretic Approach', *Environmental and Resource Economics*, **10**, 249–266.

Fankhauser, S., Tol, R.S.J. and Pearce, D.W. (1998) 'Extensions and Alternatives to Climate Change Impact Valuation: On the Critique of IPCC Working Group III's Impact Estimates', *Environment and Development Economics*, **3**, 59–81.

Freeman, A.M., III (1993) *The Measurement of Environmental and Resource Values*. Washington, DC: Resources for the Future.

Hohmeyer, O. and Gaertner, M. (1992) *The Costs of Climate Change – A Rough Estimate of Orders of Magnitude*. Karlsruhe: Fraunhofer-Institut für Systemtechnik und Innovationsforschung.

Hoozemans, F.M.J., Marchand, M. and Pennekamp, H.A. (1993) *A Global Vulnerability Analysis: Vulnerability Assessment for Population, Coastal Wetlands and Rice Production and a Global Scale* (second, revised edition). Delft: Delft Hydraulics.

Mahlman, J.D. (1997) 'Uncertainties in Projections of Human-caused Climate Warming', *Science*, **278**, 1416–1417.

Mendelsohn, R.O., Morrison, W.N., Schlesinger, M.E. and Andronova, N.G. (1996) 'A Global Impact Model for Climate Change'. Draft.

Mendelsohn, R.O. and Neumann, J.E. (eds) (1999) *The Impact of Climate Change on the United States Economy.* Cambridge: Cambridge University Press.

Mendelsohn, R.O. and Schlesinger, M.E. (1999) 'Climate-response Functions', *Ambio.*

Nordhaus, W.D. (1991) 'To Slow or Not to Slow: The Economics of the Greenhouse Effect', *Economic Journal,* **101**, 920–937.

Nordhaus, W.D. (1994) *Managing the Global Commons: The Economics of Climate Change.* Cambridge: The MIT Press.

Nordhaus, W.D. and Boyer, J.G. (2000) *Warming the World: Economic Models of Global Warming.* Cambridge: MIT Press.

Pearce, D.W., Cline, W.R., Achanta, A.N., Fankhauser, S., Pachauri, R.K., Tol, R.S.J. and Vellinga, P. (1996) 'The Social Costs of Climate Change: Greenhouse Damage and the Benefits of Control'. In: Bruce, J.P., Lee, H. and Haites, E.F. (eds) *Climate Change 1995: Economic and Social Dimensions – Contribution of Working Group III to the Second Assessment Report of the Intergovernmental Panel on Climate Change,* pp. 179–224. Cambridge: Cambridge University Press.

Peck, S.C. and Teisberg, T.J. (1992) 'CETA: A Model for Carbon Emissions Trajectory Assessment', *Energy Journal,* **13**(1), 55–77.

Plambeck, E.L. and Hope, C.W. (1996) 'PAGE95 – An Updated Valuation of the Impacts of Global Warming', *Energy Policy,* **24**(9), 783–793.

Portney, P.R. and Weyant, J.P. (eds) (1999) *Discounting and Intergenerational Equity.* Washington, DC: Resources for the Future.

Smith, J.B., Schellnhuber, H.-J., Mirza, M.Q., Lin, E., Fankhauser, S., Leemans, R., Ogallo, L., Richels, R.G., Safriel, U., Tol, R.S.J., Weyant, J.P. and Yohe, G.W. (2001), 'Synthesis'. In: McCarthy, J.J., Canziani, O.F., Leary, N.A., Dokken, D.J. and White, K.S. (eds) *Climate Change 2001: Impacts, Adaptation, and Vulnerability,* IPCC Working 2 Third Assessment Report, pp. 913–967. Cambridge: Cambridge University Press.

Sohngen, B.L. and Mendelsohn, R.O. (1999) 'The Timber Market Impacts of Climate Change on the US Timber Market'. In: Mendelsohn, R.O. and Neumann, J.E. (eds) *The Impact of Climate Change on the US Economy,* pp. 94–132. Cambridge: Cambridge University Press.

Titus, J.G. (1992) 'The Costs of Climate Change to the United States'. In: Majumdar, S.K., Kalkstein, L.S., Yarnal, B.M., Miller, E.W. and Rosenfeld, L.M. (eds) *Global Climate Change: Implications, Challenges and Mitigation Measures,* pp. 384–409. Easton: Pennsylvania Academy of Science.

Tol, R.S.J. (1995) 'The Damage Costs of Climate Change: Toward More Comprehensive Calculations', *Environmental and Resource Economics,* **5**, 353–374.

Tol, R.S.J. (1996) 'The Damage Costs of Climate Change: Towards a Dynamic Representation', *Ecological Economics,* **19**, 67–90.

Tol, R.S.J. (1997) 'On the Optimal Control of Carbon Dioxide Emissions – An Application of *FUND*', *Environmental Modelling and Assessment,* **2**, 151–163.

Tol, R.S.J. (1999a) 'The Marginal Damage Costs of Greenhouse Gas Emissions', *The Energy Journal,* **20**(1), 61–81.

Tol, R.S.J. (1999b) 'Time Discounting and Optimal Control of Climate Change: An Application of *FUND*', *Climatic Change,* **41**(3–4), 351–362.

Tol, R.S.J. (1999c) 'Kyoto, Efficiency, and Cost-effectiveness: Applications of *FUND*', *Energy Journal Special Issue on the Costs of the Kyoto Protocol: A Multi-Model Evaluation,* 130–156.

Tol, R.S.J. (1999d) 'Spatial and Temporal Efficiency in Climate Policy: Applications of *FUND*', *Environmental and Resource Economics*, **14**(1), 33–49.

Tol, R.S.J. (1999e) 'Safe Policies in an Uncertain Climate: An Application of *FUND*', *Global Environmental Change*, **9**, 221–232.

Tol, R.S.J. (2002, a) 'New Estimates of the Damage Costs of Climate Change, Part I: Benchmark Estimates', *Environmental and Resource Economics*, **21**(1), 47–73.

Tol, R.S.J. (2002, b) 'New Estimates of the Damage Costs of Climate Change, Part II: Dynamic Estimates', *Environmental and Resource Economics*, **21**(1), 135–160.

Tol, R.S.J. and Dowlatabadi, H. (2001) 'Vector-borne Diseases, Climate Change, and Economic Growth', *Integrated Assessment*, **2**, 173–181.

Tol, R.S.J. and Downing, T.E. (2000) *The Marginal Damage Costs of Climate Changing Gases*. Amsterdam: Institute for Environmental Studies D00/08, Vrije Universiteit.

Tol, R.S.J., Downing, T.E., Fankhauser, S., Richels, R.G. and Smith, J.B. (2001) 'Recent Estimates of the Marginal Costs of Greenhouse Gas Emissions', *Journal Pollution Atmosphérique – Numéro Spécial: Combien Vaut l'Air Propre?*, 155–179.

Tol, R.S.J., Fankhauser, S., Richels, R.G. and Smith, J.B. (2000) 'How Much Damage Will Climate Change Do? Recent Estimates', *World Economics*, **1**(4), 179–206.

US Country Studies Program (1999) *Climate Change: Mitigation, Vulnerability, and Adaptation in Developing Countries*. Washington, DC: US Country Studies Program.

White, D.J., Running, S.W., Thornton, P.E., Keane, R.E., Ryan, K.C., Fagre, D.B. and Key, C.H. (1998) 'Assessing Simulated Ecosystem Processes for Climate Variability Research at Glacier National Park', *Ecological Applications*, **8**, 805–823.

World Bank (2000) *Attacking Poverty. World Development Report 2000/2001*. Washington DC: World Bank.

Yohe, G.W., Neumann, J.E., Marshall, P. and Ameden, H. (1996) 'The Economic Costs of Sea Level Rise on US Coastal Properties', *Climatic Change*, **32**, 387–410.

2. Adaptation to climate variability and change: what is optimal and appropriate?

Richard J.T. Klein

INTRODUCTION

Adaptation is increasingly recognised as an appropriate and necessary response option to climate change, especially since it has been established that humans are – at least in part – responsible for climate change and that some impacts can no longer be avoided. The Intergovernmental Panel on Climate Change (IPCC) Workshop on Adaptation to Climate Variability and Change (San José, Costa Rica, 1998) provided a strong impetus to the increasing recognition of the importance of adaptation. The workshop aimed to assess and improve the current understanding of both the theory and practice of climate adaptation. It also served to produce materials for consideration by the IPCC for its Third Assessment Report, which has recently been finalised. The Working Group II contribution to the IPCC Third Assessment Report features adaptation more strongly than before in its discussions of vulnerable sectors and regions. In addition, it contains a chapter devoted entirely to adaptation in the context of sustainable development and equity (Smit *et al.*, 2001). It re-emphasises the need for adaptation and stresses the importance of enhancing the adaptive capacity of developing countries.

From an international policy perspective the importance of adaptation was first confirmed at the third Conference of the Parties (COP-3, 1997) to the United Nations Framework Convention on Climate Change (UNFCCC) in Kyoto. The Kyoto Protocol defines a Clean Development Mechanism (CDM) that explicitly mentions adaptation as an expenditure goal. At COP-4 in Buenos Aires (1998) governments decided that funding could be made available to developing countries for preparatory (so-called 'Stage II') adaptation activities. At COP-5 and COP-6 (Bonn, 1999 and The Hague, 2000, respectively) governments subsequently discussed how the CDM and the aforementioned decision made at COP-4 could be made operational. The initial failure at COP-6 to reach agreement among Parties on the implementation of the Kyoto Protocol and the functioning of the CDM seemed likely to delay its implementation and thereby the availability of adaptation funding from this source. However, COP-6bis in Bonn (2001) and COP-7 in Marrakech (2001) responded to the increasing need for adaptation, and agreement was reached on the establishment of three funds from which adaptation activities in developing countries can be financed.

Adaptation has not always been considered as important or relevant within climate science or policy. Despite the fact that the UNFCCC refers to both mitigation and adaptation, national and international climate policies to date have mainly focused on mitigation (i.e., all human activities aimed at limiting climate change by reducing the emissions or enhancing the sinks of greenhouse gases). In part this reflects the uncertainty about climate change being caused by human activity, which existed until the publication of the IPCC Second Assessment Report in 1996. It also reflects the lack of theoretical and practical knowledge about adaptation to climate change, which in turn resulted from the limited attention given to adaptation by the scientific community. In his review of the IPCC Second Assessment Report, Kates (1997) suggested the reason for this limited attention lies in the existence of two distinct schools of thought about climate change, both of which chose not to engage in adaptation research.

At one extreme Kates identified the 'preventionist' school, which argues that the ongoing increase of atmospheric greenhouse gas concentrations could be catastrophic and that drastic action is required to reduce emissions. Preventionists fear that increased emphasis on adaptation will weaken society's willingness to reduce emissions and thus delay or diminish mitigation efforts. At the other extreme one finds what Kates referred to as the 'adaptationist' school, which sees no need to focus on either adaptation or mitigation. Adaptationists argue that natural and human systems have a long history of adapting naturally to changing circumstances and that active adaptation would constitute interference with these systems, bringing with it high social costs.

Following the publication of the IPCC Second Assessment Report a distinct third school of thought has emerged, which has been labelled the 'realist' school by Klein and MacIver (1999). The realist school positions itself in between the two extreme views of the preventionists and adaptationists. Realists regard climate change as a fact but acknowledge that impacts are still uncertain. Furthermore, realists appreciate that the planning and implementation of effective adaptation options takes time. Therefore, they understand that a process must be set in motion to consider adaptation as a crucial and realistic response option along with mitigation (e.g. Parry *et al.*, 1998; Pielke, 1998). The establishment of the three funds from which adaptation activities in developing countries can be financed is a reflection of this understanding.

However, the limited theoretical and practical understanding of adaptation to climate change, combined with the considerable uncertainties that remain concerning the location and magnitude of impacts, threaten to be an impediment to adaptation investment. Adaptation is intricately linked with non-climatic developments and takes place in a dynamic societal context, in which many different actors pursue many different interests. The identification of optimal and appropriate adaptation strategies, in part based on the balancing of their costs and benefits, is therefore fraught with difficulties.

For a variety of reasons assessing the financial costs and, especially, benefits of available adaptation options is considerably more complicated than determining those of most mitigation options. Most importantly, the performance of adaptation options is more difficult to measure and express in a single metric, which constrains the comparison of alternative options. This chapter analyses the role of adaptation in reducing a system's vulnerability to adverse impacts of climate change and argues that the use of economic decision tools alone should not form the basis of international adaptation decisions. The next section discusses the various types of adaptation and how they can help to reduce impacts to climate change. The third section provides an overview of current international funding arrangements for adaptation, while the fourth section discusses uncertainty-related and methodological caveats to assessing adaptation benefits. The final section draws conclusions and places them in a broader policy context.

TYPES OF ADAPTATION

There are various ways to classify or distinguish between adaptation options. First, depending on the timing, goal and motive of its implementation, adaptation can be either reactive or anticipatory. Reactive adaptation occurs after the initial impacts of climate change have become manifest, while anticipatory (or proactive) adaptation takes place before impacts are apparent. A second distinction can be based on the system in which the adaptation takes place: the natural system (in which adaptation is by definition reactive) or the human system (in which both reactive and anticipatory adaptation are observed). Within the human system a third distinction can be based on whether the adaptation decision is motivated by private or public interests. Private decision-makers include both individual households and commercial companies, while public interests are served by governments at all levels. Figure 2.1 shows examples of adaptation activities for each of the five types of adaptation that have thus been defined.

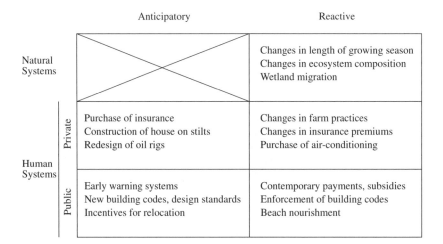

Figure 2.1   Matrix showing the five prevalent types of adaptation to climate change, including examples (based on Klein, 1998)

In addition to these, other adaptation distinctions are discussed by Smit *et al.* (2000). A useful distinction that is often made is the one between planned and autonomous adaptation (Carter *et al.*, 1994). Planned adaptation is the result of a deliberate policy decision that is based on an awareness that conditions have changed or are about to change and that action is required to return to, maintain or achieve a desired state. Autonomous adaptation involves the changes that natural and most human systems will undergo in response to changing conditions irrespective of any policy plan or decision. Instead, autonomous adaptation will be triggered by market or welfare changes induced by climate change. Autonomous adaptation in human systems would therefore be in the actor's rational self-interest, while the focus of planned adaptation is on collective needs (Leary, 1999). Thus defined, autonomous and planned adaptation largely correspond with private and public adaptation, respectively (see Figure 2.1).

The extent to which society can rely on autonomous adaptation to reduce the potential impacts of climate change to an acceptable level is an issue of great academic and policy interest. Autonomous adaptation forms a baseline against which the need for planned anticipatory adaptation can be evaluated. Some studies assume considerable faith in market mechanisms and thus in the capacity of private human systems to adapt autonomously (e.g. Mendelsohn *et al.*, 1996; Yohe *et al.*, 1996). Other studies highlight the constraints for such autonomous adaptation, such as limited information, knowledge and access to resources, and emphasise the need for anticipatory planned adaptation (e.g. Tol *et al.*, 1996; Fankhauser *et al.*, 1999).

Article 3.3 of the UNFCCC suggests that anticipatory planned adaptation (as well as mitigation) deserves particular attention from the international climate change community:

> The Parties should take precautionary measures to anticipate, prevent or minimise the causes of climate change and mitigate its adverse effects. Where there are threats of serious or irreversible damage, lack of full scientific certainty should not be used as a reason for postponing such measures, taking into account that policies and measures to deal with climate change should be cost-effective so as to ensure global benefits at the lowest possible cost.

Anticipatory adaptation is aimed at reducing a system's vulnerability by either minimising risk or maximising adaptive capacity. Five generic objectives of anticipatory adaptation can be identified (see Klein and Tol, 1997):

- *Increasing robustness of infrastructural designs and long-term investments* – for example by extending the range of temperature or precipitation a system can withstand without failure and/or changing a system's tolerance of loss or failure (*e.g.*, by increasing economic reserves or insurance).
- *Increasing flexibility of vulnerable managed systems* – for example by allowing mid-term adjustments (including change of activities or location) and/or reducing economic lifetimes (including increasing depreciation).
- *Enhancing adaptability of vulnerable natural systems* – for example by reducing other (non-climatic) stresses and/or removing barriers to migration (such as establishing eco-corridors).
- *Reversing trends that increase vulnerability ('maladaptation')* – for example by introducing restrictions for development in vulnerable areas such as floodplains and coastal zones.
- *Improving societal awareness and preparedness* – for example by informing the public of the risks and possible consequences of climate change and/or setting up early warning systems.

INTERNATIONAL FUNDING ARRANGEMENT FOR ADAPTATION

The identification of human-induced climate change as an actual rather than a theoretical phenomenon has led to increased recognition of the need to prepare for adaptation (Parry *et al.*, 1998; Pielke, 1998). In fact, Article

4.1(b) of the UNFCCC already commits Parties to: 'Formulate, implement, publish and regularly update national and, where appropriate, regional programmes containing measures (. . .) to facilitate adequate adaptation to climate change.'

The financing of adaptation measures is addressed in Article 4.3, which states that:

> The developed country Parties and other developed Parties included in Annex II[1] shall provide new and additional financial resources (. . .) needed by the developing country Parties to meet the agreed full incremental costs of implementing measures that are covered by paragraph 1 of this Article.

For developing countries that are particularly vulnerable, Article 4.4 of the UNFCCC contains another, more explicit, commitment to financing adaptation measures:

> The developed country Parties and other developed Parties included in Annex II shall also assist the developing country Parties that are particularly vulnerable to the adverse effects of climate change in meeting costs of adaptation to those adverse effects.

The Global Environment Facility (GEF) is the international entity entrusted with the operation of the financial mechanism of the UNFCCC. Until recently, the focus of the GEF has been primarily on mitigation of climate change but following COP-3 and COP-4 adaptation has risen on the priority ladder. The types of adaptation activities to be considered by the GEF were already classified at the tenth session of the Intergovernmental Negotiating Committee of the UNFCCC. Its decision was endorsed at COP-1 in Berlin in 1995 (Decision 11/CP.1). The decision identifies three stages in the adaptation process:

- *Stage I* – Planning, which includes studies of possible impacts of climate change, to identify particularly vulnerable countries or regions and policy options for adaptation and appropriate capacity building.
- *Stage II* – Measures, including further capacity building, which may be taken to prepare for adaptation, as envisaged by Article 4.1(e).
- *Stage III* – Measures to facilitate adequate adaptation, including insurance and other adaptation measures as envisaged by Articles 4.1(b) and 4.4.

According to the GEF Operational Strategy (GEF, 1996), Stage I activities could encompass the following:

- Assessment of national, regional and/or subregional vulnerability to climate change; where appropriate rely on related data-gathering systems to measure climate change effects in particularly vulnerable countries or regions and strengthen such systems as necessary; and identify a near-term research and development agenda to understand sensitivity to climate change.
- Evaluation of policy options for adequate monitoring systems and response strategies for climate change impacts on terrestrial and marine ecosystems.
- Assessment of policy frameworks for implementing adaptation measures and response strategies in the context of coastal zone management, disaster preparedness, agriculture, fisheries and forestry, with a view of integrating climate change impact information, as appropriate, into national strategic planning processes.
- In the context of undertaking national communication, building of national, regional and/or subregional capacity, as appropriate, to integrate climate change concerns into medium- and long-term planning.

With respect to financing, Decision 11/CP.1 states the following:

For Stage I, the Conference of the Parties (. . .) shall entrust to the Global Environment Facility (GEF) (. . .) the task of meeting the agreed full costs of the activities required by Article 12.1 of the Convention. This would include meeting the agreed full costs of relevant adaptation activities undertaken in the context of the formulation of national communications; such activities may include studies of the possible impacts of climate change, identification of options for implementing the adaptation provisions (. . .) and relevant capacity building.

With respect to Stages II and III, Decision 11/CP.1 states that:

Based on the outputs of the Stage I studies, as well as other relevant scientific and technical studies (. . .), the Conference of the Parties may decide that it has become necessary to implement the measures and activities envisaged in Stages II and III.

In line with this, Decision 11/CP.1 includes the provision that:

If it is decided (. . .) that is has become necessary to implement the measures envisaged in Stages II and III, the Parties included in Annex II to the Convention will provide funding to implement the adaptation measures envisaged in these stages in accordance with their commitments contained in Articles 4.3 and 4.4 of the Convention.

At COP-4 in Buenos Aires (1998) governments adopted Decision 2/CP.4, which states that:

the GEF should provide funding to developing country Parties to implement adaptation response measures under Article 4.1 of the Convention for adaptation activities envisaged in decision 11/CP.1, paragraph 1(d)(ii) (Stage II activities) in particularly vulnerable countries and regions identified in Stage I activities, and especially in countries vulnerable to climate-related natural disasters.

In spite of this decision no additional funds were made available to the GEF for Stage II projects. In addition, no clear guidance exists as to which types of activities are eligible under Stage II, which constrains the development of proposals. As it became clear that such guidance would not be provided in the foreseeable future, countries and organisations have begun to give their own interpretations to the text of Decision 11/CP.1. A number of regional project proposals have been submitted to the GEF, aimed mainly at further adaptation assessment and the identification of adaptation needs. One such project that has received GEF funding under Stage II is 'Assessments of Impacts of and Adaptation to Climate Change in Multiple Regions and Sectors' (AIACC), proposed jointly by the United Nations Environment Programme (UNEP) and the IPCC.

With the completion of the negotiations on the Kyoto Protocol to the UNFCCC at COP-7 in Marrakech (2001) agreement has been reached on the establishment of three funds that are relevant to adaptation in developing countries:

- a Special Climate Change Fund;
- a Least Developed Countries Fund;
- an Adaptation Fund.

The first two of these funds would require additional funding from Annex II Parties via the GEF, while in accordance with Article 12.8 of the Kyoto Protocol the Adaptation Fund would be financed from the share of proceeds on the Clean Development Mechanism (CDM).[2]

The text of the relevant COP-7 decisions seems to suggest that the three-stage approach of Decision 11/CP.1 is no longer the only guidance for adaptation funding. Decisions 5/CP.7 and 6/CP.7 list a number of adaptation activities that appear to go even beyond Stage III activities. For example, Decision 5/CP.7 states that the following activities shall be supported through the Special Climate Change Fund and/or the Adaptation Fund and other bilateral and multilateral sources:

- Starting to implement adaptation activities promptly where sufficient information is available to warrant such activities, *inter alia*, in the areas of water resources management, land management, agriculture, health, infrastructure development, fragile ecosystems, including mountainous ecosystems, and integrated coastal zone management.

- Improving the monitoring of diseases and vectors affected by climate change, and related forecasting and early warning systems, and in this context improving disease control and prevention.
- Supporting capacity-building, including institutional capacity, for preventive measures, planning, preparedness and management of disasters relating to climate change, including contingency planning, in particular for droughts and floods in areas prone to extreme weather events.
- Strengthening existing and, where needed, establishing national and regional centres and information networks for rapid response to extreme weather events, utilising information technology as much as possible.

The Least Developed Countries Fund is to be used in part for the development of National Adaptation Programmes of Action (NAPAs), in which least developed countries (LDCs) can communicate priority activities addressing their urgent and immediate needs and concerns relating to adaptation to the adverse effects of climate change. As stated in Decision 28/CP.7:

> The rationale for developing NAPAs rests on the low adaptive capacity of LDCs, which renders them in need of immediate and urgent support to start adapting to current and projected adverse effects of climate change. Activities proposed through NAPAs would be those whose further delay could increase vulnerability or lead to increased costs at a later stage.

It thus appears that COP-7 has removed a number of major barriers to international adaptation funding. Nonetheless, the activities listed in Decision 5/CP.7, as well as those to be identified in the NAPAs, can only be implemented if sufficient additional funding is made available. At COP-7 the government of Canada expressed its intention to contribute CAD 10 million to the Least Developed Countries Fund but this has not yet been followed up by other Annex II Parties.

Even if more money became available for the implementation of adaptation activities, two major barriers to the international funding of such activities remain. First, in line with Article 3.3 of the UNFCCC the GEF Operational Strategy prescribes that activities need to have global benefits in order to be eligible for funding. Mitigation activities, aimed at reducing atmospheric greenhouse gas concentrations, clearly have global benefits. For adaptation activities on the other hand, it is difficult to imagine how global benefits can be produced. Adaptation takes place at the scale of an impacted system, which is regional at best, but mostly local.

Second, the GEF will not cover the full costs of adaptation (however defined). The GEF assumes that some development and upgrading of systems will take place irrespective of climate change. It will fund only the incremental costs of adaptation, which are the additional costs required to maintain a system climate-safe (i.e., prepared for and able to cope with prevailing weather extremes). In theory, these costs can be estimated by comparing two impact scenarios: one with and one without climate change.[3] By then comparing the costs of alternative adaptation options with their respective benefits, one can determine the (economically) optimal option, which is the one with the highest benefit–cost ratio. In practice, however, estimates of the costs and especially benefits of adaptation to climate change are difficult to make.

BENEFITS OF ADAPTATION

Determining the benefits of adaptation is not a straightforward exercise. First of all, one needs to have a clear understanding of what adaptation benefits exactly are. As shown in Figure 2.1, one can distinguish between five types of adaptation, each yielding its own benefits. Figure 2.2 shows how these five types of adaptation relate to three types of impacts: (1) potential impacts, (2) initial impacts and (3) residual impacts.

Fankhauser (1997) and Callaway *et al.* (1998) show that, in principle, the

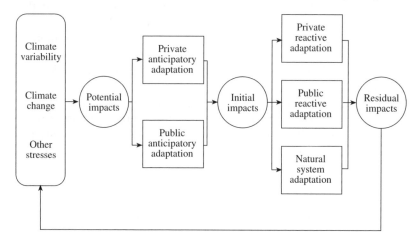

Note: Types of adaptation correspond with those defined in Figure 2.1 (modified from Klein, 1998).

Figure 2.2 The role of adaptation in determining residual impacts of climate change

benefits of adaptation (all five types taken together) would be the climate-related damage costs one avoids by taking adaptive measures (assuming that climate change would have adverse consequences). Thus, if one quantifies the *potential* impacts of climate change on a system (assuming no adaptation) as well as its *residual* impacts (assuming all five types of adaptation; see Figure 2.2), the benefits of adaptation are given by the difference between the two. From the value thus obtained one can subtract the costs of implementing the adaptation options (including transition costs) to arrive at the net benefits of adaptation. A mathematical representation and deduction can be found in Callaway *et al.* (1998).

However, there are a number of caveats involved in such analysis aimed at identifying the 'optimal' adaptation option, as prescribed by the GEF. Two types of caveats are distinguished here: those related to the uncertainty of future scenarios and methodological caveats. Both are discussed below.

Caveats Related to Uncertainty

To date, very few studies have succeeded in incorporating all types of adaptation (anticipatory, reactive, natural system, human system, planned, autonomous) in their impact analyses. Many of the early studies used a so-called 'dumb farmer'[4] scenario: they assumed present-day behaviour and activities would continue unchanged in the future, irrespective of how they may be affected by climate change. By ignoring any adaptation these studies, which are not unique for agriculture, did not distinguish between potential and residual impacts and thus their damage-cost values represent serious overestimates. On the other hand, they served to generate awareness of the potential magnitude of impacts and of the need for anticipatory adaptation.

Most studies do now consider adaptation to varying degrees. However, in doing so they invariably encounter the problem of how to deal with uncertainty: not only are impacts of climate change themselves uncertain but they will occur in a future world that is complex and uncertain as well. Some studies accommodate this problem by using a 'clairvoyant farmer' scenario, which assumes that adaptation will be perfect. The results of these studies represent serious underestimates.

Other studies take a normative – prescriptive – approach to adaptation. These evaluate what would be the *optimal* adaptation strategy given certain climate and, possibly, non-climate scenarios. Such evaluation yields quantitative results that quickly find their way to the desks of decision-makers and the computers running integrated assessment models. However, the strength of these results is also its weakness: when reduced to numbers, the results present only part of the picture. Typically, the studies assess a limited set of

– often arbitrary – adaptation options, which are assessed for their optimality without giving thought to their appropriateness in a broader societal context, or to their performance in a world in which not only the climate changes but so do most other relevant factors as well. Moreover, one tends to lose sight of the fact that the results obtained are only valid for the presupposed scenarios, which are surrounded by uncertainty.

An important uncertainty of all climate scenarios relates to the effect of a changing climate on the frequency, magnitude and spatial occurrence of extreme weather events such as floods, cyclones and droughts. To date, climate models have been unable to present unambiguous results for extreme events. Consequently most impact and adaptation studies assume only gradual changes in climate. However, as shown by West and Dowlatabadi (1999), considering extremes can lead to estimates of damage costs and hence to conclusions on optimal adaptation that differ significantly from those based only on gradual changes (see Yohe *et al.*, 1996; Yohe and Neumann, 1997). The reason for this is intuitive: most damage will not be caused by gradual changes in climate but by occasional extreme events. Reactive adaptation will therefore be triggered mainly by the impacts of extremes, while appropriate anticipatory adaptation will need to be designed to cope with these extremes.

Given the current impossibility of constructing plausible scenarios that consider all aspects that determine the costs and benefits of an adaptation option, the normative assessment of 'optimal' adaptation strategies may well be a step too far. Instead, a positive analysis of the full range of possible and appropriate adaptation options – with their costs, benefits and other implementation considerations – could be at least as informative to decision-makers.

Methodological Caveats

In addition to the above caveats associated with uncertainty there are methodological issues that constrain the assessment of adaptation benefits. These may relate to the economics of assessing future costs and benefits or to an incomplete consideration of the full process of adaptation.

To start with the latter, when calculating the costs of adaptation most studies consider only the costs of implementing adaptation options. Furthermore, they consider only those options that are well defined and (infra)structural or technological by nature (as opposed to legal, institutional, financial or behavioural options). Klein *et al.* (1999) suggested that the process of adaptation represents a continuous and iterative cycle involving four main steps: (1) information development and awareness raising, (2) planning and design, (3) implementation and (4) monitoring and evaluation

(Figure 2.3). A single focus on implementation and its costs is too limited. Such a focus ignores that successful implementation depends on the availability of various types of resources to assist the other three steps (i.e., the capacity to adapt). There is a cost to raising adaptive capacity and creating an enabling environment but this is what is required for adaptation to have any benefits at all. To assume that the full benefits of an option can be reaped only at its implementation cost is therefore misleading.

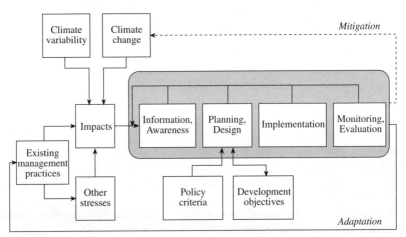

Note: The shaded area shows the iterative steps involved in adaptation to climate variability and change (generalised from Klein *et al.*, 1999).

Figure 2.3   Conceptual framework

A large literature exists on the economics of calculating future uncertain costs and benefits. This literature discusses issues such as the use of discount rates, intergenerational equity, risk assessment, opportunity costs, the precautionary principle, weighting uncertainty in cost–benefit analysis and so on. Each of these issues is a source of intense academic debate and there appears to be no consensus as to what would be the appropriate way of assessing the benefits of adaptation. Multiple 'optimal' adaptation strategies can therefore be recommended for the same expected climate impacts, depending on the methods and assumptions used. This scientific discord blurs the analytical picture and hampers the straightforward interpretation of results, both by fellow scientists and policy-makers.

An additional and recurring methodological issue is the use of what are often considered western decision tools for situations in non-western societies. The prevalent decision framework in western countries is based on maximising economic efficiency and effectiveness, with the optimal – or 'rational' – decision being the one where marginal costs equal marginal benefits. This framework presupposes that all relevant values can be expressed and compared in monetary terms. However, many non-western societies rely greatly on socio-cultural and subsistence values, which are generally considered to be inappropriate or impossible to express in monetary terms. Therefore, western decision tools cannot be universally applied to assess adaptation benefits and determine the optimality – in terms of that societal desirability – of adaptation options.

DISCUSSION AND CONCLUSIONS

This chapter has shown that the international funding of adaptation to climate change faces a number of political, as well as scientific, challenges. These challenges are not limited to the GEF: very few projects have been initiated, funded and implemented with a specific focus on climate change as part of bilateral or multilateral programmes as well. However, bilateral and multilateral development assistance has the advantage of being potentially more flexible and thus more effective than the GEF in making funding decisions. The need for such flexibility pertains in particular to the distinction between climate change and climate variability and the related issue of incremental costs.

Its mandate requires the GEF to make a distinction between adaptation to a future, scenario-based climate change and adaptation to today's climate variability. Adaptation to climate change would be eligible for funding, whereas adaptation to climate variability is not. Both types of adaptation, however, are very similar by nature and they can mutually reinforce each other. For example, both types of adaptation would include protection against weather extremes and related hazards. Weather extremes occur independently of climate change but their magnitude and frequency of occurrence is likely to be affected as a result of climate change. Adapting to extremes that result from today's variability would be a good start to prepare for the extremes associated with a future climate.

Particularly if one accepts that human-induced climate change is already taking place, the distinction between the two types of adaptation becomes highly theoretical. It assumes that one is able to identify the relative contributions to weather extremes of human-induced climate change and natural climate variability. This is not only impossible but also immoral. The attribution question and related issues of funding eligibility are highly irrelevant to people who lose their lives or livelihoods as a result of weather extremes.

As far as the calculation of incremental costs of adaptation is concerned, this too requires information of a type that is not always possible to obtain.

As explained in the third section, incremental costs are the additional costs required to keep a system climate-safe. This definition assumes either that systems that are subject to adaptation to climate change are already climate-safe; or that it is the responsibility of the individual countries to make these systems climate-safe, using alternative – possibly their own – funds.

In the example of Note 3 it is immediately clear what the incremental costs of adaptation to climate change are. However, reality is often not as straightforward. As explained in the previous section, adaptation is a process that can comprise a range of different legal, institutional, economic and structural measures. It involves information development and awareness building regarding the needs and opportunities to adapt; the planning and design of adaptation measures, and their implementation in line with existing policy criteria and development objectives; and the monitoring and evaluation of the adaptation performance (see Figure 2.3). In addition, it requires the development of an enabling environment for implementing adaptation measures.

Thus the range of measures countries may wish to take to adapt to climate change is much broader than only structural processes such as building a seawall. An adaptation strategy may include actions such as:

- Setting up a monitoring network to enable the early warning of weather-related hazards.
- Changing institutional arrangements to enhance the effectiveness of political decisions.
- Strengthening a country's legal system to improve compliance with existing regulations.
- Changing fiscal arrangements to provide adaptation incentives to the private sector.
- Supporting the role of non-governmental organisations to ensure public involvement in decision-making.

It is clear that measures like these would have benefits that go beyond those of adaptation to climate change. However, it is also clear that it will be impossible to determine the relative contributions of these measures to the various types of benefits. As a result, the incremental costs of adaptation measures that are less straightforward than building a seawall are difficult or even impossible to determine.

It goes without saying that the two issues sketched will be a major constraint when it comes to providing funds for actual adaptation to climate change by the GEF (i.e., beyond Stage III). The effectiveness of adaptation to human-induced climate change depends on a country's own initiative and ability to adapt to today's climate variability. If no funds are available for the latter type of adaptation, adaptation to climate change is unlikely to be successful.

In view of the caveats described in the last section and the consequent barriers to adaptation funding, it is concluded that the quantitative assessment of future adaptation costs and benefits should play a less significant part in determining the optimality and appropriateness of adaptation options and hence in the allocation of adaptation funds. This does not suggest that adaptation projects should not make efficient or effective use of resources. However, a project's benefit–cost ratio alone is not a good indicator for the appropriateness of the adaptation. After all, given the uncertainties surrounding future climatic and non-climatic conditions, as well as the methodological discord on the use of decision tools, any quantitative estimate of adaptation costs and benefits can and will be questioned.

Instead of concentrating on its longer-term economic aspects, one could assess the economic value of an adaptation project to today's society. Assessment of today's costs and benefits is more straightforward and not fraught with as many difficulties as the assessment of those occurring in an uncertain future. In addition, a focus on today's climate variability can be critical in terms of saving lives and livelihoods. The recent series of natural disasters in the developing world has shown that many current systems cannot be assumed to be climate-safe. Hundreds of thousands of people died in weather-related disasters in Honduras, Venezuela, India and Mozambique, illustrating the urgent need to adapt to today's climate variability.

Measures to reduce the vulnerability of these countries to climate variability will be a good starting point to reduce vulnerability to climate change. But even if climate change were not to take place such measures would still be important and beneficial and would therefore be justifiable in their own right. Analogous to 'no-regret' mitigation measures (which help to reduce greenhouse gas emissions but also have immediate benefits to society that make them worthwhile to implement irrespective of climate change), adaptation measures that have both immediate and long-term benefits can be termed 'no-regret' adaptation measures.

In addition, non-economic aspects determine the appropriateness of adaptation. Adaptation activities need to be designed keeping site-specific natural and socio-cultural circumstances in mind. No adaptation option will be successful when implemented in an environment that is not ready, willing or able to receive the option. Strengthening technological, institutional, legal and economic capacities as well as raising awareness are prerequisites for effective adaptation.

It thus appears that today there are already numerous cost-effective opportunities to invest in adaptation (which corresponds with the findings of Fankhauser *et al.*, 1999). However, investment decisions should not be dictated by questionable normative numbers but informed by sound and positive assessments of how vulnerability to climate can already be reduced now. Such adaptation could have any of the five generic objectives of anticipatory adaptation listed in the second section, with an emphasis on the latter three. These three types tend to refer to no-regret options that serve to increase adaptive capacity to climate change, while also reducing vulnerability to current climate conditions. Thus their benefits are greater than the difference between residual and potential impacts shown in Figure 2.2.

It is clear that the current funding mechanisms for adaptation have not been designed for an investment strategy as suggested. Finding the institutional means to accommodate the adaptation needs for both today and the future is therefore an important challenge to the international climate community. It appears that important steps have been taken at COP-7 in Marrakech.

NOTES

Earlier versions of this chapter were presented at the OECD workshop 'Taking Action Against Climate Change: The Kyoto Protocol' (Paris, France, 15 June 1999) and at the RICAMARE workshop 'The Socio-economics of Climate Change in the Mediterranean' (Milano, Italy, 9–10 February 2001). I thank the participants of both workshops for their valuable comments and suggestions. Parts of this chapter have also appeared in the report 'Adaptation to Climate Change in German Official Development Assistance – An Inventory of Activities and Opportunities, with a Special Focus on Africa' (Klein, 2001), which I prepared for the Deutsche Gesellschaft für Technische Zusammenarbeit (GTZ).

1. The Annex II Parties are Australia, Austria, Belgium, Canada, Denmark, the European Union, Finland, France, Germany, Greece, Iceland, Ireland, Italy, Japan, Luxembourg, The Netherlands, New Zealand, Norway, Portugal, Spain, Sweden, Switzerland, United Kingdom of Great Britain and Northern Ireland and the United States of America.
2. The purpose of the CDM is to assist developing countries in achieving sustainable development and in contributing to the ultimate objective of the UNFCCC and to assist Annex I Parties (i.e., Annex II Parties, 14 countries that are undergoing the process of transition to a market economy, Croatia, Liechtenstein, Monaco and Turkey) in limiting greenhouse gas emissions (Article 12.2 of the Kyoto Protocol).
3. The protection of a coastal area against storm surges by means of a seawall provides a simple case to illustrate what are the incremental costs of adaptation to climate change. The level at which the seawall should offer protection is essentially a policy decision and reflects the population density and the value of the land and assets in the area at risk of flooding. This protection level determines the design height of the seawall, which for today's storm-surge regime can be calculated using meteorological, morphological and hydraulic data and information. If one were to protect not only against today's storm-surge regime but also to prepare for a climate change induced sea-level rise, the design height of the seawall would have to be increased. The cost difference between a seawall that only offers protection against today's variability and a higher one that also prepares for sea-level rise reflects the incremental costs of adaptation to climate change.
4. The dumb farmer is a metaphor for any impacted economic agent that does not anticipate climate change or act on its manifestation. Instead, it continues to act as if nothing

has changed. By not responding to changing circumstances, the agent reduces its profitability or fails to take advantage of emerging opportunities. It thus incurs larger damages than would have been the case had some adaptation taken place. The clairvoyant farmer, on the other hand, has perfect knowledge and foresight and is able to minimise damages or maximise benefits. As always, reality will be somewhere in between.

REFERENCES

Callaway, J.M., L.O. Næss and L. Ringius (1998) 'Adaptation costs: a framework and methods'. In: Francis, D., C. Brooke and K. Halsnæs (eds) *Mitigation and Adaptation Cost Assessment – Concepts, Methods and Appropriate Use*. UNEP Collaborating Centre on Energy and Environment, Risø National Laboratory, Roskilde, Denmark, pp. 97–119.

Carter, T.L., M.L. Parry, S. Nishioka and H. Harasawa (eds) (1994) *Technical Guidelines for Assessing Climate Change Impacts and Adaptations*. Report of Working Group II of the Intergovernmental Panel on Climate Change, University College London and Centre for Global Environmental Research, London, UK and Tsukuba, Japan.

Fankhauser, S. (1997) *The Costs of Adapting to Climate Change*. Working Paper 13, Global Environment Facility, Washington, DC, USA.

Fankhauser, S., J.B. Smith and R.S.J. Tol (1999) 'Weathering climate change: some simple rules to guide adaptation decisions'. *Ecological Economics*, 30(1), 67–78.

GEF (1996) *Operational Strategy*. Global Environment Facility, Washington, DC, USA.

IPCC (1996) 'Summary for policymakers: scientific-technical analyses of impacts, adaptations, and mitigation of climate change'. In: Watson, R.T., M.C. Zinyowera and R.H. Moss (eds) *Climate Change 1995 – Impacts, Adaptations and Mitigation of Climate Change: Scientific-Technical Analyses*. Contribution of Working Group II to the Second Assessment Report of the Intergovernmental Panel on Climate Change, Cambridge University Press, Cambridge, UK, pp. 1–18.

Kates, R.W. (1997) 'Climate change 1995 – impacts, adaptations, and mitigation'. *Environment*, 39(9), 29–33.

Klein, R.J.T. (1998) 'Towards better understanding, assessment and funding of climate adaptation'. *Change*, 44, 15–19.

Klein, R.J.T. (2001) *Adaptation to Climate Change in German Official Development Assistance – An Inventory of Activities and Opportunities, with a Special Focus on Africa*. Deutsche Gesellschaft für Technische Zusammenarbeit, Eschborn, Germany.

Klein, R.J.T. and D.C. MacIver (1999) 'Adaptation to climate variability and change'. *Mitigation and Adaptation Strategies for Global Change*, 4(3–4), 189–198.

Klein, R.J.T., R.J. Nicholls and N. Mimura (1999) 'Coastal adaptation to climate change: can the IPCC Technical Guidelines be applied?' *Mitigation and Adaptation Strategies for Global Change*, 4(3–4), 239–252.

Klein, R.J.T. and R.S.J. Tol (1997) *Adaptation to Climate Change: Options and Technologies – An Overview Paper*. Technical Paper FCCC/TP/1997/3, United Nations Framework Convention on Climate Change Secretariat, Bonn, Germany.

Leary, N.A. (1999) 'A framework for benefit–cost analysis of adaptation to climate change and climate variability'. *Mitigation and Adaptation Strategies for Global Change*, **4**(3–4), 307–318.

Mendelsohn, R., W.D. Nordhaus and D. Shaw (1996) 'Climate impacts on aggregate farm value: accounting for adaptation'. *Agricultural and Forest Meteorology*, **80**(1), 55–66.

Parry, M., N. Arnell, M. Hulme, R. Nicholls and M. Livermore (1998) 'Adapting to the inevitable'. *Nature*, **395**, 741.

Pielke, R.A., Jr (1998) 'Rethinking the role of adaptation in climate policy'. *Global Environmental Change*, **8**(2), 159–170.

Smit, B., I. Burton, R.J.T. Klein and J. Wandel (2000) 'An anatomy of adaptation to climate change and variability'. *Climatic Change*, **45**(1), 223–251.

Smit, B., O. Pilifosova, I. Burton, B. Challenger, S. Huq, R.J.T. Klein and G. Yohe (2001) 'Adaptation to climate change in the context of sustainable development and equity'. In: McCarthy, J.J., O.F. Canziani, N.A. Leary, D.J. Dokken and K.S. White (eds) *Climate Change 2001 – Impacts, Adaptation, and Vulnerability*. Cambridge University Press, Cambridge, UK, pp. 877–912.

Tol, R.S.J., R.J.T. Klein, H.M.A. Jansen and H. Verbruggen (1996) 'Some economic considerations on the importance of proactive integrated coastal zone management'. *Ocean & Coastal Management*, **32**(1), 39–55.

West, J.J. and H. Dowlatabadi (1999) 'On assessing the economic impacts of sea-level rise on developed coasts'. In: Downing, T.E., A.A. Olsthoorn and R.S.J. Tol (eds) *Climate, Change and Risk*. Routledge, London, UK, pp. 205–220.

Yohe, G. and J. Neumann (1997) 'Planning for sea level rise and shore protection under climate uncertainty'. *Climatic Change*, **37**(2), 243–270.

Yohe, G., J. Neumann, P. Marshall and H. Ameden (1996) 'The economic cost of greenhouse-induced sea-level rise for developed property in the United States'. *Climatic Change*, **32**(3), 387–410.

PART III

Climate change and Mediterranean water resources

3. Climate change and water resources in the Middle East: vulnerability, socio-economic impacts and adaptation

M. El-Fadel and E. Bou-Zeid

INTRODUCTION

Climate change due to greenhouse gases (GHG) has been at the forefront of current research efforts in the past decade (IPCC-WGI 1996a, 1996b). The aim of these efforts was defined at the Earth Summit in Rio de Janeiro as achieving 'stabilization of greenhouse gas concentrations in the atmosphere at a level that would prevent dangerous anthropogenic interference with the climatic system'. This statement of purpose clearly recognizes that some change is inevitable and acceptable as long as it is not considered dangerous. One real challenge is to predict how GHGs interfere with the climatic system and what impacts will result. In this context, several modeling approaches have been used to simulate climate conditions under increased CO_2 concentration. The models vary from simple upwelling diffusion-energy balance models to complex general circulation models (GCMs) with atmospheric and ocean modules (AOGCM) (IPCC-WGI 1996a). However, many aspects critical to climate modeling are still not fully understood, including cloud physics, aerosol effect, and atmosphere–ocean interaction among other processes (IPCC-WGI 1996a; IHS 1999).

A critical factor hindering the development of accurate predictions for future weather is the uncertainty inherent in estimating GHG emissions and concentrations. In addition to GHG concentrations, several other factors are important for climate modeling such as aerosol concentrations. The localized cooling effect of aerosols is considered as an important aspect that cannot be neglected in climate change models (IHS 1999; IPCC-TGCIA 1999; IPCC-WGII 1997). Despite uncertainties, GCMs depict certain trends that are useful in analyzing vulnerability and setting guidelines for potential adaptation measures. GCM simulations generally indicate increasing global temperatures leading to a more active hydrologic cycle. An increase in the hydrologic cycle activity denotes increasing global evaporation and precipitation. For the Middle East, GCM simulations indicate higher future temperatures that will increase evapotranspiration and changes in climate patterns that might reduce rainfall in the region as a whole (IPCC-DCC 1999; IPCC-WGI 1996a).

Evaluating the vulnerability of a country or region to climate change is an evolving discipline. Non-climatic scenarios, describing future socio-economic and environmental changes, are being increasingly used alongside climate scenarios in impact assessments to characterize the vulnerability and capacity for adaptation. Development of such scenarios has not been explicitly used in this study; however, the potential uncertainty and variability of future socio-economic and environmental conditions has been considered. Moreover, climate scenarios developed in the early 1990s are being reviewed in the light of new research findings, and new scenarios are being developed taking into consideration policy-related issues and projection uncertainties. A risk-assessment framework is also being increasingly considered for vulnerability studies (IPCC-WGII 2001). This chapter evaluates climate change scenarios for the Middle East. For this purpose, simulations from several GCMs were used. Socio-economic implications of the projected impacts are outlined and adaptation measures are addressed in the context of regional characteristics.

CLIMATE CHANGE AND WATER RESOURCES

Vulnerability of water systems and their sensitivity to climate change have been an active research topic in the last decade (Arnell 1996; IHS 1999). In view of the uncertainties associated with climate and hydrologic models, the benefits of developing quantified predictions remain controversial (IPCC-WGII 1996). Water resources management systems are very adaptive by nature (or through institutional intervention) and the usual variations in climatic and socio-economic conditions have provided water managers with experiences that help them cope with potential changes in climate patterns (Strzepek 1998). However, the high rate of climate change and its cumulative effect might pose serious problems. In conjunction with increasing demand for water, some biophysical and socio-economic impacts on water resources expected with a potentially changing climate are summarized in Table 3.1.

Table 3.1   *Some impacts on water resources expected with changing climate*

Biophysical aspects	Major impacted components	Some potential effects
Hydrologic parameters	• Precipitation • Evaporation • Transpiration • Runoff • Recharge	• Soil moisture changes • Reduced ground water recharge • Water shortages or surpluses • Dam failure due to floods • Dam storage loss due to sedimentation
Water quality	• Water temperature • Water salinity • Pollutant concentrations • Fauna and flora	• Changes in chemical quality • Changes in biological quality • Changes in thermal quality
Aquatic systems	• Streamflows • Erosion and sedimentation • Water levels in surface water bodies • Water levels in aquifers • Water fluxes in the subsurface	• Droughts or floods • Dam failure due to floods • Dam storage loss due to sedimentation
Socio-economic aspects		
Water supply	• Water demand per capita • Agricultural water demand	• Water demand increase beyond projected levels
Water management systems	• Streamflows • Water level in surface water bodies • Water levels in aquifers	• Reduced water supply • Changing loads on water treatment systems • Changing hydropower production potential

WATER RESOURCES IN THE MIDDLE EAST

The borders of the 'Middle East' are not well established. The boundaries of this region change with changing topics, so a different approach in defining the area is used in politics, geography, history, environment, economics, and so on. For the scope of this chapter, the countries that have significantly inter-connected water resources and that do not yet rely heavily on desalination

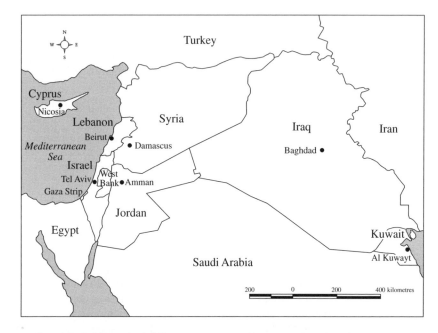

Figure 3.1   Map of Middle Eastern countries considered in this study

techniques are considered; that is, Lebanon, Syria, Iraq, Israel, Jordan, and the Palestinian Authority (West Bank and Gaza Strip) (Figure 3.1). While Turkey is the source of a significant amount of water flowing into Iraq and Syria, it is not addressed in this study due to climatic and hydrologic differences with the countries under consideration.

The Middle East and North Africa, with water resources of less than 1000 m^3 per capita in nine out of 14 countries, is the part of the world where water scarcity is the most severe and precarious (Berkoff 1994; ESCWA 1996, 1999; Postel 1993). Water shortage and uneven distribution of water supply are exacerbated by the rapid demographic and economic development in the region (Figure 3.2 and Table 3.2) which is increasing water demand at a relatively high pace. Iraq is the only country in the Middle East that appears to have sufficient water resources at present. However, Iraq is at the disadvantage of procuring more than two-thirds of its water resources as river flows from Turkey (Berkoff 1994).

It is expected that by 2025 the average annual renewable water resources for the Middle East will have fallen to 667 m^3 per capita compared to a world average of 4780 m^3 per capita (Berkoff 1994). Projections indicate significant water shortages in the future for most countries in the region (Table 3.3). Only Iraq would have adequate resources to cover its demands;

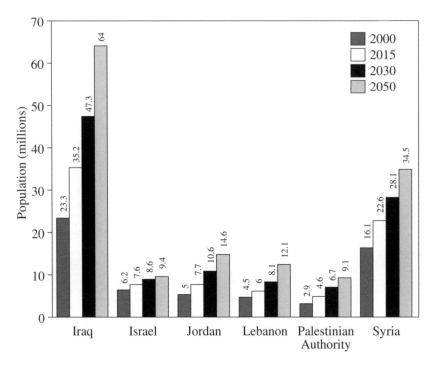

Sources: Berkoff (1994), ESCWA (1999), FAOSTAT (1999), El-Fadel *et al.* (2000).

Figure 3.2 Population projections

however, recent Turkish projects on the Euphrates and Tigris rivers threaten to reduce Iraq's supplies significantly. Table 3.3 depicts the baseline conditions, ignoring the effects of potential climate change. These estimates do not account for potential increased capacity in desalination or wastewater reuse. The ranges presented rely on varying assumptions of demographic growth, water use variation, water resources management reform, and so on. Table 3.4 depicts water demand growth for the countries under study. Note that agricultural demand accounts for 84 per cent (30 to 88 per cent for the individual countries) of the water demand in the region.

CLIMATE CHANGE IMPACTS ON WATER RESOURCES IN THE MIDDLE EAST

It is often assumed that since the Middle East region has very scarce water resources and an arid climate, the impact of climate change would be

Table 3.2 Socio-economic indicators

Country	Area (km²)	Urban population (% of total)	GNP in 1998 (billion US$)	GNP per capita			GDP growth 1999–2003 (%)	Access to safe drinking water (% of pop)
				In 1998 US$	Growth 1999–2003 (%)			
Iraq	438320	76	—[c]	540	−9.0		−6.0	77
Israel[a]	20700	91	95.2	15940	−0.3		2.0	99
Jordan	89210	73	6.9	1520	0.4		3.2	98
Lebanon	10452	89	15.0	3560	1.7		3.5	94
Palestinian Authority[b]	6263	—[c]	—[c]	—[c]	—[c]		—[c]	—
Syria	185180	54	15.6	1020	2.4		4.8	88

Notes:
[a] Area controlled by Israel before 1967.
[b] West Bank and Gaza Strip.
[c] Not available.

Sources: *Encyclopaedia Britannica* (1999), FAOSTAT (1999), World Bank (1999).

Table 3.3 Annual water resources in some Middle Eastern countries

Country	Average annual (mm)	Use of desalinated water and reclaimed waste water (% of total)	Total renewable water resources (billion m³)	Current and projected renewable water resources (m³ per capita)		
				1997	2015	2025
Iraq	154	—ᵃ	62.85–100.00	2963–4628	1832–2938	1359–2000
Israel	630	11.56	1.50–2.57	280–435	190–356	140–311
Jordan	94	5.32	0.75–1.35	168–229	78–133	70–91
Lebanon	827	0.16	2.00–3.94	766–1287	336–979	262–809
Palestinian Authority	350	1.08	0.20–0.22	72–92	43–56	34–36
Syria	252	2.56	15.00–21.48	1160–1438	759–948	535–609

Note: ᵃ Not available.

Sources: Berkoff (1994), Shuval (1994), FAO (1997), ESCWA (1999), Alatout (2000), Amery (2000), El-Fadel *et al.* (2000), Lithwick (2000), Shannang and Al-Adwan (2000).

Table 3.4　Current and projected water demand for the region
(million m³)

Country	Current and projected total water demand		Projected breakdown for 2005 by sectors		
	2000	2025	Domestic	Agriculture	Industrial
Iraq	54972	74310	4750	66000	3560
Israel	1960	3116	997	1906	206
Jordan	1257	1760	700	900	160
Lebanon	1650	3069	876	1500	693
Palestinian Authority	495	1290	800	420	70
Syria	17130	23555	2825	19430	1300

Sources:　Berkoff (1994), ESCWA (1999), FAOSTAT (1999), MFA (1999), El-Fadel et al.
(2000).

negligible (IPCC-WGII 1996). However, as noted before, water resources in the region are under heavy and increasing stress. Any alteration in climatic patterns that increased temperatures and reduced rainfall would greatly exacerbate existing difficulties. The general approach used for assessing the impacts on hydrologic regimes is to obtain climate data (representing various assumptions concerning projection period, GHG growth assumptions, etc.) from GCMs and RCMs and use them as input to basin hydrologic models. However, if long-term data on rainfall-runoff correlation and basin water balance are not available, complex hydrologic models should be avoided (IHS 1999; IPCC-WGI 1996b; Strzepek 1998). Such data are unfortunately missing or unavailable in almost all the countries under study (Lonergan and Brooks 1994; IDRC 2000). While data are available for some major basins, data collection programs are recent and do not have the time span that allows reliable statistical correlations of inputs (precipitation, runon, etc.) and outputs (runoff, evaporation, etc.) to be developed for extreme conditions. Therefore, potential climate change impacts are evaluated using GCM simulations.

Several GCMs have been used to model future climate for the whole planet under varying scenarios. Recent efforts have focused on setting standard scenarios and time-frames to ensure comparability of results from different GCM simulations (Strzepek 1998; IPCC-WGI 1996a; IPCC-WGII 1997). GCMs' relative success in reproducing global weather patterns from past data is not necessarily an assurance that they will correctly predict future climate even at the global scale.

Table 3.5   *Climate change parameters (IPCC-DCC 1999)*

Country	HadCM2	GFDL-R15	CGCM	Echam4	ΔT max
January–March mean temperature increase (°C)					
Iraq	0.9	1.7	1.6	1.1	1.7
Israel	0.6	1.2	1.2	1	1.2
Jordan	0.9	1.8	1.3	1.1	1.8
Lebanon	0.6	1.2	1.3	1	1.3
Palestine	0.6	1.2	1.3	1	1.3
Syria	0.8	1.7	1.3	1.1	1.7
June–August mean temperature increase (°C)					
Iraq	0.9	2.1	1.5	1.5	2.1
Israel	0.8	1.8	0.9	1.4	1.8
Jordan	0.9	2.1	0.8	1.2	2.1
Lebanon	0.8	1.8	0.9	1.4	1.8
Palestine	0.8	1.8	0.9	1.2	1.8
Syria	0.8	2.1	0.8	1.2	2.1
October–April mean rainfall change (mm/day)					
Iraq	0	0	0	0	0
Israel	0	−0.1	0	0	−0.1
Jordan	0	0	0	0	0
Lebanon	0	−0.1	0	0	−0.1
Palestine	0	−0.1	0	0	−0.1
Syria	0	0	0	0	0

Note: Values are for 2020s relative to the 1961–1990 period.

Source: IPCC–DCC (1999).

Climate change projections in the Middle East are compared using simulation results from four different GCMs (ECHAM4, HadCM2, CGCM1, GFDL) for the same set of assumptions (IS92a scenario). Both greenhouse gases and sulfur aerosols are accounted for in the GCMs and the projections available are for the 2020s climate conditions in comparison to the period 1961–1990.

The temperature change during the winter (January, February, March) and the summer (June, July, August), and the rainfall change during the wet season (October to April) as calculated by the different models for the countries under study are summarized in Table 3.5. These results show minor changes in mean precipitation for the region, while temperatures are projected to increase in all seasons. Mean summer temperatures, already high in the region, will rise significantly (0.8–2.1°C). Areas bordering the Mediterranean (Lebanon, Israel, Palestinian Authority, coastal Syria) would be the least affected. However, groundwater aquifers in these areas will be under the hazard of increased seawater intrusion due to higher sea levels.

The discrepancies between predictions of different models reach a maximum 1.3°C for Syria during the summer. However, the trend is clearly towards increasing mean temperatures, which will increase irrigation water demand due to higher evaporation. Extreme temperatures are predicted to increase more than mean temperature values. Increased temperature and evapotranspiration coupled with constant precipitation are highly associated with desertification. Mean winter temperatures will also increase; however, the rise is predicted to be lower than for the summer season. Higher winter temperatures will enhance evapotranspiration and reduce potential groundwater recharge. If the increased runoff due to sharper precipitation patterns is also considered, the net effect will be a reduction in groundwater recharge and hence in the baseline renewable water resources (see Table 3.3).

It is noteworthy that while most models predicted an increase in temperature, few reported an opposite trend. One particular study that coupled a nested regional model for the Middle East and southern Europe to a GCM predicted a decrease in temperature for the region ranging from 0 to 1°C due to doubling CO_2 levels (Jones *et al.* 1997). This was attributed to the cooling effect of sulfur aerosols.

SOCIO-ECONOMIC IMPLICATIONS

One of the main targets of vulnerability studies is to relate potential impacts on biophysical environments to the socio-economic effects resulting from such impacts. The simplest approaches attempt to establish and assess the direct linkages between the biophysical setting and the economic activity. Consequently, the socio-economic impacts of potential changes in the biophysical setting are reported as percentage variation in per capita GDP relative to a baseline scenario. Based on such methods, economic impact of climate change is estimated at 2 to 9 per cent of annual national GDP for developing countries (IPCC-WGII 1997) in contrast to a 1 to 1.5 per cent reduction in GDP for developed countries. The greater vulnerability of poorer regions to climate change is related to their high reliance on weather-related activities, particularly agriculture, and the low adaptation and damage restoration capacity (Tol 1996). While there is a growing trend to estimate the impacts on welfare rather than the economy, it is difficult to compare broadly different impacts and to measure them on a single scale, even when the randomness and poor understanding of socio-economic systems are overcome.

It is widely argued that many consequences of climate change are not easily amenable to monetary valuation (IPCC-WGII 1997). Examples of such consequences include loss of human life, loss of natural habitats, species loss, migration, and uneven resources distribution within a single country. Significant variations are noted when monetary valuation of such impacts is undertaken, thus resulting in differences in the estimation of financial losses. The assessment of the impacts of a 2.5°C temperature increase due to CO_2 concentration doubling on US water resources is an example. Different studies evaluate the damages to range from 6.1×10^9\$ (Cline 1992) to 13.7×10^9\$ (Fankhauser 1995).

Even when the impact assessment is not narrowed down to an economic valuation, the structure of the economy and the related development level and population distribution characteristics are necessary for vulnerability studies. Figure 3.3 depicts the distribution of the 1998 economic activity between the sectors for the countries under consideration. The sectors considered are industry, agriculture and services, which encompasses

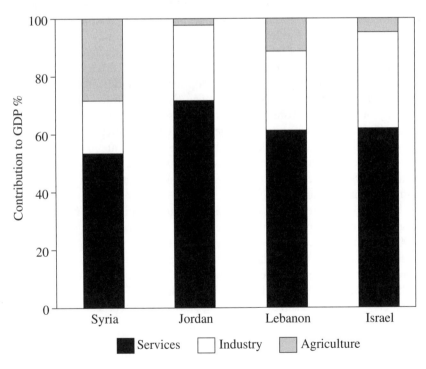

Source: World Bank (1999).

Figure 3.3 Economic activity by sector

everything else (example: banking, tourism). Note that data for Iraq and the Palestinian Authority are not available. After the Gulf War, the nascent Iraqi industry was damaged and economic activity in the country today mainly relies on oil exports, light industries, and agriculture. In addition to the three main sectors, economic activity in the Palestinian Authority relies heavily on cash flow from workers in Israel as well as external international assistance.

Economic analysis of climate change impacts can be considered at a macroscale (whole national or regional economy), a sectoral scale (economic sectors), or a project scale (effect on economic feasibility of a dam, for example). Water resources variations are assumed to impact water prices and agricultural water demand. Impacts on other economic sectors are usually indirect, through the use of agricultural products and higher water prices. Since water price elasticity is very difficult to establish, extrapolation of current conditions without regard to potential novelties and discontinuities is often used.

This review will primarily present a qualitative assessment of expected welfare implications of climate change impacts on Middle East water resources. Economic modeling should address each country separately due to the variations in economic activity characteristics and relatively low economic integration in the region. Due to the semi-arid weather of the region, water can be a limiting factor for development. This indicates that potential welfare impacts could be high. Even Syria and Iraq, which depend heavily on river flow from Turkey, could be seriously affected since transboundary water flow is expected to decrease as Turkey attempts to deal with its own water shortage problems in the future. The climate in Turkey could be characterized as semi-arid in vast regions of the country and demographic growth is expected to increase stress on water resources even if climate change is not considered.

International assessments of climate change impacts on the Middle East region often focus on the oil producing gulf countries. Some studies (Tol 1995) evaluate the cost of coastal defenses, dryland, wetland, and species loss, migration and natural hazards in the region to be insignificant. Other damages are assessed to have very low costs compared with similar costs in other regions of the world. Few studies described the climate change impacts on Middle East countries lying on the Mediterranean basin (Jeftic *et al.* 1996; IPCC-WGII 1997).

Table 3.6 summarizes the expected extent of socio-economic impacts associated with climate change effects on water resources accounting for both the importance of the impact (for example, the increased agricultural demand per hectare of agricultural land) and the significance of the impacted sector (for example, the total agricultural water demand and part

Table 3.6   *Socio-economic implications of climate change impacts on water resources in some Middle Eastern countries*

Impact	Iraq	Israel	Jordan	Lebanon	Palestinian Authority	Syria
Increased industrial and domestic water demand	**	*	*	**	*	**
Increased agricultural water demand	***	**	*	***	***	***
Water resources distribution equity decline	***	**	***	**	***	***
Flood damage	***	*	*	**	*	*
Water quality damage	***	***	***	***	***	***
Hydropower loss	*	*	*	**	*	*
Ecosystems damage and species loss	**	**	*	***	**	**
GDP reduction (%)	3–6	1–2	1–2	2–5	2–5	4–7

Note: ***: high; **: moderate; *: insignificant.

of the agriculture in the GDP). The assessment is qualitative and relies on literature addressing Middle Eastern countries considered here or countries with some similar characteristics.

Industrial water use is not significantly affected by climate change (Strzepek 1998). Domestic water demand is negatively correlated with water prices and precipitation and positively correlated with ambient temperatures (Kindler and Russel 1984). Temperature rise is expected to be highest in Syria, Iraq and Jordan while precipitation is not expected to be significantly reduced (see Table 3.5). Price variations are very difficult to forecast in the region since market mechanisms do not totally control prices in many of the countries under investigation. In addition, it can be argued that domestic water demand rises do not continually increase with temperature for countries that already have relatively warm climates. Increase in domestic water demand is not expected to be significant in Jordan, Israel, and the Palestinian Authority since the climate in these countries is already arid and water prices are expected to increase significantly with demand increase. On the other hand, Syria, Iraq and Lebanon are expected to witness some increase in domestic water demand since the length of the dry period in these countries is likely to increase and elasticity of water prices with demand is lower than for the other countries due to their relatively more abundant water resources.

Increases in agricultural water demand are expected to be significant in all countries. However, the socio-economic impacts in Jordan are expected to be insignificant since agricultural activity in the country is very minor. Israel is expected to have some moderate impacts due to the low share of agriculture to its GDP (World Bank 1999) and the relatively high adaptation capacity correlated with the high per capita GDP of Israel. Lebanon, Syria, Iraq, and the Palestinian Authority will face harder challenges to mitigate decreased water availability impact on agricultural economy.

Unequal water resource distribution impacts are expected to be most severe for rural populations that rely on agricultural production and on small-scale water management networks (European Parliament 1999). Hence, equity in water distribution is projected to decrease mostly in Syria, Iraq, Jordan, and the Palestinian Authority, where the large rural agricultural populations (see Table 3.2) will be more affected than urban populations. Lebanon and Israel have a higher percentage of urban population and less widespread rural populations that could be better served if their local water resources are depleted.

Floods can be divided into two categories: riverine floods (river overflow during thunderstorms or during the snow-melting season) and flash floods (due to severe thunderstorms causing great overland runoff). It is speculated that warmer ambient temperatures and higher evaporation rates will increase flood risk (Dracup and Kendall 1990). Damage is not expected to be significant in Syria, Israel, Jordan, and the Palestinian Authority due to scarcity of rivers and the absence of major urban areas in the vicinity of water bodies. Lebanon has high average precipitation, many rivers, and many urban settings near major rivers (for example, consider the historical flood of the Abu-Ali river in Tripoli, Lebanon). These factors indicate a potential for increased damage from flood events relative to baseline conditions. Iraq has most of its urban and agricultural population (including the capital Baghdad) in the basins of the Tigris and Euphrates rivers and floods here can cause very significant social and economic damage. However, flood risk in Iraq will be highly dependent on upstream control and Turkish dam projects Alternatively, flood protection works will be costly and will incur economic damage to the country.

Impacts on water quality are very difficult to assess due to uncertainties in predicting the biological, physical, societal, economic, and regulatory changes or adaptation measures that could affect the water environment. It is usually agreed that the impacts, if any, are mainly negative (Hanaki *et al.* 1998; Jacobi 1990). A potentially high impact was noted in Table 3.6 for all countries since water quality is already a problem in most of them and a decrease in water resources is correlated with a lower dilution potential of existing pollution. Even in countries that have significant water treatment capacity, water treatment costs will rise and economic impact will ensue. In addition to economic impacts, water quality deterioration could result in environmental damage and aquatic species loss. Water quality could also be affected by rising sea levels since many countries rely heavily on groundwater resources, and groundwater salinity is expected to rise due to an increase in seawater intrusion.

Hydropower loss is usually a concern in regions with high proportion of hydroelectric to total electric power (Gleick 1990). These proportions are insignificant in all countries since hydropower resources are scarce and untapped in the region. Lebanon is an exception as it has several hydro-power plants and plans to build other ones (El-Fadel *et al.* 2000), however, reductions in hydropower availability in Lebanon are projected to be low to moderate since fossil fuel power generation capacity is growing faster than hydroelectric capacity. If mitigation of GHG emissions reverses this trend, the country might be highly vulnerable to water flow variations.

At the latitude of the Middle East, ecosystem damage and species loss is expected to be most significant in mountainous regions where vegetation distribution is likely to shift to higher altitudes (IPCC-WGI 1997; IPCC-WGII 1997). Hence, insignificant to moderate bioclimatic changes are pro-jected for the studied countries under medium climate change scenarios due to the relatively flat topography of the region. Lebanon and some regions in western Syria are the only areas where such impact can be high due to the mountainous topography and the expected reduction in the areas of many 'wet' bioclimatic regions (the Oro-Mediterranean bioclimatic region is one example) that cover large areas in the mountainous regions of the country (UNDP 1999).

Based on ranges reported in literature (IPCC-WGI 1997), potential reduction in GDP due to climate change was projected for the six countries. Reduction is lowest for Israel and Jordan (1 to 2 per cent) due to the small contribution of weather-exposed activity to the economy. Syria and Iraq could have significant GDP reduction of up to 7 per cent due to their heavy reliance on agriculture and a currently low adaptation capacity. Finally, a detailed assessment of the health implications of water resources vulner-ability to climate change would be quite complex; however, it is expected that serious health challenges will arise due to increased temperatures and reduced water availability. Propagation of vector-borne and water-borne diseases will be particularly exacerbated due to higher temperatures and extreme weather events (Patz 1999).

While the analysis provides a prediction of potential climate change impact on water resources in the Middle East, the results can be correlated with several limitations including:

• Climate change scenarios for the region have large uncertainties and discrepancies between the different GCMs. For instance, predictions for the Nile river flow in Egypt varies from a 30 per cent increase (GISS model) to a 78 per cent decrease (GFDL model) for the same scenario depicting $2 \times CO_2$ conditions (Strzepek and Yates 1996).

- A given change in climate will produce different responses in the basins of the Middle East depending on the hydrologic characteristics of each one. Lack of data about basin characteristics and accurate water balance data hinders the use of advanced hydrologic models.

- Baseline predictions are unsure in view of the uncertainty in forecasting socio-economic, legislative, and water management conditions. Countries that have low adaptation and mitigation capacity at present might build such capacities at very different rates.

ADAPTATION MEASURES

When adaptation measures are designed or implemented before climate change, they must be flexible enough to perform their designated objectives under a wide variety of future climate conditions (Smith 1996). Measures that apply to Middle Eastern countries are discussed in the light of the expected increasing stress on water resources in the study region and the potential adverse impacts of climate change. In addition to climate change stress on water resources, water shortages will be exacerbated by population and economic growth. In fact, the baseline scenario predicts a drop in per capita water resources of about 50 per cent for the region by 2025. Therefore, most adaptation measures can be qualified as no-regret options. In other words, they would be beneficial regardless of climate change impacts. Moreover, these measures will improve the adaptability of water resources systems to natural variability in climate patterns (Conway and Hulme 1996).

The main adaptation measures and non-conventional sources of water that can be exploited in the future are summarized in Table 3.7. Adoption of any particular adaptation measure will need capital investment, institutional reforms, and capacity building. Institutional reforms should aim at strengthening institutions, removing market distortions, correcting market failure to reflect environmental damage or resource depletion, and promoting public awareness and involvement. Capacity building would be of crucial importance for monitoring and mitigating the impacts on water quality. In addition to technical adaptation measures, improvement of management systems (coordinating use of river basins, inter-basin transfer, etc.) and development of drought or flood contingency planning are essential to minimize climate change impact on water resources.

Table 3.7 Technical adaptation measures and non-conventional water resources

Adaptation measure	Potential benefits	Best uses	Cost (US$/(m³·day⁻¹))	Feasibility
Conservation	Curbs water demand increase	Domestic, industrial, agricultural demand reduction	Cost could be negative if pricing policies are adopted to reduce demand	High; inhabitants of the region are used to the notion that water is a scarce and finite resource
Use of surplus winter runoff	Collectable runoff can constitute up to 10% of rainfall	Irrigation, aquifer recharge	Not available	Low; due to the scarcity of precipitation and hence runoff
Wastewater reclamation	All collected wastewater can be reused	Irrigation, aquifer recharge	0.5–1.5	Medium-high; the technical capacity is available, the institutional capacity and financial resources might be constrained
Seawater/brackish water desalination	Unlimited water supply	Domestic, industrial	0.7–1.5	Medium-high; the technical capacity is available, the institutional capacity and financial resources might be constrained
Rainfall enhancement by seeding clouds with silver iodide crystals	Can increase precipitation by up to 15 percent in arid regions	Irrigation, aquifer recharge	Not available	Low; the technical expertise is lacking. Higher in Israel

(continued overleaf)

69

Table 3.7 (continued)

| Use of submarine springs | Submarine springs with significant flows are located along the Lebanese coastal waters (Ayoub *et al.* 2000) | Domestic, industrial, agricultural use, aquifer recharge | Not available | Low; the technical expertise is lacking and these springs have not been extensively characterized. Higher in Lebanon |

CONCLUSION

The potential impacts of climate change on water resources in the Middle East region have been presented here, with simulations of climate change predictions from several GCMs used to evaluate impacts on water resources. Climate change is expected to further exacerbate existing water shortages. Although precipitation was not predicted to decrease, temperature increases of 0.6–2.1°C would impact the water balance and reduce available resources. Similar hydrologic impacts might have different socio-economic consequences depending on region-specific characteristics. In the context of the Middle East, variations in water resources systems might have significant adverse effects including reduction of GDP, population redistribution, work force shift to alternative economic sectors, and so on.

Several potential welfare impacts were evaluated. The most critical at a regional level are expected to be increased agricultural water demand, water resources distribution equity decline, water quality damage, and GDP reduction. Serious health implications and increased propagation of diseases could also result from more extreme weather events and higher temperatures. The indirect impact of climate change on hydraulic structures should not be underestimated in view of potential increases in precipitation intensities and modifications in river flows patterns. Adaptation measures are necessary in view of increased water demand and potential decrease in available water. Most adaptation measures are no-regret options that attempt to develop non-conventional sources of water that can be exploited in the future, including use of surplus winter runoff, wastewater reclamation, seawater and brackish water desalination, rainfall enhancement by seeding clouds with silver iodide crystals, and exploitation of submarine springs. Conservation measures, as well as institutional reforms and capacity building, are also needed.

NOTE

Portions of this chapter have been accepted for publication in *ASCE, Journal of Water Resources Planning and Management.* Special thanks are extended to the United States Agency for International Development for its continuous support for the Water Resources Center and the Environmental Engineering and Sciences Programs at the American University of Beirut.

REFERENCES

Alatout, S. (2000). 'Water balances in Palestine: numbers and political culture in the Middle East', in Brooks, D.B. and Mehmet, O. (eds) *Water Balances in the Eastern Mediterranean*, pp. 59–84, International Development Research Center, Ottawa, Ontario, Canada.

Amery H.A. (2000). 'Assessing Lebanon's water balance', in Brooks, D.B. and Mehmet, O. (eds) *Water Balances in the Eastern Mediterranean*, pp. 13–28, International Development Research Center, Ottawa, Ontario, Canada.

Arnell, N. (1996). *Global Warming, River Flows and Water Resources*. The Institute of Hydrology. John Wiley and Sons, West Sussex.

Ayoub, G., Ghannam, J., Khoury, R., Acra, A. and Hamdar, B. (2000). 'The submarine springs in the Chekka Bay, Lebanon: delineation of salient features'. International Development Research Center (IDRC), Ottawa, Canada.

Berkoff, J. (1994). 'A strategy for managing water in the Middle East and North Africa'. The International Bank for Reconstruction and Development, The World Bank, Washington, DC.

Cline, W.R. (1992). *The Economics of Global Warming*. Institute for International Economics, Washington, DC.

Conway, D. and Hulme, M. (1996). 'The impacts of climate variability and future climate change in the Nile basin on water resources in Egypt'. *Water Resources Development*, **12**(3), 277–296.

Dracup, J.A. and Kendall, D.R. (1990). 'Flood and Droughts', in Waggoner, P.E. (ed.) *Climate Change and U.S. Water Resources*. John Wiley and Sons, New York.

Economic and Social Commission for Western Asia (ESCWA) (1996). 'Water legislation in selected ESCWA countries'. *Report E/ESCWA/ENR/1996/WG.1/ WP.3*, Beirut, Lebanon.

Economic and Social Commission for Western Asia (ESCWA) (1999). 'Updating the assessment of water resources in ESCWA member states'. *Report E/ESCWA/ENR/1999/WG.1/WP.3*, Beirut, Lebanon.

El-Fadel, M., Zeinati, M. and Jamali, D. (2000). 'Water resources in Lebanon: characterization, water balance and constraints'. *Water Resources Development*, **16**(4), 619–642.

Encyclopaedia Britannica (1999). <http://www.britannica.com> (17 Feb. 2000)

European Parliament (1999). 'Consequences of climate change for agricultural production'. Publication No. EP/IV/B/STOA/98/02/01, Brussels.

Fankhauser, S. (1995). *Valuing Climate Change, the Economics of Greenhouse*. EarthScan, London.

Food and Agriculture Organization of the United Nations (FAO) (1997). 'Irrigation in the Near East region in figures'. Rome, Italy.

Food and Agriculture Organization Statistics Database (FAOSTAT) (1999). <http://apps.fao.org/cgi-bin/nph-db.pl> (16 Feb. 2000)

Gleick P.H. (1990). 'Vulnerability of water systems', in Waggoner, P.E. (ed.) *Climate Change and U.S. Water Resources*. John Wiley and Sons, New York.

Hanaki, K., Takara, K., Hanazato, T., Hiromaru, H. and Kayanne, H. (1998). 'Impacts on hydrology/water resources and water environment', in *Global Warming: The Potential Impact on Japan*. Springer-Verlag, Tokyo.

Intergovernmental Panel for Climate Change, Data Distribution Center (IPCC-DCC) (1999). <http://ipcc-dcc.cru.uea.ac.uk> (24 Feb. 2000).

Intergovernmental Panel for Climate Change, Working Group I (IPCC-WGI) (1996a). *Climate Change 1995: The Science of Climate Change.* Cambridge University Press, Cambridge.

Intergovernmental Panel for Climate Change, Working Group I (IPCC-WGI) (1996b). *IPCC Workshop on Regional Climate Change Projections for Impact Assessment.* Geneva, Switzerland.

Intergovernmental Panel for Climate Change, Working Group I (IPCC-WGI) (1997). *Stabilization of Atmospheric Greenhouse Gases: Physical, Biological and Socio-economic Implications.* Houghton, J.T., Filho, L.G.M., Griggs, D.J. and Maskell, K. (eds). Geneva, Switzerland.

Intergovernmental Panel for Climate Change, Working Group II (IPCC-WGII) (1996). *Climate Change 1995: Impacts, Adaptation and Mitigation of Climate Change, Scientific-technical Analyses.* Cambridge University Press, Cambridge.

Intergovernmental Panel for Climate Change, Working Group II (IPCC-WGII) (1997). *The Regional Impacts of Climate Change, Summary for Policymakers.* Watson, R.T., Zinyowera, M.C., Moss, R.H. and Dokken, D.J. (eds). Geneva, Switzerland.

Intergovernmental Panel for Climate Change, Working Group II (IPCC-WGII) (2001). *Climate Change 2001: Impacts, Adaptation and Vulnerability, Technical Summary.* Manning, M. and Nobre, C. (eds). Geneva, Switzerland.

Intergovernmental Panel on Climate Change, Task Group on Scenarios for Climate Impact Assessment (IPCC-TGCIA) (1999). 'Guidelines on the use of scenario data for climate impact and adaptation assessment'. Version 1, Carter, T.R., Hulme, M. and Lal, M. (eds). Geneva, Switzerland.

International Development Research Center (IDRC) (2000). *Water Balances in the Eastern Mediterranean.* Brooks, D.B. and Mehmet, O. (eds). Ottawa, Ontario, Canada.

International Hydrology Series (IHS) (1999). *Impacts of Climate Change and Climate Variability on Hydrological Regimes.* Van Dam, J.C. (ed.). Cambridge University Press, Cambridge.

Jacobi, H.D. (1990). 'Water quality', in Waggoner, P.E. (ed.) *Climate Change and U.S. Water Resources.* John Wiley and Sons, New York.

Jeftic, L., Keckes, S. and Pernetta, J.C. (eds) (1996). *Climate Change and the Mediterranean.* Arnold, London.

Jones, R.G., Murphy, J.M., Noguer, M. and Keen, A.B. (1997). 'Simulation of climate change over Europe using a nested regional-climate model. II: comparison of driving and regional model responses to a doubling of carbon dioxide'. *Quarterly Journal of the Royal Meteorological Society*, **123**(538), 265.

Kindler, J. and Russel, C.S. (eds) (1984). *Modeling Water Demands.* Academy Press, London.

Lithwick, H. (2000). 'Evaluating water balances in Israel', in Brooks, D.B. and Mehmet, O. (eds) *Water Balances in the Eastern Mediterranean*, pp. 29–58. International Development Research Center, Ottawa, Ontario, Canada.

Lonergan, S.C. and Brooks, D.B. (1994). *Watershed: The Role of Fresh Water in the Israeli Palestinian Conflict.* International Development Research Center, Ottawa, Ontario, Canada.

Ministry of Foreign Affairs (MFA) (1999). 'Spotlight on Israel: Israel chronic water problem'. Jerusalem. <http://www.israel-mfa.gov.il/mfa/go.asp?MFAH00ic0> (24 Aug. 2000).

Patz, J.A. (1999). 'Climate change and health: challenges for an interdisciplinary approach'. *Environmental Management Magazine*, Air and Waste Management Association, March.

Postel, S. (1993). In Kane, H. and Ayres, E. (eds) *Water Scarcity Spreading, Vital Signs.* WorldWatch Institute, Norton & Co., New York.

Shannang, E. and Al-Adwan, Y. (2000) 'Evaluating water balances in Jordan', in Brooks, D.B. and Mehmet, O. (eds) *Water Balances in the Eastern Mediterranean*, pp. 85–94. International Development Research Center, Ottawa, Ontario, Canada.

Shuval, H. (1994) 'Proposals for the integrated management of the shared trans-boundary water resources of the Jordan River Basin'. *Water Science and Technology*, **30**(5), 187–193.

Smith, J.B. (1996). 'Development of adaptation measures for water resources'. *Water Resources Development*, **12**(2), 151–163.

Strzepek, K.M. (1998). 'Water resources', in Feenstra, J.F., Burton, I., Smith, J.B. and Tol, R.S.J. (eds) *Handbook on Methods for Climate Change Impact Assessment and Adaptation Strategies.* United Nations Environment Programme and Dutch Institute for Environmental Studies.

Strzepek, K.M. and Yates, D.N. (1996). 'Economic and social adaptations to climate change impacts on water resources: a case study of Egypt'. *Water Resources Development*, **12**(2), 229–244.

Tol, R.S.J. (1995). 'The damage costs of climate change toward more comprehensive calculation'. *Environmental Resources Economics*, **5**, 353–374.

Tol, R.S.J. (1996). 'The damage costs of climate change towards a dynamic representation'. *Ecological Economics*, **19**, 67–90.

United Nations Development Program (UNDP) (1999). 'The first national inventory of greenhouse gas emissions by sources and removals by sinks'. Ministry of Environment, Beirut, Lebanon.

World Bank (1999). 'World development indicators 2000'. Development data, country data, country tables, Lebanon, 131 <http://www.worldbank.org/data/countrydata/countrydata.html> (24 Aug. 2000).

4. Water availability for agriculture under climate change: understanding adaptation strategies in the Mediterranean

Ana Iglesias, M. Neil Ward, Manuel Menendez and Cynthia Rosenzweig

Social impacts of water scarcity in the Mediterranean are increasing and will probably be exacerbated by increasing population, urbanization, expanding irrigation areas needed to maintain food security in southern Mediterranean countries, inadequate controls of water use, lack of political will, and cultural impediments.

Climate change is likely to alter both the need for and the supply of water for irrigation. These changes could be significant, given that irrigation is the major consumer of water in the Mediterranean, using more than two-thirds of the water withdrawn from the rivers, lakes and aquifers. Projections of water availability for agriculture also relate to the expansion of cities and to industrial growth, since competition over fresh water supplies may shift between different sectors of national economies as population rises and economic development ensues.

Water management is strongly concerned with the minimization of risks in agricultural production. Much of the risk is caused by the unpredictability of future weather patterns. The most salient risks are drought on a seasonal or longer-term basis. The impacts vary between users and regions in the Mediterranean.

This chapter is concerned with the ability to understand and respond to climate variability and change as conditioned by the ongoing processes of decision-making and socio-economic transformations. The research analyzes quantitative estimates of the impacts of climate change in the water needed for irrigation in contrasting Mediterranean areas. The scenario analysis focuses on improving resource-use efficiencies that would lead to a reduction of current and future emergency actions.

75

THE REGIONAL FRAMEWORK

Climate is intrinsically linked with water resources and agriculture. The Mediterranean region has suffered from structural water deficits over the past 20 years that have forced individuals, local governments and the international community to take emergency measures (CEDEX, 2000). Many countries in the southern Mediterranean face severe shortfalls in water availability and they are classified as either water-scarce or water-stressed. The stress is expected to increase by 2025, in large part because of increases in demand resulting from economic and population growth (IPCC, 2001).

Crop production in Mediterranean countries is extremely sensitive to large year-to-year weather fluctuations and to structural water deficits. Irrigated agriculture in the region has greatly expanded to ensure food production targets and today agriculture accounts for over 80 per cent of the total water demand in southern Mediterranean countries (African) and for over 60 per cent in the northern Mediterranean countries (European). The connections between water and food production in the region are receiving increasing attention as the concerns of food experts begin to encompass the realities of current and future water availability (IPCC, 2001; Parry et al., 1999, 2001; Gleick, 2000).

In the whole of the Mediterranean basin, climate is an essential component of the natural capital and an important element of sustainable development. Water is not only a major socio-economic element but an essential cultural element as well. As a result, the policy debates related to water have been and will continue to be vigorous. Effective measures to cope with scarcity are known, but are difficult to implement due to the variety of stakeholders and inadequate means to negotiate new policies (Downing et al., 2001). Any efforts made to improve communication among the scientific and decision-making communities will have great benefits for the future of water management in the region.

Mediterranean climates are among the most variable in the world and recurrent drought problems often affect entire countries over multi-year periods, resulting in serious social problems. For example, the structural water deficit of many areas in the region has been aggravated during three periods of severe drought (1975–76, 1981–82, and 1992–95), each more severe than the previous one. During these droughts, besides the collapse of the agricultural activities, urban water supply was affected significantly. For example, the water supply of the metropolitan area of Sevilla (1 300 000 inhabitants) suffered a severe emergency in 1995 (CEDEX, 2001). Although less documented, the adverse effects of recurrent drought are more dramatic in the southern Mediterranean countries and often result in serious social problems. For example, the drought experienced in Morocco, Algeria, and Tunisia during the period 1999/2001 resulted in a dramatic disparity in their agricultural trade balance, disrupting local rural economies and contributing to migration to urban areas. In Morocco, the government and the international community responded to this extreme drought vigorously, but so far the responses have focused on the effects of drought *ex post*, rather than on anticipatory measures *ex ante*. In general, these efforts have neglected to build the capacity needed to deal with similar situations in the future. Furthermore, information on possible longer-term climate forecasts and/or development of plausible scenarios has not yet been incorporated into any specific action plans.

The social impacts of water scarcity in the Mediterranean are increasing and will probably be exacerbated by increasing population and urbanization, expanding irrigation areas needed to maintain food security in southern Mediterranean countries, inadequate controls of water use, and lack of political will due to the need for stabilizing the rural population to avoid migration to cities with extreme unemployment. Cultural impediments to limiting the use of water are an additional source of concern.

Since agriculture is both the main use of the land in terms of area (over 50 per cent of total land area) and the principal water-consuming sector (over 80 per cent of total water consumption), adverse effects of drought are perceived to be associated with agricultural activities, leading to conflicts over the use of resources. Historically, policy-makers with competence in agriculture at national and sub-national levels have been responsible for both natural and economic resource management. These agricultural managers already use short-term weather forecasts in irrigation scheduling with success, since cropping systems must be matched with seasonal water supply, a major component of risk for farmers (Iglesias et al., 2000; El-Shaer et al., 1997; Wilhite and Vanyarkho, 2000; Wilhite, 1996). These managers, therefore, have already incorporated quantitative estimates of possible climate scenarios and modeling output into their decision-making process. It is reasonable to expect that this current situation may lead to an effective dialog among resource managers and scientists on methods of quantitative assessment, therefore paving the way for improving the development of adaptation strategies for longer-term climate change. At present, water management plans that incorporate future climate scenarios have been published, for instance, by Spanish water companies.

Current policy questions require specific information on the interactions between sectors and evaluation of adaptation options for stakeholders at local and regional levels. These issues require shifting research priorities from identification of impacts to evaluation of adaptation strategies on different time and geographic scales, towards a science that addresses real-world decision-making.

THE CLIMATE CONTEXT

The climate context for the region is one of very strong variability requiring careful management, together with a modest amount of seasonal forecasting skill. However, the processes that define spatial and temporal climate patterns are poorly understood and there is limited forecasting skill in the region. While the Mediterranean region is not expected to achieve a high level of seasonal forecasting skill in the foreseeable future, research does suggest that sea-surface temperature forcing does yield some seasonal forecasts for part of the rainy season, especially in the western region where the latter part of the rainy season (March–April) is correlated with the El Nino/Southern Oscillation (Rodo et al.,1997; Ward et al., 1999). This provides specific opportunities for incorporation of forecast information into water management strategies, especially related to irrigation. The North Atlantic Oscillation (NAO) exerts a strong control on rainfall in the region, especially through the boreal winter (Lamb and Peppler, 1987; Rodo et al., 1997). Generally, there is considered to be little predictability in the NAO, though a repeating signal in NAO evolution from about August to the following March has been noted and offers prospects for some anticipation of NAO evolution (Lamb et al., 1997). In addition to these small prediction signals, the very large interannual and decadal climate variability that is now known to exist in the region itself requires careful evaluation in the context of current methods and temporal scales for communicating risk to resource managers. In Egypt, the key variable for forecasting is related to the River Nile flow. There is much ongoing work on forecasting and applying Nile flow.

The appropriate adoption of mechanisms of communicating climate information and sectoral risk should permit regional planners to reduce the devastating effects of drought and the uncertain effects of climate and weather in the more favorable seasons. Finally, we believe that 'integrated climate monitoring' is an important element of adaptation strategies. The goal is to incorporate the information about climate, soil, water supply, and potential yields in the monitoring system. Information should be in the public domain, sufficient to gauge the level of risk and make informed decisions about the future.

DEFINING COMMON PRIORITIES

The events in recent history, such as the expansion of population and irrigated agriculture in the region, are now encouraging national planning agencies to explore efficiency improvements for managing water demand and reallocating water among users. In addition, national and regional planning agencies also confront major trans-national issues, such as the dependence of Egypt on external surface water (97 per cent of the total Nile flow originates outside Egypt). Therefore, the Mediterranean region provides an exceptional opportunity for analyzing adaptation options that will ensure a balance between water users and sectors given the observed climate variability and the projected future climate.

Mediterranean policy-makers recognize the urgent need for investment in new technologies, infrastructure, and knowledge related to agriculture in response to major problems in the region: (a) increasing domestic demand, urbanization, high unemployment levels, and low rent of the traditional rural population; (b) loss of comparative advantage vis-à-vis international growers; (c) water resources competition and land deterioration (erosion, desertification, salinization, pollution, and deforestation).

Costs are rising due to environmental protection policies. As regional planners meet these challenges they will benefit from an improved understanding of the climate–agriculture–economics interactions in the region.

DEFINING FUTURE SCENARIOS

Future vulnerability and adaptation assessments require the development of environmental change scenarios for different time-scales. These scenarios should include not only estimates of changes in the climatic baseline, but also estimates of possible future changes in socio-economics. For example, drought policies or prices of agricultural commodities may vary substantially over relative short time periods in response to market and policy drivers. Ideally, the approach to this issue is to develop a range of plausible future socio-economic scenarios, and to apply these in an analogous way to the application of climate scenarios. Where possible, the socio-economic scenarios should be directly linked to the climate scenarios through the common societal and political assumptions that underpin each scenario (IPCC SRES, 2001). An important benefit of this approach is that scenarios allow the direct comparison of changes arising from either climate or socio-economic change. Thus the relative importance of socio-economic and biophysical drivers can be assessed, and the implications for policy can be highlighted.

However, predicting population growth rates and future economic conditions is equally if not more uncertain than predicting the future climate. Therefore future scenarios need to be designed carefully to address a range of possible conditions. A useful approach is to contrast 'optimistic' and 'pessimistic' views of the future. In the optimistic scenario, population growth rates are low, economic growth rates and incomes rise, environmental pollution decreases and land degradation abates. In the pessimistic scenario, population growth rates are high, economic growth rates and incomes are low, environmental pollution increases, and land degradation accelerates. A scenario of no change (i.e. present conditions) should also be included. The differential effects of climate change on current conditions, and on these two alternative scenarios of the future may then be evaluated.

CO_2 and greenhouse gas emission scenarios are needed, especially for agriculture because of the need to estimate crop responses to the CO_2 fertilization effect, as well as projections of sea-level rise. Socio-economic factors often considered in future scenarios include population, income, productivity, and technology levels. Environmental factors may include stratospheric and tropospheric ozone levels and changes in land use. Institutions and legal structures may change as well, but these are very hard to predict.

CENTRAL RESEARCH QUESTIONS

The design of effective adaptation options of water management under climate change requires evaluating and enhancing methods of communication of scientific information to stakeholders regarding climate, water use, food production, and social responses and interactions in the region. The intensification of water deficit damage has been an important factor in Mediterranean countries due to the intensification in the use of the land, and this has led to increasing conflicts between users of water and transboundary water disputes. The effects of water deficits will continue to change in the future as a result of the dynamic processes of climate, land use, and socio-economic relationships. Therefore it is necessary to develop and integrate improved quantitative assessment methodologies that permit the evaluation of plausible scenarios. Within this broad framework, key research questions include: (1) are current scientific impact assessment methods effective for communicating vulnerability of water resources to stakeholders? (2) are methods transferable across spatial scales and socio-economic systems? (3) are current strategies for water management in more developed countries a possible model for future strategies in less developed countries? An analysis across areas with different technological and socio-economic resilience to drought would contribute to regional development by testing strategies aimed at improving water management.

DISCUSSION OF DATA AND METHODS

Geo-referenced Databases of Observations and Scenarios

The construction of appropriate databases is fundamental to the understanding of current trends and the evaluation of vulnerability and adaptation options. Data are available for a range of scales and resolutions on the basis of different spatial units, such as soil map units, catchment boundaries, and administrative units. For example, climate data are available at a resolution of 0.5° latitude and longitude and at station level; soils data on a scale of 1:1 000 000; topographic data at a resolution of 2 km, and so on. These types of data may be collected within the framework of a geographical information system (GIS). The GIS is useful to rationalize the different sources and resolutions, creating a common framework for both non-quantitative analysis and modeling.

The geo-referenced database is also essential for: (a) validating the evaluation tools against the observational record; (b) construction of scenarios; and (c) helping the stakeholders in the interpretation of the climate at different time-scales.

Communicating Results at Different Levels

Evaluation methods that include different spatial and temporal scales improve the design of adaptation options. A Mediterranean basin overview is needed to make comparisons to assist policy decisions and implementation at the administrative regional level. Case studies are essential since they provide a means of cross-validating the outputs of a Mediterranean-level evaluation approach, and allow for more detailed analysis of the specific issues and processes that affect water demand and agricultural output at the local level. The combination of the two scales of evaluation allows different vulnerability evaluations to be tested and presented to local stakeholders. In theory, assessments that agree at the two levels will reduce the uncertainty associated with the vulnerability evaluation.

The development of a modeling capability is important for the engagement of stakeholders in the region. A Mediterranean-level approach enables direct comparison between and across regions, highlighting disparities as well as similarities, and allowing policy-makers to target vulnerable regions. We believe that the development of such a modeling capability should be assessed on the integration of different methodologies linked to appropriate GIS technology, to benefit from the best elements of scientific modeling approaches. Studies at local level may be easily interpreted by stakeholders since they understand the system and can validate the results with well known observational data.

Modeling Approaches

Several existing simple models may be applied and tested under a range of Mediterranean conditions and the results visualized in the form of maps. This simple Mediterranean-wide approach is essential for integrating drought, yield, and water demand indices at the Mediterranean level, thus providing a first-order evaluating tool to analyze possible adaptation strategies. Although several studies have used this approach in the European countries (ARIDE, 2001), none has included the entire Mediterranean basin.

Most of the evaluations of climate change in Mediterranean irrigation water resources have used local-level modeling approaches. The local studies analyze the sensitivity of farm management and water use to climate at that level and the implications for policy decisions that affect water management policies. Crop models typically focus on optimizing timing of the production and the efficiency of use of nutrients (primarily nitrogen) and irrigation water. This type of information is useful to national and sub-national water resource and agricultural planners for responding to the primary demands of the farming community (i.e. to maximize annual economic returns) and for addressing long-term sustainable agricultural policies (i.e. for the next 25 years).

Several crop models have been extensively used in the past to evaluate the impacts of climate scenarios in agricultural production and irrigation water demand. For a complete overview see Rosenzweig and Iglesias (2001). The crop models allow the researcher and regional planner to ask 'what if?' questions and simulate results by conducting experiments, therefore addressing environmental, sustainability, and economic issues under different crop management strategies. The DSSAT crop models have been validated and calibrated with field experiments in Spain (Iglesias et al., 2000) and in Egypt (El-Shaer et al., 1997) and have been widely used for the evaluation of climate–crop interactions (Rosenzweig and Iglesias, 1998; Strzepek et al., 1999).

Scenario Development and Stakeholder Participation

The development of adaptation scenarios should include stakeholder participation since the stakeholders are both the demand drivers and the end-users of vulnerability analysis. Stakeholders include a wide range of people ranging from local and national policy-makers to individual land managers, such as farmers.

Adaptive capacity is conceptually difficult to assess. A wide range of plausible strategies can be envisaged in response to environmental change pressure, including management options, and national and local policy initiatives. It is extremely difficult to anticipate future management changes that might arise from technological improvements. However, the use of the modeling methodology does allow different management and policy strategies to be tested against our current understanding of what is possible, since it allows the testing of alternative adaptation options in a 'what if?' approach involving the stakeholder groups. This approach is possible because adaptation options may be explicitly formulated within the rules of the modeling framework.

EXAMINING TRENDS AND PROJECTING IMPACTS

The relationship between the Mediterranean climate and its impacts on ecosystems, land use, and economic sectors has been analyzed in the context of extreme events, especially droughts, and future climate projections (the synthesis of many past and ongoing efforts is included in this volume). Previous research has sought to document the extent to which independent sectors were sensitive to individual extremes and potential mean climatic changes, excluding from the evaluations the dynamic components of climatic, social, and policy-related elements. A few initiatives related to drought monitoring and desertification provide a historical understanding of some interactions of climate with society in the region. The Mediterranean Land Use and Desertification Project (MEDALUS, 2001) has analyzed historical drivers and indicators of drought impacts (Kosmas et al., 1999).

Current new initiatives will contribute to the framework for research on the adaptation of water resources to climate change in the Mediterranean. First, the Moroccan National Drought Observatory is developing a National Drought Policy Plan, with the close institutional collaboration of both the Moroccan government and universities. The aim of this effort is to develop an institutional structure/capacity that includes an early warning system and a delivery system for information to users (D. Wilhite, personal communication). The goal here is mitigation, moving away from reactive, crisis management. This effort represents recognition of the importance of carrying out some of the activities proposed in this project.

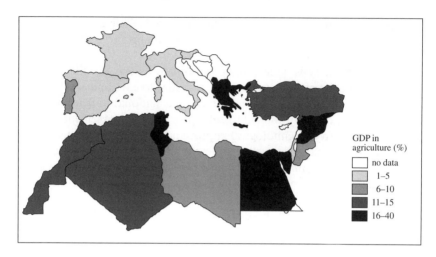

Source: FAO (2001).

Figure 4.1   Share of GDP in agriculture and location of the local-level case studies

We have assembled an initial database that includes climate variables and agricultural indicators at different temporal and spatial scales in selected Mediterranean countries. Figure 4.1 shows the percentage of GDP in agriculture in the Mediterranean countries. Table 4.1 summarizes a few characteristics of the selected countries that reflect disparities and similarities. Egypt, Morocco, Tunisia, and Spain represent major socio-economic and natural resource differences while having great similarities in the cropping and agricultural systems. Major country differences are in relation to: (a) economic development; (b) water use conflicts among sectors; and (c) agricultural policies.

In order to evaluate how each system interacts with climate in the context of climate variability and decadal change, we have analyzed the correlations of rainfall and dryland cereal production. In Spain, rainfall variability explains up to 60 per cent of the dryland wheat yield variability in southern areas (Table 4.2).

At the country level, climate is one of the components that may disrupt the agricultural sector. Figure 4.2 shows a comparison of cereal area harvested, yields, and agricultural trade in Spain and Morocco during the 1961–2000 period. The figure shows dramatic yield losses in both countries during the severe climatologic and hydrologic drought of 1992–94. This may have been a factor for the imbalance between the agricultural exports and imports in Morocco (Figure 4.3). In Spain, water is highly regulated

Table 4.1 Characteristics and indicators of the case study countries

Country 1999	Egypt	Morocco	Tunisia	Spain
Total area (1000 ha)	100145	44655	16361	50599
Total population (1000)	67226	27867	9460	39634
Total population estimated in 2030 (1000)	100371	40451	13380	35611
Agricultural area (% of total)	3	69	54	59
Fertilizer consumption per unit agricultural area (t/ha)	337	11	14	70
Irrigation area (% of agricultural area)	100	4	4	12
Population in agriculture (% of total)	37	38	25	8
Population in rural areas (% of total)	54	45	35	23
Population in rural areas estimated in 2030 (% of total)	38	29	22	15
Wheat yield (kg/ha) (average world = 2733 kg/ha)	6251	552	924	3078
Value of agricultural imports (million $)	38412	20058	8738	106784
Value of agricultural exports (million $)	5225	5841	6569	118262
GDP per capita ($)	3000	3600	5500	17300
Agricultural subsidies (national and supra-national)	Low	Low	Low	Very high
Crop/drought insurance (national or private)	No	No	No	Yes
Internal renewable water resources (million m³)	1800	30000	3520	110300
Total withdrawal (million m³)	55100	11045	3075	30750
Agricultural withdrawal (%)	86	92	89	62
Domestic withdrawal (%)	6	5	9	12
Industrial withdrawal (%)	8	3	3	26
Renewable water resources per inhabitant (m³/pers)	820	396	325	776

Source: FAO (2001).

Table 4.2 Correlation coefficients between dryland and irrigated wheat yield and current observed climate anomalies (1971–98) in the areas that include Zamora (41.48° N; −5.75° W; 667 m) and Almeria (36.83° N; −2.38° W; 20 m)

	Dryland		Irrigated	
Factor	Zamora	Almeria	Zamora	Almeria
Precipitation in April	0.41	0.62		
Temperature in April	−0.04	0.02	0.25	−0.27

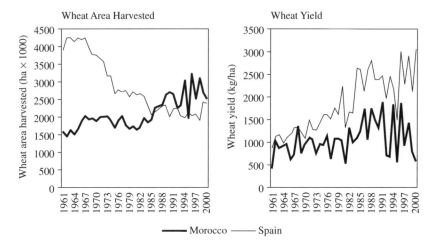

Figure 4.2   Area harvested to wheat and wheat yield in Morocco and Spain during 1961–2000

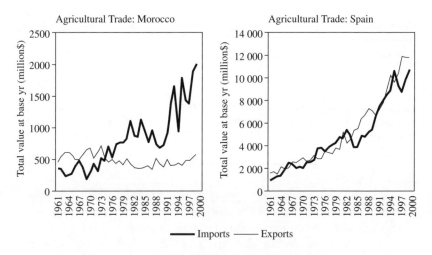

Figure 4.3   Agricultural trade in Morocco and Spain during 1961–2000

and therefore the water for irrigation may be available during periods of climatologic drought. Figure 4.4 shows that the reservoir capacity in Spain during the 1990s was greatly reduced and affected most irrigation areas in the country.

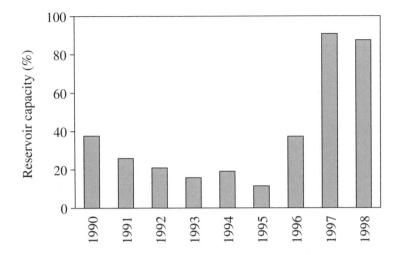

Figure 4.4   Reservoir capacity in Spain during 1990–98

IDENTIFYING VULNERABILITY AND ADAPTATION

A Survey of Previous Studies

Several hundred studies have now been completed of impacts of climate change on agriculture and water resources, and these provide an indication both of the types and magnitude of climate change likely to be most important and the possibility of future adaptation strategies. Climate variability is emerging as an important issue to be considered in identifying vulnerability and adaptation, particularly when evaluating associated risks of water shortages (Strzepek et al., 1999). Recent studies consider explicitly the impact of climatic variability in addition to climate change in the evaluations of crop responses. In regions where current interannual climate variability is a major factor determining agricultural output, there is an additional challenge for projecting climate change impacts on irrigation demand and agricultural production.

Climate change may alter the competitive position of countries with respect, for example, to water availability, exports of agricultural products, or people at risk of hunger (Parry et al., 2001). The altered competitive position may not only affect trade and local economies, but also regional and farm-level income, rural employment and, of course, the competition among water resource users. While most studies are unlikely to include an analysis of competitiveness itself, it is possible to evaluate the relative position of a region or country by studying the few analyses of climate change effects on agriculture. Indeed, some data on country-level output are available as part of the global studies (see for example Rosenzweig and Iglesias, 2001).

The Case Study of Egypt

Source: El-Shaer et al. (1997).

Background: Agriculture in Egypt is restricted to the fertile lands of the narrow Nile valley from Aswan to Cairo and the flat Nile Delta north of Cairo. Together this comprises only 3 per cent of the country's land area. Egypt's entire agricultural water supply comes from irrigation, solely from the Nile River. In 1990, agriculture (crops and livestock) accounted for 17 per cent of Egypt's gross domestic product.

Problem: The study sought to assess the potential impact of a change in climate and sea level on Egypt's agricultural sector, accounting for changes in land area, water resources, crop production and world agricultural trade. The aim was not to predict Egypt's future under a changed climate, but rather to examine the combined effects on agriculture of different natural factors and the adaptability of the economic system.

Methods: A physically based water balance model of the Nile Basin was used to evaluate river runoff and thus enable inferences to be drawn concerning water supply for agriculture. Process-based agronomic models were used to estimate crop yields and crop water requirements. External factors such as world food prices were introduced from a study of climate change which used a global food model to assess climate-change impacts on world food supply and demand. Supply and demand at national level were then input to a national agricultural sector model to determine effects on land use, water use, agricultural employment, etc.

Testing of methods: Each of the sub-models used in the study was validated against local data.

Scenarios: The current baseline adopted for the socio-economic projections was 1990 and the climatological baseline, 1951–80. The time horizon of the study, 1990–2060, was largely dictated by the climate change projections.

Impacts: An agricultural water productivity index was used to measure impacts on agriculture: total agricultural production (tonnes) divided by total agricultural water use (cubic metres). Under these $2 \times CO_2$ GCM-derived scenarios the index declined between 13 and 45 per cent.

Adaptive responses: Adaptations in water resources (major river diversion schemes), irrigation (improved water delivery systems), agriculture (altered crop varieties and crop management) and coastal protection against sea-level rise were all tested. They achieve a modest 7–8 per cent increase in agricultural sector performance compared to no adaptation, but together would be extremely expensive to implement. However, investment in improving irrigation efficiency appears to be a robust, 'no regrets' policy that would be beneficial whether or not the climate changes.

The Case Study of Spain

Source: Iglesias et al. (2000) Iglesias and Minguez (1997).

Background: Agriculture in Spain is highly subsidized. Irrigation accounts for over 60 per cent of the total water withdrawals, about 10 per cent of the agricultural area, and about 90 per cent of the total value of crop production. Water resources vary greatly between basins. The new Hydrological Law plans large inter-basin water transfers.

Problem: The study sought to assess the potential impact of a change in climate in future crop production and irrigation demand. The aim was to examine the potential increase in irrigation demand in areas already vulnerable to water use conflicts.

Methods: Process-based agronomic models were used to estimate crop yields and crop water requirements at the site level. Crop yield and irrigation demand functions were derived from the validated site results to evaluate spatial water demand and potential change in irrigation areas.

Testing of methods: Each of the models used in the study was validated against local data.

Scenarios: The current baseline adopted for the socio-economic projections was 1990 and the climatological baseline, 1951–80. Scenarios of climate change were projected for the 2050s with the HadCM2 model with and without aerosols.

Impacts: Under climate change irrigation demand increased in all regions of Spain, especially the ones with the largest current irrigation areas.

Adaptive responses: Improvement of water delivery systems compensates for increases in irrigation demand and projected irrigation area increases in the northern half of the country, but does not achieve the same results in the south-eastern part of the country.

Adaptation Options in the Mediterranean

Mediterranean countries differ in development levels (e.g. income), mechanisms of risk-sharing (e.g. insurance), technological innovations (e.g. irrigation techniques), and information delivery systems, therefore providing a framework for analyzing coping and adaptation strategies. We believe that a combination of methodologies that address adaptation to climate change at local and regional-wide levels will improve the effectiveness of management strategies and will allow a balance between water users and sectors. Adaptive capacity in the future is hard to assess since it is difficult to anticipate future management changes that might arise from technological improvements. However, the use of the modeling methodology does allow different management and policy strategies to be tested against our current understanding of what is possible, identifying the most vulnerable areas, and defining local disparities between the Mediterranean countries.

Changes in cropping systems
Adaptation options in the future for a given climate may be designed from the knowledge of changes in the crop distribution, production potential, and potential water demand, covering the whole Mediterranean region. Subsidies, restrictions and other socio-economic state variables that seek to modify the probabilities of change occurring should also be considered.

Coping with climate variability
Different strategies may be evaluated for coping with the high climate variability found in the region on interannual and decadal timescales. In addition, the analysis methodology will be used to evaluate the value of the seasonal climate forecasts (considering contrasting Mediterranean farming systems) and the implications of responses to climate forecasts for the country water balance.

Integrating results
Current policy questions require specific information on the interactions between sectors and evaluation of adaptation options for stakeholders at local, national, and regional Mediterranean levels. Adaptation is, in part, a political process, and information on options reflects different views about the long-term future of resources, economies, and societies. There is little reason to believe that rational decision-making paradigms will provide much insight into the kind of adaptation strategies that are most likely to be adopted (Downing et al., 2001). We believe that the analysis should focus on comparing options tested in different systems. The capacity to adapt to environmental change is implicit in the concept of sustainable development, and implies an economic as well as a natural resource component. Perception of the environmental and economic damage of drought is also a driver of the economic component of adaptation.

Integrated adaptation options at local and regional levels have been outlined in several IPCC reports (see for example IPCC, 1997). For example, at local level adaptation initiatives may combine pricing systems, water efficiency initiatives, engineering and structural improvements to water supply infrastructure, agriculture policies and urban planning/management. At national/regional level, priorities include placing greater emphasis on integrated, cross-sectoral water resource management, using river basins as resource management units, and encouraging sound pricing and management practices. Given increasing demands, the prevalence and sensitivity of many simple water management systems to fluctuations in precipitation and runoff, and the considerable time and expense required to implement many adaptation measures, the water resources sector in many regions and countries is vulnerable to potential changes in climate (IPCC, 2001). Water management is partly determined by legislation and cooperation between government entities, within countries and internationally; altered water supply and demand would call for a reconsideration of existing legal and cooperative arrangements (IPCC, 2001).

CONCLUSIONS

There has been remarkable progress in the science of climate and climate prediction in the last few decades. While this progress will continue, it is necessary to mainstream the climate variable into the development planning and implementation processes. This requires an understanding of how climate variability impacts on society in a country, region, or community. To advance the development adaptation strategies to include climate variability and change requires continuing strengthening of research capacities, interdisciplinary communication, and international cooperation. Successful sustainable development strategies must embody the elements of adaptation and mitigation to climate variations. Global change will alter vulnerability to water shortages and agricultural production in many areas, with potentially serious consequences at local and regional levels in the Mediterranean. Many of the world's poorest people – particularly those living in drought prone areas – are most at risk of increased vulnerability.

Other environmental problems are already major issues in the Mediterranean region, such as desertification and loss of agricultural land. The adaptation options are limited. Population and land-use dynamics, and overall strategies for environmental protection determine, and limit, possible adaptation options. Unfortunately, in most cases, current national policies for resource management and rural planning do not take into account climate change.

ACKNOWLEDGEMENTS

Funding was provided by the International Research Institute for Climate Prediction and the Columbia Earth Institute. We acknowledge the support of the Climate Impacts Group of the NASA Goddard Institute for Space Studies. Data for the study was provided by the Centro de Estudios y Experimentacion de Obras Publicas of the Spanish Ministry of Public Works.

REFERENCES

ARIDE (2001). *Assessment of the Regional Impact of Drought in Europe.* Commission of the European Union. ENV-CT97-0553.

CEDEX (Centro de Estudios y Experimentacion de Obras Publicas) (2000). *Continental Waters in the Mediterranean Countries of the European Union.* Spanish Ministry of the Environment. http://hispagua.cedex.es/Grupo1/Documentos/documen.htm.

Downing, T.E. et al. (eds) (2001). *Social and Institutional Responses to Climate Change and Climatic Hazards: Droughts and Floods.* Final Report of the SIRCH Project. ECI, Oxford.

El-Shaer, H.M., Rosenzweig, C., Iglesias, A., Eid, M.H. and Hillel, D. (1997). 'Impact of climate change on possible scenarios for Egyptian agriculture in the future'. *Mitigation and Adaptation Strategies for Global Change* **1**(3): 233–250.

FAO (2001). *AQUASTAT.* FAO's global information system of water and agriculture. http://www.fao.org/ag/agl/aglw/Aquastatweb/Main/html/aquastat.htm.

Gleick, P.H. (2000). 'The changing water paradigm: a look at twenty-first century water resources development'. *International Water Resources Association. Water International* **25**(1): 127–138.

Iglesias, A. and Minguez, M.I. (1997). 'Modelling crop-climate interactions in Spain: vulnerability and adaptation of different agricultural systems to climate change'. *Mitigation and Adaptation Strategies for Global Change* **1**(3): 273–288.

Iglesias, A., Rosenzweig, C. and Pereira, D. (2000). 'Predicting spatial impacts of climate in agriculture in Spain'. *Global Environmental Change* **10**: 69–80.

IPCC (1997). *The Regional Impacts of Climate Change: An Assessment of Vulnerability.* Watson, R.T., Zinyowera, M.C. and Mos, R.H. (eds).

IPCC (2001). *Intergovernmental Panel on Climate Change.*

IPCC SRES (2001). *Special Report on Emission Scenarios. Intergovernmental Panel on Climate Change.* Available at: http://sres.ciesin.org.

Kosmas, C., Kirkby, M. and Geeson, N. (1999). *Manual on Key Indicators of Desertification and Mapping Environmentally Sensitive Areas to Desertification.* European Commission, EUR 18882.

Lamb, P.J., El Hamly, M., Ward, M.N., Sebbari, R., Portis, D.H. and El Khatri, S. (1997). *Experimental Precipitation Prediction for Morocco for 1997–98.* Report for Moroccan Ministry of Public Works, Cooperative Institute for Mesoscale Meteorological Studies, University of Oklahoma, Norman.

Lamb, P.J. and Peppler, R.A. (1987). 'North Atlantic oscillation: concept and application'. *Bull. Amer. Met. Soc.* **68**: 1218–1225.

MEDALUS (2001). *Mediterranean Desertification and Land Use.* Working progress and references of the project. http://www.medalus.demon.co.uk/.

Parry, M., Arnell, N., McMichael, T., Nicholls, R., Martens, P., Kovats, S., Livermore, M., Rosenzweig, C., Iglesias, A. and Fischer, G. (2001). 'Defining critical climate change threats and targets'. *Global Environmental Change* **11**: 181–193.

Parry, M.L., Rosenzweig, C., Iglesias, A., Fischer, G. and Livermore, M.T.J. (1999). 'Climate change and world food security: a new assessment'. *Global Environmental Change* **9**: S51–S67.

Rodo, X., Baert, E. and Comin, F.A. (1997). 'Variations in seasonal rainfall in Southern Europe during the present century: relationships with the North Atlantic oscillation and ENSO'. *Climate Dynamics* **13**: 275–284.

Rosenzweig, C. and Iglesias, A. (1998). 'The use of crop models for international climate change impact assessment'. In: G.Y. Tsuji et al. (eds). *Understanding Options for Agricultural Production.* Kluwer Academic Publishers, Dordrecht, pp. 267–292.

Rosenzweig, C. and Iglesias, A. (2001). *Potential Impacts of Climate Change on World Food Supply.* http://sedac.ciesin.columbia.edu/giss_crop_study/.

Strzepek, K., Rosenzweig, C., Major, D., Iglesias, A., Yates, D., Holt, A. and Hillel, D. (1999). 'New methods of modeling water availability for agriculture under climate change'. *Journal of the American Water Resource Association* **35**(6, December); 1639–1655.

Ward, M.N., Lamb, P.J., Portis, D.H., El-Hamly, M. and Sebbari, R. (1999). 'Climate variability in North Africa: understanding droughts in the Sahel and the Magreb'. In: A. Navarra (ed.) *Beyond El Nino: Decadal Variability in the Climate System.* Springer-Verlag, New York, pp. 119–140.

Wilhite, D.A. (1996). 'A methodology for drought preparedness'. *Natural Hazards* **13**: 229–252. Kluwer Academic Publishers, The Netherlands.

Wilhite, D.A. and Vanyarkho, O. (2000). 'Drought: pervasive impacts of a creeping phenomenon'. In: D.A. Wilhite (ed.) *Drought: A Global Assessment* (Vol. I, Ch. 18). Routledge Publishers, London.

5. The impacts of climate change on water resources of Lebanon – Eastern Mediterranean

Mohamad R. Khawlie

INTRODUCTION

Obviously, talking about water resources in a region like the Middle East, where they are scarce (Sadek and Barghouti, 1994; ACSAD, 1998), is a matter of utmost significance. It must be made clear from the beginning that this also applies to Lebanon, in spite of the fact that some authors erroneously point out that Lebanon is rich in water (Allan, 1994).

There are increasing problems facing the water sector in Lebanon, making it more difficult to counteract them with the classical management approaches being followed (Khawlie, 1999). These approaches, as implemented by the centralized water authorities of the Ministry of Water, still capitalize on supply rather than demand management. The infrastructural services (i.e. network and maintenance) are mostly old, with considerable waste, hence needing upgrading and expansion. The sectoral demand for water is highly biased to agriculture, sometimes reaching 80 per cent, and yet old irrigation methods are still being used with high losses. No noticeable national measures have yet been taken to make use of unconventional sources of water, and many of the existing sources need better protection and maintenance. Although the need for water in the extended dry period (April to November) is increasingly felt over wider areas, especially in the coastal zone where population density is highest, the recurrence of periods with no quality control of water supply is common, leading in many instances to securing poor-quality water with resultant diseases. Another way of facing water scarcity is increasing reliance on groundwater as a major source of water supply, now tending to reach 40 per cent in agricultural and less well serviced areas. This opens the way for more people in those areas to become infected as there is poor control over sewage, and waste water being dumped into unsanitary pits and holes is a common practice. Although the water authorities have updated and upgraded relevant water legislation, there is still a long way to go in incorporating such aspects as environmental impact assessment (EIA), regulating traditional water rights, protecting spring zones or applying integrated watershed management.

Both natural causes and human interference are adding to the extent of deterioration, quantitatively and qualitatively. There is a definite need to upgrade the water sector, and to secure its sustainability.

The problem has several causes:

- improper management: conventional and non-conventional sources;
- inadequate financial resources;
- lacking accurate and total integrated information;
- inappropriate life-style (wastage);
- lacking relevant legislation and implementation;
- lacking relevant awareness (participation).

A new dimension has to be added to the above, namely the impact of climate change (CC). CC especially affects the following crucial issues of the water sector in Lebanon:

- the supplies;
- the sources;
- the demand;
- the management.

WATER DATABASES AND CLIMATE PROJECTION

The best way to reflect on this is the water balance, shown in Table 5.1, and the demand–supply picture of the country (Figure 5.1) (Khawlie, 1999). Table 5.1 shows estimates of the supply–demand which are not necessarily the most accurate, but are the best data available. One basic problem with the supply is that rain distribution varies geographically (different microclimates from arid to humid to oromediterranean) and also varies temporally, being episodic and torrential. Moreover, since in many areas the water distribution network is old or lacking, this implies considerable wastage.

Generally, there is a lack of systematic ongoing monitoring of the water quality in Lebanon. Considerable work, however, was carried out with the help of international institutions (e.g. UNESCO), or through individual researchers (Jurdi, 1995; Dia, 1995; Darwish et al., 2000). Although the results cover wide areas of Lebanon, they do not provide a reliable time-frame of updated/upgraded data. The data apply only to the time when those investigations were carried out.

As such, it is not an easy task to give an accurate updated picture of water

Table 5.1   *Ranges of estimated data on sectoral use of water resources, and supply–demand**

Total precipitation (supply) (+ snow) b.c.m. 8.6–9.7			Total demand (major uses) m.c.m. 900–1460		
surface water 1.4–4.2	subsurface water 0.6–3.8	lost out 2.3–3.0	agriculture (irrigation) 670–890 67%	residential (80–420) 28% per capita l/d	industrial 50–150 6%
				urban 250–300	rural 150–200
projected average annual decrease in precipitation = 1.11% ** (max 0.9%)**			projected annual increase in water needs = 3.52 % (2.0%)**		
An integrated estimate (b.c.m.): (Maksoud, personal communication)			total supply 8.60 – beneficial consumption 3.30 – to sea &/or out 2.31 – unutilized surface flow 2.99		

Estimated projections of available water: – 1995 = 1.46 b.c.m. →2015 = 2.70 b.c.m. (UNDP, 1997), the increase would result from more efficient use, conservation, increased dependence on subsurface water and some recycling. But still there is an expected deficit in 2015 = 800 m.c.m.

Notes:
m.c.m. = millions of cubic meters of water
b.c.m. = billions of cubic meters of water
*   As can be obviously seen in the table, there is a wide range in the estimated values of supply, demand and projections. This, unfortunately, makes arriving at an accurate baseline questionable.
** These two projections sound rather high, but they are interpreted from the last few decades, i.e. a limited span of time which does not reflect a true value. This is checked by the Beirut precipitation trend, where the regression lines of Beirut 100 years precipitation do not indicate a decrease exceeding maximum 0.9%, and expectedly closer to half that value. As for increase in water needs, several workers put it more realistically at about 2.0% maximum. This is because of water conservation and other environment-friendly practices that would be expected to be employed in the near future.

Source: Khawlie (1999) and various sources.

pollution in Lebanon, and Table 5.2 gives an overview of its status. One can clearly notice by studying Table 5.2 that all geographic areas are being exposed to different degrees of polluted water, and the picture is serious. Indeed, the recurrence of annual diseases due to water problems is very common, especially in the rural and several suburban areas.

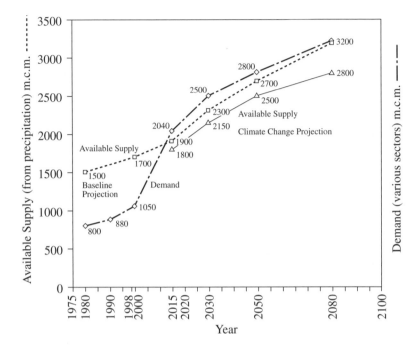

Sources: Supply demand (Jaber, 1993); Climate change protection (HadCM2/HH G–Gax).

Figure 5.1   Climate change projection, water supply–demand

Databases in Lebanon are not fully consistent and accurate, implying difficulty in interpreting correctly trends of change. Actual records on water supply, for example, precipitation, reflect a decreasing pattern over the last century. This is in agreement with predicted trends of temperature and precipitation values obtained from the GCM models over Lebanon. The HadCM2/HHGGax model predicts an average of 1.6°C increase in temperature by the year 2020, and an equivalent average of about 3 per cent less precipitation (Safi, 1999). This figure does not agree with the 1.11 per cent projected average annual increase as shown in Table 5.1, because the 1.11 per cent was obtained using a limited amount of data and covering only three decades of discontinuous precipitation records.

Indicators of change can be monitored as they are reflected in reduced water quantities and soil moisture, desertified areas, and increased water pollution and environmental deterioration. As shown in Figure 5.1, the baseline supply and demand from 1980s onward shows a positive balance (supply more than demand until around 2015). But this is misleading because the population and various sectors are not getting full and adequate

*Table 5.2 Overview of the status of water pollution in Lebanon, reflecting on its quality**

Direct	Indirect**
Sources/causes	• lack of agro-directives
a. status of waste water/sewage network	• lack of monitor/control
b. industrial enterprises (food, materials, energy)	• air pollution
c. solid waste open dumps	• non-separation of different services networks
d. farms & animal husbandries	• decrease in natural rejuvenation
e. quarries & construction debris	• increase uncontrolled pumping/exploitation
f. hospitals	• improper management
g. fuel stations & car repair shops	• lack of data
h. fertilizers & (herbi + insecti)cides	
i. salt-water intrusion	

A = Chemical		B = Biological	C = Physical
(inorganic)	(organic)	• bacteria	• sediments
Types		• virus	• suspended water
A-1. heavy metals	A-8. hydrocarbons	• algae	• heat
A-2. toxics	A-9. (h) above	• others	• color
A-3. (h) above	A-10. (f) above		• taste
A-4. salts	A-11. BOD		• smell
A-5. radioactive	A-12. organic waste		
A-6. COD			
A-7. excessive other elements			

	Extent of Pollution		
Area	High	Moderate	Low
Quality status (geographic dominance)			
Dense urbanized areas	a, b, c, f, g, i (coastal), B	A-4, A-8, A-10, A-12, C	A-1, A-2, (A-5?)
Akkar	a, c, d, h, i, B	A-12, C	b, e, f, g, A-1, A-2
Other coastal plains	a, c, i	b, f, g, h, A-12, B, C	A-1, A-2, (A-5?)
Coastal slopes (up to 1200m)	a, c, e, A-12	b, d, f, g, h, B	A-1, A-2, (A-5?), C
Mount Lebanon eastern slopes	a, c, d	e, h, B	b, f, g, A-8, A-12, C
Beka'a plain	a, c, d, h, A-12	b, e, g, i, B, C	f, A-2, A-4
Anti-Lebanon slopes	a, c, e	d, h	b, f, g, A-12, B, C

Notes:

* Wherever surface water or land surface is polluted, it is highly likely that this affects groundwater as well. This explains the high incidence of organic pollution (ranging from 70%–80%) of drinking water – see Table 5.5.

** Essentially, these aspects affect the quality of water all over Lebanon.

services even though the water is there (in nature). After about 2015, with exponential increase in demands at about 2005, the balance will tip negatively. If we add to this the effect of reduced supply due to climate change, the water deficit will become critical. The projected trends take into consideration a more efficient water sector, but nevertheless the impacts of a drier climate are already foreseen.

SOCIO-ECONOMIC IMPACTS

Figure 5.2 proposes what should constitute the major components of the socio-economic framework – that is, resources, natural and human settings; it also shows the main factors and parameters that would be affected by climate change. There are four factors under A (resources), three under B (natural settings) and eight under C (human settings). Some, under B for instance, have been given parameters (or exposure potential) which imply how likely it is that climate change is going to impact those factors (exposure impact). Clearly, space in this chapter does not allow coverage of the multitude of exposure impacts, but all these 15 factors are directly affected by any change that will impact water as expected, as a result of climate change. This reflects on the inherent inter-relationship of the socio-economic framework with water. Under each of the three components (i.e. resources, natural settings and human settings), water deficiencies would affect (or be affected) either directly or indirectly by climate change-induced problems.

Obviously, with less water one expects problems with forestry, fisheries, desertification or with wetlands and relevant ecosystems, or with any/all human practices that rely on water, as shown in the Figure 5.2.

In this regard, and in view of the overwhelming problem at hand, one could focus on what are likely to be the most significant impacts, or what is more vulnerable. Three types of study: analogues, field surveys and expert judgment, reveal an interesting picture emerging in a cross impact analysis approach (as shown in Figure 5.3). Thus analogues cover such aspects as living standards, diseases, social conflicts, forestry and agriculture. Similarly, other approaches cover other aspects as applicable. For expert judgment, different specialists were contacted to find out their opinions. In Figure 5.3 a cross-impact structural analysis is shown, with variables reflecting impact of climate change and how they are influenced by the water sector. The driving power values range from 6 to 13, which reflects how much the socio-economic aspect would be affected by water stresses relative to other aspects. Similarly, the dependency values also reflect differential effect which, when taken together, give the resultant 'interactive' influence. This is then used to

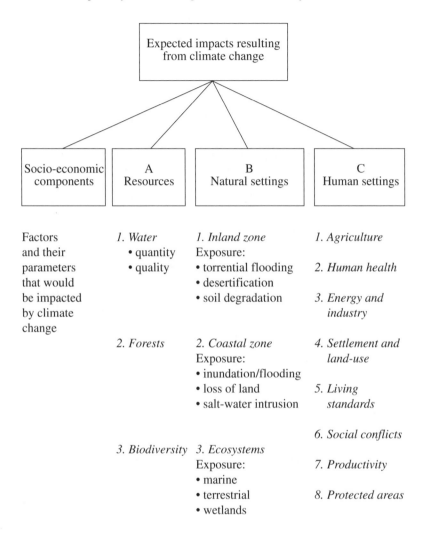

Figure 5.2   Expected impacts resulting from climate change

construct the driving power/dependency chart, Figure 5.4, which allows us to categorize the variables into four types: 'autonomous' (weak drivers and weakly dependent on climate change), 'relay' (strong drivers and strongly dependent), 'result' (strongly dependent and weak drivers), and 'forcing' (strong drivers but weakly dependent). Obviously, the most vulnerable are

Figure 5.3 Cross impact analysis

Method	Impact	Living standards	Diseases	Social conflicts	Forestry	Agriculture	Productivity	Water quality	Soil productivity	Wetlands	Hygiene	Sanitary	Ecosystems	Protected areas	Water quantity	Row sum (driving power)
Analogues	Living standards		1	1			1	1			1	1		1	1	8
Analogues	Diseases	1		1				1			1	1			1	6
Analogues	Social conflicts	1	1					1			1	1			1	6
Analogues	Forestry	1		1		1	1	1	1	1			1	1	1	10
Analogues	Agriculture	1		1	1		1	1	1	1			1	1	1	10
Analogues	Productivity	1		1	1	1		1	1	1			1	1	1	10
Field survey	Water quality	1	1	1	1	1	1		1	1	1	1	1	1	1	13
Field survey	Soil productivity	1		1	1	1	1	1		1			1		1	9
Field survey	Wetlands	1		1	1	1	1	1	1				1	1	1	10
Expert judgment	Hygiene	1	1	1			1	1				1			1	7
Expert judgment	Sanitary	1	1	1			1	1			1				1	7
Expert judgment	Ecosystems		1		1	1	1	1	1	1					1	8
Expert judgment	Protected areas	1	1		1	1	1	1	1	1					1	9
Expert judgment	Water quantity	1	1	1	1	1	1	1	1	1	1	1	1	1		13
	Column sum (dependency)	12	7	11	8	8	11	13	7	7	6	8	7	8	13	

102

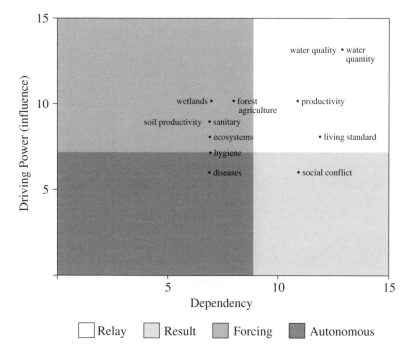

Figure 5.4   Categories of variables impacted by climate change

the 'relay' variables, particularly water quantity, water quality, productivity and living standards. Thus the impact of climate change on water would be reflected seriously in those four variables. This paves the way for better planning of adaptation measures.

ADAPTATION MEASURES AND RECOMMENDATIONS

Adaptability and adaptation are defined as follows:

> Adaptability refers to the degree to which adjustments are possible in practices, processes or structures of systems to projected or actual changes of climate. Adaptation can be spontaneous or planned, and can be carried out in response to or in anticipation of changes in conditions. (IPCC, 1996)

In this respect it is necessary to find out where or how climate change effects on a system are most pronounced. Thus, in reference to the effects on water resources, and in view of the fact that water impacts the whole social

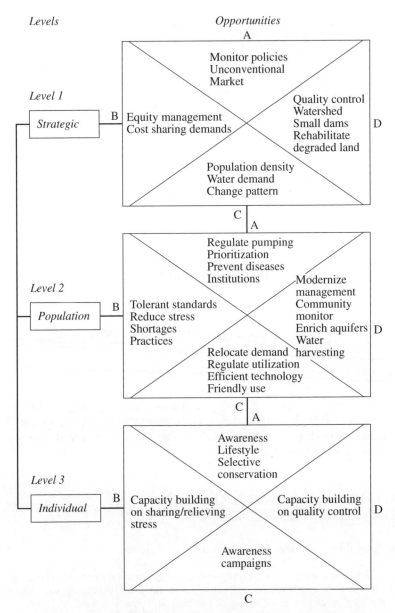

Opportunities: A = Prevention & toleration of loss   C = Changing use or location
               B = Sharing loss   D = Restoration & quality control technology

*Figure 5.5   Major adaptation opportunities for water resources facing
              climate change*

structure, it is necessary to consider adaptation at three levels: the strategic, the population, and the individual level (Klein and Tol, 1997).

Figure 5.5 reflects the major adaptation opportunities of water resources facing climate change conditions as revealed in this chapter. The strategic level considers development and implementation policies and programs to help people adapt to climate change. At the population level, the concern is geared towards protection or prevention of impacts. This leaves adaptation at the individual level which focuses on behavioral adjustments. The other data in Figure 5.5 identify the opportunities and classify them under different generic approaches for coping with the effects of climate change. As is obvious, those approaches could lead to adaptation through various means; that is through preventive measures, sharing losses, changing attitudes and restoring or applying some technologies on quality control.

The three priorities of the adaptation opportunities can also be linked to a framework of time. This serves a more pragmatic three-phase recommendation framework as follows:

Phase 1 – Immediate Implementation (within the Year 2005)

- Policies to enhance better monitoring of sectoral water use, adoption of quality standards and enforcing environmental laws.
- Short-term strategy for watershed management and upgrading of water network and services, including gauging stations nationwide.
- Assure functional operation and sectoral needs prioritization.
- Assure availability of preventive means to face water-borne diseases.
- Spreading of knowledge and capacities for appropriate practices during disasters.
- Implement local community-based monitoring systems for water quality.
- Restoration of secondary enrichment of depleted aquifers.
- Re-enhancement of water reservoirs under the 'Green Plan'.

Phase 2 – Medium-term Implementation (within the Year 2008)

- Long-term strategy on equity management of water resources.
- Policies and incentives to enhance changing patterns of water use.
- Enforce policies to control water resource quality, especially from sewage, wastewater, and agrochemicals.
- Policies and programs to implement a series of small earth dams to increase amounts of available surface water, notably on rivers of international waters.

- Long-term strategy to rehabilitate forests and degraded land in order to upgrade forestry and soil conditions.
- Upgrade institutional capabilities and capacity building in climate stations and databases.
- Devise mechanisms to reduce water stress on a geographic basis.
- Apply more efficient ways and means to face increased shortages at community level.
- Regulate all sectoral uses of water at all levels.
- Devise new technologies reusing smaller amounts of water.
- Introduce concepts and demonstrations at educational institutions on 'friendly' use and conservation of water.
- Reorganization of water management to become more effective and modern.
- Public awareness of water wastage, conservation practices, and quality control.
- Selective application of water conservation technologies.
- Capacity building for individuals to share resources, to cooperate during stress, and accept more stringent conditions of water use.
- Public awareness campaign on benefits of changing water use patterns.
- Capacity building and awareness on benefits of quality control practices.

Phase 3 – Long-term Implementation (within the Year 2015)

- Policies to develop innovative means of using unconventional sources of water.
- Policies to strengthen market mechanisms and financial incentives in water use and pricing.
- Policies to enhance cost sharing of water demand by private sector.
- Long-term strategy to reduce densely populated areas with water problems.
- Long-term strategy to reduce water-demanding activities in dry areas.
- Regulate pumping of subsurface water to prevent stressing the water table.
- Tolerable sectoral water use standards.
- R & D on efficient approaches to relocate high water demand activities.
- Accept less luxurious ways of living.

REFERENCES

ACSAD (1998). *Databank for Water Resources of the Arab World.* Arab Center for Studies of Arid and Dry Lands, Damascus (Arabic).

Allan, J.A. (1994). 'Overall perspectives on countries and regions', in: *Water in the Arab World: Perspectives and Prognoses.* Rogers and Lydon (eds), AUC Press, Egypt.

Darwish, T., Jomaa, I. and Sukkarieh, W. (2000). 'Modeling of the transfer of heavy metals from soil to groundwater'. Presented at the Workshop on Soil and Groundwater Vulnerability to Contamination. ACSAD/BGR/NCSR, Beirut.

Dia, A. (1995). 'Impact des pollutions organiques sur un cours d'eau de Jabboule (Bassin supérieur du Nahr el-A'ssi- Oronte)'. Presented at the 1st National Conference on Environmental Management for Sustainable Development in Lebanon. NCSR, Beirut.

IPCC (1996). 'Summary for policymakers: scientific-technical analysis of impacts, adaptations, and mitigation of climate change', in: *Climate Change 1995 – the Second Assessment Report of IPCC.* Cambridge University Press.

Jaber, B. (1993). *Water Issues in Lebanon.* Center for Studies, Research and Documentation, Beirut (Arabic).

Jurdi, M. (1995). 'Potable water in Lebanon: quality and quantity control program'. Presented at the 1st National Conference on Environmental Management for Sustainable Development in Lebanon. NCSR, Beirut.

Khawlie, M. (1999). *Water Resources: Assessment of Lebanon's Vulnerability to Climate Change.* Lebanon's National Communication on Climate Change. Ministry of Environment, UNDP, GEF. Beirut.

Klein, R. and Tol, R. (1997). 'Adaptation to climate change: options and technologies – an overview paper'. *Intl. Env. Studies* E97/18.

Sadek, A.K. and Barghouti, S. (1994). 'The water problems of the Arab world: management of scarce resources', in: *Water in the Arab World: Perspectives and Prognoses.* Rogers and Lydon (eds), AUC Press, Egypt.

Safi, S. (1999). *Assessment of Bioclimatic Change (Lebanon).* Lebanon's National Communication on Climate Change. Ministry of Environment, UNDP, GEF, Beirut.

UNDP (1997). 'Report of Human Development – Lebanon', Beirut.

6. Economic impacts of hydrological droughts under climate change scenarios[1]

Eva Iglesias Martínez, Almudena Gómez Ramos and Alberto Garrido Colmenero

INTRODUCTION

Climate change of anthropogenic origin is a global process whose scientific bases are fully accepted in the international scientific community. Models developed by the most advanced institutes (Hadley Centre and University of East Anglia, UK; PIZ, Germany) coincide in projecting declines in rainfall in the Mediterranean basins. The effects of climate change on available water resources are particularly difficult to project, since several factors come into play, such as changes in the characteristics of rainfall pattern, changes in the vegetation of the basin and rise in temperatures (Strzepek et al., 1998). In spite of the uncertainty surrounding these model projections, available studies indicate 20–40 per cent reduction in water resources in the Guadalquivir basin (south of Spain) as a result of climate change (Ayala and Iglesias, 1997). In addition to lower average precipitations, models project that rainfall patterns will become more variable.

Although the literature is abundant with attempts to evaluate the impact of climate change on water resources (see Strzepek et al., 1998), only a few have tackled the effects of climate change on water resources from the economic perspective. Until now, apart from the work of Balti et al. (2001) focused exclusively on agriculture, no studies aimed at evaluating the economic effect of climate change in Spain have been published. In 1998, the United Nations Environmental Programme (Feenstra et al., 1998) published a handbook for evaluating the impact of climate change which offers numerous methodologies and practical applications aimed at evaluating impact as well as adaptation strategies. The chapter covering water resources clearly reveals the difficulties involved in any attempt at evaluating, from an economic perspective, the impact of climate change on sectors that are users of, or depend on, water resources (Strzepek et al., 1998).

In this chapter, we propose a methodology to evaluate the economic impact of climate change on irrigated agriculture. A dynamic stochastic model is developed to characterise the economic results of irrigated farms that are serviced from reservoirs. The dynamics of the system is modelled as a Markovian process that integrates the stochastic nature of water inflows, engineering and hydrological constraints, institutional criteria on reservoir management and the economic aspects of irrigated farming. We apply this model to two irrigation areas in the Guadalquivir basin situated in the south of Spain and characterise the convergence path to a long-run stochastic equilibrium in both systems under different scenarios of climate change. The analyses of the economic results associated with the steady state stochastic equilibrium of the system allow us to anticipate the impact of climate change on the economic returns of irrigated farms.

The following section reviews the literature on economic evaluations of the effects of climatic change on water resources. The third section lays down the analytical framework, detailing the model and its assumptions. The fourth section describes the application of this model to two irrigation areas in the Guadalquivir basin that are run by differentiated management criteria. The results are presented and discussed in the fifth section and the sixth section summarises the main conclusions and suggests further lines of research that can contribute to a better understanding of the economic impact of climate change on water resources.

THE ECONOMIC IMPACT OF CLIMATE CHANGE ON WATER RESOURCES

It is an outstanding fact that only two of the five specific tools models for the study of water resources, mentioned in a compendium of decision tools to evaluate climate change drawn up by the Secretariat of the United Nations Convention for Climate Change (UNFCCC, 1999), contain economic analysis subroutines.

Among the few references that cover the effects of climate change on water resources from an economic perspective, one that stands out is the work of Hurd et al. (1998) among others, as well as the seminal contribution of Vaux and Howitt (1984). This lack of references is due, among other reasons, to the difficulty of integrating into the hydrological economic model, the institutional aspects that characterise water management in each region or basin. Without this critical issue, the simulation exercises would lack relevance due to overlooking important elements, such as the water assignment criteria. Another reason is the fact that the projections of climate change at the river basin level are still subject to significant statistical uncertainty.

Venema et al. (1997) formulate a model that integrates hydrological, engineering and economic aspects for evaluating plans for economic management and agricultural policy in different scenarios of climate change. After characterising time series data of water resources in the Senegal river, the authors generate several scenarios for water resources that they feed into a dynamic model for reservoir management to which hydroelectric and agricultural uses are linked. The solution of the model, that optimises a multi-objective function, makes it possible to characterise optimal management rules defined by dates and volumes of water withdrawal. The optimal rules are re-examined under three hydrological scenarios and two agricultural policy scenarios, obtaining the guarantee threshold for water stocks in each scenario.

Hurd et al. (1999) appears as the only reference that has attempted to evaluate the global economic impact of climate change on water resources in the US. Following a similar approach to the one developed by Booker and Young (1994) for the Colorado, they calibrated specific models for other important basins such as the Missouri, Delaware and the Apalachicola-Flint-Chattahoochee system. Hurd et al. obtained measures of economic welfare, consumptive and non-consumptive uses of water, reservoir levels and shadow prices of water. Standard welfare analysis based on deterministic mathematical programming models and water demand elasticities provide the economic dimension. Climate change scenarios are defined by the combination of different warming levels (from 1.5°C to 5.0°C) with rises and falls of average rainfall levels (from −10 per cent to 15 per cent). By extrapolating results to the whole USA territory, the authors conclude that the annual economic effects of climate change would range from welfare losses of 43 billion dollars in 1994 (scenario: +5.0°C, 0 per cent rainfall) to welfare gains of 9 billion dollars (scenario +1.5°C, +15 per cent rainfall). In the first case, which represents the scenario that causes the most damage, the distribution of costs would assign 73 per cent to the loss of non-consumption profits (mainly costs derived from smaller recreation options and losses due to lower water quality), 17 per cent to reduced opportunities for hydroelectricity, and only 8.5 per cent to losses in the irrigation sector.

The theoretical contribution of Fischer and Rubio (1997) is particularly outstanding. In their work, a stochastic dynamic model is developed to evaluate the qualitative impact of climate change on the level of optimal investment in hydraulic infrastructures. These authors use the steady state conditions that result from the optimal control problem to analyse how investment in the long-run equilibrium will be modified by an increase in the variance of water inflows. The results show that water storage capacity in the long run is positively correlated with increases in uncertainty if the marginal benefit of water withdrawal is convex. They also find that investment diminishes and the optimal water storage capacity follows a more stable path under climate change when costly reversibility of investment is considered. This result suggests that there might be little scope to adapt to climate change through reservoir capacity building.

THE ANALYTICAL FRAMEWORK

In this section, we lay down the analytical framework for evaluating the economic impact of climate change in irrigation systems. A dynamic stochastic model is developed to characterise the variability of farmers' profit who obtain their water allotment from a reservoir supply system. This model allows us to characterise the convergence path to the long-run stochastic equilibrium of the system in terms of expected economic profit in irrigated farming.

The dynamics of the system is characterised as a discrete Markovian process that integrates economic, institutional, and hydrological components. First, the economic profit of farmers in irrigated areas, which depends on the amount of water allotment they receive from the reservoir. Secondly, the institutional rules and decisions that govern the reservoir, such as the amount of water that is going to be released from it. We assume that institutional rules are state contingent and follow a time consistent pattern. In particular, we assume that water allotment set by the water manager in any given period t depends on the available stock of water in the reservoir at the beginning of the period. Finally, other hydrological and climatic components are specified such as the stochastic characterisation of the probability distribution of the water inflows entering the reservoir. This approach makes it possible to evaluate the economic impact of different scenarios of climate change that affect the average and variance of the distribution of the inflows regime.

We shall begin by considering the case of a particular reservoir that supplies water to an irrigation district with K heterogeneous farmers. At the beginning of the period, the river basin authority responsible for managing the reservoir notifies the farmers of the amount of available water to be released in the current period and allocates it on an equal basis among the district farmers. Each farmer k adjusts his or her production plan to the announced water allotment. Thus the profit derived from the use of the water is defined by:

$$\pi^k (w_t) = \underset{V_{kt}}{Max} \ F(V_{kt}; w_t, \phi_k) \tag{6.1}$$

where w_t represents the water allotment per hectare that each farmer receives in period t, ϕ_k is a vector of technical and economic parameters on which the farmer's profits depend, such as prices, grants, price of labour, and so on; and V_{kt} represents farmer decision variables – such as crop activities, labour and input allocation, and so on – that take optimal values for a given water allotment.

Thus annual economic results of the irrigation district, π_t, depends on the water allotment set annually by the authority that manages the reservoir or network of reservoirs and can be obtained by weighting and adding up each farmer's profit:

$$\pi(w_t) = \sum_k \frac{\alpha_k}{\alpha} \pi^k(w_t)$$

where α_k is the number of hectares of farm k and α is total hectares in the district.

We assume that the water releasing policy followed by the water manager is state contingent and time consistent. That is, we assume that the water allotment set by the water manager in any given period t depends on the stock of water available in the reservoir at the beginning of the period as follows:

$$w_t = 0, \qquad\qquad if\ S_t < S_{min} \qquad\qquad (6.2a)$$
$$w_t = W(S_t), \qquad if\ S_t > S_{min} \qquad\qquad (6.2b)$$

Where S_{min} either represents the stock level below which the remains of the reservoir are mud or sludge which cannot be withdrawn, or represents the level of stock at which other users have priority rights.

If management decisions about water releases follow a consistent pattern throughout time, then with expressions (6.2) and (6.3) we are equipped to establish a relationship between average farm profits in the district and the available stock of water in the supply system at the beginning of the period:

$$\pi(w_t) = \pi(W(S_t)) \qquad\qquad (6.3)$$

Let us now consider the simpler case of a single reservoir that supplies water to an irrigation district. The dynamics of the system follows a Markovian process that will be governed by the following stochastic equation in which several institutional and hydrological elements are integrated:

$$S_{t+1} = S_t - \alpha W(S_t) - P(S_t) - A(S_t, \tilde{W}I_t) + \tilde{W}I_t \qquad (6.4)$$

where

S_t represents the state of the reservoir at the start of period t

$W(S_t)$ represents water allotment per hectare in period t and α is total irrigated area

$P(S_t)$ are the losses of the system in period t, i.e. evaporation

$\tilde{W}I_t$ represents stochastic water inflows to the reservoir in period t

$A(S_t, \tilde{W}I_t)$ represents the water withdrawn from the reservoir in period t, which depends on the state of the reservoir and the amount of water inflows entering the reservoir

We assume that $\tilde{W}I_t$ is a random variable that follows a given distribution function. If $W(S_t)$ and $P(S_t)$ are explicitly known functions or can at least be estimated, we will be able to characterise the evolution of the system by way of the transition probability matrix $\mathbf{P}_{ij}$ with elements p_{ij} representing the probability of jumping from a given initial state in period t to any possible final state in period $t+1$.

Let S_t^i be the initial state of the reservoir in the period t, with $i = 1,..., n$ representing all possible initial states at the reservoir and let S_{t+1}^j be the state of the reservoir in the following period $t+1$, with $j = 1,...,n$, representing all possible final states at the reservoir. On the basis of equation (6.4), we can determine all the elements p_{ij} of the transition probability matrix $\mathbf{P}(i,j)$, according to:

$$p_{ij} = P(S_{t+1}^j/S_t^i) = P(WI_{ij} = S_{t+1}^j - S_t^i - G^t(S_t^i) - P(S_t^i) - A_t(S_t^i WI_{ij})) \quad (6.5)$$

where each element p_{ij} represents the probability of reaching a certain level of S_{t+1}^j in the period $t+1$, given the initial level of stock S_t^i in the preceding period. This matrix of dimension $n \times n$ exhibits homogeneity and time stability, and meets the following conditions: $p_{ij} \geq 0$ and $\sum_j p_{ij} = 1$.

Equation (6.5) expresses that the probability of the reservoir being at a given state level one period ahead depends on: (a) the state of the reservoir at the beginning of the ongoing period; (b) how much water is to be released and, implicitly, how much water is left in the reservoir for future use, which constitutes a crucial decision for the management of the reservoir; (c) the accumulated inflow to the reservoir during the period, which represents the intrinsically random component; (d) the natural losses of the reservoir; and (e) the planned withdrawals carried out in order to maintain the protection criteria defined in the overflow and flooding prevention plan. Thus defined, the Markovian process reflects the result of pure random processes, the intervention of man-made decision and the technical limitations and safety measures for the reservoir.

Given the initial state of the reservoir $S_0 = S_i$ in $t = 0$, the probability of reaching a certain level of stock S_j in the following periods will also determine the probability of obtaining a certain profit π associated with S_j. On the basis of the matrix of distribution probabilities previously obtained we can calculate the expected profit in the following periods according to:

$$For\ t=0 \quad \pi_{t=1}(S_o=S_i)=\pi(W(S_i))$$

$$For\ t=1 \quad E(\pi_{t=1}/S_o=S_i)=\sum_j P(S_j/S_i)\times \pi(W(S_j))$$

$$For\ t=2 \quad E(\pi_{t=2}/S_o=S_i)=\sum_j P^2(S_j/S_i)\times \pi(W(S_j))$$

$$For\ t=3 \quad E(\pi_{t=3}/S_o=S_i)=\sum_j P^3(S_j/S_i)\times \pi(W(S_j))$$

$$\ldots$$

$$For\ t \quad E(\pi_{t=t}/S_o=S_i)=\sum_j P^t(S_j/S_i)\times \pi(W(S_j)) \tag{6.6}$$

It is shown that this trajectory in time converges at a steady state distribution $\Gamma(i)$, if the following conditions are met (Malliaris and Brock, 1999):

$$\forall i=1,...,n \quad \Gamma(i)\geq 0 \tag{6.7}$$

$$\sum_i \Gamma(i)=1 \tag{6.8}$$

$$\sum_i \Gamma(i)P(ij)=\Gamma(j), \quad j=1,...,n \tag{6.9}$$

$$\forall j \quad \lim_{t\to\infty} p^t(i,j)=\Gamma(j) \tag{6.10}$$

Finally, we define the period of convergence T to the long-run steady state, such that:

$$For\ t\geq T \quad var(E(\pi_t^k/S_o=S_i))\leq \varepsilon \quad \forall i \tag{6.11}$$

Where equation (6.11) states that the influence of the initial state of the reservoir on the expected profit in period T or later is lower than a sufficiently small number ε. Thus, it is possible to write expected profit associated to the long-run stochastic equilibrium as:

$$E(\Pi_T^k/S_o = S_i) = E(\Pi_T^k) = \sum_j \Gamma(j) \times F(W(S_j)) \qquad (6.12)$$

Any changes in the distribution pattern of water inflows that result from climate change will alter the long-run steady state equilibrium and also the expected economic profit in irrigated areas.

We define the economic impact of climate change on water resources, V^{cc}, as the difference between the expected profit associated with the distribution of the stochastic steady state under the current climatic conditions and the expected profit associated with the stochastic steady state under a climate change scenario, that implies a change in the pattern of water inflows to the reservoir:

$$V^{cc} = \sum_j \Gamma(j)F(W(S_j)) - \sum_j \Gamma^{cc}(j)F(W(S_j)) = E(\Pi_T) - E^{cc}(\Pi_T) \qquad (6.13)$$

Where $\Gamma(j)$ represents the distribution of probabilities in the steady state corresponding to the current pattern of inflows, and $\Gamma^{cc}(j)$ is the distribution of probabilities of the steady state that results from a pattern of inflows in a certain climate change scenario.

EMPIRICAL APPLICATION

This sections presents an application of this analytical framework to evaluate the economic impact of plausible scenarios of climate change in irrigated agriculture in the Guadalquivir river basin. This river basin is located in the southern part of Spain and drains to the Atlantic Ocean, encompassing an area of 63 240 square kilometres. Being the home of almost 5 million people, its water resources have a predominantly agricultural use, which makes up about 75 per cent of water use in a normal year.

Two different management supply systems coexist in this river basin. The first and most important is the General Regulation System (GRS), which consists of a set of eight main reservoirs centrally managed by the River Basin Authority (RBA). The total capacity of the system has been expanded over time as new dams were erected, and its present storage capacity is 4046 billion cubic metres. An irrigated area of about 200 000 hectares depends annually on the water supply that originates from the resources stored in the GRS. In addition to irrigation, the GRS provides other services such as urban supply, flood control, hydropower and water quality upgrading. The RBA has the legal capacity to impose restrictions on the flows or volumes to users, based on the priority criteria laid down in the law and the availability of resources stored in the reservoirs. The second management supply system is typically characterised by a dam which serves a single group of users, who have 'special' rights over its water resources. They are placed in tributaries to the Guadalquivir, and were erected decades ago – a fact that explains the 'special' nature of the water rights – and are managed by water users' associations. Of course, they must follow a few general guidelines dictated by the RBA, but unless extreme droughts occur, they just have to inform the RBA of their reservoir operations.

Two representative irrigation districts have been selected for this empirical application. The first, called El Viar (EV), has operated since 1949, has about 500 farmers, encompasses about 12000 hectares and its water supply depends on one single reservoir that is managed by the water users' association. The second is Bajo Guadalquivir (BG), operating since 1974, with about 800 farmers, an area of 15000 hectares and its water supply originating from the pool of resources that can be stored in the eight large interconnected reservoirs centrally managed by the RBA. These two irrigation areas are also characterised by different technical features, technological levels and productive profiles. Field work carried out by Sumpsi et al. (1998) and revised field work done by the authors permitted the definition and characterisation of six and two representative farms in EV and BG districts, respectively (see Table 6.1).

Table 6.1   Descriptive features of the areas under study

Feature	El Viar	Bajo Guadalquivir
Acreage (ha)	11958	14099
Max. allotment (cm/ha)	7370	8590
Number of farmers	1500	800
Water supply system	El Pintado	General regulation
Initial date of operation	1949	1974

The Function of Agricultural Profit

The profit function for representative farms in each irrigation district is based on the results of a model of mathematical programming applied to a set of representative farms (Iglesias et al., 2000). By doing successive simulations for a complete range of possible amounts of water allotment, which go from zero to a maximum allotment, the model generates the optimal levels of other short-term decision variables, such as the crop rotation or the hiring of temporary labour, thus obtaining as a result a certain gross profit for each possible water allotment. On the basis of these results

Table 6.2   The gross margin function $\pi(w) = aw + bw^2 + c$

Coefficient	EV	BG
a (Allotment)	68.83	62.45
b (Allotment)^2	−4.25	−4.5
c	160.9	258.66
Adjusted R^2	0.99	0.99

the average gross profit function is obtained in its reduced form, which is reported in Table 6.2 for each irrigation district.

The Components of the Markovian Process

The Markovian process that characterises the evolution of the state of the reservoir is determined by the balance of the inputs and outputs in equation (6.4). In the empirical estimation of the balance equation that governs the dynamics of the stochastic process in the El Pintado reservoir, only the water releases to the El Viar community of farmers are taken into consideration, since they have exclusive rights over this regulation system. However, in the case of the GRS not only the water releases to the BG district have to be taken into consideration but also the rest of the users who are supplied with water from this system. The complete specification of these equations for both systems is contained in a previous work by the authors (Iglesias et al., 2001).

The Rules for Agricultural Water Withdrawals

It has to be pointed out that although there are certain priority rules for users, there are no other explicit criteria regarding how much water to release for irrigation purposes. Therefore, the function $W(S_t)$, has been estimated based on the annual historical data concerning the state of the reservoirs at the beginning of the period and the actual water allotments released to each irrigation district. The best adjustment is obtained by means of a quadratic model whose results are presented in Table 6.3. As has already been mentioned, the Bajo Guadalquivir irrigation district does not depend on just one reservoir, but rather on a number of reservoirs that integrate the general regulation system. Thus for this irrigation area we have devised a virtual reservoir and generated its annual water stock level by considering the data for the state of each of the reservoirs of the network weighted in relation to their relative capacity.

Table 6.3   Regression results for the functional relation between farmers' allotments and water stock levels
$[W_t = aS_t + b(S_t)^2 + cD_t^{St} + d(S_t D^{DR}) + e(S_t^2 D^{DR})]$ (t-ratios in parentheses)

Coefficient	Definition	EV (1974–98; n=25)	BG (1977–98; n=21)
a (stock)	Values recorded at 1 Febr measured as storage capacity	194 (11.33)	216 (14.84)
b (stock)²	Values recorded at 1 Febr measured as storage capacity	-1.27 (-7.26)	-1.35 (-7.23)
c (structural dummy)[a]	EV: $D_t^{st}=0$ for $t>18$, $D_t^{st}=1$ otherwise. BG: $D_t^{st}=0$ for $t>6$; $D_t^{st}=1$ otherwise	1083 (2.84)	2627 (6.06)
d (drought dummy × stock)	BG: drought dummy $D_t^{DR}=1$, for stock <25%, $D_t^{DR}=0$, otherwise		-443 (-4.15)
e (drought dummy × (stock)²)	BG: drought dummy $D_t^{DR}=1$, for stock <25%, $D_t^{DR}=0$, otherwise		17.5 (3.41)
Adjusted R²		0.88	0.95
F-stat		81.77	82.26
Durbin-Watson		2.01	1.91

Note: [a]The structural dummy was added in view of the fact that farmers' allotments were reduced after $t=6$ in BG and $t=18$ in EV.

Source: Iglesias et al. (2000).

The Pattern of Water Inflows and Climate Change Scenarios

The inflows to each reservoir are determined by the pattern of rainfall and the physical conditions under which overflow occurs in the collection area. In our model the inflows to each reservoir constitute a stochastic variable whose distribution function has been estimated based on the data collected since the reservoirs came into use.

In the case of the El Viar, the statistical analysis has been based on the inflow data to the El Pintado reservoir, the only reservoir that supplies water to the said community of irrigators, which consists of a series of historical data over a period of 50 years. The results reveal that the inflows follow a gamma distribution whose parameters are shown in Table 6.4.

In the case of Bajo Guadalquivir, the characterisation of inflows has been carried out in relative terms since the number of reservoirs in the network has increased over the past four decades. In order to carry out a consistent analysis it is assumed that the Bajo Guadalquivir obtains its water from a virtual reservoir whose annual inflows have been generated by adding up the weighted data on annual inflows for each of the reservoirs in the network.

The results show that stochastic inflows are best characterised following a gamma distribution function with a 0.05 significance level whose parameters are shown in Table 6.4.

Table 6.4   Statistical characterisation of inflows in each reservoir

Parameter	General regulation $N = 37$	Pintado $N = 50$
Gamma: shape	1.836	1.498
Gamma: scale	0.0370	0.0102
P-value	0.311	0.160

Source: Iglesias et al. (2001).

Taking into consideration the projections of the effects of climate change by Ayala and Iglesias (1997) for the Guadalquivir basin, which establish a 32 per cent reduction of inflows, two climate change scenarios have been defined: scenario 1 considers a 20 per cent reduction in average inflows and scenario 2 reflects a 40 per cent reduction. Considering the forecasts for an increase in the inter-annual variability of the inflows into the Guadalquivir basin (Balairón, 2001), a third climate change scenario has been established, defined as a reduction of 20 per cent in average inflows together with an increase in the variance of 50 per cent. Finally, scenario 0 represents the current climate regime and will be used as a base line to establish the economic impact of the former climate change scenarios.

Characterisation of the Steady State (Long-term Stochastic Equilibrium)

The complete empirical specification for the dynamic equation for both irrigation supply systems makes it possible to calculate all the elements of the transition probability matrix from a given initial state S_i to a final state S_j. Defining $n = 16$ possible levels of the state of the reservoirs, ranging from zero to full capacity, $i = 1,..., 16$ and $j = 1,...,16$, the transition matrix $P(i,j)$ of dimension 16×16 has been obtained for both systems, the Viar-Pintado and the BG-Regulación General, for the current pattern of inflows (scenario 0) and for the three climate change scenarios defined earlier.

With these matrixes, we are able to obtain the distribution of probabilities of the state of the system and the expected economic profit in successive periods for each of the systems and each of the climate scenarios, thus obtaining the convergence path of the system. $\varepsilon = 1\%$ is taken as the criterion for defining the period T at which the system converges. The distribution of probabilities corresponding to the steady state or stochastic equilibrium $\Gamma(j)$ will be given by any of the row vectors of the matrix $P^T(i,j)$. The convergence criterion thus defined establishes that the influence of the initial state $S_0 = S_i$, $\forall i$, on the probability of obtaining a certain level of profit in $t \geq T$ will be lower than 1 per cent. That is to say, for $t \geq T$ the system has lost its 'memory' and the probability of obtaining a certain economic result associated with the state S_j does not depend on the initial outset conditions. The distribution of probabilities in the steady state $\Gamma(j)$ obtained for each of the systems in the four climate scenarios under consideration is laid out in Table 6.5.

RESULTS

The economic impact of climate change on irrigated farming can be measured by comparing the expected gross margin in the long-term steady state, evaluated under the current climatic conditions, with the expected gross margin obtained under the climate conditions forecast for the year 2060. The results, presented in Tables 6.6 and 6.7, highlight the magnitude of the economic impact of climate change under any of the scenarios considered, although the most adverse results are obtained in scenario 2, where a 40 per cent reduction of the average inflows would translate into economic losses of 13 per cent in El Viar district and 24 per cent in the Bajo Guadalquivir district.

Table 6.5   Characterisation of the steady state (long-term stochastic equilibrium)

(T_j) (S_j)	13%	16%	22%	28%	34%	40%	46%	52%	58%	64%	70%	76%	82%	88%	94%	100%
BG																
SCE. 0	0.01	0.01	0.01	0.02	0.03	0.04	0.05	0.06	0.07	0.10	0.13	0.12	0.09	0.07	0.05	0.13
SCE. 1	0.06	0.04	0.05	0.06	0.06	0.07	0.08	0.08	0.07	0.09	0.09	0.07	0.05	0.04	0.03	0.06
SCE. 2	0.25	0.08	0.08	0.07	0.07	0.07	0.06	0.05	0.05	0.05	0.05	0.03	0.02	0.02	0.01	0.04
SCE. 3	0.11	0.05	0.06	0.06	0.06	0.07	0.07	0.06	0.06	0.07	0.08	0.06	0.04	0.03	0.02	0.08
VIAR																
SCE. 0	0.01	0.01	0.01	0.02	0.02	0.03	0.03	0.04	0.08	0.07	0.08	0.07	0.06	0.06	0.05	0.37
SCE. 1	0.03	0.03	0.04	0.05	0.05	0.05	0.04	0.07	0.09	0.07	0.06	0.05	0.04	0.04	0.03	0.26
SCE. 2	0.15	0.08	0.07	0.06	0.05	0.05	0.04	0.08	0.07	0.04	0.04	0.03	0.03	0.02	0.02	0.17
SCE. 3	0.08	0.05	0.05	0.05	0.05	0.05	0.04	0.08	0.08	0.05	0.05	0.04	0.03	0.03	0.02	0.24

Table 6.6 *Expected gross margin for four climatic scenarios in the Bajo Guadalquivir*

	Climate change scenarios			
	Scenario 0 Base line	Scenario 1 $\Delta WI = -20\%$	Scenario 2 $\Delta WI = -40\%$	Scenario 3 $\Delta WI = -20\%$; $\Delta \sigma WI^2 = +50\%$
Gross margin (T conv) (€/ha)	2362	2181	1803	2085
Losses (%)		7.6	24	12
T (number of years of convergence)	7	9	9	9

Tabla 6.7 *Expected gross margin for four climatic scenarios in the El Viar*

	Climate change scenarios			
	Scenario 0 Base line	Scenario 1 $\Delta WI = -20\%$	Scenario 2 $\Delta WI = -40\%$	Scenario 3 $\Delta WI = -20\%$; $\Delta \sigma WI^2 = +50\%$
Gross margin (T conv) (€/ha)	2590	2488	2259	2398
Losses (%)		4	13	7.4
T (number of years of convergence)	3	4	4	4

Comparison of the results obtained in scenarios 1 and 2 – which reflect respective drops of 20 per cent and 40 per cent in average inflows – reveals that the economic impact increases more than proportionally in the face of a progressive reduction in average inflows. This result is similar for both irrigation systems and it can be observed that in both cases the economic losses caused by the climate change in scenario 2 would multiply the losses obtained in scenario 1 by a factor of three.

The results obtained in scenario 3 and in scenario 1 allow us to evaluate the economic impact of an increase in the variance of the inflows. Comparison of these results shows that the increase in the variance notably increases the economic losses, even when average inflows remain constant. This is due to the fact that the increase in dispersion, in the right-hand tail of the distribution, increases the probability of having to release more water for security reasons. In short, this means that less water inflows can be stored to meet demands; the increase in dispersion reduces the effective capacity of managing a reservoir on an inter-annual basis, and in turn the supply of water it can offer. Furthermore, it has to be pointed out that in relative terms the economic impact of an increase in the variance is greater in El Viar where it is observed that the losses generated in scenario 3 – 7.4 per cent – are practically double those obtained in scenario 1 – 4 per cent – whereas for the Bajo Guadalquivir, although the impact is also notable, the economic losses would not be as much as double.

On the other hand, it has to be stressed that the economic impact of the climate change is considerably higher in the Bajo Guadalquivir, where the economic losses are practically twice those generated in the El Viar for any of the climate change scenarios analysed. The differences between both irrigation systems also clearly stand out in the analysis of the process of convergence to the steady state. Figures 6.1 and 6.2 represent, for each of the areas under study, the approximation paths to the said state from each of the 16 possible initial states of the reservoir. The successive periods after the initial one are represented on the horizontal axis and the gross margin associated with each period on the vertical axis.

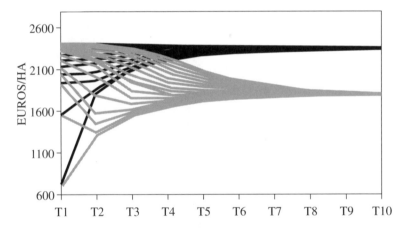

Figure 6.1   Convergence path to the steady state equilibrium in BG

The dynamics in the two systems describe clearly different approximation paths. Whereas El Viar converges to the steady state in four periods under the current climatic situation, Bajo Guadalquivir requires nine periods. Also, the possible initial states in BG are translated into a much wider range of income than in El Viar. In this respect, the differences in the management and farming regulations that apply to both systems have to be pointed out. The priority criteria implicit in the regulations for water release in the

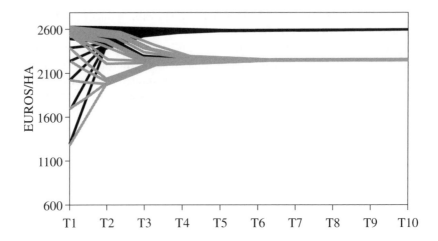

Figure 6.2   Convergence path to the steady state equilibrium in Viar

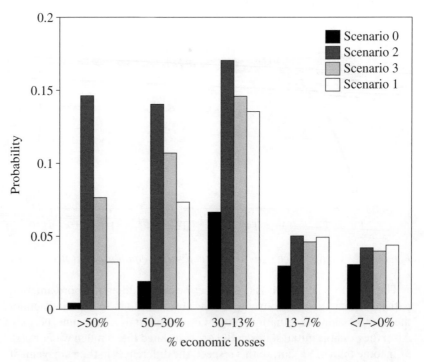

Figure 6.3   Probability of incurring economic losses in Viar district

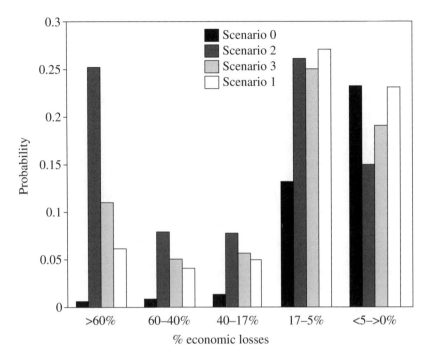

Figure 6.4   *Probability of incurring economic losses in Bajo Guadalquivir district*

General Regulation implies that the Bajo Guadalquivir receives smaller quotas for lower levels of water stocks than the El Viar, where users have exclusive rights over the El Pintado reservoir resources. In consequence, this means smaller profits for Bajo Guadalquivir when the stock levels are low.

On the other hand, it is interesting to highlight that in both systems the dispersion in the paths and in the number of periods necessary to reach convergence increases under the climate change scenarios. In the first place, this makes it possible to infer that it is going to be more 'costly' to recover from a drought or, in other words, that the economic impact of a hydrological drought is going to last longer. Secondly, this also implies that if the current pattern for water withdrawal is maintained, the probable economic results in the periods following one characterised by having a very high level of stock will describe a clearly descending path, which does not happen in the current climate scenario, whose convergence occurs at an economic level very close to the attainable maximum. This reveals that the economic risk of suffering a hydrological drought will considerably increase.

Figures 6.3 and 6.4 show the probabilities of incurring in different levels of losses. The economic losses are defined in this case as the reduction in gross margin, expressed in percentages, with regard to the gross margin that would result from having a complete allotment. These results show that the climate change significantly increases the probability and economic cost of hydrological droughts. This is particularly significant due to the fact that the probability of suffering economic losses increases to a greater extent for the highest ranges of losses. If, in the current scenario, the probability of losses being higher than 50 per cent is below 1 per cent in both systems, it is shown that it will reach 15 per cent for El Viar and 25 per cent for BG under the worst possible climatic scenario.

Table 6.8 synthesises the results of the simulation focusing on the expected probability of not incurring economic losses. These results reveal a considerable reduction in the probability of not incurring losses, the case of BG being particularly outstanding with a reduction of almost half in scenarios 1 and 3, and reduced to almost a quarter in scenario 2.

Table 6.8   Probabilities of not suffering economic losses in the different scenarios (%)

	Climate change scenarios			
	Scenario 0 $\Delta WI = -20\%$	Scenario 1 $\Delta WI = -40\%$	Scenario 2 $\Delta WI = -20\%$;	Scenario 3 $\Delta\sigma_{WI}^2 = +50\%$
Viar	87	71	49	62
Bajo Guadalquivir	60	34	17	32

CONCLUSIONS

The analysis of the Markovian process that governs the whole hydrological system and is characterised by the stochastic inflows resulting from climatic processes, and by the outflows resulting from institutional decisions on how much water to release from the reservoir, makes it possible to study the expected economic effect of a change in the pattern of inflows caused by climate change. Under assumptions of stability in water management rules, reservoir capacity and economic parameters affecting agricultural crops, a stochastic dynamic model is developed in order to obtain the economic value of the long-run steady state of the system. The results are analysed under different hypotheses of climate change in the current pattern of inflows to the systems that supply two irrigation districts of the Guadalquivir basin.

The complete characterisation of the transition processes between possible states has made it possible to determine the convergence paths to the steady state from any possible state of the reservoir at the initial period, and to determine the number of necessary periods to lose the system's memory (or convergence time). The application also allows the probabilities distribution of the economic results to be obtained for each climate change scenario, thus enabling a comparison of how the probability mass is altered between different ranges of economic loss and determination of the persistence in time of adverse economic scenarios.

Some outstanding conclusions on the management of water stockage systems and the economic effect of climate change arise from the analysis. First, it is shown that if the current pattern of releasing water to farming uses remains, climate change will have considerable impacts on the economies of farms in irrigated areas, translating into a 24 per cent reduction in the expected profits in the most unfavourable case of climate change. This justifies the need to redesign the regulations for water withdrawal, adjusting them to a pattern of inflows that will alter over the coming decades, in accordance with the best projections for climate change. The results reveal that this need is particularly crucial in the case of the Bajo Guadalquivir-General Regulation system where the theoretical allotment for farms is possibly too high.

Furthermore, the results of the study prove that the economic damage could increase more than proportionally in the face of successive reductions in the inflows, showing that a 40 per cent reduction in the average inputs would mean economic losses three times higher than those for a 20 per cent reduction. The results also show that the climate change will increase the dispersion of the economic results of the farms in irrigated areas, making them more vulnerable to meteorological drought cycles. The probability of incurring losses in adverse economic scenarios increases acutely and, what is more, it is shown that the persistence of the said scenarios will be more prolonged. From the above we can conclude that the projections for climate change will give rise to a structural change in the economies of agricultural farms that will not only have to face a severe reduction in the expected profitability of their land, but also acute variability in their income.

These results reveal the need to take the issue of climate change as a phenomenon of economic consequences of serious magnitude and lay out a future economic context in which to situate the debate on measures to mitigate and adapt to climate change. In this sense, both Article 27.2 of the Law Project for the National Hydrological Plan (Congreso de Diputados, 2001) and Article 11 of the Framework Directive for Water Policy should take into consideration the most probable scenarios of climate change when requiring the drawing up of plans to manage resources in drought situations and programmes for relevant measures. The consideration of economic projections associated with projected climate scenarios constitutes without doubt an important element in the planning and management of water resources.

NOTE

1. This work has benefited from European funding through the IV Framework Programme for R + D, with the project titled 'Societal and Institutional Responses to Climate Change and Climatic Hazards: Managing Flood and Drought Risks (SIRCH)'. Contract: n° ENV4-CT97-0447. 1998–2000.

REFERENCES

Ayala F. and A. Iglesias. (1997). 'Impacto del posible cambio climático sobre los recursos hídricos, el diseño y la planificación hidrológica en la España peninsular'. *El Campo* **137**, 201–223.

Balairón, L. (2001). 'Los escenarios del protocolo. Retos del Tercer Informe sobre el cambio climático'. *El Cultural* 11 April, 56–57.

Balti, N., A. Garrido and S. Zekri (2001). 'The impact of climate change in the Spanish and Tunisian agriculture'. Paper presented at Socioeconomic Assessments of Climate Change in the Mediterranean: Impacts, Adaptation, and Mitigation Co-benefits. FEEM, Milan, 9–10 February 2001.

Booker, J.F. and R.A. Young (1994). 'Modelling intrastate and interstate markets for Colorado river water resources'. *Journal of Environmental Economics and Management* **26**, 66–87.

Congreso de Diputados (2001). *Proyecto de Ley de PHN*, Madrid.

Feenstra, J., J. Burton, J. Smith and R. Tol (eds) (1998). *Handbook on Methods for Climate Change Impact Assessment and Adaptation Strategies*, version 2.0. United Nations Environmental Programme, Nairobi, and Institute of Environmental Studies, Vrije Universiteit, Amsterdam.

Fisher, A. and S. Rubio (1997). 'Adjusting to climate change: Implications of increased variability and asymmetric adjustment costs for investment in water reserves'. *Journal of Environmental Economics and Management* **34**, 207–227.

Iglesias, E., A. Garrido and A. Gómez Ramos (2000). 'Evaluation of drought management in irrigated areas'. Paper presented at International Conference of Agricultural Economists, August 2000, Berlin.

Iglesias, E., A. Garrido and A. Gómez Ramos (2001). 'An economic drought management index to evaluate water institutions' performance under uncertainty and climate change'. FEEM Working Papers series. Milan.

Hurd et al. (1999). 'Economic effects of climate change on US water resources', in R. Mendelsohn and J.E. Neumann (eds) *The Impact of Climate Change on the United States Economy*. Cambridge University Press, UK.

Malliaris, A.G. and W.A. Brock (1999). *Stochastic Methods in Economics and Finance*. Elsevier Science BV, Amsterdam.

Strzepek, K.M. et al. (1998). 'Water resources', in J. Feenstra, J. Burton, J. Smith and R. Tol (eds) *Handbook on Methods for Climate Change Impact Assessment and Adaptation Strategies*, version 2.0. United Nations Environmental Programme, Nairobi, and Institute of Environmental Studies, Vrije Universiteit, Amsterdam.

Sumpsi, J.M., A. Garrido, M. Blanco, C. Varela-Ortega and E. Iglesias (1998). 'Economía y política de gestión del agua en la agricultura', Secretaría General Técnica Ministerio de Agricultura, Pesca y Alimentación (MAPA), Ediciones Mundi-Prensa, Madrid.

UNFCCC (1999). *Compendium of Decision Tools to Evaluate Strategies for Adaptation to Climate Change*, Final Report. Bonn.

Vaux, H.J. and R.E. Howitt (1984). 'Managing water scarcity: An evaluation of interregional transfers'. *Water Resources Research* **20**, 785–792.

Venema, H.D., E.J. Schiller, K. Adamowski and J.M. Thizy (1997). 'A water resources planning response to climate change in the Senegal River Basin'. *Journal of Environmental Management* **49**(1), 125–155.

PART IV

Climate change and Mediterranean land uses

7. What future for Mediterranean agriculture? A proposal to integrate socio-economics in climate change scenarios

Paolo Rosato and Carlo Giupponi

INTRODUCTION

> Future climate change could critically undermine efforts for sustainable development in the Mediterranean region. In particular, climate change may add to existing problems of desertification, water scarcity and food production, while also introducing new threats to human health, ecosystems and national economies of countries. The most serious impacts are likely to be felt in North African and eastern Mediterranean countries. (Greenpeace, 1997)

Such a negative scenario of possible effects of climate change in the Mediterranean area may be considered to be pessimistic, but probably not far from the perception of people living there. It is well known that the perception of climate by people is far from objective and quantitative, but it is also clear that in recent times Mediterranean people have had the chance to experience signs of those changes and some of them are indeed currently being monitored. As a matter of fact, observational records suggest marked changes in the climate of the Mediterranean region over recent years (Piervitali *et al.*, 1997).

While it is impossible at the moment to be certain if those changes represent significant trends or depend on short- and medium-term variability, it is also clear that significant proof of changes will be available only after remarkable impacts have started to occur. It is therefore necessary to be prepared for the future evolution of climate, to identify potential impacts and the most vulnerable situations, and to define adequate strategies for the adaptation to and mitigation of the effects of climate change.

An approach common to the international literature dealing with uncertain futures (if not unknown), is based on the development of scenarios; that is, alternative images of how the future may unfold. Scenarios are not to be considered predictions or forecasts, but just hypothetical references, developed to enhance our understanding of how systems behave, evolve and interact (IPCC, 2000).

This work is aimed at presenting the current understanding in scientific literature about climate change in the Mediterranean area, focusing in particular on the agricultural sector. Moreover, based on the available knowledge, a methodological proposal is presented for designing locally consistent future scenarios to drive simulations of possible land use changes. An application of such methodology is presented for Italy.

MAIN TRAITS AND PROSPECTS FOR MEDITERRANEAN AGRICULTURAL SYSTEMS

Throughout history, water has been a means of communication and cohesion between different cultures; this was particularly true for the Mediterranean Sea, which contributed to the spreading and diffusion of ancient civilisations such as the Phoenicians, the Greeks and Romans. Today this does not seem to be true and, in fact, the countries that are along the Mediterranean shores present some of the most dramatic cultural, socio-economic and religious conflicts of the present age. To some extent this is also reflected in the way the research community and the international institutions deal with the area. It is, probably only in the field of physical sciences that it is possible to find a great wealth of studies and data for the Mediterranean area as a whole, as socio-economic analyses tend to deal with the area by splitting it into the three continents (Europe, Africa and Asia) or into the two main historical and cultural blocks (North Africa and the Middle East on one side and Europe on the other).

The utilisation of statistical data reported at the abovementioned levels of aggregation for describing the Mediterranean area is clearly meaningless. This makes integrated analyses, that consider socio-economic and environmental approaches together, particularly difficult. Analyses targeted to the agricultural sector are even more complicated, because even data at national level may be unsuitable for describing the Mediterranean specificities (e.g. in case of states such as France with great north–south differentiations).

Given the aforementioned limitations, nevertheless, a survey of the most recent statistics published by dedicated international organisations (FAO and CIHEAM in particular[1]) may allow an overall picture to be drawn of the agricultural systems of the Mediterranean area.

The agricultural sector plays a diversified role in the countries around the Mediterranean. Table 7.1 presents some relevant economic traits suitable for the comparison of various Mediterranean countries and their

Table 7.1   Gross domestic product (GDP), agriculture ratio to GDP (AGDP), AGDP per agricultural employee (reference year 1998) and AGDP growth rates

Country	GDP (10⁶ US$)	GDP/inhabitant (US$)	AGDP/ GDP (%)	AGDP/Ag. empl. (US$)	AGDP growth rate (%) 1997	1998	1999
Albania	2460	649	63.0	2026	1.0	5.0	4.0
Algeria	49585	1664	12.0	2459	−24.0	11.4	0.1
Egypt	88781	1320	17.0	1552	3.4	n.a.	3.7
France	1395204	23607	1.8	26201	1.3	1.5	2.5
Italy	1140976	19898	2.4	19344	0.9	1.2	3.1
Morocco	35545	1279	16.0	1296	−25.6	24.2	−19.8
Portugal	106862	10718	1.9	2971	−5.2	−17.2	28.0
Spain	580297	14720	3.0	11903	−1.3	4.0	−2.1
Tunisia	21031	2223	14.1	3340	0.4	0.1	11.0
Turkey	198006	3120	26.0	3415	−2.3	4.5	−4.6

Source: CIHEAM (2000).

135

agriculture. The main evidence from the cited table is the diversity in both the economies as a whole and in the agricultural sectors around the Mediterranean. It is not simply a matter of north–south contrasts, because the economic figures present great differences also from east to west and within European and Middle East countries. The specific feature of Mediterranean agriculture that is more relevant for the present context is presented in the right part of the table, which clearly shows the *annual variability* of agricultural productions in general, strictly related to meteorological events and in particular to the droughts that frequently affect the area.

Table 7.2   Mean yield of different crop types (t/ha), FAOSTAT database for the period 1979–98

Country	Cereals	Oil-crops	Root-tuber crops	Vegetables
Albania	2.59	0.18	10.79	16.88
Algeria	0.87	0.44	13.37	10.59
Egypt	6.33	0.44	20.18	25.31
France	6.87	0.95	35.95	17.85
Greece	3.61	0.50	19.31	30.87
Croatia	4.57	0.50	9.59	8.64
Israel	1.88	0.62	39.88	28.72
Italy	4.84	0.63	23.20	24.31
Lebanon	2.37	0.40	22.34	23.04
Libya	0.72	0.40	7.26	14.39
Morocco	1.01	0.27	17.56	17.86
Spain	2.70	0.37	20.59	27.21
Tunisia	1.19	0.13	13.70	14.14
Turkey	2.15	0.43	24.35	23.43

Another aspect of such variability is clearly evident when examining the statistics about agricultural productions of Mediterranean countries. Table 7.2 presents a selection of data of mean yields; in reading the table one can immediately interpret the widest *geographical variability* of yields as due to one or more of the various socio-economic and environmental factors affecting agricultural production. Even without considering the more obvious north–south variations, along the northern shore, cereal yields range between 2.6 and 4.8 t/ha for Albania and Italy respectively or, to the south, between 0.9 and 6.3 t/ha for Algeria and Egypt.

A first attempt to understand the socio-economic meaning of those figures in the southern and eastern parts of the Mediterranean can be made by comparing *total productions and national demand* and by analysing the

temporal trends, as reported in Table 7.3. It is evident in the FAO's estimates that production of wheat and coarse grains may not keep up even
with lowering growth of demand. Production grew about 3 per cent per
annum in the 1970s and the 1980s, while the average growth rate of the
1990s (1990–99) was 1.4 per cent. Moreover, production was 79 million
tonnes in the latest 3-year average, 1997/99, which was almost the same as
the 78 million tonnes of 1990/92.

Table 7.3   *Cereal balances for the Near East/North Africa (NE/NA)*
                  region

	Demand						
	Per head (kg)		Total (t × 10⁶)				
	Food	All uses	Food	All uses	Production	Net trade	Self-sufficiency rate
1964/66	174	292	28	47	40	−5	86
1974/76	190	307	40	64	55	−13	85
1984/86	203	365	56	100	65	−38	65
1995/97	208	357	75	129	84	−43	65
2015	209	359	108	186	110	−76	59
2030	205	367	130	232	131	−102	56

Source: FAO (2000).

The evaluation of the possible land-yield combinations in the future, as
well as the prospect that there will be no return to the heavy production subsidies some countries provided in the past, does not permit optimism
concerning the possibility that growth of aggregate wheat and coarse grains
production of the region could exceed 1.5 per cent per annum in the next
two decades. Hence the need for growing net imports to maintain the,
admittedly fairly high, per head consumption (FAO, 2000).

Projected production paths for meat to 2015 and 2030 generally follow
those projected for consumption worldwide, except for this region and East
Asia. NE/NA projections foresee an increase in meat production from the
present 6 million tonnes to 11 in 2015 and 16 in 2030. Large increments are
estimated in particular for poultry meat and eggs. Large deficits are thus
expected to develop: meat imports are projected to increase from 1.2 in
1995/97 to 4.7 million tons by 2030 (FAO, 2000).

A general conclusion from these considerations with regard to
Mediterranean agriculture is that the already widely recognised unsustain-
ability of existing systems and trends in the Mediterranean region may

become more evident in the future and the impacts of climate change could seriously undermine efforts to reorient Mediterranean societies toward sustainable development (Greenpeace, 1997).

There is therefore the need for coordinated efforts to design directions for future development inspired by the concept of sustainability, as defined by the 'Brundtland Commission' (WCED, 1987). This means recognising that sufficient resources should be retained or renewed to allow both current and future generations to meet their needs. In general, the concept of socially efficient resource management (water in particular), should be implemented, which considers not only resource consumption, but also the outflows or indirect uses; that is, the generation of pollutants, and other effects (e.g. erosion) known as negative externalities (MAP, 2000).

All those necessary efforts should be based on an in-depth understanding of the most likely climate change consequences and their potential impacts on Mediterranean agriculture.

POSSIBLE DIRECT AND INDIRECT CONSEQUENCES OF CLIMATE CHANGE

Significant uncertainties surround predictions of regional climate changes: first, uncertainty related to including different sources of errors within the assessments (e.g. climate scenarios, crop experiments, models and spatialisation procedures), secondly, the uncertainty linked with unpredictable directions of future social, economic, political and technical changes and, finally, unpredictable dynamic and combined effects of biophysical, social, economic, political and technological drivers.

Global circulation models (GCMs) have been widely used to examine climate changes and to construct climate scenarios over the Mediterranean basin (see for instance Houghton *et al.*, 1990 and 1992; Palutikof *et al.*, 1992 and 1997).

Bearing in mind the problem of uncertainty of prediction in its various forms, there is a certain consensus in the international literature that the temperatures in the Mediterranean region will rise significantly during the subsequent decades. The outlook for precipitation is much less certain, but most projections point to more precipitations in winter and less in summer over the region as a whole (Rosenzweig and Tubiello, 1997; Palutikof and Wigley, 1996). It is generally accepted that precipitation will decrease in the southern Mediterranean region (south of latitude 40–45°N) and will increase in the northern Mediterranean region (Cubasch *et al.*, 1996; Barrow and Hulme, 1995; Palutikof and Wigley, 1996). The variability of climate and the frequency of extreme events (droughts and storminess) could also increase (Houghton *et al.*, 1996; Jeftic *et al.*, 1996). Even areas receiving more precipitation may get drier than today due to increased evapotranspiration and changes in the seasonal distribution of rainfall and its intensity (Jeftic *et al.*, 1996; Palutikof *et al.*, 1994). As a consequence, the frequency and severity of droughts could increase across the region (Parry, 2000).

A long list of possible consequences of climate change in the Mediterranean has been proposed by various authors, including direct environmental effects and indirect socio-economic consequences:

- coastal flooding, erosion, sea water intrusion in aquifers;
- increase in extent and severity of desertification;
- increased frequency of water shortages and decline in water quality;
- food security threatened by falls in production and world price rises;
- new, widespread risks to public health;
- losses of valuable ecosystems;
- economic activity undermined in coastal zones;
- losses to national economies.

All of these may have significant effects on Mediterranean agricultural systems.

Agriculture sensitivity to climate depends on both direct and indirect effects (Parry, 2000). In concise and simplified terms we can state that crops are sensitive to the *incoming solar radiation*, which regulates the photosynthesis processes; *air temperature*, which controls the duration of the growing period and other processes linked with the accumulation of dry matter (i.e. leaf area expansion, respiration); and *rainfall and soil water availability* affecting the duration of growth (i.e. leaf area duration and photosynthetic efficiency). Livestock production is instead affected by the effect of *climatic variables* in general on metabolic processes of reared animals and, indirectly by the *availability and quality of water, forages and other foodstuff*.

Yields of grains and other crops could decrease substantially across the Mediterranean region due to increased frequency of drought, even if potential production should rise thanks to increased CO_2 concentrations. Some crops (e.g. maize) could be forced out of production. Livestock production would suffer due to deterioration in the quality of rangeland associated with higher concentrations of atmospheric carbon dioxide and to changes in areas of rangeland (increase of unproductive shrub land and desert).

The main consequences of the possible *direct* influence of future climate changes on crop and livestock production are listed below:

- current differences in crop productivity between northern and southern countries will increase under climate change;
- inter-annual variability of crop yields will increase, especially in regions such as southern Europe, where crop production is affected by water shortages;
- changes in availability and prices of grains for feeding (cereals, pulses and other feed grains);
- changes in productivity of pastures and forage crops;
- change in distribution of livestock diseases;
- changes in animal health, growth, and reproduction (direct effects of weather and extreme events);
- change in the turnover and losses of nutrients from animal manure, both in houses, stores and in the field, influencing the availability of manure in organic farms.
- adaptive strategies (changing variety and altering sowing date) may alleviate yield losses by reducing the risk of low yields in most situations;

Possible *indirect* consequences of climate change may be:

- crop production would be further threatened by increases in competition for water from other sectors;
- world prices for many key commodities such as wheat, maize, soybean meal and poultry could rise significantly as a result of global climate changes and macroeconomic factors;
- not only might Mediterranean countries lose in economic terms, but the combination of population growth, higher prices and yield losses would lead to a deterioration in levels of food security, particularly in southern countries.

Not only may agriculture be affected by indirect effects driven by other sectors, but it could also produce broader cascade effects (positive or negative) on the socio-economy (Parry, 2000). First, the food industry may be affected by changes in the productivity and quality of agriculture and horticulture induced by climate change (especially for local high quality food specialities). Service industries (e.g. biotechnology, farming technology) may be benefited by adjusting agricultural practices to the effects of global change. Insurance may be affected by an altered frequency of extreme weather events (e.g. storms, hail or floods) that will lead to lower or higher damage costs.

Most of these possible and, unfortunately, generally negative consequences of climate change in the Mediterranean region have water in common as the most crucial and threatened resource. Climate change is in fact expected to exacerbate the existing problems of water scarcity, both in quantitative and qualitative terms. Water is also the main environmental and social source of concern for the projected development of the economies of Mediterranean countries in the 21st century, therefore, competition for water resources should be considered as an issue of primary strategic relevance. In relatively water-abundant and developed communities, competition is between consumptive and non-consumptive uses; in water-scarce ones competition still primarily results from the difficulty of satisfying the increasing demands for 'traditional' consumptive water uses. In the Mediterranean basin both forms of competition can be observed, but countries on the southern shores are experiencing a continuous decrease in their ability to satisfy 'basic needs'.

A first conclusion of the brief analyses presented here is that climate change tends to exacerbate existing environmental and socio-economic problems (desertification, food security, etc.), rather than creating new ones, but the concurrent macroeconomic trends could lead to amplified negative interactions between environmental and economic variables and amplified social impacts. Water resources should be considered the main source of concern.

POSSIBLE IMPACTS AND ADAPTATION OPTIONS

Existing studies show that, on the whole, global agricultural production will not be harmed by climate change, and that total agricultural production might even be maintained in the midst of global warming (Odingo, 1998). Despite the substantial lack of systematic studies for the countries around the Mediterranean, agricultural impact studies, however, have suggested very different implications for developing countries, including the southern and eastern shores of the Mediterranean. Scientists tend to agree that global climate change will lead to more significant agricultural productivity losses in the tropics where a majority of these countries lie (Winters *et al.*, 1998). In general we can state that negative effects of climate change will depend on:

- relationships of each economy with the international market;
- substitution possibilities within the economy;
- relative importance of agriculture;
- composition of production in the agricultural sector.

The specific vulnerability of Mediterranean agro-ecosystems to climate change should not mean that some areas may become completely unsuitable for agriculture, but a reduction of suitable areas for traditional crops is predicted, with a likely need to introduce new crops. Marginal regions suitable for production of traditional crops will be particularly sensitive and in some cases vulnerable to climate changes.

In the Mediterranean area climate changes are expected to damage summer crops in particular, for several reasons; first the problem of *water shortage* may be enhanced by the combined increase in temperature and reduction in precipitation during summer as predicted by future climate scenarios. Secondly, the increases in *climatic inter-annual variability* and extreme events may also affect crop production, causing lower yield (shorter growing season, increase in water shortage, heat stress) and higher yield variability (increase in extreme events).

Mediterranean farmers could experience negative effects of CC both in terms of crop yields and of crop choices, the consequence of that being a stronger rigidity of farms to market changes (Rosenzweig and Tubiello, 1997). Therefore, economic and agronomic adaptation strategies will be important to limit losses and exploit possible positive effects (Reilly, 1996). The economic strategies are intended to render the agricultural costs of climate change lower by comparison with the overall expansion of agricultural products, while the agronomic strategies intend to offset, either partially or completely, the loss of productivity caused by climate change.

A crucial point for the selection of the most appropriate strategies is the evaluation of their adjustment time, both short- and long-term strategies should be identified, planned and implemented by competent actors. Reilly (1996) estimated the adjustment times of adoption for major adaptation measures in agricultural systems, with values ranging from a few years for changes in management and crop varieties, to several decades in the case of strategies based on the construction of new water networks, dams or irrigation systems.

Short-term adjustment strategies are the first defence against climate change and aim at optimising production with minor system changes through alternative management of cropping systems and interventions for the conservation of soil moisture (Parry, 2000).

Alternative management of cropping systems may consider changes in crop varieties in a search for higher thermal and water efficiencies and more stable yields, a diversification of cultivars, adjustments in agronomic practices (e.g. sowing dates, fertiliser and pesticide uses). The conservation of soil moisture considers mostly the introduction of more efficient irrigation schemes and new tillage systems (minimum tillage, mulching, etc.)

Long-term adaptation strategies try to overcome negative effects caused by climate change through major structural system changes, such as crop substitution or re-allocation, taking into account the changed land suitability, or even the introduction of new cultivars especially designed to adapt to climatic stresses (heat, water, pest and disease, etc.). These strategies should be introduced in combination with adapted nutrient management to reflect the modified growth and yield of crops, and also changes in the turnover of nutrients in soils. In some instances microclimate modification to improve water use efficiency in agriculture may also be feasible.

Several authors have tried to estimate the potential effects of the various adaptation strategies. Rosenzweig and Parry (1994) estimated the potential effects of two levels of adaptation options roughly corresponding to the short- and long-term strategies described earlier. Having estimates of potential losses of agricultural production due to climate change at global level ranging between 10.9 and 19.6 per cent, depending on the global circulation model (GCM) scenarios used, they estimated first the positive photosynthetic effect of increased CO_2 to reduce losses by between 1.2 and 7.6 per cent. Then they simulated the potential effects of short-term adaptations, obtaining losses ranging from 0 to 7.9 per cent, and long-term ones, estimating potential effects ranging from an increase in production of 1.1 per cent to a loss limited to 2.4 per cent. Such global average figures were also distinguished between developed and developing countries, obtaining for the first more positive and for the latter more negative results due to the effects of both climate change and adaptation potentials.

CONCEPTS AND DEFINITIONS FOR SCENARIO DEVELOPMENT

The analyses of Mediterranean agriculture and its future prospects presented so far have demonstrated the complexity of the theme and the great difficulties encountered when systematic and integrated studies are attempted. In such a context, predictions of socio-economic trends in an environment dramatically changing in space and time are clearly impossible. In recognising this, the global change literature has made growing use of various approaches to imagine the possible futures, based on the concept of *scenarios*.

The scenario approach is widely used by physical, economic and social sciences in a variety of circumstances and for widely different purposes. Even the definition of 'scenario' is not unique and the word is often used with different meanings. For the IPCC (Intergovernmental Panel on Climate Change) a scenario is a coherent, internally consistent and plausible description of a possible future state of the world (McCarthy *et al.*, 2001), but still within the climate change literature the term scenario is used with different meanings. In some cases it simply consists of a set of values deriving from

GCMs, which describe one hypothetical future climatic situation, but it may also consist of a complex set of quantitative and qualitative components (including driving forces of change) associated with a narrative description, like in the case of the SRES (Special Report on Emission Scenarios) scenarios of the IPCC (2000). It may then be useful to define in general the concept of what a scenario should include. According to Rotmans (cited in Rotmans *et al.*, 2000) scenarios should in general present *hypotheses* and consist of *causally related* states, driving forces, events, consequences and actions, describing *dynamic processes* starting from an initial state (usually the present) and depicting a final state in the *future*.

A key aspect, which is instead commonly accepted in the whole international literature, is that scenarios are not predictions or forecasts of the future, but then, what could they be useful for? Some authors identify the main role of scenarios as providing insight to the present, by learning from the proposed projections of the future. It is important to realise that the main issue is not to understand whether a certain situation may or may not be realistic for the future, but instead to identify what are the most likely consequences and, even more importantly, how we should prepare *in the present* to cope with possible events, of unknown probability. For the climate change literature this is a fundamental concept on which the research about climate change impacts and strategies for mitigation and adaptation are based.

In general, global change studies rely on scenario development to describe causal processes representing the dynamic of climate in the future. In the case of the multiple scenarios families developed by the IPCC for its Third Assessment Report (TAR), their main purpose was to explore uncertainties of future development trends and greenhouse gas (GHG) emissions in relation to their main driving forces. An important distinction should be made at this point between *climatic* and *non-climatic* scenarios, the latter providing the socio-economic and environmental context in which the climate variables evolve, both being necessary as inputs for assessments of impacts, vulnerability, and mitigation and adaptation options.

Many other distinctions should be mentioned to go deeply into the concept of scenario development. The first is between *descriptive* or *exploratory* scenarios (which project expected futures) and *normative* ones, which project desired or un-desired futures. The first category is quite commonly used and in the simplest instance they are a mere extrapolation of past trends to the future, while the second category typically includes scenarios developed for policy design, for mitigation or adaptation measures.

Another classification of scenarios relevant to the scope of the present work concerns the approaches used for their development. A whole range of solutions exist between two extremes: on the one hand scenarios may be developed with *complex quantitative, formal and mechanistic models*, while, on the other, they may consist of *qualitative, narrative descriptions* elaborated on the basis of analogies with past events and/or of the judgement of experts. In many cases both approaches are adopted; for example, the SRES scenarios have a narrative part called 'storylines' and a number of corresponding quantitative model-based scenarios for each storyline (IPCC, 2000).

A final aspect relevant for introducing the methodological proposal presented in the following section regards the issue of scales. The *temporal scale* is obviously relevant for defining the time horizon of the projections to the future and may be one of the main determinants of the level of uncertainty of the resulting scenarios (the longer the projections, the higher the uncertainty).

The spatial scale issue is one of the most relevant in the current scientific debate. A great wealth of literature has been published in recent years about methodologies for downscaling global scenarios to the regional level. Unfortunately those methodologies generally focus on the downscaling of climatic variables only, and thus a proposal for a comprehensive multi-disciplinary approach for integrated climate change scenarios at regional level is substantially lacking.

A METHODOLOGICAL PROPOSAL FOR BUILDING LOCALLY CONSISTENT AGRICULTURAL SCENARIOS

The variable availability of data and studies on agriculture in Mediterranean countries and the possible evolution driven by expected climatic changes, calls for an integrated approach for designing future scenarios. This approach should be based on a methodology that is realistically applicable in the various countries of the area.

As previously stated, no comprehensive mechanistic models are as yet available and so a combination of various models, that use synthetic and/or empirical approaches and expert judgements must be integrated to construct climatic and socio-economic scenarios at local level. The current climate change literature commonly refers only to global or regional levels and thus there is a need to design a downscaling process to build local scenarios, which maintain the internal consistency of the original, larger scale scenarios.

The following sections present a methodology developed by the authors for building such locally consistent agricultural scenarios, within an ongoing European research project, called ACCELERATES,[2] and briefly refer an exploratory application carried out at national level, in Italy.

The ACCELERATES project aims at evaluating the relationship between agricultural land use responses to environmental change drivers and environmental protection, as reflected specifically in the management of biological resources. The overall aim of the project is to assess the vulnerability to environmental change of European managed ecosystems, in support of the conventions of climate change and biological diversity. This aim will be achieved through an assessment of:

- the rate, extent and dynamics of agricultural land use change arising from climate, policy and socio-economic pressures;
- the impact of agricultural land use and climate change on biological resources;
- the vulnerability of agro-ecosystems in terms of both their sensitivity and capacity to adapt to change.

A specific task under the responsibility of the authors of this chapter is targeted at the development of integrated scenarios of future changes in both the socio-economic and climate baselines for Europe for 2020, 2050 and 2080.

The ACCELERATES modelling will be driven by the use of environmental change scenarios. The approach adopted within the project is to develop a range of plausible future socio-economic scenarios to be applied in an analogous way to the climate change scenarios. This approach requires an investigation of how the socio-economic scenarios may be directly linked to the climate change scenarios through the common social and political assumptions that underpin them. An important benefit of this approach is that scenarios allow the direct comparison of changes arising from either climate or socio-economic change. Thus the relative importance of socio-economic and biophysical drivers can be assessed, and the implications for policy can be highlighted.

The IPCC Third Assessment Report (TAR) has identified necessary requisites of scenarios as being *coherency, internal consistency and plausibility* (McCarthy *et al.*, 2001, p. 147), which is in accordance with the definition given by Rotmans *et al.* (2000) for 'integrated scenarios', characterised by being coherent and consistent. Therefore, climate change studies require the development of integrated scenarios, which should be coherent, internally consistent and plausible. They should thus include all the relevant dimensions and interlinkages between the processes examined and should be based on assumptions or theories that could be checked for their internal consistency and reproducibility.

The procedure designed in this chapter for the quantification of socio-economic impacts on agriculture in future climate change scenarios is

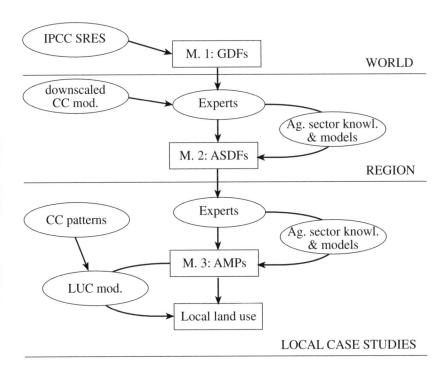

Figure 7.1   *Graphical representation of the integrated approach, allowing downscaling from global change models to local land use scenarios*

based on the most recent acquisitions of the literature in the field. During several decades studies of the evolution of the agricultural sector have developed various methodologies to evaluate the impacts of future policy and socio-economic scenarios. They vary from general equilibrium econometric models, to more specific approaches such as sector, regional or even farm-scale models.

For the present research an integrated approach was designed (see Figure 7.1), in which the available evidence and research results from climate change literature are elaborated together with a socio-economic approach and further synthesised in subsequent steps (Matrices 1 to 3), by integrating quantitative algorithms with expert judgement, with the aim of:

1. managing, organising and sharing the available information for elaborating evaluations and judgements;
2. defining a common approach for the formulation of judgements.

IPCC scenarios drive the setting of global driving forces (GDFs) in Matrix 1, which represents the reference background at global level for a panel of experts belonging to socio-economic and agricultural disciplines. Information deriving from downscaled climate change models,[3] together with expert knowledge and model results (e.g. statistics and outputs of general equilibrium models) allow the panel to compile a table (Matrix 2) which presents the changes of agricultural sector driving forces (ASDFs), from the present situation to the future scenarios, at regional level (i.e. the Mediterranean area, or the EU, for instance).

In a following step, the expert panel utilises the ASDF data stored in Matrix 2, to identify their effects on agricultural model parameters (AMPs) at local level (Matrix 3), with the help of data about local agricultural systems and climate change patterns. AMPs are the values required for running land use change (LUC) models, such as the expected changes in the profitability of crops suitable for being grown in the area considered.[4]

The proposed approach, holistic and synthetic, is coherent with the approach developed by the IPCC for the Third Assessment Report, in which it is recognised that, owing to the present degree of understanding of global change phenomena formal modelling techniques, should often be coupled with expert judgement to obtain projections (McCarthy *et al.*, 2001). This requires the setting up of expert panels and the design of adequate tools, such as questionnaires, to collect information useful for estimates of future changes.

From the socio-economic viewpoint two different scales are adopted (see Figure 7.2):

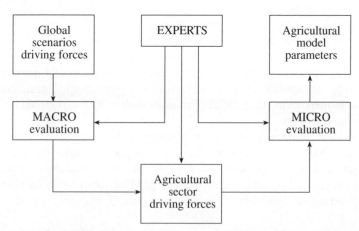

Figure 7.2   Graphical representation of experts' involvement to obtain projections

1. First evaluations are developed at the *macro level* (i.e. regional or even global) to identify and examine the pressure exerted on the agricultural sector by the major driving forces in the selected climate change scenarios (e.g. the SRES scenarios of the IPCC).
2. Secondly, evaluations at the *micro level* are targeted at identifying and quantifying the impacts of the macro drivers and pressures, as defined by the adopted scenarios, on the agricultural systems and land use.

The methodology developed for guiding the work of experts is based on systematic comparisons between present situation (PS) and future scenarios, in which current values of parameters considered in the matrices are set to 100. The pairwise comparison approach is adopted to obtain quantitative judgements from verbal comparative judgements of experts. This procedure foresees the application of a series of phases described in Figure 7.3.

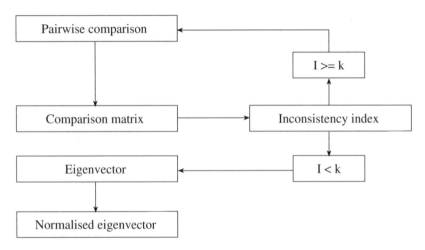

Figure 7.3   The pairwise comparison procedure

The evaluation is done by comparing pairs of situations (e.g. the role of European Union Agricultural Policy now and in 2020) and by formulating judgements of relative importance based on the ranking system proposed by Saaty (1980). This system allows the transformation of qualitative judgements into quantitative figures, as reported in Table 7.4. Given the aims of this work, the original scale proposed by Saaty, which ranges between 9 and 1/9 has been used together with two other more compact scales ranging between 5 and 1/5, or 3 and 1/3, thus obtaining eigenvectors in the matrix of pairwise comparison with smaller ranges. These possibilities of less diverse judgement provide better performances in cases like the

Table 7.4   The pairwise comparison approach

Comparative judgement	Numerical equivalent 1st	Numerical equivalent 2nd	Numerical equivalent 3rd
Absolutely more important	9	5	3
Much more important	7	4	2,5
More important	5	3	2
Slightly more important	3	2	1,5
Equal importance	1	1	1
Slightly less important	1/3	1/2	2/3
Less important	1/5	1/3	1/2
Much less important	1/7	1/4	2/5
Absolutely minor importance	1/9	1/5	1/3

Table 7.5   An example of a comparison matrix ('EUAP market' role)

	WM	RE	GS	LS
PS	More important	Slightly more to more important	Equal to slightly more important	Equally important
WM		Equal to slightly less important	Equal to slightly less important	Slightly less important
RE			Equal to slightly more important	Equal to slightly more important
GS				Equal to slightly less important

present one, in which rather than ranking alternative options, the identification of trends is pursued.

An example of a pairwise comparison matrix is given in Table 7.5 for the evaluation regarding the role of European Union Agricultural Policy (EUAP) in 2020, as compared with the present situation, in four alternative scenarios deriving from the IPCC SRES families (IPCC, 2000).[5]

Judgements are formulated by examining the present situation (PS) and 2020 scenarios on the rows with respect to those on the columns. In practice the contribution of experts is collected by asking them questions, having given them the Saaty scale as a reference for answers. For example:

Q: What is the role of the EUAP in the present situation as compared to the hypothetical scenario WM in 2020?
A: More important.

After having compiled the matrix it is necessary to choose, from the three scales proposed, the one to be adopted for transforming verbal judgements into numeric values. This choice should be based on the maximum range that is considered to be reasonable for the eigenvector that will be produced from the pairwise comparison matrix in question. In other words this choice may be expressed in terms of the expected intensity with which the parameter under evaluation may affect the future scenarios: the smaller the expected effect, the smaller the range of the comparison scale. After the conversion of verbal judgements into numeric values, eigenvectors are calculated, to obtain a synthesis of the judgements expressed during the pair comparison. The reliability of eigenvectors can be tested through the consistency of the matrix, which may be affected by problems deriving mainly from lack of transitivity of judgements. The calculation of the 'inconsistency index' provides a quantitative assessment of the reliability and robustness of the results of the pair comparison, with respect to an ideal situation of perfect consistency. In accordance with Saaty, the inconsistency index may be calculated as follows:

$$k = \frac{\lambda_1 - n}{n - 1}$$

where λ_1 is the eigenvalue associated with the maximum eigenvalue

$$n = \sum_{i=1}^{n} \lambda_i.$$

With $k = 0$ the matrix is perfectly consistent while, with $k = 1$ it is perfectly inconsistent. In general, for the original Saaty (1980) scale (9–1/9) an inconsistency index of 0.1 is considered the threshold for the acceptability of the matrix.

Following the example given for the EUAP, the resulting eigenvector calculated from the pair comparison matrix expressed with the scale 3–1/3 is:

- PS   100
- WM   52
- RE   90
- GS   74
- PS   85

Which means that the importance of the EUAP in the future scenarios is expected to decline in particular for scenarios WM and GS, and the results can be considered as internally consistent, given the inconsistency index of 0.01.

The results of a preliminary application of the proposed methodology with reference to the most important crops in Italy, having 2020 as the reference year for future scenarios[6] are reported in Tables 7.6 and 7.7.

Table 7.6   Agricultural sector driving forces at regional level (Matrix 2 for the EU)

	Present situation	2020 scenarios			
		WM	RE	GS	LS
EU AP 'market'	100	52	90	74	85
EU AP 'rural development'	100	58	106	100	163
Environmental policy pressure	100	85	97	183	173
EU enlargement	100	108	67	92	53
Resource competition	100	161	123	92	52
World demand/supply	100	172	106	121	79
WTO role	100	188	70	124	61

Table 7.7   Agricultural production profitability (Matrix 3 for Italy)

Italy	Present situation	2020 scenarios			
		WM	RE	GS	LS
Maize	100	89	98	64	66
Wheat	100	112	108	124	108
Sugarbeet	100	73	120	84	84
Soybean	100	102	113	157	137
Milk	100	137	116	115	157
Meat	100	147	96	109	71
Wine	100	130	104	127	100
Olive	100	87	90	111	196

Results presented in Table 7.6, for example, clearly highlight the state of ASDFs, as affected by the expected general revision of the objectives of the EU agricultural policy: all the scenarios show the progressive reduction of the intervention of the EU on the agricultural commodities market. This reduction is more evident in the global scenarios (WM and GS), but is considered likely also to occur, even though to a lower extent, in the scenarios dominated by localism (RE and LS), as a result of an increasing attention to public spending and of the declining role of agriculture in economic development.

The results of the proposed methodology for Matrix 3 are given in Table

7.7, presenting the variation in crop profitability caused by the ASDFs shown earlier, for Italy in 2020. Maize, for example, shows a reduction in profitability in both the global scenario and the more protectionist one. A slight drop is brought on by the liberalisation of the market in the WM scenario and by environmental constraints on production techniques in the GS and LS scenarios. The profitability of maize should remain stable only in the RE scenario. With regards to wheat, profitability should increase due to the same factors that will cause the decrease in profitability for maize. The expansion of the population and the economy should reward the price of wheat, even in the presence of environmental protection. Wheat, essentially should be advantaged by the introduction of environmental measures and crop rotations, also due to its cultivation period in autumn, favouring the protection of soil from erosion and limiting the runoff of nitrogen and phosphorus.

A substantial reduction in profitability is expected for sugar beet in the WM scenario, caused by the competitiveness of sugar cane. Its profitability is therefore tied to a protectionist scenario (RE). The introduction of environmental policy measures, caused by the high impacts productive techniques (pesticides) should penalise it. Soybean should not register any significant reduction in price due to an increase in demand of future scenarios (the demand of protein increases with the increase of income and population) and to the competitive advantage in the 'conservationist' scenarios (GE and LS), given the low environmental impact of cultivation techniques. Milk production foresees an increase in profitability due to the growth of demand at the global level (WM, RE) and the role that this production could have in the management of the marginal areas of developed countries (LS).

The profitability of meat can be linked essentially to global and consumerist scenarios, e.g. WM. Therefore there will not be significant variations in the RE scenario, given the limits to market globalisation and in the GS scenario given the environmental restrictions, compensated by the positive effect of globalisation. Only in the LS scenario the profitability of meat production will suffer a significant reduction as a result of limited economic development, which decreases demand, and of the concomitant environmental restrictions to production techniques and manure management. Wine production registers a remarkable success continuing to the immediate future, especially in the more global sensitive scenarios (WS and GS). On the other hand, olive production could suffer significantly in the consumerist scenario caused by the competition of alternative oil products (WM), and by other local productions in the use of resources, especially labour (RE). On the contrary, the profitability of this type of cultivation develops in the conservationist scenarios due to the high environmental value (GS and LS).

CONCLUDING REMARKS

Investigations and projections of the future are, by definition, uncertain. Research on climate change is therefore always characterised by various sources and degrees of uncertainty. On the other hand, adequate strategies for the mitigation of possible impacts and for adaptation policies should be planned well in advance, on the basis of possible future events. The considerations here have driven the attention of researchers to the development of sets of plausible alternative scenarios, with the intent to imagine and describe 'how the future may unfold' (IPCC, 2000).

In some cases the research interests are focused on the effects of single drivers or on their impact on single sectors, thus requiring the treatment of the complex socio-economic and environmental systems as separate entities, among which some variables are kept constant and others are treated with sector models, to assess specific dynamics and/or variables.

In other instances, such as the present research, the investigation of the future with an integrated approach is proposed, in order to be able to deal with interactions between a wide set of socio-economic and environmental drivers. In this case, multidisciplinary and integrated models, characterised by extreme complexity and high degrees of uncertainty, would be necessary. Unfortunately, the current modelling science and the available tools are not adequate for applying such analyses to regional and local levels, with an adequate level of accuracy. Thus the need arises for integrating the results of partial models with synthetic judgements given by experts. Only if this latter source of information is acquired and managed with robust, structured and transparent methodologies can it be integrated with modelling results without compromising their significance with uncontrolled sources of subjectivity and uncertainty.

This is particularly true for the Mediterranean and, even more, for what concerns the future of its agriculture. Around that sea are countries characterised by economic, political, social and environmental situations that are very diversified but, at the same time, strictly connected.

Moreover, Mediterranean agriculture is located in an area where the research on global change has identified the transition between potential benefits, in the case of central and northern Europe, and uncertain contrasting effects or even concordant negative consequences, in the case of the southern and eastern shores of the sea, where future climates could exacerbate environmental and socio-economic situations that are currently already critical.

It is hoped that the proposed methodology may contribute to the scientific debate on the development of climate change scenarios and, in particular, for what concerns the integration between socio-economic and environmental approaches at various spatial scales.

Regarding the results produced by the proposed methodology, it should be pointed out that there are various possible uses of the information provided by Matrix 3 in the field of agricultural policy. Among others the most relevant are: (1) agri-environmental policy; (2) farmers' income support; and (3) rural development policy.

First, from the profit variations forecast in Matrix 3, it is possible to derive the evolution of farmland use that would allow an estimation of the evolution in the environmental impact of agricultural systems and, consequently, the setting up of an appropriate policy. Secondly, the profit evolution of the cultivations could supply the evolution of the profitability of the agricultural activities. That could be useful in order to forecast future requirements of the farmers' income support. Finally, the evolution of crop profitability could be used to characterise the basic guidelines of the rural areas development policy, especially where a single crop (monoculture) prevails. The forecasts could be useful in order to identify the areas at underdevelopment risk and, consequently, where stronger public interventions will be needed to reorient the agricultural activities.

NOTES

This work was partially funded by the European research project ACCELERATES (Assessing Climate Change Effects on Land use and Ecosystems: from Regional Analysis to The European Scale), contract EVK2–2000–00567, and partially by the Fondazione Eni Enrico Mattei. The first four sections of the work are due to C. Giupponi, the methodological proposal was developed and referred jointly by the two authors, with P. Rosato contributing to the socio-economic aspects and C. Giupponi to the climatic ones. The authors wish to thank Vasco Boatto, Edi Defrancesco and the anonymous referee for their useful comments.

1. Food and Agriculture Organization of the United Nations and Centre International de Hautes Etudes Agronomiques Méditerranéennes, respectively.
2. ACCELERATES is the acronym of Assessing Climate Change Effects on Land use and Ecosystems: from Regional Analysis to The European Scale, more information about the project can be found in http://www.geo.ucl.ac.be/accelerates.
3. In the present research the IMAGE model (Integrated Model to Assess the Greenhouse Effect of the National Institute for Public Health and Environmental Hygiene (RIVM) is adopted (Alcamo *et al.*, 1998).
4. In the ACCELERATES project, SFARMOD (Audsley, 1993) will be adopted as a farm scale simulation model, together with the RO-IMPEL (Rounsevell, 1999) model for simulating crop performances as affected by local climate changes.
5. In the present work, the four of the six marker scenarios of the IPCC were selected and were named as: A1FI: World Market (fossil fuel intensive) (WM); A2: Regional Enterprise (RE); B1: Global Sustainability (GS); and B2: Local Stewardship (LS).
6. In the ACCELERATES project further projections are foreseen also for the year 2050 and 2080.

REFERENCES

Alcamo, J., Leemans, R. and Krieleman, E. (eds) (1998). *Global Change Scenarios for the 21st Century. Results from the IMAGE 2.1 Model.* Elsevier, London.

Audsley, E. (1993). 'Labour, machinery and cropping planning'. In: E. Annevelink, R.K. Oving and H.W. Vos (eds) *Farm Planning. Labour and Labour Conditions. Computers in Agricultural Management.* Proceedings XXV CIOSTACIGR V Congress Wageningen, The Netherlands. Wageningen Pers, pp. 83–88.

Barrow, E. and Hulme, M. (1995). 'Construction of regional scenarios'. In: R. Harrison, A.R. Butterfield and T.E. Downing (eds) *Climate Change and Agriculture in Europe. Assessment of Impacts and Adaptations.* Environmental Change Unit, University of Oxford, Oxford, pp. 21–30.

Berkhout, F., Hertin, J., Lorenzoni, I., Jordan, A., Turner, K., O'Riordan, T., Cobb, D., Ledoux, L., Tinch, R., Hulme, M., Palutikof, J. and Skea, J. (1999). *Non-climate Futures Study. Socio-economic Futures Scenarios for Climate Impact Assessment. Final Report.* SPRU, Brighton.

Bonazzi, M. and Gomez y Paloma, S. (2000). *CAP and the Euro-Mediterranean Free Trade Area: Regional Lessons.* http://www.jrc.es/iptsreport/vol25/english/MED6E256.htm

Brochier, F. and Ramieri, E. (2001). 'Climate change impacts on the Mediterranean coastal zones'. *FEEM Note di Lavoro* **27**, 81.

Carter, T.R. (1996). 'Developing scenarios of atmosphere, weather and climate for northern regions'. *Agricultural and Food Science in Finland* **5**, 235–249.

Carter, T.R., Hulme, M. and Viner, D. (1999). *Representing Uncertainty in Climate Change Scenarios and Impact Studies.* ECLAT-2 Workshop Report No. 1, Climatic Research Unit, University of East Anglia, Norwich.

CIHEAM (Centre International de Hautes Etudes Agronomiques Méditerranéennes) (2000). *Development and Agri-food Policies in the Mediterranean Region. Extracts from Annual Reports 1998, 1999, 2000.* CIHEAM, Zaragoza.

Cubasch, U., Von Storch, H. Waszkewitz, H. and Zorita, E. (1996). 'Estimates of climate change in Southern Europe derived from dynamical climate model output'. *Climate Research* **7**, 129–149.

FAO (Food and Agriculture Organization of the United Nations) (2000). *Agriculture Towards 2015/30, Technical Interim Report, April 2000.* http://www.fao.org/es/esd/at2015/toc-e.htm.

Giupponi, C., Rosato, P. and Rounsevell, M. (1998). 'Integrated model to predict European land use: climate change and land use in the Venice Lagoon Watershed'. In: T. Tempesta and M. Thiene (eds) *Proceedings of the 6th Joint Conference on Food, Agriculture and the Environment.* U. Padova-U. Minnesota, Padova, 271–287.

Greenpeace (1997). *Climate Change and the Mediterranean Region.* http://www.greenpeace.org/~climate/science/reports/desertification.html.

Houghton, J.T., Callender B.A. and Varney, S.K. (eds) (1992). *Climate Change 1992: The Supplementary Report to the IPCC Scientific Assessment, Working Group I.* Cambridge University Press, Cambridge.

Houghton, J.T., Jenkins G.J. and Ephraums, J.J. (eds) (1990). *Climate Change: The IPCC Scientific Assessment.* Cambridge University Press, Cambridge.

Houghton, J.T., Meira Filho, L.G., Callender, B.A., Harris, N., Kattenberg, A. and Maskell, K. (eds) (1996). *Climate Change 1995: The Sciences of Climate Change,*

Contribution of Working Group I to the Second Assessment Report of IPCC. Cambridge University Press, Cambridge.

IPCC (Intergovernmental Panel on Climate Change) (2000). *Summary for Policymakers: Emission Scenarios.* WMO-UNEP.

Jeftic, L., Keckes, S. and Pernetta, J.C. (1996). *Climate Change and the Mediterranean. Vol. 2.* Edward Arnold, London.

McCarthy, J.J., Canziani, O.F., Leary, N.A., Dokken, D.J. and White, K.S. (2001). *Climate Change 2001: Impacts, Adaptation, and Vulnerability.* Cambridge University Press, Cambridge.

MAP (Mediterranean Action Plan) (2000). *Water, Population and the Environment in the Mediterranean for the 21st Century.* Plan Bleu – UNEP.

Odingo, R.S. (1998). 'The likely impacts of global warming and climate change on the agricultural resources of the Mediterranean Basin'. In: *Proceeding of 'The International Conference on the Impacts of Climate Change on the Mediterranean Countries'.*

Openshaw, S. and Turner, A. (2000). *Forecasting Global Climatic Change Impacts on Mediterranean Agricultural Land Use in the 21st Century.* http://www. geog.leeds.ac.uk/people/a.turner/papers/21stC/21stC.html.

Palutikof, J.P., Goodess, C.M. and Guo, X. (1994). 'Climate change, potential evapotranspiration and moisture availability in the Mediterranean basin'. *International Journal of Climatology* 14, 853–869.

Palutikof, J.P., Guo, X., Wigley, T.M.L. and Gregory, J.Y. (1992). 'Regional changes in climate in the Mediterranean basin due to global greenhouse gas warming'. *UNEP-MAP Technical Report Series* (66).

Palutikof, J.P. and Wigley, T.M.L. (1996). 'Developing climate change scenarios for the Mediterranean region'. In: L. Jeftic, S. Keckes and J.C. Pernetta (eds) *Climate Change and the Mediterranean, Vol. 2.* Edward Arnold, London, pp. 27–56.

Parry, M. (ed.) (2000). *Scenarios of Climate Change for Europe: The Europe ACACIA Project.* University of East Anglia, Norwich.

Parry, M.L., Hossell, J.E., Jones, P.J., Rehman, P.J., Tranter, R.B., Marsh, J.S., Rosenzweig, C., Fisher, G., Carson, I.G. and Bunce, R.G.H. (1996). 'Integrating global and regional analyses of the effects of climate change: a case study of land use in England and Wales'. *Climatic Change* 32, 185–198.

Piervitali, E., Colacino, M. and Conte, M. (1997). 'Signals of climatic change in the central western Mediterranean basin'. *Theoretical and Applied Climatology* 58, 211–219.

Reilly, J. (1996). 'Climate change, global agriculture and regional vulnerability'. In: F. Bazzaz and W. Sombroek (eds) *Global Climate Change and Agricultural Production. Direct and Indirect Effects of Changing Hydrological, Pedological and Plant Physiological Processes.* John Wiley and Sons, Chichester, pp. 237–265.

Rosenzweig, C. and Hillel, D. (1995). *Potential Impacts of Climate Change on Agriculture and Food Supply.* http://www.gcrio.org/CONSQUENCES/ summer95/agriculture.html.

Rosenzweig C. and Parry, M.L. (1994). 'Potential impacts of climate changes on world food supply'. *Nature* 367, 133–138.

Rosenzweig, C. and Tubiello, F.N. (1997). 'Impacts of global climate change on Mediterranean agriculture: current methodologies and future directions. An introductory essay'. *Mitigation and Adaptation Strategies for Global Change* 1(3), 219–232.

Rotmans, J., van Asselt, M., Anastasi, C., Greeuw, S., Mellors J., Peters, S.,

Rothman, D. and Rijkens, N. (2000). 'Vision for a sustainable Europe'. *Futures* **32**, 809–831.

Rounsevell, M. (ed.) (1999). *Spatial Modelling of the Response and Adaptation of Soils and Land Use Systems to Climate Change – An Integrated Model to Predict European Land Use (IMPEL)*. Project Summary.

Saaty, T.L. (1980). *The Analytic Hierarchy Process*. New York, McGraw-Hill.

UK National Foresight Programme (1999). *Environmental Futures*. Office of Science and Technology, Department of Trade and Industry, London.

UNEP (United Nations Environment Programme) (1997). *Climate Change Information Kit*. UNEP.

Watson, T.R., Zinyovera, M.C. and Moss, R.H. (1994). *IPCC Special Report on the Regional Impacts of Climate Change. An Assessment of Vulnerability*. UNEP-WMO-IPCC.

Winters, P., Murgai R., de Janvry, A., Sadoulet, E., Frisvold, G. and Kuhn, B. (1998). 'Climate change and agriculture: effects on developing countries'. In: A. de Janvry and G. Frisvold (eds) *Global Environmental Change and Agriculture: Assessing the Impacts*. Edward Elgar, Cheltenham UK and Lyme, USA, pp. 239–296.

WCED (World Commission on Environment and Development) (1987). *Our Common Future*. Oxford University Press, Oxford.

8. Development of a Decision Support System for the integrated assessment of policies related to desertification and land degradation in the Mediterranean

Guy Engelen

METHODOLOGICAL APPROACH

Integrating Existing Scientific Material

In the past decade, as part of its successive Framework Programmes, the European Union has enabled major research efforts in the domains of land degradation and desertification. This research has generated large amounts of data, methodologies and models, which have been instrumental in getting a much better understanding of both the physical and human causes and effects of land degradation and desertification in Southern Europe. Based on the work carried out, many of the research projects made 'scientifically based' suggestions and recommendations, on ways to mitigate, stop or reverse the process of land degradation. However few of the measures and interventions proposed found their way through the policy-making process and were implemented. Thus, and from a practical policy-making point of view, little use has been made so far of the studies carried out. This is mostly due to the fact that much of the research was primarily carried out for scientific reasons and with the purpose of better understanding the processes causing or caused by land degradation. This type of research tends to be very sectorial and in depth, rather than integral and multi-faceted in nature. It may produce output, which is extremely valuable in its narrow discipline, but overly specific and fragmented for the policy-maker who needs a broader societal view on the problems in need of solutions.

With a view to boost the policy use of material developed for scientific purposes, the MODULUS project posed the following research question: *Can existing scientific material, obtained from different complementary research projects, be integrated and made useful to policy-makers?* MODULUS did not intend to answer this question in a universal manner, rather it set out to tackle this subject in a very practical, even pragmatic manner, and built and applied a spatial Decision Support System aimed at integrated socio-economic and environmental policy preparation in the domains of land degradation, desertification and sustainable water management in the Northern Mediterranean. In order to achieve this aim, the following guidelines and activities were listed at the beginning of the project:

- To make use, to the extent possible, of existing scientific knowledge, methods, models and databases available from recent 'EU Environment Programme' projects. In particular, scientific material developed in EFEDA, ERMES, ModMED and ARCHAEOMEDES, and to a lesser extent MEDALUS was assessed for integration. These projects were selected because of the complementary nature of the research carried out.
- To review existing models dealing with physical, ecological and socio-economic aspects of land degradation and adapt them in view of their integration into a multi-scale, multi-temporal dynamic modelling framework and Decision Support System (DSS) aimed at better understanding and mitigating the processes of land degradation and desertification in Europe.
- To involve from the start and for the duration of the exercise, potential end-users of the intended DSS from local planning and decision-making authorities, to explore the wider range of issues that preoccupy them, and to include in the models those policy indicators and variables that they consider relevant for their practical policy preparation work.

It was the explicit aim of MODULUS to build a Decision Support System with a high level of flexibility and generic applicability enabling the end-user to gain access to state-of-the-art knowledge about the processes causing and caused by land degradation, and providing appropriate tools for the design and evaluation of policy options in an integral, interactive, transparent and user-friendly manner.

From the following short project descriptions, it may be clear that there is both complementarity and overlap between the projects selected. The complementarity permitted an integrated representation covering the essential physical, ecological, economic and social processes, while the overlap permitted selection of the most appropriate and compatible model components from the alternatives available.

The EFEDA Project

The EFEDA project (see for example Burke *et al.*, 1998) examined the inter-action between types of land surface and hydrological change associated with desertification and meso-scale climatic impacts. EFEDA developed methods and models to investigate the interaction between the land surface and climate processes within the context of changing surface properties. One of the main outputs of research was the PATTERN ecosystem model, devel-oped to investigate the impact of climatic variability and climatic change on surface and sub-surface hydrology and plant ecology (Mulligan, 1996, 1998a). The model is a tightly coupled hydrology and plant growth model developed for semi-arid environments. It incorporates all of the major hydrological fluxes as well as ecological processes of germination, growth, biomass partitioning, death and competition for up to three plant functional types at any one time. It includes a rainfall, storm and weather generator in addition to the tightly coupled hydrology and plant growth model that forms its core. The model was originally designed as a cellular slope model applied at the 100 m^2 scale. It was later coupled with a GIS and applied to the whole Guadiana catchment (Castilla La Mancha, central Spain) for analysis of the impact of land use and climatic change on groundwater recharge.

The ERMES Project

As part of the ERMES project (see for example Oxley *et al.*, 1998) multi-scale models have been developed concerning the effects of changing land-use patterns on vegetation cover, erosion risks, water run-off and infiltration, changes in ground water and channel flows, and evapotranspi-ration. The models developed capture the effects of various processes of water flow and storage as a function of biological activity that operates in the system. These are very small-scale processes involving the water storage capacity and permeability of the soils as a function of the vegetation cover, slope, soil type, aspect and detailed spatial and temporal patterns of rain-fall. This allows representation at more aggregate levels of the behaviour of successive scales of sub-basins within a catchment, and of the complex impacts of land use on the channel flows at local and larger levels, as well as on the recharge rates for ground water, and the stability and fertility of soils within the catchment.

The ModMED Project

The focus of the ModMED project (see for example Legg *et al.*, 1998; ModMED, 1998) was on the study and modelling of natural vegetation dynamics, thus, on the biological and ecological processes characterising land covered by freely colonising and growing plant species. However, the space available to natural vegetation enabling the recovery of spontaneous plant cover is largely dependent on socio-economic dynamics. Where human pressure is increasing, loss of biodiversity and the complete destruction of habitats occur but where old types of land-use practices are abandoned, new re-colonisation and succession takes place, restoring the dominance by shrubs and eventually forest species. In turn, the latter may lead to the loss of some ancient communities of grass- and shrub-land vegetation with a high biodiversity and conservation value. Although these processes are increasingly understood, the timing of the related landscape changes and the biological mechanisms behind such changes (species dissemination, establishment and competition) still need to be studied to a more satisfactory extent. ModMED addressed these problems by integrating three different levels of ecosystem analysis: individual plant, plant community, and landscape. A modelling environment was developed consisting of hierarchically nested modules operating at different spatial and temporal scales.

The ARCHAEOMEDES Project

The ARCHAEOMEDES project (see for example Leeuw, 1998) investigated how the changing socio-natural dynamics of Southern Europe (urbanisation, agro-industry, infrastructure) relate to the problems of degradation and desertification in the area. Its central themes were: (1) the definition of the various levels of structuration that drive the dynamics involved, (2) the investigation of the ways in which the dynamics at these various levels articulate, (3) the development of decision support models of these dynamics which facilitate the investigation of alternative scenarios for the future, and (4) the development of ways in which to map these dynamics in geographical time–space. The project used a combination of fieldwork, analysis, interpretation and modelling focused on the relationship between the social dynamics responsible for perception, decision-making and action and the natural dynamics, which sometimes are subject to human action, and at other times, trigger and constrain it. The phenomena are investigated at four spatial levels, each representing the interaction between two levels of structuration ranging from the European level to the level of the individual.

CHOICE OF THE PILOT REGIONS

It was one of the aims of the MODULUS project to develop models and a Decision Support System with a high level of generic applicability in the

Northern Mediterranean region. The system was applied to two pilot regions in order to test its adaptability and transferability. The Marina Baixa in Spain, and the Argolida in Greece were selected based on the following scientific and practical considerations:

1. *Policy relevance.* Both regions are coastal watersheds, some 40 by 40 km in size. They are predominantly limestone systems with a rugged, mountainous landscape and elevations ranging from sea level to $+/-1500$ metres. The socio-economic activities are concentrated in the semi-arid, coastal, lowlands suitable for the practice of Mediterranean rain-fed polyculture (olives, vines and cereals). However, the traditional agriculture has been largely replaced by monoculture and intensive fruit cultivation, based on irrigation: citrus in the Argolida and medlar in the Marina Baixa. Both are valuable but delicate cash crops, which demand capital-intensive cultivation and cause a lot of stress on the limited drinking water supplies. In the Argolida more than in the Marina Baixa the income generated in the agricultural sector depends on European export subsidies, a system that is not sustainable in the long run. In the Marina Baixa, the rising importance of the tourism industry generates ever-increasing demands for water and conflicts with the farmers are an emergent issue. Thus, in both regions, there are non-trivial problems of land degradation and depletion of drinking water that require integrated assessment and urgent policy intervention.

2. *Focus.* From the many sites where EU Environment Programme projects were carried out, two were selected where the researchers participating in MODULUS studied physical, natural and socio-economic processes. Sites also where the consequences of human practices (crop rotation schemes, irrigation, abandonment of agricultural land, return of natural vegetation cover) on slope dynamics and on the aquifer (depletion, pollution, salt intrusion) had been documented and modelled in ways that fit the dynamic and integrated approach to water management, desertification and land degradation taken in MODULUS.

3. *Data availability.* The MODULUS project did not allow for an intensive data acquisition programme, rather it proposed to work to the extent possible with existing data. For both regions selected, data of sufficient quality, including GIS data, were readily available to calibrate and run the integrated models.

4. *Model availability.* MODULUS integrates existing models, methods and knowledge. As few as possible new models were to be developed. Both regions were selected because ERMES and ARCHAEOMEDES carried out combined research in these regions in an effort to pool up-to-date understanding of the linked natural and socio-econonic

dynamics. Models to that effect were available or under construction. EFEDA and ModMED had been active in different regions. They had been involved in predominantly natural dynamics and came up with more easily 'portable' insights and models.

POLICY-MAKERS

The development of a Decision Support System is an expensive and time-consuming venture, only to be undertaken in cases where problems exist that need a lasting surveillance of a complex system and where choices and interventions, aimed at keeping this system on course, need to be assessed. But DSSs are sophisticated technical instruments with a logic of their own. Irrespective of their level of sophistication, they provide, through their models and tools, a partial representation of the real-world system. In order to assure their effective use for policy and planning exercises, the way in which they represent the real-world system needs to be understood and supported by the intended end-users. To that effect, the latter should partake in the development of the DSS as much as possible. From the start, they should feel that the end product is useful in solving their problems in ways that make intuitive sense to them (see for example Holtzman, 1989).

The intended end-users for the MODULUS system are regional planners and policy-makers, defined as: *high-level technicians actively involved in the design and evaluation of regional public policies. They perform policy work of a formal/analytic nature in support of the administrator or politically appointed person responsible for taking the actual decision and starting the actual policy implementation.* Thus this policy-maker is not a politician; rather, he or she is a technician, and is not setting the agenda; rather his or her superior, the public, or the media sets the latter. Most often, the policy-maker will work under a lot of stress due to time constraints and rapid changes in the emphasis and relevance of the policy work itself.

Hence, our intended user is a key responsible person involved in the design, analysis and evaluation of policies related to, among others, land use planning, water(shed) or river management, agricultural policy, urban and regional development. He or she is in need of an integrated approach to the issues of concern and is active at the regional level: provinces, departments, prefecture, counties and possibly the national level.

However, involving the intended end-users from both pilot regions in the development of the DSS was more difficult than anticipated as problems were met that find their origin in the research activities carried out, as well as in the policy-making organisations aimed to work with (see Engelen *et al.*, 2000):

1. As will be explained in more detail in the next section, there are great differences between *policy models* and *research models*. These differences are deeply rooted in the scientific discipline and thus in the minds of the researchers producing models. As a result, it is a very hard bargain for a modeller to simplify his or her model. When developing an integrated model, the process of simplification and aggregation is an iterative one, as step-by-step a model is tuned to its position and role within a larger entity. This process is not trivial and it takes time, certainly when it takes place before or while the original research models are under development. Thus the modelling materials available and the model developers were not necessarily and entirely ready for the exercise.

2. In both pilot regions selected, the scientific work had been carried out for research purposes and not for policy-making strictly speaking. Hence, local and regional policy-makers had not been involved. Nor had a network of potentially interested institutions or persons been established. As a result, MODULUS had to contact potential end-users and convince them of the usefulness of yet another research project. This process was slow and tedious, more so, because at the beginning of the project there was not much to be shown to the end-users. In fact, most of the models considered useful for integration were still under construction as part of the projects that initiated their development. Thus they could not be demonstrated in a running version. It was only in month 18 of this 24-month project that a reasonable demonstrator was available which could convince the end-users of its usefulness. This was close to 12 months later than required and originally expected.

3. In the Argolida, it was reasonable to assume that the institution benefiting most from the MODULUS DSS would be the Prefecture of Argolida, as the pilot region is fully encompassed within the jurisdiction of the prefecture. Moreover, the prefecture is an institution deciding on land use, agricultural and water management policies. These are precisely the domains dealt with by the MODULUS DSS. However, in the Marina Baixa, it was less clear which policy-making institution should take ownership of the MODULUS DSS, because it is a less self-contained administrative or policy-making entity. Potential end-users could be found either in the larger municipalities that are part of the region, such as Benidorm, Altea, or Callosa, or in administrative entities that are larger than the Marina Baixa, such as the Province of Alicante, or the Comunidad Valenciana. In the Marina Baixa, none of these institutional bodies expressed much interest. More positive reactions were obtained from stakeholder organizations, such as the water companies and the farmers' cooperatives (see Engelen *et al.*, 2000).

4. In retrospect, some of the problems encountered reflect rather naïve views on the true differences between the world of the researcher and that of the policy-maker. In some West European countries there exists a long tradition of involving scientifically trained technicians in the policy preparation process. Other countries are still in a phase of setting up the institutional frameworks within which these people are or will become active. In Greece and for the Argolida for example (see Engelen *et al.*, 2000), regional agricultural policy preparation takes place at the level of the district and the prefecture. This institutional structure is very new: the level of the district has existed since 1997, while the level of the prefecture has been in place since 1994. For both institutions, the intended technical staff were not hired at the time of the project (April 1999–June 2000). Precisely these technicians are the prototypical end-users of the MODULUS system. Thus MODULUS departed from a very technocratic West European view on policy-making and intended to implement it in regions where the infrastructure and the people to support it were not present. As a result, it was extremely difficult to find in the pilot regions even a few end-users of the system.
5. Although it is well understood in a scientific context that problems of land degradation and water management need to be addressed in an integrated manner, policy-making institutions are still organised in a strictly sectoral manner. Hence, the technicians within these institutions are often more interested in the analysis of 'sectoral management solutions' rather than 'integrated policy options'. Thus the MODULUS DSS does not always offer them the level of detail that they find suitable; instead it offers them a level of complexity that they find confusing. Hence, it is difficult to name the precise user of the DSS in the policy-making organisation as well as to define its precise role.
6. Only at the end of the project (month 21) did we finally get through to real end-users. There were limited contacts only, insufficient and too late to change anything substantial in the system. Mostly they got to see the prototype system developed in a few demonstrations and in a workshop organised in both pilot regions. The results of these workshops were overall very positive.

In the absence of real policy-makers in the early stages of the project, and in order not to slow down the technical work, the project team decided to define a 'virtual' policy-maker and 'typical' policy problems. The intention was to replace these with 'real' policy-makers and their 'real' policy problems later on, but we only got to this stage at the very end of the MODULUS project.

'RESEARCH MODELS' VERSUS 'MODELS TO SUPPORT POLICY-MAKING'

Despite the fact that the terms 'integrated' or 'integral' model are widespread in the scientific literature, and that the use of integrated models is strongly advocated in new disciplines such as integrated assessment (see for example Gough *et al.*, 1998), very few recipes or procedures for model integration are available from the literature. Hence, model integration seems more an art than a science at this moment.

The integration of models is clearly a multi-criteria and multi-objective problem as problems need to be solved that deal with the *end use, scientific,* and *technical* aspects of the integration. Although we treat them here separately, it is clearly understood that this sub-division is rather artificial:

- *End-use integration* deals with the end use and the end-user of the model. It seeks an answer to the questions: what is useful to be integrated with a particular end use in mind and what are the needs, expectations and constraints of the end-user. Public policy problems are very often 'complex problems' rather than 'complicated problems' in the sense that although the problems touch the near complete system, they can be given an adequate answer if a limited formal description of the whole system would be available to support the search for solutions. The development of the integral MODULUS model involved foremost a simplification and aggregation effort with minimal loss of content and accuracy in order to enable policy use of models that were originally developed for research purposes.
- *Scientific integration* is about what can and what cannot be integrated from a scientific point of view. It involves constraints on the type of models (for example qualitative vs. quantitative, dynamic vs. static, equilibrium vs. non-equilibrium, etc.) on the temporal dynamics and time scales, on the spatial dynamics and spatial resolutions, on the details that matter, and on rigorous methods for aggregation and simplification. Once sub-models have been selected and integrated, a thorough analysis of the resulting product is required in order to find out whether the component models are correctly and sufficiently coupled, whether their synchronisation and information passing is correctly handled, and whether the integrated model is an appropriately complete and correct representation of the real-world system. Such analysis should bring about the missing elements and processes in the representation.
- *Technical integration* deals with the ways in which existing models, their software representation, databases, user interfaces, input and

output devices can be coupled into a single system, running on the end-user's computer platform. In the computer sciences, technical integration has been given a lot of attention in the last decade. It has become much easier, at the least for the software technicians among us, with the advent of object-oriented and component-based development methods and frameworks.

The approach taken in MODULUS was clearly bottom-up: based on a reasonable understanding of the characteristic processes and problems typifying the pilot regions (and many similar Mediterranean regions) and, based on a fair amount of complementary modelling material, an integrated model was designed and constructed. On the basis of information available before the start of the project, the decision was taken to limit the number of models considered for integration to those developed as part of the four projects described earlier in this chapter. These projects were deliberately selected on the basis of the complementary nature of the research carried out: from a preliminary analysis it was concluded that the potential for integration was real. This decision limited from the start greatly the number of models to be analysed and evaluated with a view to their integration in the MODULUS model. But, this does not exclude that other models, from other EU Environment and Climate projects, could have been integrated and could have resulted in a much better DSS than what is available today. At the end of MODULUS, however, we are much better equipped to consider the possibility of exchanging MODULUS models for more appropriate ones or complementing them with additional ones. At this moment, unlike at the beginning of the project, it is much better understood what the precise role of 'other' models would be within MODULUS and why this role is insufficiently covered by the actual MODULUS model. The factual possibility of extensions or modifications of this kind is one of the virtues of the open architecture of the MODULUS system.

End Use Integration

Models are 'a simplified representation of a system (or process or theory) intended to enhance our ability to understand, predict, and possibly control the behaviour of the system' (Neelamkavil, 1988, p. 29). However, there are important differences between 'research' models and 'policy' models. Consequently research models are not automatically useful for policy purposes; rather important adaptations may be required (Mulligan, 1998b).

Research models are strongly process oriented. Their temporal scales, their spatial scales, and also their level of complexity are determined by the characteristics of the process that is the subject of the modelling exercise. The model is mostly mono-sectorial. The model developers aim at a representation that is as accurate as possible. They use the model to test hypotheses and push the level of understanding with an eventual aim to enable 'prediction'. In this endeavour, they are encouraged to make use of scientifically innovative techniques and will develop a model that is as complex as required. Often this will pose difficulties in validating the resulting model. But, in a quest for new knowledge, the development of the model is a purpose in its own right as it raises new questions that help in furthering and deepening the level of knowledge. In the process, new data needed for the model will be gathered as required from field sites or other sources. The processing speed and the interactivity of the model are not considered a criteria. Nor are the transparency of the model and its user-friendliness, as the model developer is usually the only user of the model.

Policy models are foremost problem oriented. The policy problems that are in need of solutions determine the time horizon of the calculations performed as well as the temporal and spatial resolution at which processes are represented. The levels of detail, complexity and spatial resolution are most often determined by the availability of data. Policy models are only interesting when they deliver usable output. In order to achieve this, robust, extensively tested, and proven methodologies will preferentially be applied to perform the mathematical operations. The policy model might be complex, but it is kept as simple as possible. Quite often it is superficial, but addresses the problem in an integrated manner. The processing speed and the interactivity of the model are determining factors for its success, mostly so if the model is used in participatory and exploratory exercises involving policy-makers and/or stakeholders. Also the transparency and the user-friendliness of the system are crucial factors. And, as the model is very much problem oriented, the involvement of the problem owner during its development is very important.

In the selection of component sub-models for the integrated MODULUS model, the following list of key *end-user requirements* was taken as a guideline (see Engelen *et al.*, 2000):

- *All processes.* The MODULUS model should adequately represent all the important processes necessary to provide the required policy outputs.
- *Scientifically proven.* The process descriptions within the MODULUS model should be well understood and scientifically proven. A well understood, proven but crude process description is preferred above an innovative but poorly documented and less proven one. The model results should be as robust, reliable and accurate as possible.

- *Spatial scale.* The MODULUS model should be spatial and operate at a regional level. It should provide information at a sufficient level of spatial resolution to reflect the scale of variation in the most important physical, environmental and socio-economic variables. This should also be a spatial resolution at which policy problems occur and can be addressed in public policies.
- *Time horizon.* The MODULUS model should be dynamic and operate at time scales and temporal resolutions representing realistically the autonomous dynamics of the system modelled. The time horizon also should be relevant for policy design, implementation and assessment.
- *Routine data.* The MODULUS model should be sufficiently simple in order to run as much as possible from routinely measured data. Routinely available data may include data collected by government or intergovernmental agencies such as the EU.
- *Scenario based.* The MODULUS model should provide easy to understand scenarios that the user can be taken through. These may be for environmental changes, anthropic impacts, and management options.
- *Output centred.* The MODULUS model should be output centred. It will be judged mostly on the quality of its output and less on its scientific or technical innovative character. It should provide appropriate results using indicators or variables that directly interface with the policy implementation process rather than more abstract scientific or technical variables.
- *Interactive.* The MODULUS model should be fast, responsive and interactive and should cater for a very short attention span. A response time of 15–60 minutes per simulation run covering a period of 20–30 years should be aimed for. Clever models, fast algorithms, and efficient code are required to achieve this.

Scientific Integration

With a view to their integration, the models were evaluated on the basis of an informal evaluation of their content and their conceptual, paradigmatic, spatial, dynamic, and technical characteristics using a set of agreed criteria (Engelen *et al.*, 2000). A more profound scientific evaluation would also have considered the performance of the models in terms of their capacity to generate validatable output. However, many of the models available from the four projects were not sufficiently operational to permit this kind of analysis. The following criteria were taken into consideration for their selection and evaluation:

- *Time scales and temporal dynamics.* Only dynamic models are considered. Models have to span a strategic time horizon (10–20 years) and operate at appropriate (simulation) time steps reflecting the real-world processes and decision-making time frame (1 day–1 year). With a view to simplifying or aggregating the model, the effect of increasing or decreasing the time step on the performance of the model is a criterion.

- *Spatial resolution and spatial dynamics.* Only spatial models or models that can be spatialised are considered. Models need to be applicable to a relatively large regional entity and operate at an appropriate spatial resolution reflecting realistically the real-world processes, the spatial variability across the region, and the individual geographical entities subject to decision- and policy-making (1 ha–1000 km^2). With a view to simplifying or aggregating the model, the effect of increasing or decreasing the spatial resolution on the performance of the model is a criterion.

- *Compatibility of scientific paradigms.* Models are considered that from a scientific/operational point of view can be integrated. Thus the basic assumptions and constraints on which the models are developed are evaluated. Most of the models selected in MODULUS are spatial, dynamic, non-equilibrium or quasi-equilibrium models that are solved by means of simulation. Hence, few problems with clashing scientific paradigms were detected.

- *Models that fit the total integration scheme.* Models were considered that fulfilled a task within the MODULUS integration scheme which was not dealt with by any other (sub-)model. They compute a subset of the total set of state variables and exchange the necessary information between one another at the right temporal and spatial scales during the calculation.

- *Level of sophistication.* The models selected for integration are in most cases simplified versions of 'the ultimate' or 'the best available' models. In order to fit the integrated scheme, and to work at the right level of abstraction, models need to be simplified and stripped of details that are not directly relevant in the process represented, the pilot regions and/or the problems studied. The value of the integral model is as good as the weakest element in the web of linked sub-models. Hence, it is better to improve this weakest element rather than to add details to the other sub-models.

From the model descriptions provided by the developers at the beginning of the project, Tables 8.1 and 8.2 were compiled. In both tables, black cells indicate the time and space resolution at which the models appropriately

Table 8.1 Models considered for integration in MODULUS; spatial resolution as specified by the developers

Name of model	Project	Spatial resolution (in metres)					
		Non-spatial	irregular	1<10	10<100	100<1000	>1000
Cellular automata land use	RIKS			■	■		
Forest fire model*	ModMED			■	■		
Grazing model*	ModMED			■	■		
Seed dispersal**	ModMED			■	■		
Community model (RBCLM2)	ModMED	1<100					
Catchment model	ERMES		>1000				■
Slope model*	ERMES			■	■	■	
Aquifer model (IERC)	Archaeomedes					■	
Aquifer model (AUA)	Archaeomedes					■	
Decision-making model	Archaeomedes	■					
PATTERN weather & storms	EFEDA	.001–100000					
PATTERN hydrology model	EFEDA	.001–100000					
PATTERN plant growth model	EFEDA	.001–100000		■	■	■	

Notes:
* refers to models useful for integration, but not integrated as yet.
** this model has been re-implemented entirely in a different form.

Table 8.2   *Models considered for integration in MODULUS; temporal resolution as specified by the developers*

Name of model	Project	Non-dynamic	Temporal resolution — Time step				
			variable	hours	days	months	years
Cellular automata land use	GEONAMICA						■
Forest fire model*	ModMED				■	■	■
Grazing model*	ModMED					■	■
Seed dispersal**	ModMED					■	
Community model (RBCLM2)	ModMED					■	■
Catchment model	ERMES				■	■	
Slope model*	ERMES				■	■	
Aquifer model (IERC)	Archaeomedes				■		
Aquifer model (AUA)	Archaeomedes				■		
Decision-making model	Archaeomedes				■		
PATTERN weather & storms	EFEDA		▨	■			
PATTERN hydrology model	EFEDA			■			
PATTERN plant growth model	EFEDA			■			

Notes:
* refers to models useful for integration, but not integrated as yet.
** this model has been re-implemented entirely in a different form.

represent the processes modelled. Non-spatial models, such as the RBCLM2 model; or spatial models running on irregular geographical spaces, such as the catchment model; or running at variable time steps, such as the PATTERN weather & storms model, are represented by means of a grey cell in the appropriate columns.

These tables helped in defining a set of minimum requirements for the integrated product in relation to the temporal and spatial resolutions at which it was to run and enabled the modellers to get a better view of the effort required to narrow down the differences in temporal and spatial resolution of the component sub-models. Finally, from the tables an estimate could be made of the type and resolution of data required to run the integrated product.

The analysis of the two tables led us to conclude initially that an integrated MODULUS model would be grid based, running at a spatial resolution of 1 ha (100 by 100 metres) and at a temporal resolution in the order of 1 week to 1 month. The output generated with this model would suffice for most relevant policy questions in both pilot regions. A spatial resolution of 1 ha would be appropriate for the majority of the processes represented, and a large amount of GIS data are available at this resolution. Also, this spatial resolution allows for the inclusion of models running on irregular (administrative) areas if the borders of these are redrawn to coincide with the edges of cells. The errors thus made are minimal.

However, the choice of a monthly or weekly time step was not appropriate for a number of the models. In particular, the PATTERN weather & storms model (see Engelen *et al.*, 2000) requires a much finer time step. This is because soil and hydrological processes in desertified areas are very strongly determined by the intensity and quantity of precipitation generated during individual storms. As a result, the decision was made to develop the MODULUS model running at an hourly time step. While the simulation is stepping through time, sub-models are invoked as required and the information that is exchanged between them is aggregated over days, weeks or months as needed.

Straightforward Integration, Adaptation, Rebuild

The key trade-offs in the selection process were very much between accuracy (of the data and of the model process representation) and simplicity (of models and of data). The resulting model needed to have sufficient spatial and temporal detail and sufficient model complexity to accurately represent the processes but needed to achieve this over large areas in a fast and responsive manner with a minimum of data. From the preceding paragraphs it will be clear that this is not automatically achieved; rather that important adaptations to the research models were required before they were effectively integrated.

In this respect, MODULUS has developed solutions at three levels:

- *straightforward integration* when the model represents the process adequately and efficiently, and when the interactions with other component models are possible;
- models are *adapted* if only minor repairs or reformulations of the model, its algorithms or its code are required to have it perform its tasks more appropriately;
- finally *rebuilding* is considered when the model needs major repair and adaptation in order for it to fit in the modelling scheme.

Clearly, the more a model has been designed and developed with a generic purpose in mind, the more a straightforward integration is possible. However, the rebuild solution is often the only one that will meet all the user requirements fully. In MODULUS we have gained experience with all three levels of integration: the land-use model, and the AUA aquifer model were integrated as they are; the farmer decision-making model, the natural vegetation community model and the catchment model have undergone adaptations, and the weather, hydrology and plant growth models have basically been rebuilt.

Technical Integration

As all of the models discussed so far are also digital, the problem of technical integration is very much a hard- and software problem: how can we efficiently link pieces of executable code so that they together perform the operations specified in the integrated model at the right time and so that data are exchanged in a way that is consistent with the temporal and spatial logic of the model? Is it possible to do this in a manner that enables reconfiguring the model in a straightforward manner?

In MODULUS the question of re-use was clearly posed: as a result of different EU projects, the participating researchers have models written as monolithic applications in whatever programming language they master. Most often this application is their model: they have worked on the code for a long time, have tested it and trust it. Rather than re-coding this material in yet another programming language to develop yet another monolithic application, MODULUS chose to integrate the material on the basis of state-of-the-art components technology. The constraints of time and budget, the availability of ready to use modelling material, as well as the objective of producing a running system applied to two pilot regions made us decide to tackle the problem from a practical angle. The issue of technical integration was very much reformulated as: is the existing component-based development a usable methodology to develop a DSS for environmental policy-making?

Software components are pieces of software that are designed for re-use: 'a coherent package of software artefacts that can be independently developed and delivered as a unit and that can be composed, unchanged, with the other components to build something larger' (D'Souza and Wills, 1999). The ideal software component is platform independent and can be plugged into a software system like a plug into a socket. In the last decades, several software component technologies have been developed; some of which are platform independent. On the basis of a list of technical criteria (see Engelen *et al.*, 2000) we have chosen the COM/ActiveX technology developed and supported by Microsoft for the PC platform (see for example Rogerson, 1997).

GEONAMICA® was used to implement the MODULUS DSS. To that effect it was partly redesigned and extended to make extensive use of the COM/ActiveX technology. GEONAMICA® is a spatial modelling environment and Decision Support System Generator developed on the Windows (NT/95/98) platform by RIKS b.v. GEONAMICA® enables the development of integrated dynamic models, operating at multiple time scales and spatial resolutions. These models are supplemented with state-of-the-art analysis, presentation and decision support tools and become available as part of dedicated, transparent, interactive and easy to use spatial Decision Support Systems (Uljee *et al.*, 1996; Huizing *et al.*, 1998; Engelen, 1999).

THE INTEGRATED MODULUS MODEL

Screening the available models against the *end use integration* and *scientific integration* criteria enabled us to decide on a preliminary scheme for an integrated MODULUS model, consisting of linked sub-models. For some of these such as the slope model, alternative models were available for integration, which were ranked from most to least adequate (see Figure 8.1). The models ranked first were implemented first. This resulted in a reasonably adequate model, but other integration schemes could have been considered for implementation. This also resulted in 'white spots' for which no models were available in the integration scheme. More in particular the choice of the PATTERN hydrology & slope model rather than the ERMES slope model resulted in the need for an additional model called the irrigation model. The latter was developed and added to the model base.

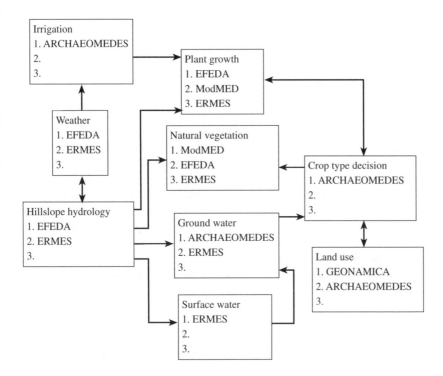

Note: The MODULUS model integrates a number of sub-models (shown as boxes). Each sub-model is a model developed as part of EFEDA, ERMES, ModMED or ARCHAEOMEDES. For each of the boxes, the available models, named after the projects that generated them, have been ranked from most to least adequate. After a thorough analysis, the models ranked first were implemented. The arrows in the scheme represent the main conceptual linkages between the sub-models only.

Figure 8.1   The MODULUS Model

This preliminary integration scheme had the great merit of covering an important part of both the natural and the socio-economic system. From an extensive analyses it was concluded that sufficient data were available in both pilot regions to run the integrated model, and that the sub-models produced and exchanged the appropriate information required in the integration scheme (see Engelen *et al,.* 2000). This in itself is a remarkable result, since each of the models had been developed within different research contexts and with different purposes in mind. However, the fact that the integration exercise led to a *scientifically* acceptable model did not mean that the *end use of* the integral instrument was automatically guaranteed. The first tests performed showed that a single run of the integrated model for the entire Argolida region, consisting of nearly 240 000 cells of 1 ha each, took nearly 12 days. In this test the sub-models were running at the appropriate time step (1 minute–1 year), for a period of 30 years. It goes without saying that a model that takes more than 10 days to perform a single simulation run is not a very practical tool for policy preparation. It quickly loses all its potential as a tool for analysis, for explorative learning, and for communication. Hence, a lot of effort was put into reducing the execution time of this first MODULUS model.

The performance of the models was improved in one of three ways. First, more efficient ways of performing the calculations were tried out and faster algorithms were implemented. Second, the levels of detail, spatial, and temporal resolution applied in the models were re-evaluated against the problems that they were to solve and the data material available to run them. Third, and only when the previous two failed, the models were simplified at the level of the process representation and the modelling methodology itself. The final version of the model resulting from this exercise takes, depending on the pilot region, some 45 minutes for the same run mentioned earlier. The full model will only run on PCs equipped with a minimum of 256 Mb internal memory (see Figure 8.2).

In its final version the integrated model is also represented in the user interface of the MODULUS DSS, as depicted in Figure 8.2. Each model included in the scheme is dynamic and spatial. The typical spatial resolution of the integrated model is the 1 ha grid. The role of the individual models in the connection scheme can be summarised as follows:

- *Climate and weather:* (from EFEDA, PATTERN weather & storms model, available as a C++ software model, resolution 1 ha). This model runs daily. It calculates for each day the time of sunrise and sunset and the average solar radiation map at the top of the atmosphere between sunrise and sunset. The average solar radiation is then corrected for cloudiness and the slope and aspect of each cell. The average temperature per cell is updated monthly. Further the model generates for the day a detailed time series for precipitation (expressed as a fixed amount of rain per variable amount of time, called bucket-tip time) for the study areas based on data from at the least one AWS weather station. Both temperature and precipitation for the future are corrected for climate change affecting the pilot regions as calculated by the HADCM2, GFDL or ECHAM global circulation models.
- *Hillslope hydrology:* (from EFEDA, PATTERN hydrology & slope processes model, available as a C++ software model, resolution 1 ha). This model runs daily, but integrates internally over bucket-tip

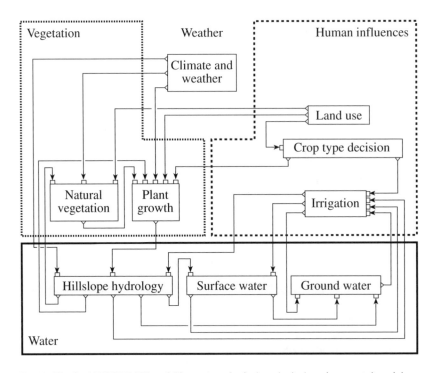

Note: The final MODULUS model integrates physical, ecological, environmental, social and economic processes each running at the appropriate temporal scale and spatial resolutions.

Figure 8.2   The final MODULUS model

times. It deals with the soil hydraulic properties and calculates the water budget: interception, infiltration, soil moisture (Figure 8.3), transpiration, soil evaporation, overland flow, surface recharge, and erosion.

- *Natural vegetation:* (from ModMED, RBCLM2 community model, available as a PROLOG software model, resolution 25 ha). This model runs once a month. It represents the processes of growth, succession and decline of the natural vegetation at the community level (Figure 8.4). It calculates the leaf area index, the vegetation cover fraction, and the rooting depth. The natural vegetation model is a rule-based model, applied to each individual 25 ha cell of the pilot regions. It is supplemented with a cellular seed diffusion model, a C++ software model, which produces a seed biomass map and thus links the community level cells at the landscape level.

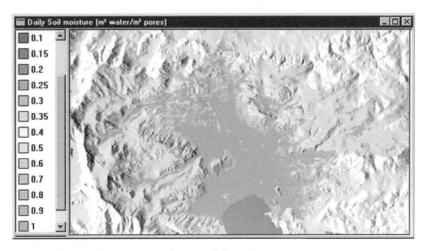

Figure 8.3   Soil moisture in the Argolida in January

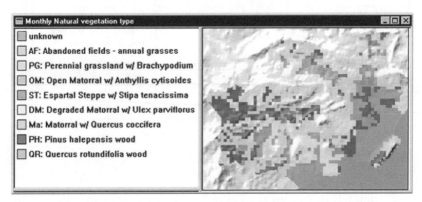

Figure 8.4   Natural vegetation types in the Marina Baixa, modelled on a 500 metre grid

- *Plant growth:* (from EFEDA, PATTERN plant growth model, available as a C++ software model, resolution 1 ha). This model runs daily. It represents the processes of growth of commercial crops and natural species on the basis of soil and hydrologic properties and calculates the leaf biomass, root biomass, leaf area index and the vegetation cover fraction.
- *Ground water:* (from ARCHAEOMEDES, two versions of the aquifer model are retained: the (Agricultural University of Athens) AUA-ModFlow model and the (International Ecotechnology Research Centre) IERC aquifer model. The ModFlow model is avail-

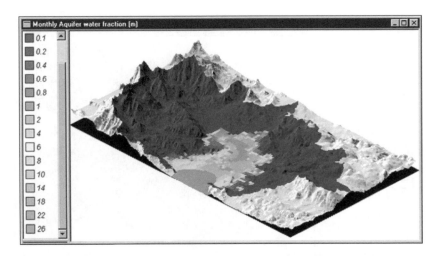

Note: The Aquifer is modelled on a 500 by 500 m grid and using monthly time steps. The water fraction of the aquifer in April is represented.

Figure 8.5   The main watershed modelled in the Argolida and the location of the aquifer within it

able as a FORTRAN software model, while the IERC model is available as a POWER BASIC software model).

Due to the very complex and discontinuous nature of the aquifer in the Marina Baixa, the aquifer model is only applied in the Argolida region. This model represents the depletion, recharge and pollution of the aquifer. It calculates the aquifer water height, salt concentration and the fluxes between cells. The ModFlow aquifer model runs monthly and on a spatial resolution of 500 by 500 m (Figure 8.5). The IERC aquifer model is developed to run on daily time steps and on a 1 ha resolution, however for computational reasons and due to the lack of appropriate data, it is installed to run, like the AUA modflow model, on a monthly time step and on a 25 ha resolution.

- *Surface water:* (from ERMES, catchment model, available as a POWER BASIC software model). This model runs on a daily basis. It represents the river, canal, and water reservoir system, and the water quality of the surface water. It calculates the river flows per stream order (Figure 8.6), the sinkhole flows, the catchment recharge flows, and the river PO_4 and NO_3 charges. The model runs on irregular shaped, natural defined areas: the catchments and sub-catchments.

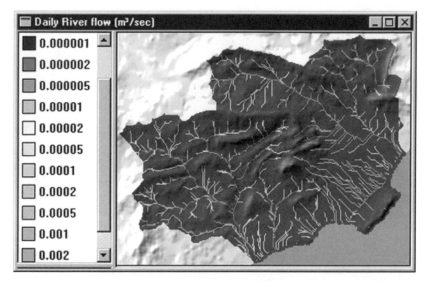

Figure 8.6   Daily river flow in the Marina Baixa for a day in January

- *Crop type decision:* (from ARCHAEOMEDES, farmer's decision-making model, available as a POWER BASIC software model, resolution 1 ha). This model runs on a yearly basis. It is a rule-based model representing the crop choices made by farmers as a function of changing physical, socio-economic and institutional conditions and circumstances (Figure 8.7). It is applied to each 1 ha cell and calculates the crop type, crop water requirements, water source, presence of boreholes, borehole depth, pumping capacity, anti-frost-device deployment and the total yearly long-term exploitation costs.
- *Irrigation:* (extracted from work done in ARCHAEOMEDES by IERC, available as a POWER BASIC software model, resolution 1 ha). This model runs twice daily. It is a rule-based model representing the farmers' decisions to switch on the water pumps and start the irrigation with water from the aquifer or the (river) canals. It is applied to each 1 ha cell and calculates the pump status, volume to be pumped from the aquifer (or extraction from the canals), volume of frost water, frost water salt concentration, irrigation water volume, irrigation water salt concentration, and the total (yearly) exploitation costs.
- *Land use:* (GEONAMICA constrained cellular automata model, available as a C++ software model). This model runs yearly. It is a cellular automata based model which allocates in a detailed manner (1 ha grid) the land claims resulting from demographic changes, as well as the

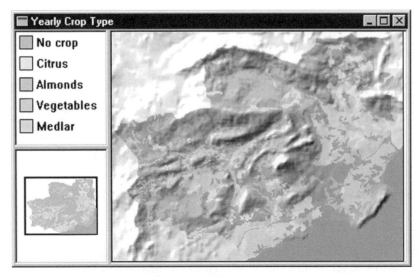

Figure 8.7   Crop types in the Marina Baixa

dynamics in the agricultural and non-agricultural part of the economy (Figure 8.8). The allocation methodology takes into consideration the activity specific attractivity of cells in terms of their suitability, zoning regulations and accessibility to the road transportation infrastructure (see for example Engelen *et al.*, 1995; White and Engelen, 1997).

The MODULUS model presented relies heavily on GIS data. As an input it requires some 25 GIS raster maps, mostly at 100 metres resolution. During a simulation, which typically covers the 30-year period between 1990 and 2020, it generates and updates at every simulation time step some 50 output maps. All the output maps are simultaneously available to the user for visualisation and analytic purposes. Thus, during the simulation he or she can watch the evolution of the modelled region by means of any combination of the mapped variables. Some of the output maps represent a final output variable of the integrated model, but others are generated or updated by one model to serve as an input to another.

USING THE MODULUS MODEL AND DECISION SUPPORT SYSTEM[1]

The use, role and usefulness of models and Decision Support Systems in policy-making has been the subject of rich scientific debate and literature,

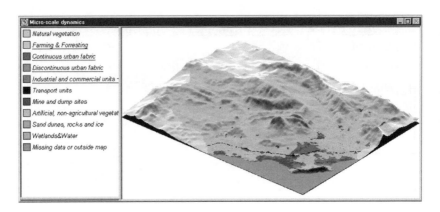

Figure 8.8   Land use in the Marina Baixa in 2020

and extreme views have their advocates. In this chapter we do not have the room to dwell on this discussion. However, inherent in the aims of the MODULUS project, is the somewhat positivistic view that the use of research models can improve the policy-making process. More in particular, MODULUS adheres to the view that *better informed* policy-makers are *better equipped* to make *better policies* that bring the systems they are to manage on a path towards sustainability. Thus the prime role of the models and the Decision Support Systems is awareness building and education, rather than the decision-making act itself. The models therefore should give an adequate and truthful representation of the real-world system, and the policy-maker should be enabled to work with the models in a well-structured, well-guided and flexible manner. To this effect, the system has been equipped with a graphical user interface (Figure 8.9), enabling easy access to the models, the data and the maps by invoking menu commands or selecting interface objects on the screen. The same interface increases the transparency of the model by enabling access to context-sensitive on-line model documentation: at any point in time, the user can gain access (by pushing the Fl key) to the technical background information required to understand the process modelled, the output generated and the input required. Without this information, the models would remain black boxes and no learning would take place.

In the Decision Support System, the real-world system is represented by means of the integrated MODULUS model. Users can try out *policy interventions* by changing policy relevant parameter values in one or more models. They can test the robustness of the system and their policy interventions if the system is subjected to *scenarios,* defined by other parameters, representing mostly exogenous elements. Finally, they can see how

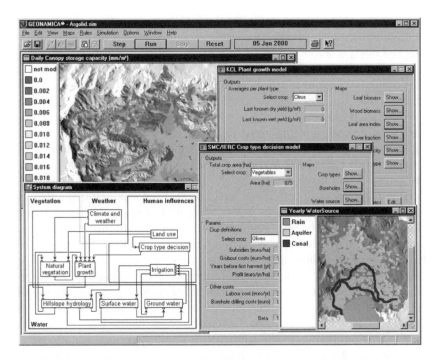

Note: The user gets access to the individual sub-models by clicking the boxes in the systems diagram (shown in bottom left). He or set sets parameters in the dialogs (shown upper left), can run simulations, and open any combination of (dynamically updated) maps on the display.

Figure 8.9 User interface of the MODULUS system

their policy interventions and/or scenarios affect the system in terms of policy relevant variables or *indicators*. In this way the impact of interventions can be tested and tuned in an interactive session between the policy-maker and the modelled system and catastrophes can perhaps be avoided in the real-world system.

The DSS takes input data in standard readable formats, .TXT for simple data, and .IMG IDRISI, or ARC/INFO grid .ASC for the GIS maps. A number of dedicated editors: text editors, graph editors, map editors, and formula editors are available to the user for entering data and setting the specifics of a simulation exercise. While a simulation is running data are written into an MS Excel Workbook, which is opened and linked dynamically to a simulation if and when this option is invoked. In a similar manner, dynamic map output can be stored in so-called .LOG files for future analysis and visualisation by means of a dedicated ANALYSE-Tool. Or it can be animated and visualised in the form of .GIF movies. Thus the dynamic output of a simulation exercise is available to the end-user for further analysis and interpretation.

The individual sub-models in the DSS have been validated and tested for both pilot regions to some degree: for the AUA aquifer model, the validation has been very elaborate and in detail, for others, such as the land-use model, it has been rather partial and limited to ensure that the results are sensible and appropriate to the environment and conditions in the pilot regions. The integrated MODULUS model has been run and tested under a wide range of conditions by the model developers in isolation or as part of 'test drive workshops' involving field researchers, modellers and software developers. These tests revealed a considerable number of problems in the component sub-models or the integrated model that never showed up before. Problems were detected in the assumptions underlying the models, the formulation and implementation of the models, the coupling and synchronisation of the models, and the exchanges of data, both the actual numbers and the units of measurement. At the end of the project we can only conclude that more time and effort will be required for the validation of the integrated MODULUS model in a systematic manner (Muetzelfeldt, 2000). Such validation however should go hand in hand with, or come after, a critical review of the integrated model and its component sub-models. For instance, we know that there are possibilities for intensifying the linkages between the sub-models. In some cases this requires only minor changes, aimed at improving the representation of (part of) a process. In other cases more drastic changes are required including replacing sub-models with more appropriate versions.

Only a very limited number of policy exercises have been carried out with the integrated model. These were mostly for demonstration purposes and dealt with, among other things, water management and irrigation issues in the Marina Baixa (see Engelen *et al.*, 2000). The results of these exercises show the usefulness of the system developed: its interactive, integrated, spatial and dynamic approach. The results produced are easy to visualise and communicate to the end-users. Notwithstanding this, it is a fact that the DSS remains an overly cumbersome instrument, producing output that is of more interest to the researcher than the policy-maker. For instance, the failure or success of a cropping season is expressed in terms of leaf biomass, instead of euros or tonnes of fruit; hence, not the kind of indicator that makes intuitive sense to the farmers in the regions.

In spite of all these reservations, the MODULUS DSS can be useful in the design and assessment of a large number of policy relevant matters. The list provided is not intended to be complete. It only is a record of exercises already worked out:

1. *Zoning regulations, land-use and land cover policies, urbanisation schemes.* Among others the land-use model features zoning maps for different types of land uses which can be drawn, imported, or changed interactively by the user. The effects of zoning regulations on the system as a whole, or in particular areas, or on particular land uses and linked variables can thus be analysed.
2. *Location of crops or other activities.* As the crop growth is linked right through to soil properties, soil moisture and the proximity of irrigation waters, the potential for alternative types or other combinations of crops can be tried out in an explicitly geographic and dynamic manner.
3. *Irrigation systems.* Irrigation puts a lot of stress on the availability of drinking water for household use or use in the industrial and tourism sector. Dedicated parameters in the model enable simulation of the application of alternative irrigation technologies and analysis of the consequences of these on the aquifers and other water users.
4. *Types of crops, mono- and multi-cropping systems.* The change from traditional rain-fed multi-cropping to irrigated mono-cropping systems has brought a lot of wealth to both pilot regions studied. However, it also has caused stress on the traditional life style and social cohesion in the regions. More so, it caused severe land degradation and economic dependency on one or a few staple crops. The potential for a partial restoration of the multi-cropping system could be evaluated. The MODULUS system will enable assessment of the best locations for these activities and will value alternatives in terms of output generated, water consumed, number of farmers employed and families involved.
5. *Climate and weather scenarios.* With the PATTERN^{LITE} sub-model, the weather in both pilot regions is generated. This is done within the general trends set by a changing climate as forecast by one of three General Circulation Models. The far-reaching consequences of these changing weather patterns on the physical environment, the vegetation, the commercial crops and the surface and sub-surface hydrology is calculated throughout the entire MODULUS model.
6. *Artificial recharge of aquifers.* In the Argolida the artificial recharge of the aquifer is currently tried out in an experimental set-up. The potential for this technique seems real. In MODULUS, and in particular by means of the aquifer sub-model, it is possible to estimate the consequences of this practice: the volumes required to replenish, the state

of the aquifer through the years and the effects on the existing salina-
tion, and potential new pollution of the ground water. Further to this,
other sub-models enable estimation of the benefits of this technical
solution.

7. *Creation of storage lakes.* In the Marina Baixa, where aquifers are
   small, heavily fragmented, and affected by salt intrusion, most of the
   drinking water is obtained from storage lakes. The latter store water
   pumped in from outside the region or from local springs. The catchment sub-model enables experimenting with alternative configurations
   and different numbers of storage lakes in different locations. The consequences of the availability of this water can be analysed.

8. *Alternative EU policies and regulations, subsidies.* In their cost–benefit
   calculation and crop decision-making, farmers are influenced by
   subsidies and other regulations at regional, national or European level.
   Changes in these will have immediate consequences in the crop choices
   and through these on other aspects modelled.

9. *Alternative employment and economic activities.* If water scarcity keeps
   on threatening employment in the agricultural sector, then the potential and need for alternative forms of employment and the location of
   such activities need to be assessed, as do the consequences of these
   regarding land degradation.

CONCLUSIONS

The Policy Relevance of MODULUS

The ultimate success of an instrument like MODULUS is its use in the
policy-making process. This is the only motive for the investment and effort
that goes into its development. MODULUS has been developed for use in
the Northern Mediterranean. To apply it to another region and to assess a
set of 'typical' policy problems, it suffices, in theory at least, to fill it with
the new data. In practice however, regions and their problems are
sufficiently different so that the system will need adaptations that are more
substantial, both in technical terms and policy content. The open architecture of the system makes the technical adaptations rather straightforward,
at the least for a competent software technician. But more effort is required
in attuning the system to the precise questions, possible policy solutions,
actors and issues involved, and so on.

In the Marina Baixa and the Argolida, MODULUS is usable for technical calculations and policy analysis of a large number of issues covered
by its individual models. But it offers unique potential when it comes to

questions requiring calculations through the linked models, interfering with complex feedback loops, and causing non-linear behaviour and irreversible change in the system. Thus it is most powerful if questions are raised relative to a combination of the following:

- *Direct and indirect consequences of policies.* For instance the effects of EU subsidies for production and exports of citrus fruits on the urban expansion and the loss of valuable natural areas such as coastal wetlands.
- *Immediate and the longer-term effects of policies.* For instance the changeover from rain-fed polyculture to irrigated monoculture on the drinking water consumption, the depletion of the aquifer, and the intrusion of salt water into the aquifer, and finally the loss of valuable agricultural lands due to salinisation.
- *Spatial consequences of policies.* For instance the effects on the agricultural output of the Marina Baixa due to the construction of a water-consuming tourist facility near the coast in Benidorm. The effects also, even further inland, on the regions from where water is imported.
- *External effects not under the control of the policy-maker.* For instance the effects of a warmer and dryer climate on the natural vegetation, the agricultural production, the tourist sector, and the wealth of the inhabitants. The effect also of a drop in the world price of agricultural goods such as olive oil, citrus fruits or almonds.
- *Early anticipation of threats and the design of a plan of action.* For instance to be ready for a changeover from one crop to another before the soil moisture is below the critical level due to a drying climate or a lack of irrigation water.
- *Monitoring of the system against preset criteria.* For instance to verify whether an urbanisation programme and the ensuing demand for drinking water are on scheme with the estimates and to know when and how to intervene if not.

The End-users and MODULUS

MODULUS encountered great difficulties in defining and locating the end-users of the Decision Support System that it intended to create. The reasons for this have been briefly presented: lack of the appropriate network, insufficient knowledge of the institutional organisation and the policy-making culture in the pilot regions, and not least, a lack of good demonstration material to convince potential end-users of the benefits they were to get from the project and the final product.

Two months before the end of the project, two major workshops, one in Argos (Greece) and one in Alicante (Spain), were organised, in which the system was demonstrated to, and discussed with, a group of some 80 interested potential end-users, consisting of politicians (including the Prefects of the Argolida and Corinth region) technicians, stakeholders from industry, water companies, farming organisations, and researchers. Technically speaking, these workshops came at the right time in the project: we had finally reached the right kind of policy people, and we had a working system, capable of demonstrating the use of this kind of instrument in the region of the end-users and on real problems and examples. However, from a project management point of view, these workshops should have taken place 12 months earlier. As it happened, they came too late in the project to have the impact on the activities they deserved to have.

In general the product, the MODULUS DSS, generated good discussions and got a good response. There was agreement that there is a match between the models and the problems in the pilot regions; hence, that this system has a great deal of potential. But, and at the same time, it was also obvious that there is still a great mismatch between the policy questions that need straightforward answers and the outputs generated by the model. This is more than a mismatch in terminology only, it rather points at 'white spots' in the model: aspects and processes not incorporated as yet. One good example of this is the absence of a module taking care of the accounting of policy alternatives: what are the costs and what are the benefits, now and in the future 'and in Euros if possible'. Some questions raised and comments made touched on very fundamental technical aspects too, such as the operational status and usability of the system, its integrated nature, its data hunger, its correctness and accuracy, its ability for upgrading to new situations, new problems, changing world views and knowledge. These made us realise that the product developed so far is more the beginning than the end of a development cycle, which will take a while before it will come to an end. However it was also a stimulus for the developers, in that many of the problems raised could have been solved with very little extra effort: a change in terminology, the incorporation in the models of ten commercial crops rather than six or an extra equation here or there.

Other points raised are not unique to MODULUS; rather they are typical for systems and models like MODULUS. 'Is this a management system or a policy support system?' Although we build these instruments for policy-makers with a view to enable them to explore and fine tune their policies in a long-term, integrated context, they mostly end up in the hands of managers and are evaluated on their sectoral and short-term forecasting capabilities. Also, 'is this a system for analysis, for training and education, or for communication?' Again, we build them for the purpose of analysis, which automatically includes some form of education, yet they often end up being used as tools for communication. 'Is this a database or is it a knowledge base?' Although the emphasis is very much on the knowledge embedded in these systems in an operational form, users will often look at them as instruments containing data on related topics, thus devaluing the system to an ill-designed and very incomplete database.

Finally comments are made relative to the way in which these systems can be made useful in the organisation of the policy-maker. This is a very fundamental issue that is very often overlooked, certainly by the scientists whose role it is to build the models. Systems like MODULUS attain a very high level of sophistication, hence they cannot be handed to the end-user on a simple CD-ROM with user manual. Rather they require guidance and, in most cases, an intensive training programme. In the Argolida, for instance, the prototypical end-user of MODULUS does not have a PC on his or her desk, let alone the state-of-the-art PC required. Further this user is not very proficient in English, hence would like a system and documentation in Greek rather than English. Once the organisation takes the system on board as a tool for policy assessment, procedures need to be developed that give it a clear institutional position and role in the organisation and the assignments of its employees. None of the above are trivial problems to tackle. Moreover they require the involvement of specialists with skills different from those available from scientists involved in EU environment and climate research projects.

The Integration Carried out in MODULUS

While we interpreted 'integrating existing material' rather loosely while carrying out the scientific and end-use evaluation of models, we took this expression much more factually while carrying out the technical integration. This was not accidental, rather we wanted to find out what state-of-the-art component technology has to offer to consortia like ours involved in the joint development of an integrated model and the encompassing decision support framework. Two rather conflicting views on integration come to the surface. On the one hand, the technological solutions offered by today's component technologies are very promising and indeed enable the integration of material that was never designed for that purpose before. On the other hand, this requires very able software developers spending a lot of time and effort on many programming solutions that are not nice, not efficient and unable to improve the bad performance of the constituent components. The same technicians, with much less effort, can design much better software products with the same or better 'modelling' functionality. Similarly, the scientists may be able to develop models with the same functionality as the MODULUS model in a scientifically much nicer, much more reliable manner. However, before any of this can happen, an exercise like the one carried out in MODULUS is required to bring the scientists, the programmers, the end-users and the material together, to cut the odd corners of the individual models, to find ways in which they can be simplified, spatialised and aggregated in manners that make them fit a linking scheme defined with a particular end use in mind. In our opinion, this is where the true value of the MODULUS methodology lies: it plays its role in an intermediate stage, a 'bottom-up' phase in which existing material is gathered, and where a synthesis needs to be made. A stage in which the available material is selected and evaluated in a new context, with other end-users and end uses in mind, and for applications in other regions with different problems. A stage, in which specialists from different disciplines get together to construct an end product from semi-finished products. This is where components technology is useful, because it enables different parties to work at a distance, to come to agree on the tasks and functionalities of models, tools and final products, and work on it in an environment (both physical and software) that is theirs. From the MODULUS project we can conclude that this works, that a tool can be developed within reasonable constraints relative to budget, human resources and development time. This phase however is not the final one in a development path of a Decision Support System for practical regional policy-making. On the contrary, it needs to be followed by an in-depth evaluation of the integrated model and its constituting sub-models, the way in which it covers the decision domain(s), the way in which it links the sub-systems within the domain(s), and the way in which the spatial and temporal dynamics are dealt with. Also an evaluation of the DSS by the end-users is pertinent. Is their decision domain represented in a way that they consider complete and adequate? Does the system speak their language? Does it work in a way that they find useful and pleasant? With the answers to these questions a more or less major redesign of the DSS is possible and a 'top-down' development phase can start. In the latter, and with a view to improving both the functionality and the performance of the system, each of the components needs to be worked on very seriously and all the elements that do not fulfil the performance or functionality criteria should be considered for major repair or re-implementation. Also at this stage, components technology has a lot to offer in that it enables us to compartmentalise the system, develop it in a distributed manner, and keep much better track of the advancement of the work in progress.

Given its limited financial and human resources and given also its short lifetime, the MODULUS project embarked on a very ambitious endeavour. It succeeded nevertheless in bringing together and re-using research material in a policy context, a context for which it was not developed. The project succeeded also in developing an integrated model and encompassing Decision Support System and applied it in two pilot regions. This model has been only partly validated and has not as yet been used by its intended end-users to solve real policy problems. It is fair to conclude that the greatest enemy of the project was the lack of time – it takes more than 24 months to go through the full development cycle of a DSS of this complexity. A third year would have enabled us to involve the end-users much more intensely and implement their remarks and suggestions. This certainly would have led to a more appropriate product for practical policy-making.

NOTES

This research is supported by the Commission of the European Union Directorate General XII Environment (IV) Framework Climatology and Natural Hazards Programme contract ENV4-CT97-0685 (DG12-EHKN).
The consortium carrying out the work described consists of:
Research Institute for Knowledge Systems b.v., P.O. Box 463, 6200 AL Maastricht, The Netherlands.
Guy Engelen (co-ordinator), Maarten van der Meulen, Bernhard Hahn, Inge Uljee, Panagiotis Giannoulopoulos.
Department of Geography, King's College London, Strand, London WC2R 2LS, UK.
John Thornes, Mark Mulligan, Sim Reaney.
International Ecotechnology Research Centre, Cranfield University, Cranfield, Bedford MK43 0AL, UK.
Peter M. Allen, Tim Oxley, Condelynia Blatsou, Macarena Mata-Porra, Spiros Kahrimanis.
Universitá di Napoli 'Federico II', Istituto di Botanica Generali e Sistemica, Facoltá di Agraria, Via Universitá 100, I-80055 Portici (Napoli), Italy.
Stelano Mazzoleni, Adele Coppola, Brian McIntosh.
The Spatial Modelling Centre on Human Dimensions of Environmental Change, Rymdhuset, Österleden 15, S-981 28 Kiruna, Sweden.
Einar Holm, Nick Winder.
Université de Paris I (Panthéon-Sorbonne),UFR 03, 3 rue Michelet, 75006 Paris, France
Sander van der Leeuw.
1. The MODULUS DSS is available from http://www.riks.nl/projects/MODULUS./

REFERENCES

Burke S., Mulligan M. and Thornes J.B., 'Regional estimation of groundwater recharge and the role of changing land use', in: Bromley J. (ed.) *EFEDA-2: Hydrology Group Final Report*, EU-DG12 (Contract EV5V-CT93-0282), 1998.
D'Souza D.F. and Cameron Wills D., *Objects, Components, and Frameworks with UML. The Catalysis Approach*, Addison-Wesley, Reading, MA, 1999.

Engelen G., *BOS Integraal beheer van Estuariene en Waddensystemen*, Stichting LWI, Gouda, 1999.

Engelen G., van der Meulen M., Hahn B., Uljee I., Mulligan M., Reaney S., Oxley T., Blatsou C., Mata-Porras M., Kahrimanis S., Giannoulopoulos P., Mazzoleni S., Coppola A., Winder N., van der Leeuw S. and McIntosh B., *MODULUS: A Spatial Modelling Tool for Integrated Environmental Decision-making*, Final Report, EU-DG12 (Contract ENV4-CT97-0685), Brussels, 2000. This report is downloadable from: http://www.riks.nl/projects/MODULUS/

Engelen G., White R., Uljee I. and Drazan P., 'Using cellular automata for integrated modelling of socio-environmental systems', *Environmental Monitoring and Assessment*, **34**, pp. 203–214, 1995.

Gough C., Castells N., and Funtowics S., 'Integrated assessment; an emerging methodology for complex issues', *Environmental Modeling and Assessment*, **3**, pp. 19–29, 1998.

Holtzman, *Intelligent Decision Systems*, Addison-Wesley, Reading, MA, 1989.

Huizing, J., van de Ven K., Pothof I. and Engelen G., 'WadBOS: Een prototype van een kennissysteem voor beleidsanalyse van de Waddenzee – Eindrapport'. Rijkswaterstaat Directie Noord-Nederland, Leeuwarden, 1998.

Leeuw van der, S. (ed.) 'Understanding the natural and anthropogenic causes of land degradation and desertification in the Mediterranean basin', The ARCHAEOMEDES project – Volume Synthesis, EU-DG12 (EV5V-CT91-0021),1998.

Legg C., Papanastasis V.P., Heathfield D., Arianoutsou M., Kelly A., Meutzelfeldt R. and Mazzoleni S., 'Modelling the impact of grazing on vegetation in the Mediterranean: the approach of the ModMED project, in: Papanastasis V.P. and Peter D. (eds) *Ecological Basis of Livestock Grazing in Mediterranean Ecosystems*, Proceedings of the International Workshop held in Thessaloniki, Greece, pp. 189–199, 1998.

ModMED, *ModMED, Modelling Vegetation Dynamics and Degradation in Mediterranean Ecosystems*, Final report, EU-DG12 (Contract ENV4-CT95-0139), Brussels, 1998.

Muetzelfeldt R., 'Evaluation of the MODULUS spatial modelling tool for environmental decision-making', Report produced as part of Contract ENV4-CT97-0685, EU-DGXII, Brussels, 2000. This report is downloadable from: http://www.riks.nl/projects/MODULUS/

Mulligan M., 'Modelling the complexity of landscape response to climatic variability in semi arid environments', in: Anderson M.G.A. and Brooks S.M. (eds) *Advances in Hillslope Processes*, John Wiley, Chichester, pp. 1099–1149, 1996.

Mulligan M., 'Modelling the geomorphological impact of climatic variability and extreme events in a semi-arid environment', *Geomorphology*, **24**: 1, pp. 59–89, 1998a.

Mulligan M., *Modelling Desertification, EU Concerted Action on Mediterranean Desertification*, Thematic Report, King's College London, 1998b.

Neelamkavil F., *Computer Simulation and Modelling*, John Wiley & Sons, Chichester, 1988.

Oxley T., Allen P. and Lemon M., 'The integration of dynamic socio-economic and biophysical models: a model of slope dynamics in the Marina Baixa'. IERC, Cranfield. Final report for the ERMES II Project EU-DG12 (ENV4-CT95-0181), Brussels, 1998.

Rogerson D., *Inside COM*, Microsoft Press, Redmond, Washington, 1997.

Uljee I., Engelen G. and White R., *Rapid Assessment Module for Coastal Zone Management*. *RamCo Demo Guide*, Coastal Zone Management Centre, National Institute for Coastal and Marine Management, The Hague, The Netherlands, 1996.

White R. and Engelen G., 'Cellular automata as the basis of integrated dynamic regional modelling', *Environment and Planning B*, **24**, pp. 235–246, 1997.

9. Climate change and agriculture: an Israeli perspective

N. Yehoshua and M. Shechter

INTRODUCTION

The overall objective of this study is to assess – in monetary terms – the potential damage associated with the impacts of climate change due to the greenhouse effect in Israel. The socio-economic impacts will affect water resources, agricultural production, biodiversity resources, forestry resources, coastal regions (due to sea level rise), tourism, health levels, and population migration due to desertification and related phenomena. Damage is estimated for a future point in the 21st century when CO_2 levels in the atmosphere will double from pre-industrial levels. This is a common reference benchmark in the literature, given that there is still a great deal of uncertainty regarding which of the global greenhouse gas (GHG) emission scenarios will actually materialize. There is a widespread tendency in the literature, however, to associate this doubling with the period 2030–2050. The study aims to sum-up damage by sectors, employing the 'bottom-up' approach, assuming present or (when possible) forecast future technological know-how. This is in contrast to the 'top-down' approach that is based on econometric and macroeconomic models.

In this chapter we assess the impacts of climate change on Israeli agriculture. During the past 50 years, Israel's highly sophisticated agricultural[1] sector has increased yields 16-fold while introducing a variety of new crops. In more recent times, as is the case in other developed economies, the comparative advantage of agriculture has declined, and the sector's output has amounted to only 2.4 per cent of GDP (1995). The labor employed in agriculture was 3.4 per cent, and agricultural exports were 4 per cent of total exports, valued at $740 million. Agriculture's share of export has declined over the years, as well as its composition. Currently, field crops make up 10 per cent of the total value of output, vegetables, potatoes and melons 15 per cent, citrus 8 per cent, other fruits 15 per cent, flowers 8 per cent, poultry 18 per cent, and cattle 16 per cent. The total cultivated area in 1995 was 367000 hectares, out of which 199300 are irrigated.

The damage estimates are derived using a simple production function approach, like that employed by a number of similar studies, using a number of rather strong assumptions on adaptability potential or the lack thereof. Despite making these assumptions, we believe the study provides a useful order of magnitude estimate of damage with and without some adaptation, which would be of value in policy making regarding proactive adaptation as well as Israel's contribution to the global mitigation efforts under the Kyoto Protocol. We further believe that it is a useful exercise to focus on irrigation water shortage as the major determinant of agriculture's response to climate change in the semi-arid region where the country is located

In general, there are three independent categories of costs related to climate change: direct damage (designated as D), adaptation costs (A), and net (of ancillary benefits) mitigation costs (P). Mitigating GHG emissions in turn affects the magnitude of damage, or reduces the need for adaptive measures. Similarly, adaptation reduces exposure to damage. The policy objective is to minimize total costs (T), the sum of the three categories: D + A + P. In this study we focus on the first two cost categories: direct damage and adaptation costs. Clearly, a region the size of Israel or even the whole eastern Mediterranean basin has a negligible impact on total global GHG emissions and concentration. Therefore, a benefit–cost framework comparing mitigation costs with damage and adaptation costs would make sense only on a global level, due to the common-property nature of the earth's atmosphere with regard to the impact of GHG on the global and regional climate.

We employ commonly used assumptions for the economic calculations:

- According to the average emission scenario ('IS92') of the Inter Governmental Panel on Climate Change (IPCC), doubling CO_2 is expected to occur in 2055–2060 (IPCC, 1996a).
- Average temperatures in the eastern Mediterranean are expected to rise by up to 2°C, taking into account the cooling effect of aerosols (polluting particles that 'swallow' part of the returned radiation) (IPCC, 1996a).
- Sea level rise by 2060 is expected to range between 10 and 55 cm, with an average prediction of a rise of 25 cm (IPCC, 1996a).

Specifically, our estimates are based on a recent research study (Dayan and Koch, 1999) which has produced climatic forecasts for the coastal region of Israel. The study's forecasts are on a global circulation model (GCM) developed in the University of East Anglia (Palutikof et al., 1996). According to this study, the expected changes in temperature for Israel are:

2020:0.3–0.4°C; 2050:0.7–0.8°C; 2100:1.6–1.8°C. With corresponding changes in precipitation: 2020:(−2)–(−1) per cent; 2050:(−4)–(−2) per cent; 2100:(−8)–(−4) per cent.

The chapter first surveys relevant climate change factors and their potential impact on agriculture in Israel. It then reviews a number of relevant studies and the methodologies employed by them. A brief review of the Israeli agricultural sector is then followed by a description of the methodology and specific assumptions used in this study and their application to the Israeli data. As expected, given the highly sophisticated nature of this sector in Israel, there is a wide variation between estimates assuming no adaptation, compared with those based on optimal crop selection and adaptation to the change in climatic variables, specifically precipitation changes.

AGRICULTURE AND CLIMATE CHANGE

Agriculture (and commercial forestry) are the most vulnerable production sectors that would be influenced by climate change, due to their great dependence on climatic variables. The factors that affect agriculture and which are related to climate change can be classified into several subcategories.

1. Climatic factors: temperature, precipitation and soil moisture.
2. Factors that accompany climate change: the effect of CO_2 levels on plant development (fertilization effect), and the impact of other gases such as tropospheric ozone and SO_2.
3. Factors related to human activity in coping with climate change, such as adaptation measures in various fields.

Climatic Factors

Temperature largely controls the rate of plant growth, flowering and fruiting responses, seed development, the water vapor flux, plant water status, soil drying, and irrigation practices. At the individual plant level, we can observe that different crops reach their optimum at different ranges of temperature (IPCC, 1996b). For crops in temperate climates the optimal range is between 30 and 35°C (Parry et al., 1988). Changes in temperature can directly influence livestock, as well as indirectly influence pest distribution (weeds and insects). Another change related to temperature is the length of the growing season. Global warming significantly reduces frost danger for all the Mediterranean region climates. It enables crops to be planted earlier in the season and lengthens the harvest season. On the other hand, higher temperatures accelerate development, shorten the growing period and decrease yields if the reduced growing period is not compensated by enhanced development of the plant (Ellis et al.,1990).

Precipitation is likely to become the most critical component in the structure of stresses that agriculture could face in the future. Any amount of global warming will increase water demand of almost all crops. Changes in annual precipitation affect agriculture directly through soil moisture and non-irrigated crops, and indirectly through refilling water reservoirs. In addition to the total annual rainfall, there is a great importance to the distribution of the precipitation over the year. It should be mentioned, however, that most of the Global Circulation Models (e.g. GISS and UKMO (IPCC, 1996a)) do not provide a uniform picture regarding the predicted changes in precipitation, and forecasts differ from one region to another and from one model to the other.

One of the more significant impacts is the rise in drought incidents. Drought is the most common cause of yield loss, especially in arid to semi-arid regions. Drought is an example of broader phenomena, namely, annual fluctuations in precipitation (and temperature), which influence agriculture.

Other factors are the *moisture* and the amount of *solar radiation* to which the plant is exposed. Moisture affects plant growth rate, fruiting period, evaporation rates and water demands. A constant level of moisture is essential in most phases of crop development. Generally, the hydrological cycle is about to increase with climate change, including precipitation and moisture.

Future agriculture will face a serious challenge due to *soil degradation*. Among its causes are enhanced erosion, loss of organic matter and accumulation of salts. Climate change is expected to enhance such effects because of changes in intensities and amounts of precipitation, higher radiation levels and extreme weather events.

Pest impacts are another factor. The predicted changes in temperature and CO_2 level will influence the distribution and range of different kinds of pests (weeds, insects and disease-borne organisms). This will probably aggravate the damage to crops. Their influence will be most noticeable in shorter crops, and additional prevention and control costs will become necessary (Rosenzweig and Hillel, 1998).

Atmospheric Changes

Future changes in CO_2 levels are the most important change. This has been studied a great deal recently, in terms of the rise in CO_2 concentrations in the atmosphere. This change is predicted to enhance photosynthesis and plant water-use efficiency. The average response of C3 group crops (most of the crops, excluding sugar canes, maize and several cereals) to doubling CO_2 levels is an increase of 30 per cent in yields, ranging between -10 per cent and $+80$ per cent. The factors that affect the response include temperature, soil fertility and precipitation (IPCC, 1996b). A recent study, using the FACE method (Free Air Carbon Dioxide Enrichment), found that CO_2 concentration of 550 ppm would cause a 15–16 per cent increase in yields. Other studies point out the effects of changes of CO_2 concentration on the form, shape and compound of crop yields. For example, rice grown under higher CO_2 concentration will contain higher concentration of amylose, while iron levels will be lower (Seneweera and Conroy, 1997).

Another change expected to influence agriculture is the level of plants' exposure to tropospheric ozone. Its concentration has doubled in the last century, and has caused an estimated drop in yields in the range of 1–30 per cent (IPCC, 1996b). The depletion of the ozone layer leads to higher exposure to UV-B radiation that has been proved to affect crops. This radiation damage is manifested mainly at high altitudes.

Human Induced Factors

Crop adaptation is becoming an important component in the process of agriculture's adjustment to climate change. However, research that has examined the independent adjustment capability of crops to changes in growth conditions has not yielded encouraging results. Human activity in this field can be divided into two major categories: choosing an optimal crop mix and biotechnological development. In selecting new genotypes, the factors that should be taken into account are high sensitivity to CO_2 concentration, the maintenance of yield levels even when higher temperatures cause enhanced development, and sustainability in the face of heat waves and water shortage in the growth and reproduction phases. Biotechnology is open to research and development of more sustainable crops for a changing environment.

A SHORT METHODOLOGICAL SURVEY

To date, numerous studies have dealt with the impact of climate change on agriculture (IPCC, 1996b). The earlier ones forecast future responses on the basis of statistical regressions on past data. More recent studies using 'dynamic crop models', attempt to model the principal physiological, morphological, and physical processes involving the transfer of energy and mass within the crop and between the crop and its environment. From such relationships, these models derive predictions of crop performance under various conditions (Rosenzweig and Hillel, 1998). These studies rely on climate scenarios derived from a variety of GCM. Among them are CERES, a dynamic crop model applied to several crops such as wheat and maize (Ritchie et al., 1989; Godwin et al., 1990) and SOYGRO for soy crops (Jones et al., 1989). A number of works incorporate market responses and long-range adaptation options. Failing to incorporate market reactions probably leads to an overestimation of the impact of climate change and should be classified in a 'worst case scenario' category.

More recently, attempts have been made to combine crop responses and economic models in order to evaluate future changes in production and welfare. These works can be divided into two main groups: research based on structural models and evaluations based on spatial models.

Structural models, such as the study by Adams (Adams et al., 1998) specifies the production process and incorporates it into an economic optimization. The main advantage of this approach is that it can estimate the impact of climate change on market equilibrium. The main omission to date has been overlooking adaptation potential.

Spatial ('Ricardian') models rely on econometric evaluation and are based on historical data. They estimate the relationship between economic data such as land and other asset values, and climatic variants. An example is the work by Mendelsohn (Mendelsohn et al., 1994), which has examined the impact of the warming in a Ricardian approach, in a partial equilibrium framework (agricultural land markets), on the basis of land prices in over 3000 counties in the US. Thus it implicitly reflects (past and present) adaptations to climate-related variables throughout the US. Application of the model to climate change scenarios reveals lower future impacts due to climate change. While including adaptation options, this approach cannot represent production processes specifically, and therefore cannot, for example, take explicit account of phenomena such as CO_2 fertilization.

In an attempt to apply this methodology, we examined official documents of the Ministry of Agriculture which provide normative assessments of profitability by crop groups. In theory, we could have used these values as proxies for land prices, assuming land is the only fixed input, and the calculated net profits (after returns to labor) represent computed (i.e. not observable) land rents. Given that most of the agricultural land in Israel is state-owned, and that effectively there is no fully functioning agricultural land market, these computed values could have been used as proxies. However, these values are national averages and, consequently, are useless in the present context, since regional climatic variability cannot be factored out of the data.

OTHER MEDITERRANEAN COUNTRIES STUDIES

Naturally, studies with the highest relevance to this study are those which have examined neighboring countries. However, comparisons are not easy to make, since one would expect to find differences in methods used (models, the inclusion of adaptation, etc.), the nature of basic climate change assumptions (climate scenarios, CO_2 fertilization), and the type of crops examined.

The Lebanese Ministry of Environment (Republic of Lebanon, 1999), for the UNDP and the Global Environmental Facility (GEF), prepared a major study. It examined the vulnerability of Lebanese agriculture to climate change. The study divides Lebanese agriculture into four main crop groups: apple orchards, citrus, olives and sugar cane. Three approaches have been employed by the researchers: (1) 'analogue' – assuming that following climate change, agricultural regions would assume characteristics similar to those of presently lower altitudes; (2) field studies relying on past data; (3) 'expert judgment'. The study's results have been expressed largely in qualitative terms. They predict a drop in yields and a rise in production costs for apples and citrus; inconclusive results for olives, and a negligible impact on sugar cane production. It should be pointed out that the study assumes more severe climate scenarios than ours (a rise of 1.6–4.1°C by 2080).

The Egyptian Environmental Affairs Agency (1999) conducted a similar study, which also examined the influence of climate change on the major crops in Egypt for standard GCM predictions, as well as arbitrary climate change assumptions (+2°, +4°, and 10–20 per cent change in precipitation). The study reports a decrease of 18–19 per cent in wheat and maize yields, and an increase of 17 per cent for cotton. Adaptation options were examined using three models: COTTAM, TEAM, and DSSAT3. The most important adaptation measures presented by the models are: (1) improvement of wheat and maize cultivars; (2) switching from maize to cotton, and replacing wheat with winter crops; (3) changing agricultural techniques, such as planting dates, water and nitrogen applications, and plant density; (4) removing crops with high water consumption.

Yet another study, reported in the second IPCC report, examined Egyptian agriculture in 2060 (with $2 \times CO_2$) (Yates and Strzepek, 1998). The study is based on GCM scenarios GFDL, UKMO, and GISS A1. It investigated crop response to climate change with and without adaptation, and included the CO_2 fertilization effect. The forecast (prepared for wheat, rice, other cereals and fruits) indicated a decrease in yields of -5 to -51 per cent for wheat, -5 to -27 per cent for rice and -2 to -21 per cent for other cereals and fruits. The study states that yield damage could decrease by up to 50 per cent if proper adaptation measures are taken, such as changes in crops, fertilizers, and seeding and watering patterns. An earlier study (Eid, 1994) also investigated climate change impact, using the same scenarios. It predicted a more noticeable decrease in yields; for wheat: -18 to -75 per cent and for maize: $+6$ to -65 per cent.

ASSESSING THE DAMAGE TO ISRAELI AGRICULTURE

Assumptions

A number of simplifying assumptions were made in this rather preliminary study. A major one limits the impact to one climatic factor – namely, precipitation. That is, climate change would affect the agricultural sector only through the availability of water (including soil moisture) for crop production.[2] The assessment is therefore based on the impact on water supplies, and further assumes that all such shortages, if and when they occur (around 2060) will have to be absorbed by agriculture. However, given the elastic nature of the demand for irrigation water (compared with household demand), this is not a too heroic assumption. The branches included in the calculations are field crops, vegetables and plants alone.[3]

A couple of additional strong assumptions underlie the estimated damage to agriculture; namely, no structural changes will take place due to adaptation, and the relative (real) price levels for agricultural output will remain constant.

A number of important reasons underlie the approach and assumptions adopted for the present analysis:

1. The available climate change data for Israel is scant, at best. Israel's small land area requires climatic forecasts of a very high resolution, which are still lacking. This leads to high uncertainty regarding predicted warming. Recall that according to the forecast used here, only a rise of less than 1°C (Dayan and Koch, 1999) is predicted for the coastal region of Israel. This makes it hard to estimate impacts using standard models, such as Dynamic Crop Models.
2. The most limiting factor of Israel's agriculture is water. This will be aggravated in the future given the expected rise in domestic and industrial water demand.
3. Because of the nature of land ownership in the Israeli agricultural sector (most of the land is owned by the state), there is no developed market for agricultural land, and therefore there is no possibility to apply the spatial model approach.

4. Only partial consideration is given to adaptation. Adaptation options that have not been analyzed are: (1) crop mix changes (including cultivar development); (2) development of new agro-technologies in agriculture and water management; (3) changes in crop location.
5. The study does not incorporate the CO_2 fertilization effect and other atmospheric changes that might alter crop yields significantly.

Damage Calculations

A number of factors will affect water supplies in connection with climate change: a decrease in precipitation, enhanced evaporation from water reservoirs (as a result of the rise in temperature), aquifer salinization due to over pumping and sea water intrusion. Since it is not easy to evaluate the impact of the three last factors in quantitative terms, we use only the predicted precipitation shortfall (Dayan and Koch, 1999), employing the upper limit of 4 per cent as a 'worst case' scenario. Given that the average annual supply is 2000 million cm, the supply shortfall assumed in the calculations is 80 million cm.

As mentioned earlier, the approach used in this assessment is the production function approach; that is, using an estimated production function for water (other inputs held fixed) for a number of key crops, we estimated the drop in yields due to cuts in irrigated water and natural precipitation. We used recently estimated production functions by Vered (Vered, 2000), which examined crop yield responses to water of different quality (fresh, recycled, and brackish).

The production function with water as a single variant, and all other inputs constant (evaluated at their means and added to the intercept) was:

$$Y_i = a + b(W_i) + c(W_i)^2$$

where

Y_i = yield per dunam (0.1 hectare) for crop i
W_i = irrigation water input per dunam of crop i
a = constant (incorporates yield with only natural rainfall)
b, c = coefficients.

The estimated functions in Vered (2000) incorporate additional variables which influence output beside water quantity and quality; these are the geographical region (there are significant differences in climatic and soil characteristics between regions) and the type of irrigation system (dripping, etc.). However, for our purpose (crop yields as a function of water input) we assumed them to remain constant, and incorporated them into the constant term.

The crops were divided into several groups, and a representative crop was selected in each group as given in Table 9.1.

Table 9.1   Crop groups

Group	Selected crop
Citrus	Oranges
Fruits (non citrus)	Avocado, apples
Cereals and oils	Wheat
Fibers	Cotton
Vegetables	Tomato, watermelon, potato[4]

Note: [a] Because of the large size of the vegetables group, three representative crops, equally weighted, were taken for it.

Scenario I (the 'naive' scenario)
The underlying assumption in this scenario is that production cutbacks will be undertaken in an arbitrary fashion due to the water shortfall and there will be a proportionate cutback in water use by each crop group, relative to its present water consumption. Total damage is given therefore by summing the value of yield cutbacks for all groups; namely,

$$TD = \sum_{i=1}^{n} \Delta Yi \times Pi \qquad (9.1)$$

Where:

TD = annual damage in monetary terms
i = crop group
Pi = average price per tonne for crop group i[4]
ΔYi = change in yield for crop group i.

Yield change is a function of the change in water allocation to the respective crop group and the change in the value of the constant coefficient (due to decline in rainfall), given by equation (9.2).

$$\Delta Yi = f(\Delta Wi) + \Delta a \qquad (9.2)$$

where

Wi = amount of water consumed by crop group i
ΔWi = the change in the amount of water consumed by crop group i.

The change in the water allocated to each crop group is proportionate to its present consumption,

$$\Delta Wi = \Delta W \times \frac{Wi}{TW} \qquad (9.3)$$

where

TW = total amount of water consumed by all groups
ΔW = total change in water consumption
$\Sigma \Delta Wi = \Delta W$.

From the assumption that production will be affected not only by irrigation cutbacks but also because of decline in rainfall, one must incorporate this impact as well. The intercept in the response function is supposed to capture this effect, as well as other factors not explicitly represented in the model specification. We estimated its weight to be around 66 per cent of the value of the intercept.[5] This part of the intercept would therefore need to be re-calculated along with the change in the irrigation water input,[6] as given in equation (9.4):

$$\Delta a = 0.66 \times 0.04 \times a \qquad (9.4)$$

Table 9.2 summarizes the loss in production value in the naïve scenario. The total annual loss is about $208 million in present prices.

Table 9.2   Annual damage by crop group, scenario I

Subgroup	Total damage (mil. $)
Cereals and oils	5.5
Fibers	51.7
Citrus	86.5
Vegetables	48
Fruits (without citrus)	16.5
Total	208

Scenario II: partial adaptation
It is most likely, even certain, that in reality costs will be significantly lower, given the agricultural sector's ability to carry out adaptive measures over

time. Here we assume that (partial) adaptation will be in the form of economic adjustment, by which we mean adjusting crop areas according to the water-use efficiency of the different crops. The naïve scenario ignores adaptation altogether, and therefore overlooks significant savings in production costs due to a response in the form of crop adjustment (among many others, of course).

In scenario II we consider two components of damage (given in equation (9.5)):

1. Decrease in precipitation as an element having an impact on all crop groups (equation 6).
2. Cutbacks in water allocated to crops whose water use efficiency is relatively low, based on the *marginal value product* (MVP) of water (which is the partial derivative of the response function of the representative crops with respect to the water input, evaluated at the average water input per irrigated dunam of the given crop, multiplied by the average price per tonne).

$$TD = \sum_{i=1}^{n} (\Delta Yi \times Pi) + \Delta Yj \times Pj \qquad (9.5)$$

$$\Delta Yi = f(\Delta a) \qquad (9.6)$$

where

j = the crop group for which MVP is the lowest and

$$\frac{\partial Yj}{\partial W} \times Pj \le \frac{\partial Yj}{\partial W} \times Pi \text{ for all } i.$$

However, we should also consider the possibility that whenever a cutback in irrigation reduces a given crop acreage (and not just yield per dunam), there will be a corresponding reduction in production costs. Consequently, *net* damage costs will be correspondingly lower. Production costs for the different crops were taken from the annual agricultural survey (CBS, 1998). The calculation of net damage for the second scenario is given by:

$$Dj = f(\Delta Wj) - \lambda TC(\Delta Yj) \qquad (9.7)$$

$$\lambda = \frac{\Delta Yj(w)}{Yj(w)} \qquad 0 \le \lambda \le 1 \qquad (9.8)$$

$$\Delta Wj = \Delta W \qquad (9.9)$$

where:

Dj = total damage value to group j

ΔYj = yield change, group j

TC = total production costs for group j

ΔWj = change in water consumption of group j.

Table 9.3 gives the MVP for the different crop groups.

Table 9.3   Marginal revenue of water by crop groups

Subgroup	Marginal revenue ($/cm)
Cereals and oils	0.195
Vegetables	2.3
Citrus	2
Fruits	17.75
Fibers	0.4

The crop group with the lowest MVP is cereals and oils. It turns out that if it absorbed the entire needed cutback to meet the projected drop in precipitation, production will drop by about 66 per cent, with a corresponding annual decline in output valued at $105 million. However, net damage, after taking into account the corresponding decrease in production inputs (equation (9.5)) is $40 million.

In addition to the cutback achieved through the reduction in crop acreage of crop group j, we should take into account the impact of precipitation decrease on all crops, $i = 1,\ldots n$, represented by $= \Delta Y_i$ in equations (9.5) and (9.6). Table 9.4 gives the monetary value of this impact on crops. Thus the total annual damage due to a projected decrease in mean precipitation levels amounts to $62 million. Combining the two components of the forecast impact $(62 + 40)$, total annual damage under this scenario adds up to $102 million.

The outcome is described in Figure 9.1, which depicts the demand (= MVP) for and supply of irrigation water in agriculture. The expected impact of climate change through the decline in precipitation is depicted by the leftward shift in the supply schedule. The decline in economic welfare (i.e. social damage costs) is given by the triangle formed by the intersection of the demand and the two supply curves.

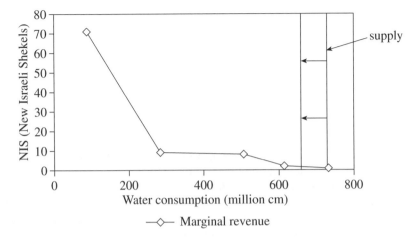

Figure 9.1   Water supply and demand in Israel's agriculture

Scenario III
The third scenario considered in this study examined the possibility of augmenting domestic freshwater water supplies with desalinated water at current production costs. In this case damage represented by the replacement costs of supply shortage due to climate change will be the sum of the damage resulting from precipitation decrease (Table 9.4) and the costs of desalinating 80 million cm (the assumed water shortage). This is described by equation (9.10):

$$TD = \sum_{i=1}^{n} (\Delta Yi \times Pi) + TCs(\Delta W) \qquad (9.10)$$

where TCs = total desalination costs. The current cost of desalination stands at about 80 cents per cm, so this yields an annual bill for this scenario of about $126 million (see Table 9.5).

Table 9.4   Annual damage by crop group, scenario III

Subgroup	Damage (mil. $)
Vegetables	
Cereals and oils	1.5
Fibers	43
Fruits	2
Citrus	9
Total	61

Table 9.5   Total damage by scenario (million US$)

Scenario	I	II	III
Total damage	208	101.5	125.5

SUMMARY

Our aim in this exploratory study has been to provide a range of rough preliminary estimates of expected future damage to agriculture in Israel resulting from climate change. In addition to the inherent uncertainty in forecasting climate change impacts, there is the uncertainty regarding what adaptation options will be available to farmers several decades from now, the nature of demand for water, and the role of agriculture in the national economy. There are also several additional climatic factors which we were not able to incorporate in the analysis due to a lack of usable data for Israel: change in temperature, climatic fluctuations (temperature and precipitation), the role of CO_2 fertilization, and more.

However, even this modest exercise tells us a great deal about the importance of adaptation and the correct proactive planning in counteracting the adverse effects of climate change. In addition to providing a range of quantitative economic estimates of costs, this is probably the major lesson of the study.

The authors are planning to carry out similar exercises to assess the economic impact on other sectors believed to be affected by climate change. We hope these studies will serve to stimulate further, more rigorous and detailed studies, in order to provide a better understanding of climate change through estimates that are of direct relevance for informed policy decisions in this important, emerging area of environmental decision making.

NOTES

1. The information presented here is taken from Publication No. 2 of Israel's CBS, 'Jubilee Publications' series.
2. According to the Israel National Report on Climate Change (Ministry of Environment, 2000) the decreased annual rainfall and lengthened intervals between rains, coupled with increased temperatures and evaporation, will reduce plant productivity, with a concomitant decrease in soil organic matter. This will reduce water holding capacity and soil permeability. An increase in runoff velocity and intensity will erode the most fertile topsoil, further reducing productivity. Soil salinity will increase due to higher evapotranspiration and lower leaching effect of the reduced rains.

3. Flowers and livestock were not included in the calculation due to lack of relevant data. In any case, we assume that these branches will not incur any water cutbacks.
4. This price is calculated according to data from the *Agriculture Statistics Quarterly* (CBS, 1997) containing total products (tonnes) and total monetary return in average prices for 1995.
5. Based on discussions with Vered.
6. Greenhouse crops (e.g. tomatoes) were excluded because there is no significance for precipitation in their growth.

REFERENCES

Adams, R.M., McCarl, B.A., Segerson, K., Rosenzweig, C., Briant, K.J., Dixon, B.L., Conner, R., Evenson, R.E. and Ojima, D. (1999). 'The economic effects of climate change on US agriculture'. In: R. Mendelsohn and J.E. Neumann (eds) *The Impact of Climate Change on the U.S. Economy*. Cambridge: Cambridge University Press.

CBS (Central Bureau of Statistics) (1997). *Agricultural Quarterly*, Vol. 28. Jerusalem: CBS.

Dayan, U. and Koch, J. (1999). *Implications of Climate Change on the Coastal Region of Israel*, Mediterranean Action Plan. Athens: UNEP.

Egyptian Environmental Affairs Agency (1999). *The Arab Republic of Egypt: Initial National Communication on Climate Change*. Prepared for the UNFCCC.

Eid, H.M. (1994). 'Impact of climate change on simulated wheat and maize yields in Egypt'. In: *Implications of Climate Change for International Agriculture*. Washington, DC: US Environmental Protection Agency, pp. 1–14.

El-Shaer, H.M., Rosenzweig, C., Iglesias, A., Eid, M.H. and Hillel. D. (1997). 'Impact of climate change on possible scenarios for Egyptian agriculture in the future'. *Mitigation and Adaptation Strategies Global Change* 1(3), 233–250.

Ellis, R.H., Headley, P, Roberts, E.H. and Summerfield, R.J. (1990). 'Quantitative relations between temperature and crop development and growth'. In: *Climate Change and Plant Genetic Resources*. London: Belhaven, pp. 85–115.

Godwin, D.C. et al. (1990). *A User's Guide to CERES-Rice-V2.10*. Muscle Shoals, AI: International Fertilizer Development Center.

Iglesias, A., Rosenzweig, C. and Pereira, D. (2000). 'Predicting spatial impacts of climate in agriculture in Spain'. *Global Environmental Change* 10, 69–80.

IPCC (1996a). *Climate Change 1995: The Science of Climate Change*, Houghton, J.T., Jenkins, G.J. and Ephraums, J.J. (eds) Cambridge: Cambridge University Press.

IPCC (1996b). 'Agriculture in a changing climate: impacts and adaptation'. In: Watson, R.T., Zinyowera, M.C., Moss, R.H. and Dokken, D.J. (eds) *Impacts, Adaptation and Mitigation of Climate Change: Scientific-Technical Analysis*. New York: Cambridge University Press.

IPCC (2001). 'Ecosystems and their goods and services'. In: Chianziani, O.F., Dokken, D.J., Leary, N.A., McCarthy J.J. and White, K.S. *Climate Change 2001: Impacts, Adaptation and Vulnerability*. New York: Cambridge University Press.

Israel, Ministry of Environment (2000). *Israel National Report on Climate Change*, Gabbay S. Jerusalem: Ministry of Environment's Publications Unit.

Jewish Agency to Israel, Agricultural Planning and Development Authority, 1975–1996. *Agricultural Branches*. Tel-Aviv.

Jones, J.W. et al. (1989). 'SOYGROv5.42 soybean crop growth simulation model: users' guide'. *Florida Agriculture Experimental Station Journal*, University of Florida, Gainesville.

Kol, N. (1998). *Agriculture, Publication No.2* from 'Jubilee Publications'. Jerusalem: Central Bureau of Statistics.

Mendelsohn, R., Nordhaus, W.D. and Daigee, S. (1994). 'The impact of global warming on agriculture: a Ricardian analysis'. *The American Economic Review* **84**, 754–771.

Palutikof, J.P., Gou, X. and Wigley, T.M.L. (1996). 'Developing climate change scenarios for the Mediterranean region'. In: Jeftic, L., Keckes, S. and Pernetta, J.C. (eds) *Climate Change and the Mediterranean*, London: Arnold, Vol. 2, pp. 27–56.

Parry, M.L., Carter, J.H., Konijn, N.T. (1988). *The Impact of Climate Variation on US Agriculture, Vol. 1, Assessment in Semi-arid Regions.* Dordrecht, Netherlands: Kluwer Academic Publishers.

Pinter, P.J. Jr, Kimball, B.A., Garcia, R.A., Wall, G.W., Hunsaker, D.J. and LaMort, R.L. (1996). 'Free air CO_2 enrichment. Responses of cotton and wheat crops'. In: *Carbon Dioxide and Terrestrial Ecosystems.* San Diego, CA: Academic Press.

Republic of Lebanon, Ministry of Environment (1999). 'Climate change assessment agriculture'. In: *Technical Annex to Lebanon's First National Communication. Final Report.* Republic of Lebanon: UNDP, Global Environment Facility.

Ritchie, J.T., Baer, B.D. and Chou, T.Y. (1989). 'Effect of global climate change on the agriculture in the Great Lakes region'. In: Smith, J. and Tirpak, D. (eds) *The Potential Effect of Global Climate Change on the United States.* Washington DC: Office of Policy, Planning and Evaluation, US Environmental Protection Agency, Appendix C, pp. 1.1–1.21.

Rosenzweig, C. and Hillel, D. (1998). *Climate Change and the Global Harvest.* New York: Oxford University Press.

Seneweera, S.P. and Conroy, J.P. (1997). 'Growth, grain yields and quality of rice in response to elevated CO_2 and phosphorus nutrition'. *Soil Science and Plant Nutrition* **43**, 1131–1136.

Vered, A. (2000). 'Yields function according to water quality', MSc thesis, Hebrew University, Faculty of Agriculture, Rehovot, Israel.

Wittwer, S.H. (1995). *Food, Climate, and Carbon Dioxide.* Boca Raton, FL: CRC Press.

Yates D.M. and Strzepek, K.M. (1998). 'An assessment of integrated climate change impacts on the agricultural economy of Egypt'. *Climate Change* **38**, 261–287.

10. Assessing the ancillary socio-economic benefits of mitigating greenhouse gases from municipal solid waste management

O. Ayalon, M. Shechter and Y. Avnimelech

INTRODUCTION

The increased concern about environmental problems caused by inadequate waste management, as well as the concern about global warming, promotes action toward a sustainable management of the organic fraction of the waste. The waste sector in Israel contributes 13 per cent of total CO_2-equivalents (CO_2-eq.) emitted in Israel (Avnimelech et al., 1999) for a 100 years time range. This significant contribution is due to the fact that most of the waste, containing a high percentage of degradable organic material, is being landfilled without any methane recovery. International concern about global warming is the driving force in recent legislation in Europe to reduce the biodegradable organic fraction of waste entering landfills (EU, 1996; Petersen, 1997) with Germany leading (Stegmann, 1997), as well as several US states (e.g. Friesen, 1999). It is expected that changing the technology of waste treatment could lead to a substantial greenhouse gas (GHG) reduction with relatively low marginal costs and within a short time. In addition, better waste management is associated with ancillary socio-economic benefits, such as increased crop yield and reduced fertilizer production and consumption due to the use of MSW compost. The aim of this chapter is to identify and assess these benefits.

We believe that the principles demonstrated here are relevant to many Mediterranean countries, also characterized by similar waste composition and rather poor waste management practices. Implementation of improved technologies to manage the waste could not only reduce the amount of GHG emitted at rather low marginal costs, but it could also contribute to additional environmental benefits in these countries as well.

EXTERNAL IMPACTS OF LANDFILL SITES

Due to the fact that almost 90 per cent of the waste in Israel is being landfilled (*Israel Environment Bulletin*, 1997) the externalities from waste management should be spelled out and assessed. These externalities include land use (typical figures in Israel: 20 ha for medium sites receiving 500 tonnes of waste per day, 30–40 ha for 1000–3000 tonnes per day sites); disamenity effects (i.e. odors, view); potential water pollution by leachates; release of conventional air pollutants (i.e. SOx, NOx); release of toxic air pollutants (VOC, heavy metals); attraction of animals and spread of disease; attraction of birds that endanger civil and military aviation; resource depletion; externalities from transportation to and from the landfill, including road congestion, accidents, air pollution, and noise. Finally, as mentioned before, degradation of organic matter in landfills is an anaerobic process, leading to the generation of biogas (landfill gas, LFG) containing roughly 50–60 per cent methane (CH_4) and 40–50 per cent CO_2 (e.g. EPA, 1989). The most significant factors influencing methane generation in landfills include the following:

- Waste composition – the higher the proportion of organic components the higher the production of GHG; the waste in Israel is characterized by a high percentage of wet organic components, with more than 70 per cent including kitchen residuals (almost 40 per cent), paper products (22 per cent), yard waste and disposable diapers (10 per cent) (*Israel Environment Bulletin*, 1997).
- Physical factors such as moisture content, pH, and temperature influence the production of methane.
- The last factor affecting methane production in landfills is waste disposal practices (i.e. daily cover, type of soil used for daily cover, compaction).

In several studies conducted in Europe and in Israel, the external costs of landfilling due to leachates, air pollution including GHG emissions and transportation impacts were evaluated to be in the range of 5–10 US$/tonne waste (DoE report, 1993, Coopers & Lybrand, 1996). In Israel, it was estimated that the external costs of landfills is 5.5$, while 5$ are related to GHG emissions (Enosh Consultants, 1996). None of the above estimates include disamenities or resource depletion.

WASTE MANAGEMENT ALTERNATIVES

Different waste management alternatives could lead to a significant decrease in GHG emissions. In order to reduce GHG emissions, the aim is to convert CH_4 to CO_2 (i.e. by incineration). It should be noted that some of the methods could be applied to the entire amount of the waste (incineration or landfilling) and in some methods only the organic part of the waste could be treated (e.g. composting, anaerobic digestion). Pretreatment of the waste can include incineration, aerobic composting or anaerobic digestion (AD). Table 10.1 summarizes the alternative ways of processing waste in order to minimize the amount of methane produced. In addition to GHG reduction, each alternative has also ancillary socio-economic benefits (advantages) or costs (disadvantages) listed in the table.

The situation in Israel, where about 90 per cent of the waste generated in 1996 (base year for calculation of GHG emissions) was landfilled, without any extraction of LFG, serves as the reference point. Extraction and burning of LFG reduces the emissions of methane, yet recovery rate efficiencies vary from 40 per cent to 90 per cent (White et al., 1995; Meadows et al., 1997). In our analysis we assumed 50 per cent LFG collection efficiency. When LFG is used for energy production, CO_2 emission is further reduced indirectly as a result of the production of electricity and replacement of the equivalent CO_2 emissions from conventional power plants. It was estimated (Meadows et al., 1997) that by the year 2025, only 40–50 per cent of LFG will be collected in North America, Western Europe and Oceania and just 10 per cent in developing countries. These figures emphasize the need to implement other waste management technologies in order to achieve a more significant reduction in GHG mitigation.

A very effective means to reduce GHG emissions is to incinerate the waste. This process is assumed to convert all carbon to CO_2 and thus to reduce GHG emissions to only 4 per cent of Israel's national emissions inventory. In cases where energy is recovered, it was assumed (Enosh Consultants, 1996) that 1 tonne of Israeli waste will produce 468 kWh and thus the process is further credited by 138 kg CO_2 for avoiding electricity production in conventional power plants.

The third group of options is to treat the organic fraction biologically, either by using aerobic composting (see Epstein, 1997; Haug, 1993) or anaerobic process and subsequent burning of the biogas, generally with energy recovery (see Speece, 1996). For both technologies, about one half of the organic carbon remains in the compost, and is slowly released to the soil (Epstein, 1997). Part of the carbon is sequestered in the soil for a long time period. Compost is used in farmland to raise soil fertility and crop yield. In a series of farm scale experiments, conducted in several parts in Israel, it was shown that expected yield increase is 10–20 per cent for an application of about 10 tonnes of compost per hectare (Avnimelech, 1995). These figures are equivalent to an increased carbon fixation in the order of 2 tonnes CO_2 per one tonne of dry compost.

Table 10.1 Waste management alternatives

Alternative	Advantages	Disadvantages
Landfilling With LFG flare (assuming 50% efficiency)	• Credit for long-term carbon storage in landfills • Partial conversion of CH_4 to CO_2	• External impacts (land use, disamenity, water and air pollution, resources depletion and transportation to and from landfill) • GHG (50%)
With LFG energy recovery (assuming 50% efficiency)	• Credit for long-term carbon storage in landfills • Partial conversion of CH_4 to CO_2 • Avoided emissions from conventional energy sources.	• External impacts (land use, disamenity, water and air pollution, resources depletion and transportation) • GHG (50%)
Incineration With energy recovery	• Total conversion of CH_4 to CO_2 • Avoided emissions from conventional energy sources • Disposal of 20% of original amount of waste	• N_2O emissions • Possible toxic emissions • Transportation emissions to and from plant
Biological treatment Aerobic composting (assuming 90% efficiency)	• CH_4 conversion to CO_2 • Increased soil carbon storage • CO_2 sequestration • Increased crop yield • Nutrient content of the compost • Avoided fertilizer production	• Energy input • N_2O emissions * • Transportation emissions to and from composting plant • Compost-machinery emissions

Anaerobic digestion (assuming 100% efficiency)	• Total conversion of CH_4 to CO_2 • Avoided emissions from conventional energy sources • Increase in soil carbon storage • CO_2 sequestration • Increased crop yield • Nutrient content of the compost • Avoided fertilizer production	• N_2O emissions* • Transportation emissions to AD plant
Reduction, recycling Source reduction	• Decrease in energy consumption due to lower production • Decrease in process emissions • Avoided production and transportation emissions • Less consumption of wood and paper products increases forest carbon storage	• Specific information needed for each component
Recycling	• *In some products:* Decrease in energy consumption due to *lower* energy requirements (compared with manufacture from *virgin* inputs) • Paper recycling prevents logging and increases forest carbon sequestration	• Transportation emissions to and from recycling plant • Specific information needed for each component

Note: * poor data, needs further research.

217

Finally, waste minimization and/or recycling of industrial raw materials (especially paper) obviously lead to direct and indirect reduction of GHG emissions. These options should be dealt with specifically according to each component of the waste and its relative contribution to GHG mitigation.

ECONOMIC EVALUATION OF GHG EMISSION ABATEMENT AND ALTERNATIVES ASSESSMENT

There is a need to assess the environmental, economic and social aspects of the alternative ways to manage waste in order to abate GHG. In order to appraise the abatement costs of GHG emissions, the investment cost of each alternative was evaluated. Operating and maintenance (O&M) costs were not included in this valuation due to the fact that they are site specific, highly variable and are a function of factors such as salaries, transportation, insurance rates, taxes and prices obtained for recyclables or energy sales, and so on. It should be noted that there is a rough correlation between investment costs and O&M costs. As a rule of thumb, O&M represent about 40 per cent of the costs of landfilling (Glebs, 1989) and 35–40 per cent of incineration costs (excluding revenues from energy sales).

Investment cost estimations for GHG mitigation from MSW for a representative city producing 2800–3000 tonnes MSW per day (1 million tonnes per year) are given in Table 10.2. Reduction costs of 1 tonne of CO_2-eq. were calculated using methane GWP of 21 for the time horizon of 100 years (values in parentheses are calculated according to a global warming potential of methane of 56 for a time horizon of 20 years).

The investment to reduce one tonne of CO_2-eq. by collecting and burning the LFG in landfills is rather low, less than 20 US$, and more than twice for a system containing energy recovery (EPA, 1997a, 1997b). Incineration of MSW is the most effective GHG-reducing technology, yet the investment is the highest. Another potential energy recovery system is anaerobic digestion (AD), producing both biogas and compost. Systems containing energy recovery devices are credited for selling energy. For example, selling electricity at 0.05$/kWh will reduce the tipping fee (TF) at the gate of an incineration plant by 9.4$ per tonne of waste (Enosh Consultants, 1996); at an AD plant by 3.5$/tonne (de Laclos et al., 1997) and at a landfill that recovers energy from LFG by 1.6$/tonne (DoE Report, 1993). In addition, as mentioned before, these alternatives are further credited for reducing emissions from conventional power plants. The investment required to reduce a tonne of CO_2-eq. by aerobic composting using the windrow technology is the lowest, and the efficiency of this method to reduce GHG emission is high. Therefore, the least cost alternative to mitigate GHG emissions

Table 10.2   Investment costs for GHG mitigation by various waste management alternatives

Alternative	Investment per plant (10^6 $)*	Size of typical plant (TPD)	Number of plants needed	Total investment (10^6 $)	Investment costs of reduction ($/tonne CO_2-eq.)	Annualized costs (15 y) ($/tonne CO_2-eq.)
Landfilling						
With LFG flare (50% collection efficiency)	2	400	7	14	18 (6)	**1.21** (0.41)
With LFG (50% collection and energy recovery efficiency)	5	400	7	35	45 (16)	**3.02** (1.03)
Incineration	50	500	6	300	194 (67)	**12.94** (4.43)
Biological treatment						
Aerobic composting (90% efficiency)	1	250	12	12	9 (3)	**0.58** (0.21)
Anaerobic digestion	10	500	6	60	39 (13)	**2.59** (0.9)

Note: * The plant sizes were chosen following different performance efficiencies. For each alternative, the total investment was calculated according to the number of plants needed to treat all waste produced.

Sources: EPA (1997b); Coopers & Lybrand (1996); Commercial entrepreneurs engaged in waste management in Israel that asked specifically not to be identified.

from the waste sector in Israel is to construct composting plants. In this option, organic waste will be processed, part of the materials (i.e. paper, plastics etc.) will be recycled and only the non-recyclable waste that does not produce GHG will be landfilled. By adopting the integrated waste management approach, a reduction of 5000 CO_2-eq. Ktonne/year, which is 8–9 per cent of total GHG emissions, could be achieved at reasonable costs.

The final decision regarding waste management alternatives will not concentrate solely on the amount of CO_2-eq. mitigated, but also on local conditions such as availability of land, waste composition, feasibility of implementation of each alternative, direct and environmental costs, and so on (Ayalon et al., 1999). The chosen integrated waste management system should deliver both economic and environmental sustainability.

DISCUSSION AND CONCLUSIONS

The increased concern about global warming, as well as the awareness of the environmental problems caused by inadequate waste management in developing countries, provide an important additional rationale for sustainable management of the organic fraction of the waste.

The investments required to abate GHG emissions from other sectors (e.g. switch from coal to natural gas in power stations, clean and renewable energy sources, improved energy production and industrial processes, improvements in transportation) are very high and a long time-period is needed for their implementation. Reducing GHG emission by proper treatment of waste is cheaper than these alternatives and it is even cheaper than the price of carbon permits (if an emission trading mechanism is available). Therefore, on a national basis, there is a clear incentive to invest in these infrastructures and even possibly to create available permits for international trade. One can visualize the financing of waste treatment facilities by the industry or the industrial countries, based on transfer of emission permits. Expeditious reduction in the waste sector is needed for an immediate transition period as an interim solution to enable the development of long-range environmental changes in other sectors. The major effects of these steps are aimed at a short to medium transition period.

It was found that by comparing the alternatives within the waste sector, the most cost-effective alternative to reduce GHG emissions from MSW is to compost it aerobically. The composting option that does not require high investments and produces a product that can be readily utilized by the agricultural sector seems to be an available interim solution to mitigate GHG emission by most countries. In addition, the composting option carries a positive credit for the production of compost, an efficient soil additive, especially in arid, semi-arid and other impoverished soils, typical in Mediterranean countries. It should be emphasized, however, that stricter regulations regarding open composting plants and demand for closed ones might change the overall picture and call for further studies.

The approach presented here calls for expansion of these efforts and for them to be widened worldwide, especially in the developing countries that are characterized by a high organic matter fraction in their MSW. This is based on the assumption that changes in the waste sector are publicly and politically accepted, technically feasible, the time needed for implementation is short and the effect is significant.

Judging from the Israeli case study, it may be assumed that a concentrated effort in this direction may reduce national GHG emissions by more than 5 Mtonne CO_2-eq. per year (10 per cent of the total emissions). This seems to be a doable and affordable short and medium range alternative that deserves concentrated national and international effort. The dominant effect of MSW on GHG emissions and global climate change calls for intensive scientific, economic and political efforts in order to minimize the emissions from this sector. The benefits from a proper waste management policy will not only contribute significantly to the reduction of GHG emissions, but will play a significant role in other environmental areas, such as sustainable management of the waste as well as resource conservation. Reducing GHG emission by proper waste management is not the only means, but this is the most available and feasible one. However, further technological and scientific efforts should be devoted to the development of other sustainable, long-term solutions.

REFERENCES

Avnimelech, Y. (1995). 'Agronomic utilization of MSW compost: principles and application'. In: Bidlingmaier, W. and Stegmann, R. (eds) *Proceedings – First International Symposium – Biological Waste Management A Wasted Chance?* University of Essen, Technical University of Hamburg.

Avnimelech, Y. (ed.) et. al. (1999). *Policy Document – Mitigation of GHG Emissions.* Submitted to the Ministry of Environment, Israel. The S. Neaman Institute For Advanced Studies in Science & Technology.

Ayalon, O., Avnimelech, Y. and Shechter, M. (1999). 'Issues in designing an effective solid waste policy: the israeli experience'. In: Sterner, T. (ed.) *The Market and the Environment: The Effectiveness of Market Based Instruments for Environmental Reform.* Edward Elgar, Cheltenham, UK and Northampton, MA, USA, pp. 389–406.

Coopers and Lybrand (1996). *Cost–Benefit Analysis of the Different Municipal*

Solid Waste Management Systems: Objectives and Instruments for the Year 2000. Final report to the European Commission, DGXI.

de Laclos, H.F., Desbois, S. and Steinmuller, C. (1997). 'Anaerobic digestion of source sorted waste: results of Valorga full-scale plant in Tilburg (NL)'. In: Stentiford, E. (ed.) *ORBIT 97*. Zeebra Publishing, Manchester, pp. 25–28.

DoE Report (1993). *Externalities from Landfill and Incineration.* A study by CSERGE and EFTEL. HMSO Press, Edinburgh.

Enosh Consultants Ltd. (1996). *Analysis of Waste Management Externalities.* Report to the Ministry of Environment (Hebrew).

EPA (1989). *Decision-makers Guide to Solid Waste Management.* EPA/530-SW-89-072.

EPA (1997a). *Energy Project LFG Utilization Software (E-PLUS).* EPA # 430-B97-006, www.epa.gov/globalwarming.

EPA (1997b). *Feasibility Assessment for Gas-to-Energy at Selected Landfills in Sao Paulo, Brazil.* EPA # 68-W6-0004.

Epstein, E. (1997). *The Science of Composting.* Technomic Publishing Company, Inc., Lancaster, PA.

EU (1996). *Strategy Paper for Reducing Methane Emissions Communication from the Commission to the Council and the European Parliament. COM* (96) 557, http://europa.eu.int/comm/dg11/docum/96557en.pdf.

Friesen, B. (1999). 'Composting key to meeting landfill organics ban'. *BioCycle* **40**(2): 31–33.

Glebs, R.T. (1989). 'Subtitle D: how will it affect landfills?' *Waste Alternatives, the Magazine of Waste Options,* **1**(3): 56–64.

Haug, R.T. (1993). *The Practical Handbook of Compost Engineering.* Lewis Publishers, Boca Raton.

Israel Environment Bulletin (1997). 'Integrated solid waste management'. *Israel Environment Bulletin* **20**(2): 2–6.

Meadows, M., Franklin, F., Campbell, D. and Riemer P. (1997). 'Global methane emissions from solid waste disposal sites'. In: Christensen, T.H., Cossu, R. and Stegmann R. (eds) *Proceedings of Sardinia 97, 6th International Landfill Symposium.* CISA Environmental Sanitary Engineering Centre, Cagliary, Vol. IV, pp. 3–10.

Petersen, H. (1997). 'Commission of the European Communities: proposal for a Council Directive on waste landfilling'. In: Christensen, T.H., Cossu, R. and Stegmann R. (eds) *Proceedings of Sardinia 97, 6th International Landfill Symposium.* CISA Environmental Sanitary Engineering Centre, Cagliary, Vol. V, pp. 25–46.

Speece, R.E. (1996). *Anaerobic Biotechnology for Industrial Wastewaters.* Archae Press, Nashville, TN.

Stegmann, R. (1997). 'German landfill regulations and related problems'. In: Christensen, T.H., Cossu, R. and Stegmann R. (eds) *Proceedings of Sardinia 97, 6th International Landfill Symposium.* CISA Environmental Sanitary Engineering Centre, Cagliary, Vol. V, pp. 3–8.

White, P.R., Franke, M. and Hindle, P. (1995). *Integrated Solid Waste Management: A Life Cycle Inventory.* Blackie Academic & Professional, London.

PART V

Climate change and Mediterranean coastal areas

11. Assessing the impacts of climate change in the Mediterranean coastal zones

Dimitris G. Georgas

INTRODUCTION

The increasing atmospheric concentrations of greenhouse gases resulting from human activities are expected to lead to unavoidable changes in climate. It seems likely that these changes will occur at a faster rate than any that have occurred during mankind's recorded history. Although there is a continuing evolution in the expected climatic scenarios, predictions concerning the future rate and magnitude of climatic changes have high levels of uncertainty. Those for eustatic sea level and global mean surface temperature are less certain than predictions of parameters such as rainfall or changes in storm frequency. Changes in climatic parameters will be different in different areas across the Mediterranean. There is a consideration that these changes may have already started and their continuation may now be inevitable. However impacts from the expected rises in regional temperature and local precipitation patterns for arid coastal areas and islands have not been clearly estimated yet. The changes in mean sea level rise across the great diversified Mediterranean coastline have been assessed by means of a sequence of selective case studies, since 1987. Today the coastal zone hosts 70 per cent of the population, 80 per cent of industrial activities and 90 per cent of tourism income. Impact studies have been presented to selected local authorities. Although in the near future the vulnerability from climatic changes is expected to be among the major consequences for coastal planning, sound central policy options are almost absent.

The first attempt to assess the likely impacts of climatic change on coastal systems was triggered by United Nations Environment Programme (UNEP) in 1987. This systematic specific study for the impacts on the estuarine systems has attempted to analyse the potential qualitative implications of the predicted climatic changes on the natural and man-made environment and activities.

Realizing in early 1987 the potential threat of predicted climatic changes to marine and coastal systems, the Oceans and Coastal Areas Programme Activity Centre of the United Nations Environment Programme (UNEP), in cooperation with the Intergovernmental Oceanographic Commission (IOC) of UNESCO, launched a systematic approach to assess the likely impacts of climatic changes in the geographical areas covered by the UNEP-sponsored Regional Seas Programme. As a result, 11 task teams were established for regions covered by the Programme (Mediterranean, Caribbean, South Pacific, East Asian Seas, South Asian Seas, South-west Pacific, West and Central Africa, Eastern Africa, Persian/Arabian Gulf, Black Sea and Red Sea). The task of the teams was to assess the environmental, economic and social problems of coastal seas and the adjacent terrestrial areas that are likely to follow on the heels of predicted climatic changes, and to identify suitable response measures and policy options that may be adopted to mitigate or avoid the negative impacts of these changes.

During the work on the Mediterranean regional study (UNEP, 1989a) carried out between 1987 and 1989 by UNEP's Coordinating Unit for the Mediterranean Action Plan (MEDU), it was felt that, although the general effects might be similar throughout the Mediterranean region, considerable differences in the impact of climatic changes could be expected at different sites and that, consequently, different response options would be required. Moreover, it became clear that, as in the case of global predictions, regional predictions may be used only for general policy guidance and that only site-specific studies could lead to practical management and policy decisions and actions of relevance to each particular location.

This is particularly true when assessing the impacts of future climatic changes given the influence of local geographic factors on rainfall and temperature patterns and microclimate, and in the case of sea level where tectonic movements, sediment compaction and extraction of oil, gas and usually water may result in local sea level changes several orders of magnitude greater than the predicted global mean sea level rise.

Therefore, in the framework of the Mediterranean regional study, six site-specific case studies were prepared during the period 1988–89 on estuarine systems, such as deltas of the rivers Ebro, Rhone, Po and Nile; Thermaikos Gulf and Ichkeul/Bizerte lakes. The final results of this work were published by Jeftic et al. (1992).

As a follow-up to the studies completed by 1989, a 'second-generation' series of five Mediterranean site-specific studies was prepared during the period 1990–93: Island of Rhodes (UNEP, 1994a), Kaštela Bay (UNEP, 1994b), the Syrian coast (UNEP, 1994c), the Maltese Islands (UNEP, 1994d), and the Cres-Lošinj archipelago (UNEP, 1994e). A third-generation series of three studies was then launched (Fuka-Matrouh region in Egypt, the

Albanian coast, Sfax region in Tunisia) in the framework of the wider Coastal Areas Management Programmes (CAMPs) of the UNEP-sponsored Mediterranean Action Plan. Since then, an effort is being made to include, when feasible, climatic change studies in the framework of relevant CAMPs.

This is an overall presentation compiling the results and experience gained through the Mediterranean regional study. The methodology of 14 completed first-, second-, and third-generation site-specific case studies in the Mediterranean region is reviewed (Jeftic et al. 1996).

THE CASE STUDIES

Methodology

First-generation case studies
In the absence of a generally accepted and tested methodology that could have been applied in a practical way to the development of the six, first-generation case studies on estuarine environments (deltas of the rivers Ebro, Rhone, Po and Nile; Thermaikos Gulf and Ichkeul/Bizerte lakes) completed by 1989, they were based on a set of general principles, assumptions and a good deal of common sense, taking into account the best available assumptions of the possible consequences of the predicted climatic changes and the best evolving scenarios – by that time – resulting from the work of the UNEP/WMO Intergovernmental Panel on Climate Change (IPCC) (Mitchell et al., 1990; IPCC, 1990).

Three of the six case studies were prepared by individual experts, one by collaboration of two experts familiar with the study area, and the remaining two by UNEP staff with the assistance of nine and 24 co-workers, respectively.

The studies were expected to have three recognizable components:

- a general description of the environment and the environmental conditions of the study area, as well as the socio-economic structures and activities that may be affected by climatic change;
- an assessment of the likely effect of expected climatic changes on the environment, man-made structures and economic activities; and
- a summary of the major conclusions with recommendations for possible actions that may mitigate or avoid the identified potentially negative impacts, or measures that may ease adaptation to these impacts.

Data already available from various sources were used as the basis for the studies and no new research was conducted during their preparation. As background to the preparation of the studies, a bibliography containing more than 1500 references on the effects of climatic change and related topics was compiled and published (UNEP, 1989b).

In preparing the first-generation case studies it became apparent that the assessment of likely impacts was constrained by the absence of scenarios of future climates on a regional, sub-regional and local scale. Therefore, the Climatic Research Unit of the University of East Anglia (CRU/UEA) was commissioned by UNEP to attempt to produce a Mediterranean basin scenario and to develop scenarios of future local climate for the selected case study areas.

The scenario covering the Mediterranean basin (Palutikof et al., 1992), and the more focused sub-regional and local scale scenarios, were completed only after the first-generation case studies themselves completed. Therefore, the assumptions concerning the magnitude and rate of climatic change used in the Mediterranean regional study and in the first-generation site-specific studies were those accepted at the UNEP/ICSU/WMO International Conference in Villach, 9–15 October 1985 – that is, increased temperature of 1.5–4.5°C and sea level rise of 20–140 cm before the end of the 21st century (UNEP/ICSU/WMO, 1986). For the time-horizon of the year 2025 (the time at which a greenhouse gas concentration equivalent to a doubling of pre-industrial CO_2 levels was deemed likely to have occurred), a temperature elevation of 1.5°C and sea level rise of 20 cm were assumed.

Second-generation case studies
Using the experience of the first-generation case studies, the preparation of five second-generation site-specific case studies (Island of Rhodes; Kaštela Bay; the Syrian coast, the Maltese islands; and the Cres-Lošinj archipelago) was initiated in 1990. The preparation of these studies was entrusted to national multidisciplinary task teams with relevant local knowledge and experience, established and guided by UNEP/MEDU, in close cooperation with the relevant national authorities. Each team was led by a national coordinator, and consisted of about ten national experts and a few (two or three) external members who assisted the overall work of each team.

At a preparatory meeting, each of the teams was briefed by the external members of the team on:

- IPCC's most recent scientific assessment of the anticipated magnitude and rate of global climatic and sea level change;
- the regional Mediterranean scenario of climatic change and the more specific sub-regional temperature, precipitation and sea level change scenarios relevant to the particular study area; and

- the main impacts that could be expected to result from climatic change. At the same meeting, the objectives and contents of the study were determined, and specific tasks assigned to each member of the team. Although individual members of each team had specific tasks assigned to them, the studies finalized by each team were the collective work of the team as a whole.

The overall objectives of the studies were identified as being:

- to identify and assess the possible implications of expected climatic change on the natural and man-made terrestrial, aquatic and marine ecosystems; population, including public health and demographic changes; land- and sea-use practices; coastal structures; and economic activities and development plans;
- to determine the areas, systems, structures and activities that appeared to be most vulnerable to the expected climatic changes; and
- to suggest policies and measures which may reduce, avoid or allow adaptation to the negative effects of the expected impact through changes in planning and management of coastal areas and resources.

These objectives were expected to be met using the presently available data and assumptions, and the best possible extrapolations from these data and assumptions. No research generating new data was carried out under the studies, although some existing data-sets were re-analysed and synthesized, to examine evidence for past trends.

Assumptions used in the studies were those accepted by the Second World Climate Conference – that is, an increase in temperature of 2–5°C, and a sea level rise of 65±35 cm by the end of the 21st century (UNEP/WMO/ICSU, 1990), as modified by the regional and relevant sub-regional scenarios prepared by the CRU/UEA, and the information available on local tectonic trends. The CRU/UEA scenarios for temperature and precipitation were based on the combined output of four general circulation models, statistically correlated with meteorological records from the Mediterranean basin. Although, generally, these scenarios indicate that in the Mediterranean basin the temperature change due to the greenhouse effect would be similar to the changes in global mean temperature, scenarios also show that the coastal regions, particularly in the north, are zones of very rapid transition, which emphasizes the need for the highly detailed scenarios. Regarding precipitation, scenarios indicate that it would probably increase in autumn and winter, but decrease in summer, particularly in the eastern Mediterranean.

In preparing the studies, increased air and sea-surface temperatures, and changes in local climate and weather (patterns of rainfall and winds in time and space; geographic distribution, intensity and frequency of storms) were taken into account as first-order impacts resulting from climatic changes. Consideration was also given to second-order impacts, such as changes in relative humidity, runoff and river flow rates; soil conditions, coastal biome distribution, coastal currents, wave regimes and sea water stratification and mixing; location and/or persistence of oceanic frontal systems; salinity and coastal water chemistry; patterns of coastal flooding and other episodic events; and human health and comfort.

Special consideration was given to the potential social and economic impacts of:

- changes in precipitation and temperature patterns modifying relative humidity and altering evapotranspiration rates, and thus likely to affect the hydrological cycle and local water balance; animal distribution and abundance, including pests and disease vectors; productivity of natural and agricultural systems; soil decomposition processes and fertility; human drinking water supplies; freshwater management practices; and coastal marine ecosystems, fisheries productivity and mariculture through changes in salinity and mixing of coastal waters; and

- changes in sea level, which may lead to increased frequency and intensity of flooding, as well as increased inland extent of flooding; rearrangement of coastal unconsolidated sediments and soils; increased soil salinity in areas previously unaffected; changed wave climates; accelerated dune and beach erosion; upward and landward retreat of the boundary between freshwater and brackish waters; greater upstream intrusion of saltwater wedges; shifts in bank and wetland vegetation; changes in the physical location of the terrestrial–aquatic boundary, changes in coastal water clarity, coastal water circulation patterns and sediment sink volumes; modification of offshore bottom profiles; changes in Marin and coastal terrestrial productivity; and alterations in sediment and nutrient flux rates, with consequent changes in marine primary production.

UNEP's guidance and coordination ensured that the structure and content of the studies were harmonized in order to facilitate the comparison of the findings on a Mediterranean scale.

The main findings, conclusions and recommendations of the case studies were presented and reviewed by a meeting of experts (Malta, September 1992) drawn from all five task teams (UNEP, 1992). The meeting proved to be very useful in providing the opportunity for a strong interaction between the task teams and for the comparison of their results. This led to a more balanced assessment of the relative significance of the impacts identified in the individual studies. As a consequence of this interaction, a number of conclusions and recommendations contained in the individual studies were revised or presented in a new, more sharply focused context, thus making them more useful for policy makers and managers.

Third-generation case studies
The third-generation case studies (the Fuka-Matrouh region in Egypt, the Albanian coast and the Sfax region in Tunisia) followed the methodology adopted and used for the preparation of the second-generation studies. The only changes were:

- setting the years 2030 and 2100 as the time horizons for the assessment of the impacts;
- preparing the studies in the wider framework of CAMPs for management and planning of land use and the use of resources in the same geographic areas/sites in the conditions of climatic change; and
- the use of assumptions as presented in 1992 to IPCC (IPCC, 1992) – that is, a global temperature elevation of 0.3°C per decade, and scenarios of elevated global temperatures of 0.9°C and 2.5°C were adopted for the years 2030 and 2100, respectively, as modified by the relevant sub-regional or local-scale scenarios prepared by the CRU/UEA; a global sea level rise of 16 cm by 2030 and 48 cm by 2100 was assumed on the basis of Wigley and Raper's analysis (Wigley and Raper, 1992), as modified by the available information on local tectonic trends, land movements and past trends in relative sea level.

The objectives of the studies were broadened by the addition of three specific items:

- to formulate recommendations for the planning and management of coastal areas and resources, as well as for the planning and design of major infrastructures and other systems;
- to provide an input into other projects and developments relevant to the subject of the study; and
- to provide useful information for policy and decision makers, managers, economists, and the general public.

Fourth-generation case studies
Three Coastal Areas Management Programmes (CAMPs) were approved in 1993 (Israel, Lebanon and Malta). In the framework of these programmes, studies on implications of climatic changes on respective coastal

Table 11.1   Major potential impacts identified in the studies

Site	Potential impact
Delta of Ebro, Spain	Increased coastal erosion; reshaping of coastline; loss and flooding of wetlands; reduced fisheries yield
Delta of Rhone, France	Erosion of unstable or threatened parts of coastline; reduction of wetlands and agricultural land; increased impact of waves; increased salinization of coastal lakes; destabilization of dunes; intensified tourism
Delta of Po, Italy	Increased flooding and high-water events; increased coastal erosion; retreat of dunes; damage to coastal infrastructure; salinization of soils; alteration to seasonal water discharge regimes; reduced near-shore water mixing and primary production; increased bottom water anoxia
Delta of Nile, Egypt	Increased coastal erosion; overtopping of coastal defences and increased flooding; damage to port and city infrastructure; retreat of barrier dunes; decreased soil moisture; increased soil and lagoon water salinity; decreased fisheries production
Ichkeul-Bizerte, Tunisia	Increased evapotranspiration leading to decreased soil moisture, reduced lake fertility and enhanced salinity; increased salinity of the lakes and shift to marine fish fauna; reduced extent of wetlands and loss of waterfowl habitat
Thermaikos Gulf, Greece	Inundation of coastal lowlands; saline water penetration in rivers; drowning of marshland; increased sea water stratification and bottom anoxia; decreased river runoff; salinization of ground water; decreased soil fertility; damage to coastal protective structures; extension of tourist season
Island of Rhodes, Greece	Increased coastal erosion; salinization of aquifers; increased soil erosion
Maltese Islands, Malta	Salinization of aquifers; increased soil erosion; loss of freshwater habitats; increased risk to human health, livestock and crops from pathogens and pests
Kaštela Bay, Croatia	Inundation of Pantana spring and Zrnovica estuary; increased salinization of estuaries and ground water; negative impact on coastal services and infrastructure; accelerated deterioration of historic buildings; increase in domestic, industrial and agricultural cultural water requirements
Syrian coast, Syria	Increased soil erosion; modification of vegetation cover due to increased aridity; increased salinization of aquifers; erosion of beaches and damage to coastal structures and human settlements due to exceptional storm surges

Table 11.1 (continued)

Site	Potential impact
Cres-Lošinj, Croatia	Increased salinization of lake Vrana; extension of tourist season; increased risk from forest fires
Albanian coast	Salinization of coastal aquifers and shortage of adequate quality drinking water; soil erosion (physical); extension of summer drought; extension of tourist season
Fuka-Matrouh, Egypt	Increased evapotranspiration and decreased rainfall; extension of summer aridity; increased coastal erosion; flooding in eastern part; decreased soil fertility
Sfax coastal area, Tunisia	Salinization of ground water; increased rainfall; possible flooding

areas were initiated during 1995/1996. Findings of these studies have not been integrated into this study.

COMPARATIVE ANALYSIS OF THE MAIN FINDINGS

Potential Impacts of Expected Climatic Changes on Natural Systems and Socio-economic Activities

Table 11.1 summarizes the major potential impacts of climatic changes identified in the case studies analysed in this chapter.

Not surprisingly, increased erosion of unstable or presently threatened parts of the coastline, inundation of coastal flatlands, loss of wetlands, and salinization of lagoons and coastal lakes, were singled out as the most probable negative consequences of climatic changes common to the four studied deltaic regions and the Thermaikos Gulf. A combined impact of relative sea level rise, decreased water and sediment flows, and the likely increased frequency and intensity of storms and waves were perceived as the principal factors contributing to these effects.

Salinization of aquifers due to sea level rise was identified as potentially the most important impact of climatic changes common to all studied islands, Kaštela Bay, Sfax, Albania and the Syrian coast. Due to hydrological processes occurring at a distance from the coast reducing recharge to important water bodies such as lake Vrana, salinization may not be restricted to coastal aquifers. Reduced ground water recharge to this lake may enhance saline water penetration.

Superimposed on these widespread effects would be the specific impacts on agriculture and fisheries (e.g. in the deltas of Ebro, Nile and Rhone); coastal infrastructures and harbour installations; functioning of gravitational sewerage systems of settlements barely above the present mean sea level (e.g. Split) coastal defence systems (deltas of the Po and Nile, Thermaikos Gulf); and monuments of historic and artistic importance (e.g. Venice, Rhodes and Osor on Cres).

Increased soil erosion and the concomitant decrease in soil fertility would be aggravated in a number of areas (islands of Rhodes and Malta, Fuka-Matrouh, Thermaikos Gulf, Syrian coast). Hazards from forest fires, already a major problem in some areas (island of Rhodes, Cres-Lošinj archipelago), would increase considerably with the predicted increase in the aridity of these areas. The expected increase in the intensity and frequency of episodic events, such as extended droughts and temperature extremes, would affect agriculture, particularly in regions presently stressed by such events (e.g. the delta of Rhone).

The Ichkeul-Bizerte lakes would share many of the problems identified in the deltaic areas, and would experience a considerable shift from their present fresh and brackish water to marine flora and fauna. Similar shifts could be expected in deltaic areas with large coastal lagoons and lakes (e.g. lake Manzala in the delta of Nile). These shifts, combined with the potential reduction in the area of wetlands, would significantly affect migratory birds, many of which depend on the availability of suitable Mediterranean habitats for over-wintering and transit areas during their north–south migrations.

Not all the impacts of predicted climatic changes were considered as necessarily harmful. Tourism was singled out in several studies (e.g. the delta of the Rhone, Albania, islands of Rhodes and Malta, Cres-Lošinj archipelago) as one sector of the economy that may potentially benefit from climatic changes, mainly due to the extended duration of the tourist season. Agriculture and aquaculture, aided by modern agricultural techniques, genetic engineering, introduction of new species and cultivation of better varieties of traditionally used species, were also seen as potential beneficiaries of climatic changes in certain areas (the delta of Ebro, Cres-Lošinj archipelago).

Realizing that during the time horizons adopted for the studies, the main driving forces shaping the economies and social changes of the study areas would be only very marginally related to climatic changes, no serious attempt was made in any of the studies to assess the economic or social costs and benefits that may be associated with the impact of climatic changes.

As a consequence of the high uncertainty surrounding the scenarios used in the preparation of the studies, the assessment of impacts in the first-generation studies and, to a lesser extent, also in the second-generation studies, is largely qualitative. For instance, a rise in sea level would undoubtedly enhance coastal erosion but the magnitude of this erosion is difficult to evaluate without precise figures for the rates of change at local level. Despite such uncertainty, the case studies clearly indicate that the overriding feature of future impacts of climatic changes will be an exacerbation of existing environmental problems. It was also recognized that these impacts, particularly in the short term, will be of only minor significance when compared with the impacts caused by non-climate related factors such as inadequate freshwater management regimes, and poor land use planning and management, coastal and soil erosion.

Actions Suggested to Avoid, Mitigate and Adapt to the Predicted Impacts

Table 11.2 clearly indicates that the first-generation case studies produced recommendations of little value to policy and decision makers since they emphasize the nature and extent of the inadequacies of existing databases, without clearly articulating what the longer term value of such data might be for planning and management of coastal areas under conditions of future climatic change and sea level rise. One study (Ichkeul-Bizerte lakes, Tunisia) made no recommendations or suggestions for response measures, while the remaining five emphasized the need for better models, and improved monitoring, information and databases, risk assessment and response scenario building.

In contrast, the second- and third-generation studies generated more concrete proposals for response measures, including the need for changes to codes and standards such as those covering construction and engineering works, and the need to take the identified potential impacts into consideration in the future planning and management plans for coastal areas and resources.

The difference in perspective between the recommendations of the first- and second-/third-generation studies reflects, at least in part, the nature of the experts involved in completing the site-specific studies. The first-generation studies were completed on the whole by natural scientists, concerned more with the theoretical basis for impact assessment and the uncertainties surrounding their predictions of future impact, rather than with the day-to-day realities facing coastal zone managers. Managers must respond to the exigencies of present problems and require a clear statement of likely changes and the levels of uncertainty associated with quantitative estimates of change, if they are to assess adequately the comparative costs and benefits of alternative courses of action. By including 'end-users' in the task teams assembled for the second-generation case studies, the management perspective was incorporated from the outset and hence the recommendations for

Table 11.2   Major potential response measures identified in the studies

Site	Potential response measures
Delta of Ebro, Spain	Basic research on hydrology; detailed mapping and risk assessment; study of coastal processes; establishment of long-term data series; assessment of possible changes in insect pest populations; redefinition the Ebro management unit; re-evaluation of the existing delta development plans in the light of findings of the case study
Delta of Rhone, France	Improved documentation of recent environmental trends; mapping of areas at risk; identification of natural indicators of vulnerability and plants suitable to counter erosion; modelling biological system response under differing environmental conditions
Delta of Po, Italy	Creation of information systems; monitoring and modelling of trends; analysis of future trends and preparation of scenarios
Delta of Nile, Egypt	Elaborate scenarios of future environmental and socio-economic conditions; establishment of database for future planning purposes
Thermaikos Gulf, Greece	Monitoring of long-term trends; mapping of high-risk areas; readjustment of present flood defences; possible damming of Thessaloniki Bay and engineering control of water level
Island of Rhodes, Greece	Coastal zone management (land use, set-back zones) and readjustment of coastal building standards; water resources management and exploration for additional water resources; reforestation; study of the consequences of the changes to tourist season and services in relation to the island economy and population
Maltese Islands, Malta	Local and national development plans to take into consideration the possible impact of climatic change; assessment in detail of the impact of sea level rise and the local climatic changes on the local aquifers; prevention of soil erosion by maintenance of existing dry stone walls and terrace systems and by planting of trees; assessment of vulnerability of humans, livestock and crops to future increase in pests and pathogens
Kaštela Bay, Croatia	Taking into account the findings of the study for ongoing and future construction projects in the region; re-evaluation of existing land-use plans and zoning policies for buildings; revision of major policies and programmes of flood-hazard mitigation measures

Table 11.2 (continued)

Site	Potential response measures
Syrian coast, Syria	Integrated coastal zone management and planning, which should include development of water management plans, solution to problems of soil and coastal erosion and increased salinization; monitoring programmes and establishment of a data bank on natural and cultivated vegetation
Cres-Lošinj, Croatia	Trapping and storage of peak flow of karstic rivers over the Kvarner mainland; artificial recharge of the karstic underground aquifers during the prolonged summer dry season; elevation of coastal defence structures in order to protect valuable existing buildings and structures; periodic revision of physical and urban development plans; assessment of the requirement of the extended tourist season in the light of demand for additional space and services; application of suitable protective measures against forest fires
Albanian coast	Integrated planning of the coastal area; development of a strategy for the prevention of climatic impacts, including a monitoring system and local inventories of impacts
Fuka-Matrouh, Egypt	Installation of coastal protection measures in critical areas; promotion of drought-tolerant vegetation; fresh water management;
Sfax, Tunisia	Preparation of climatic atlas; collection of relevant quality data; management of water resources; prohibition of agriculture development; replanting of littoral zone with suitable species.

response measures include many actions that could be immediately acted on by the responsible authorities and institutions.

Learning from the experience of the impact studies carried out in the Mediterranean and other regions of the world, the following principles should be considered:

- Case studies should be prepared either at the explicit request of prospective end-users or following a firm confirmation of support from a potential user of the case study.
- The potential end-users should be involved in the formulation of the outline and participate in carrying out the study.
- The climatic impact study should be prepared within the framework of more broadly based integrated coastal zone management plan.

- The studies should contain recommendations for policy options to mitigate and avoid negative impacts of expected climatic changes.
- Social and economic considerations should be considered for the response options.

CONCLUSIONS

Although future global mean temperature can be predicted using global circulation models (GCMs) with a reasonable degree of certainty, local temperature change is more difficult to predict given the strong influence of physical and biological features such as topography, wind, precipitation and vegetation cover. The forecasts of future precipitation on local and sub-regional scales developed for various climate scenarios by the CRU/UEA have significantly higher degrees of uncertainty than do those for temperature. Nevertheless, it is clear from these models and forecasts that significant regional and local variations in extent and magnitude of changes will occur in the Mediterranean basin. Even where the extent of future climatic changes is similar, the nature of the impacts may differ significantly. Reducing rainfall in Malta by 10 per cent would have far greater impacts on the natural environment and human drinking water supply than reducing rainfall by a comparable amount in the Cres-Lošinj archipelago, for example. Similarly, predicted sea level rise will have more significant impacts in low-lying deltas such as those of the Po, Rhone, Ebro and Nile, than in the relatively steep rocky shorelines of Malta, the Cres-Lošinj archipelago, Kaštela Bay and the Syrian coast. The analysis of the 14 Mediterranean case studies amply demonstrates that the impacts will be highly site-specific, and therefore effective adaptation to these impacts should also be eminently site-specific. Unfortunately, there are no universally applicable methodologies for the assessment of the risks and benefits that may be associated with climatic changes, and for the determination of the most vulnerable sites, systems or processes. A good deal of common sense, inspired insight, and intellectual intuition, are still among the best, and indeed the only, tools available to scientists, managers and policy makers. In spite of the shortcomings in the present approaches to the assessment of climatic change impacts, and the inherent uncertainties underlying the assumptions on which such assessments are based, certain generalized conclusions and recommendations can be drawn from the completed Mediterranean case studies reviewed here:

- For annual mean temperature, the greatest sensitivity to greenhouse warming was shown for the mainland areas to the north-east, and in the south-west. Temperature increases lower than the global mean temperature change were indicated over the islands and southern coast of the Mediterranean Sea. It is important to note that the Mediterranean coast was generally shown to be a zone of rapid transition, emphasizing the need for the detailed scenarios as a basis for the CAMPs. The scenarios for precipitation are much more difficult to evaluate since the confidence that can be placed in sub-grid-scale scenarios of precipitation is low. Areas of increase for annual precipitation are shown to lie mainly over the northern part of the study area, and over the central Mediterranean between Italy and Tunisia.

- Potential evapotranspiration is likely to increase throughout the Mediterranean. Coupled with increases in temperature this would lead to an increase in land degradation, deterioration of water resources and, in the long run, may affect agricultural production and practices, as well as natural vegetation and aquatic ecosystems. Exceptional events of drought or rainfall and floods, marine storms, tidal surges, and enhanced coastal water stratification and eutrophication could increase in frequency.

- At the level of the case study sites, the smallest annual temperature change is indicated for Sfax and Fuka-Matrouh (0.7–0.8°C by 2030; 2.0–2.3°C by 2100), while the greatest annual warming may occur over Cres-Lošinj Islands (1.8–2.0°C by 2030; 3.5–3.9°C by 2100). In the case of precipitation, the scenarios suggest an increase in the annual total for Rhodes, Kaštela Bay and Sfax and a reduction for Fuka-Matrouh and the Syrian coastal region. For Malta and Cres-Lošinj, the scenarios suggest little change. Since summer precipitation is negligible over much of the Mediterranean basin, changes in the annual total are less significant than changes between autumn and winter, and for all case study areas, with the exception for Malta, scenarios indicate an increase in precipitation during the winter. A decrease in summer precipitation, while it has little impact on the annual total, may nevertheless have significant effects on plant growth through extension of the summer period of water stress.

- The CRU/UEA scenarios represent a considerably improved basis on which to assess the future impacts of climatic change, when compared with the low spatial resolution associated with scenarios constructed directly from GCM output. However, it must be recognized that the uncertainties associated with the resultant scenarios in precipitation are much greater than those associated with the temperature scenarios. Assessing second-order impacts, such as changes in vegetation distribution patterns, evapotranspiration and soil fertility, is further constrained by the fact that the parameters modelled on global, regional and sub-regional scales, while they may serve as crude indicators of the direction of change in biological communities, are generally not the key variables determining biotic distribution patterns. Factors such as the length of the growing season, frost occurrence and length of drought periods are generally more significant determinants and reliable indicators of species distribution, reproduction and survival than mean annual temperature or total annual precipitation.

- By developing seasonal scenarios for the case study areas, the CRU/UEA has potentially addressed this issue, but even so the climate data required to quantify future biological changes adequately are far from complete. Work on improving the precision of area/site-specific scenarios should continue as one of the fundamental prerequisites for reducing the uncertainties associated with impact assessment. At the same time, work is required in developing scenarios for those climate variables that are considered of critical importance in determining the distribution and abundance of biota and, hence, the overall productivity of natural and anthropogenically managed systems.

- The physical impact of sea level rise on the Mediterranean lowland coasts can be predicted, and even modelled quantitatively on the basis of the presently available data and information on morphology, hydrodynamics, sediment budgets, land subsidence and the effects of artificial structures. Equally, the impacts of altered rainfall distribution on surface and ground water could be modelled quantitatively, and the effects of increased air temperatures and changed soil-water parameters on biological systems can be estimated, at least qualitatively, thus providing some idea of impacts on agriculture and fisheries. What is much more difficult to estimate, however, is the impact of these physical and biological changes on the future socio-economic framework of these threatened lowlands, and the future anthropogenic impacts on the environment.

- In the next few decades, the impacts of non-climatic factors, such as population dynamics and present development plans, on the natural, social and economic systems of the Mediterranean, will most probably far exceed the direct impacts of climatic changes. Nevertheless, longer-term changes in climate may contribute quite significantly, particularly along the southern shores of the Mediterranean and at some vulnerable sites elsewhere, to the vulnerability of coastal communities to adverse environmental conditions, and impair the sustainable development of coastal areas. The sectors of the economy most likely to be affected may well be tourism and agriculture. Traditional fisheries are already overexploiting the productive capacity of the Mediterranean Sea, and climatic change will probably add little to this stress. Aquaculture may benefit from future environmental changes. Coastal wetlands and low-lying areas, and deltas may suffer, with consequent effects on agriculture and migratory birds.

- The marine and coastal terrestrial environment of the Mediterranean is strongly influenced by climate-driven events and processes, frequently originating at a considerable distance from the site of impact. Examples of such teleconnections include exchange of water masses through the Straits of Gibraltar; the hydrology of the North Adriatic drainage basin; the structure and movement of Levantine water masses; and the cyclogenesis of the Mediterranean basin.

- Expected climatic changes will affect surface and ground water flows and river regimes; the availability of surface and ground water; the incidence of floods and the amounts of sediment and nutrient transported and delivered to the sea; the movement of marine water masses (waves, currents, tides), especially the direction and intensity of storms and of extreme high and low water limits (tidal ranges); natural ecosystems, through increased temperature and its effects on water and soil qualities; and human use of the coastal lowland regions (0–5 m) as a consequence of sea level rise and altered conditions for agriculture, fishing, industry, tourism and environmental quality.

- The effects of sea level rise are most predictable even though the extent of sea level rise is difficult to foresee. A global mean eustatic rise in sea level of about 20 cm by 2025 would not, in itself, have a significant impact in the Mediterranean, except locally. However, local sea level changes could be substantially greater than this in some areas because of natural land subsidence, which may be enhanced by excessive ground water extraction. The negative impacts will be felt in low-lying areas, deltas and coastal cities.

- Among the most likely consequences of sea level rise will be increased direct wave impact on exposed coasts (e.g. the coastal barrier of Venice lagoon, beach resorts of the Rhone delta) and on harbour installations (e.g. Alexandria, Port Said, La Golette-Tunis); increased frequency and intensity of flooding of estuaries, canals and lagoons, with potentially serious consequences for agriculture, aquaculture, lagoonal fisheries and wildlife (e.g. the delta of the Ebro and Ichkeul/Bizerte); and worsening of existing shore erosion problems (e.g. the deltas of the Nile and Rhone).

- By the middle of the century, the impact on coastal settlements and construction (e.g. harbours, coastal roads) might be considerable in places where they are only slightly above the present mean sea level (e.g. Venice). Historic settlements and sites may require special, often quite expensive, protection measures, while the problem of other structures should be addressed through their gradual transformation or translocation.

- Many unprotected shorelines and low-lying regions of the Mediterranean currently suffer from erosion and experience periodic inundation during high sea level conditions (e.g. storms). Any increase in the mean sea level, or in the frequency and intensity of episodic events affecting that level, would worsen the present situation. However the dynamic character and the long-term non-climatic coastline changes are not legislatively recognized. Usually back shore space is lacking to accommodate the retreating coastline. Only the application of highly site-specific combinations of adaptive and protective measures can mitigate or avoid the problems caused by erosion and inundation. For the Mediterranean situation preference should be given, whenever applicable, to soft, non-engineering solutions.

- Sea water intrusion into coastal aquifers will intensify with an elevation of mean sea level, and worsen the already quite widespread freshwater supply difficulties experienced in a number of locations (e.g. Malta) along the shores of the Mediterranean. The best response to the expected impact would seem to be the timely adoption of more rational freshwater management policies and measures, based on realistic analyses and projections of future freshwater demand. Such projections are dependent on realistic scenarios of future socioeconomic conditions.

- Regarding sea level change, responses options can be either preventive or reactive. For example, in some instances entire economically important coasts and lagoon margins can be walled in to protect irreplaceable coastal uses and values (e.g. harbours, towns of historical or artistic value, lagoonal resources, specialized agriculture), while in others uneconomic crops could be gradually replaced with lagoons or ponds to make them into aquaculture and nature reserves and to act as a buffer zone, since their inner margins can be more easily protected than the exposed coast.

- Until the middle of the 21st century, the impact on marine resources, natural vegetation and crops is not likely to be significant, except in regions where climatic or soil conditions are already marginal, although forested areas may experience increased risk from fires. Due to changes in precipitation and temperature, gradual latitudinal and altitudinal shifts in vegetation belts may occur in some areas. The positive economic impacts and opportunities created by these shifts may be considerable, particularly if combined with modern agricultural practices (e.g. genetic engineering, introduction of species to areas where they cannot grow under present conditions).

- The changes in climatic conditions are expected to have only a very limited effect on the distribution and dynamics of the Mediterranean coastal human population, which will remain strongly influenced by non-climatic factors. In areas where tourism development is at present limited by temperature conditions, an increase in temperature could lead to a gradual extension of the tourist season, with concomitant environmental problems and economic benefits.

Sectoral approaches addressing the impacts of climatic changes will not lead to their successful long-term solution. The most promising general policy option to avoid or mitigate the eventual negative impacts of expected climatic changes is the broad application of integrated coastal zone planning and management, which takes into account, among other factors, the long-term trends in climatic conditions. In this context, long-term national socio-economic development plans will have to be re-examined in order to take into account not only the presently obvious trends and available resources, but the influence the changed climate may have on these trends and on the utilization of the resources.

Raising public awareness about the problems that may be associated with expected climatic changes is of great importance as it may facilitate societal decision making and generate the necessary public support for measures and expenditures that may seem, by an uninformed public, to be unjustified.

However, the dynamic character and the long term non-climatic coastline changes have not yet been factored into coastal legislation. Under the current coastal land uses, late response options could be particularly difficult, as most of the back shore urban space is unsuitable to accommodate any possible future retreat of the economically important coastal activities Only application of high site-specific combinations of adaptive and protective measures can be viable to mitigate or avoid potential problems caused by increasing erosion as a result of rising sea level.

On the other hand the gradual changes in climatic conditions are expected to have only a very limited effect on the distribution and the dynamics of the coastal human population, which is expected to remain strongly influenced by non-climatic factors. For the current Mediterranean situation preference should be given, whenever applicable, to soft, non-engineering solutions, reinforcing the long-term coastal integrated planning option.

In conclusion, the early preparation of the Mediterranean climate impact studies could be considered as a very cost-effective and successful exercise through which countries and their own interdisciplinary experts, including managers, planners and policy makers, were mobilized to consider the potential threat that climate change may pose to their environment and socio-economic development.

REFERENCES

IPCC (1990), *Strategies for Adaptation to Sea Level Rise,* Report of the Coastal Zone *Management Subgroup,* Response Strategies Working Group.

IPCC (1992), *IPCC Working Group 1: Climatic Change 1992: The Supplementary Report to the IPCC Scientific Assessment,* edited by J.T. Houghton, B.A. Callander and S.K. Varney. Cambridge University Press, Cambridge, pp. 1–22

Jeftic, L., S. Keckes and J. Pernetta (1996), *Climatic Change and the Mediterranean,* Vol. 2. Edward Arnold, London.

Jeftic, L., J.D. Milliman and G. Sestini (1992), *Climatic Change and the Mediterranean.* Edward Arnold, London.

Mitchell, J.F.B., S. Manabe, V. Meleshko and T. Tokioka (1990), 'Equilibrium climatic change – and its implications for the future'. In: *Climate Change: The IPCC Scientific Assessment,* Houghton, J.T., Jenkins, G.J. and Ephraums, J.J. (eds) Cambridge University Press, Cambridge, pp. 131–174.

Palutikof, J.P., X. Guo, T.M.L. Wigley and J.Y. Gregory (1992), *Regional Changes in Climate in the Mediterranean Basin Due to Global Greenhouse Gas Warming.* MAP Technical Reports Series No. 66. UNEP, Athens.

UNEP (1989a), Sestini, G., L. Jeftic and D.J. Milliman, *Implications of Expected Climate Changes in the Mediterranean Region: An Overview.* MAP Technical Reports Series No. 27. UNEP, Athens.

UNEP (1989b), *Bibliography on Effects of Climate Change and Related Topics.* MAP Technical Reports Series No. 29. UNEP, Athens.

UNEP (1992), *Report of the Meeting on Implications of Climate Changes on Mediterranean Coastal Areas (Island of Rhodes, Kaštela Bay, Syrian Coast, Malta and Cres/Lošinj Islands). Valletta, 15–19 September 1992.* UNEP(OCA)/ MED WG.55/7. UNEP, Athens.

UNEP (1994a), *Implications of Expected Climatic Changes on the Island of Rhodes.* UNEP(OCA)/MED WG.55/2 rev. UNEP, Athens.

UNEP (1994b), Implications of *Expected Climatic Changes on Kaštela Bay.* UNEP(OCA)/MED WG.55/4 rev. UNEP, Athens.

UNEP (1994c), *Implications of Expected Climatic Changes on the Syrian Coast.* UNEP(OCA)/MED WG.55/6 rev. UNEP, Athens.

UNEP (1994d), *Implications of Expected Climatic Changes on Malta.* UNEP(OCA)/MED WG.55/3 rev. UNEP, Athens.

UNEP (1994e), *Implications of Expected Climatic Changes on Cres-Lošinj Islands.* UNEP(OCA)/MED WG.55/5 rev. UNEP, Athens.

UNEP/ICSU/WMO (1986), *Report of International Conference on the Assessment of the Role of CO_2 and other Greenhouse Gases in Climate Variations and Associated Impacts.* Villach, 9–15 October 1985. WMO, Geneva.

UNEP/WMO/ICSU (1990), 'Statement by the UNEP/WMO/ICSU International Conference on the Assessment of the Role of Carbon Dioxide and Other Greenhouse Gases in Climate Variations and Associated Impacts' (Geneva, 29 October–7 November 1990). In: *The Greenhouse Effect, Climatic Change and Ecosystems.* SCOPE Report No. 29, John Wiley, London, pp. xx–xxiv.

Wigley, T.M.L. and S.C.B. Raper (1992), 'Implications for climate and sea-level of revised IPCC emissions scenarios'. *Nature,* **357**: 293–300.

12. Climate change and coastal zones: an overview of the state-of-the-art on regional and local vulnerability assessment

Horst Sterr, Richard J.T. Klein and Stefan Reese

(WHY) ARE VULNERABILITY ASSESSMENTS NEEDED?

Human population is attracted to coastal zones to a greater extent than to other regions. Urbanisation and the rapid growth of coastal cities have therefore been a dominant population trend over the last decades, leading to the development of numerous megacities in all coastal regions around the world. At least 200 million people were estimated to live in the coastal floodplain in 1990 (in the area inundated by a 1 in 1000 year flood) and it is likely that their number will increase to 600 million by the year 2100 (Nicholls and Mimura, 1998). Collectively, this is placing growing demands on coastal resources as well as increasing people's exposure to coastal hazards. In historic times, but even more pronounced in recent years, coastal populations around the world have suffered from serious disasters caused by storm floods and related wave and wind attack and precipitation. A dramatic example could be seen in the coastal region of eastern India (State of Orissa), where a tropical storm in October 1999 caused thousands of deaths and the displacement and impoverishment of millions of residents in a large coastal area.

Global climate change and the threat of accelerated sea-level rise exacerbate the already existing high risks of storm surges, severe waves and tsunamis. Climate change may not only enhance the most threatening extreme events (e.g. through increasing storminess) but also aggravate long-term biogeophysical effects, such as sea-level rise, shoreline erosion, sediment deficits, saltwater intrusion into coastal aquifers and the loss of coastal wetlands.

Unlike many other anticipated consequences of climate change, global sea-level rise is already taking place. Over the last 100 years, global sea level rose by 1.0–2.5 mm/year. Present estimates of future sea-level rise induced by climate change, as presented in the IPCC Second Assessment Report and shown in Figure 12.1, range from 20 to 86 cm for the year 2100, with a best estimate of 49 cm (including the cooling effect of aerosols). Moreover, model projections show that sea level will continue to rise (although at a slower rate) beyond the year 2100, owing to lags in climate response, even with assumed immediate stabilisation of greenhouse gas emissions.

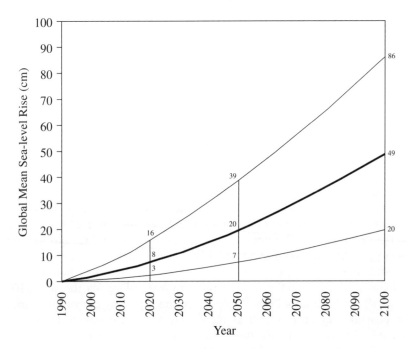

*Figure 12.1   Projected sea-level rise for the period 1990–2100, using
scenario IS92a ('Business-as-Usual')*

In view of these existing hazards and increasing risks in coastal regions, there is a great need to gain as much insight as possible into the exact nature and extent of possible risk increases related to future climate trends. Thus it is essential to carry out analyses of the coastal systems' biogeophysical responses to climate-change impacts as well as to assess the threats posed to human society. As Klein and Nicholls (1998) have stated, vulnerability to impacts is a multi-dimensional concept, encompassing biogeophysical, economic, institutional and socio-cultural factors. Vulnerability of coastal zones has been defined as 'the degree of incapability to cope with the consequences of climate change and accelerated sea-level rise' (Bijlsma *et al.*,

1996). Thus vulnerability assessment includes the assessment of both anticipated impacts and available adaptation options.

Knowledge of vulnerability enables coastal scientists and policy-makers
to anticipate impacts that could emerge as a result of sea-level rise. It can
thus help to prioritise management efforts that need to be undertaken to
minimise risks or to mitigate possible consequences. In view of the high
natural and socio-economic values that might be threatened and/or lost in
coastal zones, it is therefore important to identify the types and magnitude
of problems that different coastal areas may have to face, as well as to identify possible solutions. In some cases, assistance may be needed to overcome
these problems. Socio-economic data are of great importance for estimating the potential costs and benefits of possible adaptation strategies, such
as protection, retreat or accommodation. Experience shows that these
response options are best imbedded into the process of integrated coastal
zone management (ICZM), but that developing an ICZM framework is
usually a longer-term rather than a short-term issue in most coastal regions
(WCC '93, 1994).

A SPATIAL PERSPECTIVE ON THE VULNERABILITY OF COASTS

Since 1990, a number of major efforts have been made to develop guidelines and methodologies to assess coastal vulnerability to sea-level rise.
When assessing impacts of sea-level rise, it is the local change (or rate of
change) in relative sea level that matters, not the global or regional average.
Relative – or observed – sea level is the level of the sea relative to the land.
While it is affected by absolute changes in sea level, relative sea level is also
influenced by vertical movements of the land, which may be of regional or
only local extent. These vertical movements are mostly natural phenomena,
but human activities may be important as well. First, extraction of water
and hydrocarbons can induce or enhance subsidence of coastal lowlands.
In specific regions, this subsidence can equal or exceed the previously mentioned projected global sea-level rise. Often-quoted examples of cities that
have subsided as a result of groundwater exploitation include Venice
(Italy), Bangkok (Thailand), Shanghai (China) and Tokyo (Japan). Second,
removal or reduction of sediment supplies in deltas makes natural subsidence more apparent, as it inhibits compensating accretion. Third, in
reclaimed coastal lowlands, oxidation and compaction of peat can lead to
considerable declines in land level which can equal or exceed the projected
global sea-level rise (Klein and Nicholls, 1999).

Irrespective of the primary causes of sea-level rise (climate change, natural or human-induced subsidence, dynamic ocean effects), natural coastal systems can be affected in a variety of ways. From a societal perspective, the six most important biogeophysical effects are:

1. increasing flood-frequency probabilities and enhancement of extreme flood-level risks;
2. erosion and sediment deficits;
3. gradual inundation of low-lying areas and wetlands;
4. rising water tables;
5. saltwater intrusion;
6. biological effects.

It is clear that these effects would usually not occur in isolation. Along tropical coastlines such as in Senegal, for example, sea-level rise causes accelerated offshore transport of fine sediments (i.e. erosion), leading to destabilisation of mangroves and, subsequently, to enhanced flood risks and rising water tables (Nicholls *et al.*, 1995).

PAST VA EXERCISES: THE BENEFITS AND DRAWBACKS OF THE COMMON METHODOLOGY

In 1992, the former Coastal Zone Management Subgroup of the Intergovernmental Panel on Climate Change (IPCC) proposed a Common Methodology for Assessing the Vulnerability of Coastal Areas to Sea-level Rise. The Common Methodology was drafted to assist countries in making first-order assessments of potential coastal impacts of and adaptations to sea-level rise. The Common Methodology and similar approaches have been applied in about 25 national assessments and one global assessment. These studies have served as preparatory assessments, identifying priority regions and priority sectors and providing a first screening of possible measures. They stimulated a methodological debate on the estimation of climate change impacts in coastal areas, but also the development of alternative approaches.

In addition to the Common Methodology, the generic IPCC Technical Guidelines for Assessing Climate Change Impacts and Adaptations have been developed (Carter *et al.*, 1994) and then elaborated into a form appropriate for coastal regions (Klein and Nicholls, 1998). Both the Common Methodology and the Technical Guidelines comprise seven consecutive analytical steps for vulnerability assessment. However, they are not identical. In Figure 12.2, the Common Methodology and the Technical Guidelines are compared.

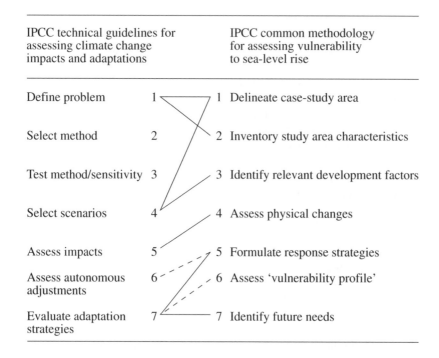

IPCC technical guidelines for assessing climate change impacts and adaptations		IPCC common methodology for assessing vulnerability to sea-level rise
Define problem	1	1 Delineate case-study area
Select method	2	2 Inventory study area characteristics
Test method/sensitivity	3	3 Identify relevant development factors
Select scenarios	4	4 Assess physical changes
Assess impacts	5	5 Formulate response strategies
Assess autonomous adjustments	6	6 Assess 'vulnerability profile'
Evaluate adaptation strategies	7	7 Identify future needs

Figure 12.2   The IPCC Common Methodology compared with the IPCC Technical Guidelines

The difference between the two approaches in large part reflects the fact that the Common Methodology was developed specifically for application in coastal zones, whereas the Technical Guidelines have been designed to serve as a more generic framework for any natural or socio-economic system. Therefore, some of the steps outlined in the Technical Guidelines do not appear in the Common Methodology. For example, the definition of the problem and the selection of the method are steps 1 and 2 of the Technical Guidelines, while they are only implied in the Common Methodology. Testing the method is also not included as an explicit step in the Common Methodology, although the wide application of the Common Methodology and other similar approaches has allowed for extensive evaluation (e.g. WCC '93, 1994). Further, the assessment of autonomous adjustments is considered explicitly in the Technical Guidelines, but not in the Common Methodology. The final step of the Technical Guidelines, the evaluation of adaptation strategies, is again made up of seven consecutive steps, which approximate steps 5, 6 and 7 of the Common Methodology.

In spite of these differences, it is important to realise that no other methodology to assess coastal vulnerability has been applied as widely and evaluated as thoroughly as the Common Methodology. The Common Methodology has contributed to understanding the consequences of sea-level rise and encouraged long-term thinking about coastal zones. The results of comparative national vulnerability studies according to the Common Methodology show considerable variation in the degree of impacts from country to country, reflecting that certain settings are more vulnerable than others. Small islands, deltaic settings and coastal ecosystems appear particularly vulnerable (Bijlsma *et al.*, 1996).

With respect to the social and economic implications of sea-level rise and the issue of adaptation, a set of six vulnerability indicators has been outlined and applied in the Common Methodology. These are:

1. people affected;
2. people at risk;
3. capital value loss;
4. land area loss;
5. protection/adaptation costs;
6. wetland loss.

The indicators are used to establish national or regional vulnerability profiles, using the information from Table 12.1 for (semi-) quantification. In Europe, the countries that have carried out comprehensive assessments according to the Common Methodology are The Netherlands, Poland and Germany (Nicholls and Mimura, 1998).

Table 12.1   Vulnerability classes developed and used in the Common Methodology

	Vulnerability classes			
Impact categories	Low	Medium	High	Critical
People affected (no. of people/total population) × 100%	<1%	1–10%	10–50%	>50%
People at risk Σ (no. of people × flood probability)/1000	<10	10–100	100–500	>500
Capital value loss (total loss/1990 GNP) × 100%	<1%	1–3%	3–10%	>10%
Land loss (area loss/total area) × 100%	<3%	3–10%	10–30%	>30%
Protection/adaptation costs (annual cost/1990 GNP) × 100%	<0.05%	0.05–0.25%	0.25–1%	>1%
Wetland loss (area loss/total area) × 100%	<3%	3–10%	10–30%	>30%

The available results all emphasise the large potential impacts of sea-level rise on coastal societies, economics and ecology in Europe, where large concentrations of the population and economic infrastructure exist in coastal areas. Local studies (e.g. Turner *et al.*, 1995; Nicholls and Leatherman, 1995; Hamann and Hofstede, 1998) further support the conclusion that sea-level rise alone, notwithstanding other climate-related impacts, should be of great concern to national and regional governments. In all three European countries, the socio-economic impact potential is rather high, yet in terms of adaptation costs, Poland appears to be more vulnerable than The Netherlands and Germany (Table 12.2; Nicholls and Mimura, 1998).

In spite of the obtained valuable results, a number of problems have been identified with the Common Methodology (Klein and Nicholls, 1998). These problems can be summarised as follows:

- Many case studies that have used the Common Methodology have faced a shortage of the accurate and complete data necessary for impact and adaptation assessment. In particular, it has often been difficult to determine accurately the impact zone in many countries owing to the lack of basic data, such as the coastal topography.
- Many studies have been directed towards a single global scenario of sea-level rise (1 metre by 2100), often owing to a lack of more detailed data on coastal elevations, while most studies have ignored the spatial distribution of relative sea-level rise and other coastal implications of climate change, owing largely to a lack of regional climate scenarios.
- Although the Common Methodology encourages researchers to take into account the biogeophysical response of the coastal system to sea-level rise, lack of data and models for describing the complicated non-linear coastal processes have hindered detailed quantitative impact assessment. Many case studies have carried out a simple linear, first-order assessment by shifting the coastline landward by an amount corresponding with the sea-level rise scenario.
- As to adaptation, the Common Methodology has been less effective in assessing the wide range of technical, institutional, economic and cultural elements present in different localities. There has been concern that the methodology stresses a protection-orientated response, rather than consideration of the full range of adaptation options.
- Market-evaluation assessment frameworks, as applied in the Common Methodology, have proved inappropriate in many subsistence economies and traditional land-tenure systems.

Unfortunately, these problems are quite fundamental for any approach to vulnerability assessment and cannot be solved overnight. Therefore,

Table 12.2 Results from impact assessments using the IPCC Common Methodology, carried out for the coastal regions of The Netherlands, Germany and Poland

Country	SLR scenario (m)	People affected		People at risk		Capital value loss		Land loss		Wetland loss (km²)	Adaptation/protection costs	
		No. of people (1000s)	% total	No. of people (1000s)	% total	million US$	% GNP	km²	% total		million US$	% GNP
The Netherlands	1.0	10000	67	3600	24	186000	69	2165	6.7	642	12300	5.5
Germany	1.0	3200	3.9	309	0.3	7500	0.05	13900	3.9	2000	23500	2.2
Poland	0.1	N/A	N/A	25 (18)	0.1 (0.05)	1800	2	N/A	N/A	N/A	700+4	2.1+0.01
	0.3	N/A	N/A	58 (41)	0.1 (0.1)	4700	5	845	0.25	N/A	1800+8	5.4+0.02
	1.0	235	0.6	196 (146)	0.5 (0.4)	22000	24	1700	0.5	N/A	4800+400	14.5+1.2

both the Common Methodology and the Technical Guidelines only represent a step in an ongoing process, rather than an endpoint. In the immediate future, a more comprehensive effort needs to be made to develop tools and techniques that more readily meet the requirements of vulnerability assessment in an environment as dynamic as the coastal zone. In particular, more attention has to be devoted both to the hazardous effects of changing frequencies, intensities and occurrences within the area of extreme weather events and to the consideration of 'residual' risks reflecting existing adaptation policies.

A CONCEPTUAL FRAMEWORK FOR VULNERABILITY ASSESSMENT AND THE ROLE OF ADAPTATION

The potential socio-economic impacts of sea-level rise can be categorised as follows:

- direct loss of economic, ecological, cultural and subsistence values through loss of land, infrastructure and coastal habitats;
- increased flood risk to people, land and infrastructure and the above-mentioned values;
- other impacts related to changes in water management, salinity and biological activity.

Owing to the great diversity of natural coastal systems and to the local and regional differences in relative sea-level rise and other climatic changes, the occurrence of and response to these impacts will not be uniform around the globe. Vulnerability studies first need to analyse the extent to which the biogeophysical effects mentioned will occur in the natural system of a study area before the potential socio-economic impacts can be assessed. Table 12.3 lists the most important socio-economic sectors in coastal zones, and indicates from which biogeophysical effects they are expected to suffer direct socio-economic impacts. Indirect impacts (e.g. human health impacts resulting from deteriorating water quality) are also likely to be important to many sectors, but these are not shown in the table.

One can distinguish between natural system vulnerability and socio-economic vulnerability to climate change, although they are clearly related and interdependent. Figure 12.3 shows a conceptual framework for coastal vulnerability assessment that makes this distinction explicit. This framework helps to define the various concepts involved in vulnerability assessment and shows how these are related (Klein and Nicholls, 1999).

As shown in Figure 12.3, proper analysis of socio-economic vulnerability

Table 12.3   Qualitative synthesis of direct *socio-economic impacts of climate change and sea-level rise on a number of sectors in coastal zones*

	Biogeophysical effect					
Sector	Flood frequency	Erosion	Inundation	Rising water tables	Saltwater intrusion	Biological effects
Water resources			√	√	√	√
Agriculture	√		√	√	√	
Human health	√		√			√
Fisheries	√	√	√		√	√
Tourism	√	√	√			√
Human settlements	√	√	√	√		

to sea-level rise requires prior understanding of how the natural system would be affected. Hence, analysis of coastal vulnerability always starts with some notion of the natural system's *susceptibility* to the biogeophysical effects of sea-level rise, and of its natural capacity to cope with these effects (*resilience* and *resistance*). Susceptibility simply reflects the coastal system's potential to be affected by sea-level rise (e.g. a subsiding delta versus an emerging fjord coast), while resilience and resistance determine the system's stability in the face of possible perturbation. As applied in ecology, 'resilience' describes the speed with which a system returns to its original state after being perturbed, while 'resistance' describes the ability of the system to avoid perturbation in the first place. Susceptibility, resilience and resistance together determine the coastal system's *natural vulnerability* to biogeophysical effects of sea-level rise.

Resilience and resistance are functions of the natural system's capacity for *autonomous adaptation*, which represents the coastal system's natural adaptive response to sea-level rise. As opposed to susceptibility, which is largely independent of human influences, resilience and resistance are often affected by human activities. The effect of human activities need not only be negative: *planned adaptation* can serve to reduce natural vulnerability by enhancing the system's resilience and resistance and thereby adding to the effectiveness of autonomous adaptation (Klein and Nicholls, 1999).

The biogeophysical effects of sea-level rise give rise to a range of potential socio-economic impacts. This *impact potential* is the socio-economic equivalent of the natural system's susceptibility (see earlier), although now it is clearly dependent on human influences. In parallel with a coastal zone's natural vulnerability, which is a function of susceptibility and resil-

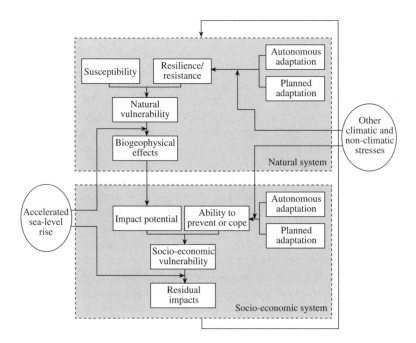

Figure 12.3   A conceptual framework for coastal vulnerability assessment

ience/resistance, *socio-economic vulnerability* is determined by the impact potential and society's technical, institutional, economic and cultural *ability to prevent or cope* with these impacts (i.e. its capacity to adapt within the time-scale of natural changes). As with the natural system's resilience and resistance, the potential for *autonomous adaptation* and *planned adaptation* determines the social system's ability to prevent or cope.

Finally, it is important to acknowledge the dynamic interaction that takes place between natural and socio-economic systems. Instead of being considered as two separate systems that exist independently of each other, natural and socio-economic systems are increasingly viewed as developing in a co-evolutionary way. This co-evolution is shown in Figure 12.3 by the feedback loop from the socio-economic system to the natural system.

INFORMATION GAINS FROM VULNERABILITY ASSESSMENTS AND THE ISSUE OF SCALE

The assessment of coastal vulnerability to climate-related impacts is a basic prerequisite for obtaining an understanding of the risks of climate change to the natural and the socio-economic coastal system. At global level, vulnerability assessment can serve to underpin the overall significance of sea-level rise for coastal societies and allows a comparison of the regional variations of sea-level rise-related risks (Hoozemans *et al.*, 1993; Nicholls and Mimura, 1998). On this scale, vulnerability assessment demonstrates that anticipated impacts might exceed the coping ability of some coastal regions and nations. At national and local level, vulnerability assessments are needed to identify the specifically vulnerable areas and sectors and reflect on the status of adaptation strategies designed to cope with adverse impacts such as flooding and erosion.

It becomes clear that first-order assessments carried out at global level will not be sufficient to achieve all of these objectives. Instead, descriptions and analyses are needed to explain in greater detail the conditions that lead to site- or area-specific exposures to risks of inundation, erosion or saltwater intrusion. Only on the basis of detailed and comprehensive information will it be possible for national and local policy-makers to design the most appropriate response strategies; that is, to decide whether and which protection, accommodation or retreat options are most suitable for minimising risks while optimising future coastal resource use. This is why in Germany, where adaptive policies are the responsibility of state governments, it has been decided to elaborate on an initial (first-order) national vulnerability assessment and refine the information base by means of a downscaling analytical procedure. Decisions on flood defence schemes at state level can now draw on specific topographic and economic data obtained from meso-scale studies. Furthermore, for particularly vulnerable coastal sections, even more detailed (micro-scale) databases are being put together, allowing for the informed evaluation of adaptation options.

PRACTICAL EXPERIENCES IN VULNERABILITY ASSESSMENT: METHODS, DATA AND TIME

In spite of the considerable interest in assessing coastal vulnerability to climate change, efforts are often hindered by the limited availability of data and resources for assessment. Sometimes there has also been a mismatch between the available data, the level of effort and the sophistication of the models utilised in vulnerability assessments. In some cases, this has led to inappropriate expectations concerning the outcomes of the assessment studies. To help to structure the approach, to optimise the level of effort, and to make the likely outcome of studies more explicit, it is useful to consider three levels of increasingly complex assessment (Table 12.4):

Table 12.4 Three levels of assessment in coastal zones, showing the respective requirements and the factors to be considered

Level of assessment	Requirements			Factors to consider		
	Time	Level of detail	Prior knowledge	Socio-economic factors	Other climatic changes	Non-climate changes
Screening assessment	2–3 months	Low	Low	No	No	No
Vulnerability assessment	6–12 months	Medium	Medium	Yes	Possible	No
Planning assessment	Continuous	High	High	Yes	Yes	Yes

Table 12.5   *Examples of the four different types of scenarios that can be used in coastal vulnerability assessment*

	Environmental changes	Socio-economic developments
Climate-induced	• Accelerated sea-level rise • Changes in rainfall patterns • Changes in sea-surface temperature • Changes in wind and wave patterns • El-Niño-related changes • Sediment-budget changes	• Autonomous adaptation • Planned adaptation
Not climate-induced	• Vertical land movement • Sediment-budget changes	• Population changes • Land-use changes • Changes in gross domestic product

- screening assessment (SA);
- vulnerability assessment (VA);
- planning assessment (PA).

As its name implies, SA is a screening approach, which – by its quick nature – focuses on one aspect of vulnerability: susceptibility. VA is a more comprehensive analysis, including explicit assessment of biogeophysical effects, socio-economic impacts and adaptation. PA involves analysis at an integrated level suitable for detailed coastal planning and would take place in the wider context of coastal management. This three-level approach relates to the issue of scale, as discussed in the previous section, in that more specific (policy-relevant) results will be obtained by a downscaling procedure, as also known from climate modelling (e.g. Warrick *et al.*, 1996).

Analysis in the framework of a country study should start with SA. The results of the SA can then be used to plan how VA might be most effectively implemented. VA will provide broad concepts and ideas concerning impacts and possible adaptation. PA might be viewed as the link between VA and detailed coastal planning and management (see later). PA asks more precise questions and, hence, the recommendations concerning possible adaptation measures would be more precise.

The remainder of this section presents a summary overview of important steps for coastal vulnerability assessment and of methods and tools that are available to complete these steps, as presented by Klein and Nicholls (1998, 1999).

Delineation of the Study Area

The study area, at a minimum, needs to be defined so that it at least encompasses the areas that might be physically affected by sea-level rise. It is advisable not to delineate the area too narrowly so as to account for the broad range of uncertainty that is involved in vulnerability assessment. The Common Methodology suggests consideration of all the land area below the contour line that corresponds with the height of a once-every-1000 years storm surge, given projected sea-level rise by the year 2100. In addition, the study area should consider saltwater intrusion and increased river flooding. In deltaic and estuarine areas, sea-level rise could cause these effects to extend tens of kilometres inland.

In the absence of the required data or other clear criteria to delineate the study area, it is recommended to use the contour line 2 metres above extreme high tide as the landward demarcation, unless the physiography or socio-economic structure of the area suggests that this arbitrary boundary will not suffice. This would be the case when impacts may also be expected to occur further inland (e.g. because of saltwater intrusion, extreme storm surges or increased river flooding) or, conversely, only much closer to the coast. The seaward extension of the study area should be based on the area that is likely to be subject to biogeophysical effects of sea-level rise, such as coral reefs, intertidal areas and wetlands, but may also include coastal waters containing valuable living resources.

Scenarios for Vulnerability Assessment

Scenarios for vulnerability assessment reflect plausible future conditions of all environmental and socio-economic parameters of interest. Some parameters can be considered universally important, while others are more site-specific. Relevant parameters have two degrees of freedom: environmental or socio-economic, and climate-induced or not climate-induced. This defines the matrix that is shown in Table 12.6.

Coastal vulnerability studies have focused primarily on scenarios of climate-induced changes in environmental conditions – especially sea level – of a given area (i.e. the upper left-hand box of Table 12.5). The lower part of Table 12.5 represents changes that will occur independently of climate change. As such, they form a reference case of what could be the environmental and socio-economic conditions in the absence of climate change. Scenarios of environmental and socio-economic developments not induced by climate change are increasingly being used in combination with climate scenarios. However, the fact that climate change will trigger socio-economic developments that in turn affect the manifestation of coastal impacts, is as yet often ignored (i.e. the upper right-hand box of Table 12.5). These developments embrace autonomous and planned adaptation. The potential for adaptation and the dynamic effects of its implementation need to be considered as an integral part of vulnerability assessment, for example by linking impact and adaptation scenarios.

For some coastal areas it could be worthwhile also to consider climatic changes other than sea-level rise (Bijlsma *et al.*, 1996). In mid- to high-latitude regions, a decrease in the return period of extreme rainfall events appears likely. This will be especially relevant for low-lying coastal areas prone to flooding. For cold temperate seas like the Baltic, but also for coral reefs and atolls, increasing seawater temperature could be important as this could affect the period of sea ice coverage and the coral growth potential, respectively. Reductions in sea ice and coral growth could reduce the coasts' ability to withstand wave impacts and erosion processes.

Other climatic changes that could have significant consequences for coastal zones, such as changes in wind direction and intensity, remain highly uncertain. The construction of plausible scenarios using the output of general circulation models is as yet impossible. However, sensitivity analyses using trend analysis (e.g. Zeidler *et al.*, 1997) or arbitrary scenarios (e.g. Peerbolte *et al.*, 1991) could be helpful in providing insight into the possible consequences.

Irrespective of the need to consider multiple scenarios, relative sea-level change remains the most important variable for coastal vulnerability assessment. As relative sea-level rise is the sum of global sea-level rise, regional oceanic effects and vertical land movements, it follows that scenarios for relative sea-level rise can be expressed as:

$$S_{r,t} = S_{g,t} + S_{o,t} + V \cdot t$$

where: $S_{r,t}$ = relative sea-level rise in year t (m);
$S_{g,t}$ = global sea-level rise in year t (m);
$S_{o,t}$ = regional sea-level change induced by oceanic changes in year t (m);
V = vertical land movement (m/year);
t = number of years in the future (base year 1990).

Given the uncertainties surrounding $S_{g,t}$, it is important that scenarios are selected so they encompass the likely change (see Figure 12.1). Therefore, a maximum scenario in which $S_{g,t}$ equals 1 metre in 2100 is quite appropriate for a screening approach. Not much information is usually available on the value of $S_{o,t}$, in which case this parameter should be neglected. Values for V can be assessed from a number of different sources, including geological analysis, geodetic surveys and the analysis of long-term tide-gauge records. Note that the equation above assumes that (1) vertical land movement is responsible for all the deviation of relative sea-level rise from global sea-level rise, and (2) vertical land movement is linear and will continue unchanged in the future. However, in areas subject to human-induced subsidence, future vertical land movements may be uncertain, as they will depend on human action, necessitating scenarios for subsidence.

Data Collection

The fundamental starting point for any assessment study is the acquisition of basic data on a number of important parameters that characterise the study area. Relevant characteristics of the natural coastal system include the following:

- coastal geomorphology/topography;
- relative sea-level changes;
- trends in sediment supply and erosion/accretion patterns;
- hydrological and meteorological characteristics;
- meteo-oceanographic characteristics;
- ecosystem characteristics.

Additionally, it is necessary to collect data on the important socio-economic characteristics of the study area. These include:

- demographic developments;
- trends in resource use and economic development;
- land use and ownership;
- infrastructural and other economic assets;
- cultural assets; and,
- institutional arrangements.

First, it is essential to review critically any available material (maps, aerial photographs, satellite images) and previous studies that may have yielded results or contain background information relevant to vulnerability assessment. Various national and international organisations have developed sites on the World Wide Web that contain coastal bibliographies, databases and tools as well as numerous links to other relevant information and organisations on the Internet.

Assessment of Biogeophysical Effects

For five of the six coastal biogeophysical effects of sea-level rise previously identified, assessment methods are presented. Each method is described in some detail, but given the scope of this chapter, it is impossible to present all the peculiarities involved.

Increasing flood frequency probabilities

One of the first consequences of a rise in sea level on low-lying coastal zones is an increased flood risk associated with storm surges and extreme precipitation and runoff events. The degree to which coastal land is at risk of flooding from storm surges is determined by a number of morphological and meteorological factors, including coastal slope and wind and wave characteristics. Together these factors determine a coastal zone's flood frequency probability curve (also referred to as flood exceedance curve). The information provided by flood frequency probability curves can be used to plot design water levels on a topographical map. Design water levels are contour lines that indicate the probability of a particular area being flooded.

Hoozemans *et al.* (1993) defined the risk zone as the land area between the coastline and the 'maximum' design water level, which is defined as a flood frequency probability of once per 1000 years, taking into account global sea-level rise and regional and local aspects such as subsidence, tidal range and storm characteristics (wind and wave set-up and minimum barometric pressure). Hence, the delineation of the risk zone requires the calculation of the maximum design water level.

Erosion and inundation

Sea-level rise can activate two important mechanisms that result in the loss of land: erosion and inundation. Erosion represents the physical removal of sediment by wave and current action, while inundation is the permanent submergence of low-lying land. The primary mechanism at any location depends on the geomorphology of the coast. Many factors other than sea-level rise can play a part in determining land loss (e.g. vegetation, sediment supply), yet at the intended level of analysis it is justified not to consider them. More sophisticated analyses would require considerably more data on the coastal sediment budget, and the development of more site-specific models. Such analyses are therefore likely to face severe time and funding constraints in many coastal areas.

Sea-level rise contributes to the erosion of erodible cliffs, coral-reef islands and gravelly, sandy and muddy coasts by promoting the offshore transport of sedimentary material. The best known and most widely applied model for estimating erosion has been developed by Bruun (1962) for application to straight sandy shores. In other erodible coastal environments, alternative erosion models have to be used, which, however, are often based on the Bruun rule.

Low-lying coastal areas such as deltas, coastal wetlands and coral atolls may face inundation as a result of sea-level rise. Land loss resulting from inundation is simply a function of slope: the lower the slope, the greater the land loss. In addition, the survival of coastal wetlands is dependent on sediment availability and/or local biomass production, as well as on the potential for these ecosystems to migrate inland. Flood embankments can inhibit this natural adaptation of wetlands to sea-level rise. Healthy, unobstructed wetlands in settings with continuing sedimentation are expected to be able to cope with projected global sea-level rise, although ecosystem characteristics may change (see Figure 12.4).

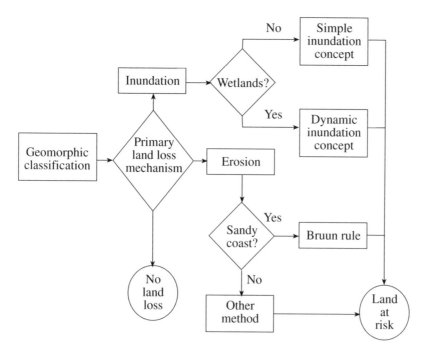

Note: Wetlands embrace marshes, mangroves and coral atolls/keys.

Figure 12.4   *Flow diagram to identify the appropriate method to determine land at risk from erosion or inundation*

Rising water tables
Sea-level rise could be associated with a rise in coastal (ground) water tables. The distance inland that a water table will be affected by sea-level rise depends on a range of factors, including elevation and subsurface permeability. In some locations, particularly deltas, rising water tables can

occur as far as several tens of kilometres inland. The need to assess rising water tables depends on the potential for saltwater intrusion in groundwater as well as impacts on foundations, drainage systems and underground services. As these impacts occur almost exclusively in urban areas, this is where attention should be focused.

Saltwater intrusion

As sea level rises, fresh groundwater and surface water could be displaced by saline water, which could have substantial adverse impacts on agriculture and drinking-water supply. To allow for these impacts to be assessed, it is essential to acquire knowledge on the spatial and temporal extent of saltwater intrusion. It is important to note that saltwater intrusion is already occurring in many coastal regions, owing to overexploitation of surface water and groundwater. With growing populations in coastal regions, saltwater intrusion of this cause is expected to occur more widely, and may enhance the rate of saltwater infiltration. Therefore, it is likely that sea-level rise will exacerbate an already adverse situation.

Assessing the extent of saltwater intrusion in groundwater is difficult as it depends on many factors that are locally variable, and often poorly understood. These factors include subsoil characteristics such as porosity and conductivity of the aquifer, hydraulic resistance of the aquitard and hydraulic variables such as groundwater flow and recharge. Also the geo(hydro)logy is important, as this determines whether a freshwater aquifer is confined, semi-confined or unconfined. Note that sea-level rise will not result in saltwater intrusion in confined aquifers. Saltwater intrusion in groundwater can be assessed using analytical methods or mathematical modelling.

Table 12.6 lists the methods that are available for assessments of biogeophysical effects of sea-level rise and indicates for which level of assessment they can be applied. It also shows the requirements for application – in terms of data, time, skill and resources – and gives an indication of the reliability and validity of results.

Assessment of Socio-economic Impacts

In addition to the biogeophysical effects discussed above, the socio-economic implications of increased flood risk and potential land loss need to be considered. This will be done using a distinction between three fundamental socio-economic impact categories:

- (human) population;
- marketed goods and services;
- non-marketed goods and services.

Table 12.6 *Summary of the available methods to assess biogeophysical effects of sea-level rise*

Biogeophysical effect	Assessment method	Requirements				Reliability and validity
		Data	Time	Skill	Money	
Increasing flood frequency probabilities	• Use of current flood frequency data	3	2	3	2	2
Erosion	• Individual-component method	3	3	3	2	2
	• Bruun rule of thumb	2	1	1	1	1
	• Bruun rule	3	3	3	2	2
	• Sediment-budget approach	5	5	5	4	3
Inundation	• Simple inundation concept	1	1	1	1	1
	• Dynamic inundation concept	2	2	3	2	2
	• Landscape modelling	5	5	5	5	3
Rising water tables	• Mazure equation	3	3	3	3	1
Saltwater intrusion	• Analytical methods (sharp-interface approach)	3	2	3	2	1
	• Mathematical modelling	5	5	5	5	3

Note: Scores from 1 to 5 indicate increasing requirements and reliability/validity.

For the latter two categories, the techniques considered here are aimed at expressing these impacts in economic terms, recognising that this may be impossible or undesirable for all values at stake. The first category applies a risk-based approach, using the design water levels calculated as suggested in the section above.

Population

Assuming no protection, the (human) population affected by sea-level rise can be divided into two categories: (1) population at risk (of flooding), and (2) population to respond. Population to respond comprises people *potentially* displaced by land loss resulting from erosion and inundation.

The population at risk is defined as the number of people experiencing flooding in a typical year (Hoozemans *et al.*, 1993; Baarse, 1995). This number is estimated by multiplying the total number of people living in an area potentially affected by flooding by the probability of flooding in any year, as determined for each risk zone. For example, if 3 million people were exposed to a flood frequency probability of 1/10 years, the population at risk would be 300000 people per year (see also Tables 12.1 and 12.2).

Marketed goods and services

Assessment of the increased risk or potential loss of marketed goods and services is a somewhat more complicated exercise. In principle, an inventory needs to be made of all economic assets and activities that can be found in the coastal area affected (both now and in the future), as well as a quantitative assessment of the degree to which these assets and activities will be subject to damage as a result of sea-level rise. Sea-level rise may also lead to costs that are not related directly to the economic assets and activities identified (e.g. evacuation). Further, benefits accruing from new opportunities, if any, should also be taken into account. Turner and Adger (1996) have provided specific guidance for the application of economic valuation methods to coastal zones. Even more detailed, and originally written for application to the United Kingdom, is the manual by Penning-Rowsell *et al.* (1992).

The most important goods and services that could be at risk of sea-level rise, and which are readily quantifiable in monetary terms include:

- land;
- physical (building) structures;
- agricultural and industrial productivity.

Either these values can be irreversibly lost as a result of erosion or inundation, or they can be exposed to a higher risk of flooding, which can cause temporal losses. Also, rising water tables may result in increased likelihood of foundation failure, existing drainage services may be made obsolete and underground services in urban areas would be impacted.

If the risk zone's contribution to a country's gross national product (GNP), is known, the GNP at risk from sea-level rise can be estimated. An approach utilised by Turner *et al.* (1995) to assess GNP at risk assumes equal annual incremental rises in sea level between 1990 and 2050, the impacts of which are a linear function. Since a time horizon of 60 years is used, 1/60th of the total capital value and activity would be at risk after one year, 2/60ths after two years, and so on. In addition to estimating GNP at risk, it is important to assess potential losses in capital assets such as land, property and infrastructure. These are to be valued based on the accelerated depreciation cost of the capital assets and, particularly in the case of land, their opportunity costs. Once an inventory has been made of the capital value in the risk zone, a similar analysis can be conducted as for population at risk. Thus capital value at increased risk over time can be assessed.

Alternatively, the timing of the occurrence of losses can be estimated based on relative sea-level rise scenarios. All losses that would occur within the time horizon of interest are summed up to arrive at the total potential loss, which can then be discounted to the net present value. In addition, it could be useful to make a distinction between temporal and permanent losses, using threshold times at which permanent losses occur. Details of this approach can be found in Turner *et al.* (1995).

Non-marketed goods and services

As the term implies, non-marketed goods and services are not traded on markets. Therefore, they cannot be readily expressed in financial terms, because no pricing mechanism exists. This does not suggest, however, that they do not possess economic value. Examples of non-marketed goods and services include recreational values, cultural and subsistence values (e.g. community structures), and natural values (e.g. a wetland's capacity to buffer wave energy and assimilate waste). To date, economic assessment of non-marketed goods and services has been directed primarily at quantifying the value of coastal recreation and indirect-use values such as storm protection and waste assimilation (e.g. Klein and Bateman, 1998). More guidance and references on the valuation of non-marketed coastal goods and services can be found in Turner and Adger (1996).

COASTAL VULNERABILITY IN THE MEDITERRANEAN

A number of studies have been conducted to assess the vulnerability to sea-level rise of coastal zones around the Mediterranean Sea. These include local studies, especially on the deltas of the Ebro (Sánchez-Arcilla *et al.*, 1998), Rhone (Ibanez *et al.*, 1999), Po (Bondesan *et al.*, 1995) and Nile (El-Raey, 1997), national studies (as collected in De la Vega-Leinert *et al.*, 2000a and 2000b), as well as regional aggregations (Nicholls and Hoozemans, 1996; Brochier and Ramieri, 2001). These studies tend to focus on the assessment of impacts, with relatively little attention devoted to adaptation or adaptive capacity. An exception is the case of Venice, Italy, for which the feasibility of preserving the great historic value of the city has been analysed from a range of different perspectives (e.g. Bandarin, 1994; Penning-Rowsell *et al.*, 1998).

The studies show that there is considerable variation in coastal vulnerability to sea-level rise in the Mediterranean. The deltas are particularly susceptible as they are already subsiding because of natural and human factors which exacerbate sea-level rise. Other human factors add to this susceptibility. For example, the Ebro delta has lost 97 per cent of its sand supply since the 1950s. In Venice, a 30 cm rise in relative sea level over the 20th century (largely due to subsidence following groundwater withdrawal) has greatly increased flooding and damage.

Mediterranean beaches tend to erode as they experience sea-level rise. Beach erosion destroys a valuable natural and economic resource and exposes human activities and infrastructure landward of the beach to increased wave and flood action. Intense recreational use of beaches around the Mediterranean makes this erosion a particular problem.

The northern Mediterranean is also susceptible to wetland loss. As a result of its morphology and tidal regime, a relatively small rise in sea level could lead to considerable losses of saltmarsh and intertidal areas.

WORKING ON THREE SCALE LEVELS: THE GERMAN EXPERIENCE

The issues and questions that have been raised in the previous sections are now briefly considered and discussed in the context of the vulnerability of the German coastal zone. In Germany, assessments have been carried out on three different scale levels. The various information bases and management strategies from national down to local level may shed some light on the use of assessment results.

Within the context of applying and testing the IPCC Common Methodology (IPCC CZMS, 1992), a national case study was carried out for the German coastal region. Northern Germany is subdivided into five coastal states (counties), three of which (Lower-Saxony, Hamburg, Bremen) border the North Sea, while one state (Mecklenburg-Vorpommern) borders the Baltic Sea and another (Schleswig-Holstein) shares a coastline with both seas. The state (regional) governments are individually responsible for policies on coastal development, protection and management, with the national government playing a subordinate part in most coast-related policies. The case study had primarily the following objectives:

1. to identify the coastal areas that would be exposed to risks from flooding – according to coastal topography – in case of an accelerated sea-level rise (scenario of +100 cm sea-level rise to the year 2100);
2. to determine the critical flood water levels along the North Sea and Baltic Sea coasts;
3. to approximate the likely socio-economic vulnerability in each of the five coastal states;
4. to delineate sub-regions most susceptible to flooding within these states;
5. to assess to what degree coastal protection schemes (dikes, sea-walls, dunes, etc.) would be insufficient in the case of the assumed scenario;
6. to determine the approximate costs of adjusting the coastal protection schemes so they could withstand a higher sea level;
7. to assess additional vulnerability of the low-lying coastal areas, in particular with respect to local drainage and decreasing wetland stability (Wadden Sea).

The data collected for the national vulnerability study were put together in a GIS database, combining (for the first time) contingent topographic and economic information for the whole coastal region of Germany (Ebenhoeh *et al.*, 1996; map scale 1:200000). The use and application of GIS for risk assessment and management planning turned out to be as time consuming as valuable (see Box 12.1). From the case study results it soon became clear, however, that the data, aggregated on the basis of statistical information at county level (macro-scale), were not specific and conclusive enough for the regional authorities to consider in detail the existing coastal defence and adaptation schemes. Therefore, it was decided that a more detailed analysis should be done on a meso-scale level for the state of Schleswig-Holstein. This region was chosen for two reasons. First, it comprises all types and elements of vulnerable coastal systems in both the North Sea and the Baltic Sea region. Second, the state authorities were in the process of revising and adjusting the coastal defence master plan for the next 30-year period and were thus particularly interested in taking results from a specific vulnerability assessment for the state into consideration.

BOX 12.1   THE ROLE OF GIS IN COASTAL RISK ASSESSMENT, ADAPTATION AND MANAGEMENT

GIS combines computer mapping and visualisation techniques with spatial databases and statistical, modelling and analytical tools. It offers powerful methods to collect, manage, retrieve, integrate, manipulate, combine, visualise and analyse spatial data and to derive information from these data. One simple, first-order application of GIS in coastal adaptation would be overlaying scenarios of sea-level rise with elevation and coastal-development data to define impact zones. More sophisticated applications may include morphodynamic modelling. GIS technology is evolving rapidly and is increasingly used for sophisticated modelling. Hence, GIS can provide excellent support to coastal managers for making decisions about adaptation.

GIS can contribute to each of the steps towards vulnerability assessment and adaptation. Collected data can be stored in a GIS, combined to develop new insights and information, and visualised for interpretation and educational purposes. In combination with scenarios of relevant developments and models to assess and evaluate changes in important natural and socio-economic variables, GIS can assist planners to identify appropriate adaptation technologies as well as their optimal locations for implementation. It allows for the non-invasive, reversible and refinable testing of specific adaptation technologies before these are implemented in the real world. After implementation, newly acquired data can be analysed to evaluate technology performance. Once created, a GIS database will have further utility in other aspects of coastal management.

In spite of its clear utility, GIS cannot substitute for fieldwork or common sense. It will never eclipse the importance of economic, institutional, legal and socio-cultural factors in coastal management. In addition, true three-dimensional modelling in GIS (e.g. for sediment budgets) remains problematic. Finally, some commentators have questioned whether GIS can always be used effectively in developing countries. Specific issues in this regard include:

- the costs of computer hardware and most GIS software;
- the lack of raw data to input to the system;

- the lack of consistency between data sets;
- restrictions on free access to information for strategic, political, economic or other reasons;
- limited salaries and career opportunities for GIS-literate operators compared with the industrialised world;
- the prevailing western conceptual model of geographical space, which may be different from local ways of perceiving and interpreting spatial relationships;
- the fear that the introduction of GIS could lead to or facilitate oppressive government, misuse of power, civil unrest or other non-democratic activities.

The rapid ongoing developments of all aspects of GIS may remove some of these concerns. There is no doubt that GIS presents great potential for societies wishing to anticipate and understand the consequences of climate change and to develop adaptation strategies to cope with the potential impacts.

In the lower-scale study for Schleswig-Holstein (map scale 1:25000) it could be shown that not all of the area up to the +5 metres contour line (which was the inward boundary at the macro-scale) would actually be at risk of sea-level rise. Instead, local topographic features such as second dike lines or road dams were used to delineate the vulnerable areas more precisely. On the other hand, there are a number of elements in terms of socio-economic values at risk, such as technical, tourist and traffic infrastructure, which are relevant for risk assessment but could not be included in the overview study. Moreover, the detailed information on the prevailing adaptation to storm flood hazards, in particular on the existing dikes, needed to be considered in greater detail in order to realistically describe the present and future exposures of coastal segments to flooding risks. Technically, the previously established coastal GIS needed to be refined and specified to meet the requirements of policy-addressed conclusions from the state-wide vulnerability assessment (Hamann and Hofstede, 1998; see Figure 12.5).

The major benefit of the meso-scale analysis was to show to what extent coastal protection and accommodation strategies may be necessary when considering sea-level rise and storm flood scenarios on a regional scale. With respect to the assessment of economic and ecological vulnerability as well as possible options for improvement of adaptation, there were still shortcomings observed in the meso-scale results. A lesson learnt from recent studies by Yohe *et al.* (1995) and West and Dowlatabadi (1999), who studied sea-level rise impacts on developed coasts in the United States on

DATA SOURCES AND DATA FLOW IN THE VALUATION STUDY

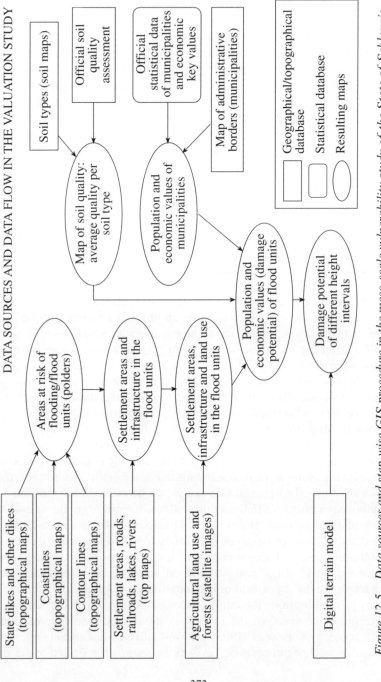

Figure 12.5   Data sources and step-wise GIS procedure in the meso-scale vulnerability study of the State of Schleswig-Holstein

a community scale, it is not sufficient to look only at the incremental depreciation of existing values and the benefits of gradual adaptation processes. Instead, the local effects of all impacts, including extreme storm events, have to be taken into account and balanced against the incremental adjustments likely to occur in coastal communities.

When considering the German conditions, it is essential to know that a range of adaptation measures fall within the communities' responsibility, while other measures would be the responsibility of the state government (according to the master plan). Therefore, decisions of how to respond to a given threat, for example by building a seawall or enhancing beach nourishment activities, must be based on community-based assessments of flooding or erosion risks. Similarly, it is only at this micro-scale level that the coastal population can make decisions on the possible benefits of flood insurance or on site-specific economic investments. The complex interrelations between results from local risk assessment and economic as well as policy-oriented decisions are demonstrated in an ongoing case study for the German island of Sylt, the major tourist attraction along the North Sea coast of the state of Schleswig-Holstein. In Sylt, risks of sea-level rise are estimated to be rather high, but trust in local adaptation schemes has still led to ongoing tourist development. From a scientific point of view, the case of Sylt appears to be a critical issue where local private judgements towards adjustment to sea-level rise are not in line with those of the public and policy-makers.

GENERAL CONCLUSIONS AND FURTHER WORK ON VULNERABILITY AND ADAPTATION

To identify the most appropriate coastal-adaptation strategy, one must consider the full context in which impacts of climate change arise, and realise that the three dominant strategies – protect, retreat, accommodate – happen within a broader policy process. Within this process, increasing resilience by reversing maladaptive trends could be an important option to reduce coastal vulnerability to climate variability and change. This approach will often address more than climate issues alone and will generally involve a change in adaptation strategy, for example, nourishing beaches instead of constructing seawalls, or introducing a building setback instead of allowing construction next to the coast (Table 12.7).

Data collection and information development are essential prerequisites for vulnerability assessment as well as for coastal adaptation. The more relevant, accurate and up-to-date the data and information available, the more targeted and effective adaptation can be. Coastal adaptation requires data

Table 12.7   *Examples of important technologies to protect against, retreat from or accommodate sea-level rise and other coastal impacts of climate change (see also Bijlsma et al., 1996 and Klein et al., 2001)*

Application	Technology
Protect	
• Hard structural options	– Dikes, levees, floodwalls
	– Seawalls, revetments, bulkheads
	– Groynes
	– Detached breakwaters
	– Floodgates and tidal barriers
	– Saltwater-intrusion barriers
• Soft structural options	– Periodic beach nourishment
	– Dune restoration and creation
	– Wetland restoration and creation
• Indigenous options	– Afforestation
	– Coconut-leaf walls
	– Coconut-fibre stone units
	– Wooden walls
	– Stone walls
(Managed) retreat	
• Increasing or establishing set-back zones	– Limited technology required
• Relocating threatened buildings	– Various technologies
• Phased-out or no development in susceptible areas	– Limited technology required
• Presumed mobility, rolling easements	– Limited technology required
• Managed realignment	– Various technologies, depending on location
• Creating upland buffers	– Limited technology required
Accommodate	
• Emergency planning	– Early-warning systems
	– Evacuation systems
• Hazard insurance	– Limited technology required
• Modification of land use and agricultural practice	– Various technologies (e.g. aquaculture, saline-resistant crops), depending on location and purpose
• Modification of building styles and codes	– Various technologies
• Strict regulation of hazard zones	– Limited technology required
• Improved drainage	– Increased diameter of pipes
	– Increased pump capacity
• Desalination	– Desalination plants

Table 12.8   *Examples of important technologies to collect data, provide information and increase awareness for coastal risk and adaptation to climate change (see also Klein et al., 2001)*

Application	Technology
Coastal-system description	
• Coastal topography and bathymetry bathymetry	– Mapping and surveying
	– Videography
	– Airborne laserscanning (lidar)
	– Satellite remote sensing
• Wind and wave regime	– Waverider buoys
	– Satellite remote sensing
• Tidal and surge regime	– Tide gauges
• Relative sea level	– Tide gauges
	– Historical or geological methods
• Absolute sea level	– Satellite remote sensing
	– Tide gauges, satellite altimetry and global positioning systems
• Land use	– Airborne and satellite remote sensing
• Natural values	– Resource surveys
• Socio-economic aspects	– Mapping and surveying
• Legal and institutional arrangements	– Interviews, questionnaires
• Socio-cultural factors	– Interviews, questionnaires
Climate-impact assessment	
• Index-based methods	– Coastal vulnerability index
	– Sustainable capacity index
• (Semi-)quantitative methods	– IPCC common methodology
	– Aerial-videotape assisted vulnerability assessment
	– UNEP impact and adaptation assessment
• Integrated assessment	– Coupled models
Awareness raising	
• Printed information	– Brochures, leaflets, newsletters
• Audio-visual media	– Newspapers, radio, television, cinema
• Interactive tools	– Board-games
	– Internet, World Wide Web
	– Computerised simulation models

and information on coastal characteristics and dynamics, and patterns of human behaviour, as well as an understanding of the potential consequences of climate change (Klein *et al.*, 1999). It is also essential that there is a general awareness among the public and coastal planners and managers of these consequences and of the possible need to act (Table 12.8). In countries where the central government has neither the means nor the expertise to address problems in every part of the coast, the information is used most effectively when targeted at the most influential people in the community.

REFERENCES

Baarse, G. (1995), *Development of an Operational Tool for Global Vulnerability Assessment (GVA): Update of the Number of People at Risk due to Sea-level Rise and Increased Flood Probabilities*. CZM Publication No. 3. The Hague, Ministry of Transport, Public Works and Water Management.

Bandarin, F. (1994), 'The Venice Project – a challenge for modern engineering'. *Proceedings of The Institution of Civil Engineers – Civil Engineering*, **102**(4), 163–174.

Bijlsma, L., C.N. Ehler, R.J.T. Klein, S.M. Kulshrestha, R.F. McLean, N. Mimura, R.J. Nicholls, L.A. Nurse, H. Pérez Nieto, E.Z. Stakhiv, R.K. Turner and R.A. Warrick (1996), 'Coastal zones and small islands'. In: *Impacts, Adaptations and Mitigation of Climate Change: Scientific-technical Analyses*, R.T. Watson, M.C. Zinyowera and R.H. Moss (eds) *Contribution of Working Group II to the Second Assessment Report of the Intergovernmental Panel on Climate Change*. Cambridge University Press, Cambridge, pp. 289–324.

Bondesan, M., G.B. Castiglioni, C. Elmi, G. Gabbianelli, R. Marocco, P.A. Pirazzoli and A. Tomasin (1995), 'Coastal areas at risk from storm surges and sea-level rise in Northeastern Italy', *Journal of Coastal Research*, **11**(4), 1354–1379.

Brochier, F. and E. Ramieri (2001), *Climate Change Impacts on the Mediterranean Coastal Zones*, Nota di Lavoro 27.2001. Fondazione Eni Enrico Mattei, Milano, Italy.

Bruun, P. (1962), 'Sea-level rise as a cause of shore erosion'. *Journal of the Waterways and Harbour Division*. Proceedings of the American Society of Civil Engineers, **88**, 117–130.

Carter, T.R., M.L. Parry, S. Nishioka and H. Harasawa (eds) (1994), *Technical Guidelines for Assessing Climate Change Impacts and Adaptations*. Report of Working Group II of the Intergovernmental Panel on Climate Change, University College London and Centre for Global Environmental Research, London and Tsukuba.

De la Vega-Leinert, A.C., R.J. Nicholls and R.S.J. Tol (eds) (2000a), *Proceedings of the SURVAS Expert Workshop on European Vulnerability and Adaptation to Accelerated Sea-Level Rise*, Hamburg, Germany, 19–21 June 2000. Flood Hazard Research Centre, Middlesex University, UK.

De la Vega-Leinert, A.C., R.J. Nicholls, A. Nasser Hassan and M. El-Raey (eds) (2000b), *Proceedings of the SURVAS Expert Workshop on African Vulnerability and Adaptation to Accelerated Sea-Level Rise*, Cairo, Egypt, 5–8 November 2000. Flood Hazard Research Centre, Middlesex University, UK.

Ebenhoeh, W., H. Sterr and F. Simmering (1996), 'Potentielle Gefährdung und Vulnerabilität der deutschen Nord- und Ostseeküste bei fortschreitendem Klimawandel'. Case study based on the Common Methodology of the IPCC, unpublished report.

El-Raey, M. (1997), 'Vulnerability assessment of the coastal zone of the Nile delta of Egypt to the impacts of sea level rise'. *Ocean and Coastal Management*, **37**(1), 29–40.

Hamann, M. and J. Hofstede (1998), 'GIS applications for integrated coastal defence management in the federal state of Schleswig-Holstein Germany'. In: *German Geographical Coastal Research – The Last Decade*, D.H. Kelletat (ed.), pp. 169–182.

Hoozemans, F.M.J., M. Marchand and H.A. Pennekamp (1993), *A Global Vulnerability Analysis: Vulnerability Assessment for Population, Coastal Wetlands and Rice Production on a Global Scale*, 2nd edn. Delft Hydraulics and Ministry of Transport, Public Works and Water Management, Delft and The Hague.

Ibanez, C., J.W. Day and D. Pont (1999), 'Primary production and decomposition of wetlands of the Rhone delta, France: interactive impacts of human modifications and relative sea level rise'. *Journal of Coastal Research*, **15**(3), 717–731.

IPCC CZMS (1992), 'A common methodology for assessing vulnerability to sea level rise, 2nd revision'. *Global Climate Change and the Rising Challenge of the Sea*. IPCC CZMS, Ministry of Transport, Public Works and Water Management, The Hague, Appendix C.

Klein, R.J.T. and I.J. Bateman (1998), 'The recreational value of Cley Marshes Nature Reserve: an argument against managed retreat?' *Journal of the Chartered Institution of Water and Environmental Management*, **12**(4), 280–285.

Klein, R.J.T. and R.J. Nicholls (1998), 'Coastal zones'. In: *Handbook on Climate Change Impact Assessment and Adaptation Strategies*, J.F. Feenstra, I. Burton, J.B. Smith and R.S.J. Tol (eds) United Nations Environment Programme and Institute for Environmental Studies, Vrije Universiteit, Nairobi, Kenya, and Amsterdam, The Netherlands, version 2.0, pp. 7.1–7.35.

Klein, R.J.T. and R.J. Nicholls (1999), 'Assessment of coastal vulnerability to climate change'. *Ambio*, **28**(2), 182–187.

Klein, R.J.T., R.J. Nicholls, and N. Mimura (1999), 'Coastal adaptation to climate change: can the IPCC Technical Guidelines be applied?' *Mitigation and Adaptation Strategies for Global Change*, **4**(3–4), 239–252.

Klein, R.J.T., R.J. Nicholls, S. Ragoonaden, M. Capobianco, J. Aston and E.N. Buckley (2001), 'Technological options for adaptation to climate change in coastal zones'. *Journal of Coastal Research*, **17**(3), 531–543.

Nicholls, R.J. and F.M.J. Hoozemans (1996), 'The Mediterranean: vulnerability to coastal implications of climate change'. *Ocean and Coastal Management*, **31**(2–3), 105–132.

Nicholls, R.J. and S.P. Leatherman (eds), (1995), 'The potential impact of accelerated sea-level rise on developing countries'. *Journal of Coastal Research*, Special Issue **14**, 13–24.

Nicholls, R.J., S.P. Leatherman, K.C. Dennis and C.R. Volonté (1995), 'Impacts and responses to sea-level rise: qualitative and quantitative assessments'. *Journal of Coastal Research*, Special Issue **14**, 26–43.

Nicholls, R.J. and N. Mimura (1998), 'Regional issues raised by sea-level rise and their policy implications'. *Climate Research*, **11**, 5–18.

Peerbolte, E.B., J.G. de Ronde, L.P.M. de Vrees, M. Mann and G. Baarse (1991), *Impact of Sea-level Rise on Society: A Case Study for The Netherlands*. Delft Hydraulics and Ministry of Transport, Public Works and Water Management, Delft and The Hague.

Penning-Rowsell, E. and M. Fordham (1992), *Floods across Europe – Flood Hazard Assessment, Modelling and Management*. Middlesex University Press, London.

Penning-Rowsell, E., P. Winchester and J. Gardiner (1998), 'New approaches to sustainable hazard management for Venice'. *Geographical Journal*, **164**(1), 1–18.

Sánchez-Arcilla, A., J.A. Jiménez and H.I. Valdemoro (1998), 'The Ebro delta: morphodynamics and vulnerability'. *Journal of Coastal Research*, **14**(3), 754–772.

Turner, R.K. and W.N. Adger (1996), *Coastal Zone Resources Assessment Guidelines*. Land–Ocean Interactions in the Coastal Zone Reports and Studies No. 4, IGBP/LOICZ, Texel, The Netherlands.

Turner, R.K., W.N. Adger, and P. Doktor (1995), 'Assessing the economic costs of sea level rise'. *Environment and Planning A*, **27**(11), 1777–1796.

Warrick, R.A., J. Oerlemans, P.L. Woodworth, M.F. Meier and C. le Provost (1996), 'Changes in sea level'. In: *Climate Change 1995: The Science of Climate Change*, J.T. Houghton, L.G. Meira Filho and B.A. Callander (eds) *Contribution of Working Group I to the Second Assessment Report of the Intergovernmental Panel on Climate Change*. Cambridge University Press, Cambridge, pp. 359–405.

WCC '93 (World Coast Conference) (1994), *Preparing to Meet the Coastal Challenges of the 21st Century*. Report of the World Coast Conference, Noordwijk, 1–5 November 1993. Ministry of Transport, Public Works and Water Management, The Hague.

West, J.J. and H. Dowlatabadi (1999), 'On assessing the economic impacts of sea-level rise on developed coasts'. In: *Climate, Change and Risk*, T.E. Downing, A.A. Olsthoorn and R.S.J. Tol (eds). Routledge, London, pp. 205–220.

Yohe, G., J. Neumann and H. Ameden (1995), 'Assessing the economic cost of greenhouse-induced sea level rise: methods and application in support of a national survey'. *Journal of Environmental Economics and Management*, **29**, S.78–S.97.

Zeidler, R.B., M. Skaja, G. Rozynski and J. Kaczmarek (1997), 'Wind- and sea level-induced shore evolution in Poland'. *Proceedings of the 25th International Conference of Coastal Engineers*, American Society of Civil Engineers, New York, pp. 4364–4375.

13. Impacts of climate change on tourism in the Mediterranean: adaptive responses

Allen Perry

The Mediterranean is currently the world's most popular and successful tourist destination with 120 million visitors every year. Its climate is perceived, quite erroneously, by many tourists as idyllic, benign and delightful. They ignore the heatwaves, floods and strong winds that can plague the region at times. With its renowned radiance and clarity of light, it has remained seductive to north European visitors since the habit of escaping from the cold and dark of the northern winter became well established by the upper classes last century. Yeo (1882) described the weather of the Côte d'Azur as 'a tonic, stimulating and exciting'. Several countries with Mediterranean shorelines, including Spain and France are now among the most visited countries in the world and in these countries international tourism receipts account for just over 2 per cent of gross domestic product. In Greece 10 per cent of total employment is in the tourist industry. Tourism is also very significant in terms of core–periphery divisions within the European Union . There is large-scale capital transfer from the tourist demand areas of north-west Europe to the generally poorer Mediterranean countries. Climate constitutes an important part of the environmental context in which recreation and tourism takes place and, because tourism is a voluntary and discretionary activity, participation will often depend on favourable conditions. Climate and weather are among the most important factors affecting participation in leisure and tourism activities, since for many activities there are critical threshold levels beyond which participation and enjoyment levels fall and safety may be endangered.

THE LURE OF THE SUN

The betterment of health has been a common motive for travel for centuries. In Roman times during the height of summer, Rome was notorious for its unhealthy conditions and the city was deserted by all but the poor.

By the eighteenth century a sojourn in winter by the shores of the Mediterranean, especially on the Côte d'Azur, by the rich aristocracy of northern Europe was deemed, if not to cure them, then at least to alleviate their condition (Kevan 1993) The 'season' lasted from mid-October to early May (Howarth 1977). The curative worth of Italian climates, and especially the Italian Riviera was also recognised, although the inconvenience posed by cold winds from the north to the more delicate was noted (Hoolihan 1989). When a summer respite was required these well-off early tourists tended to flock to the mountains, and especially the Alps. In general, until the twentieth century there was a general aversion to seeking the sun and indeed pale, consumptive complexions were prized, a suntan being seen as evidence of lower-class manual work. It was not until the development of mass transportation systems and a change of cultural values in the 1940s and 1950s that a suntan culture developed. Only then do we see the development of what has become known as 'sun-lust' tourism. Starting in the west on the Spanish 'Costas' and along the North Italian Adriatic coast, mass summer tourism has spread to ever more peripheral areas, preferably inaccessible to the masses, by fashion seekers searching for social segregation. Thus in turn, Italy, Greece, Cyprus and Turkey became the new focus of seasonal migrations from northern Europe by large numbers from all social classes in the summer months, in search of more certain sunshine than could be expected at home. Until very recently a holiday in the sun has been perceived by increasing numbers as vital to their well-being and the acquisition of a suntan as important as the acquiring of consumer durables for the home. We would be deluding ourselves if we thought that this desire to travel abroad was motivated by interest in other cultures or landscapes. A UK survey suggested that for over 80 per cent of tourists better weather than can normally be found in the UK in summer was the primary reason for choosing an overseas holiday. Concern about skin cancer and worries about UV-B radiation have so far tended to modify behaviour rather than cause a change of destination. The beach has become a fun palace, a place of ease and entertainment. While the search for a salubrious, amenable climate was once the prerogative of the wealthy or privileged classes of society, the search for 'endless summer' has now become a mass phenomenon.

KEY SENSITIVITIES TO WEATHER AND CLIMATE

Major holiday decisions within many of the 'tourist exporting' countries of Northern Europe are subject to a push and pull effect. The higher temperatures and settled weather of the Mediterranean summer exert a big attraction, but better summers at home will reduce overseas holiday bookings. Giles and Perry (1998) have shown that the exceptional summer of 1995 in the UK led to a drop in outbound tourism and a big reduction in the peak demand for Mediterranean package holidays. Large numbers of people indulged in short-term opportunistic decision-making and switched their normal holiday preferences to take account of the unusually favourable conditions at home. Such limited evidence does suggest that climate warming might alter the competitive balance of holiday destinations with adverse effects on high season tourism in the Mediterranean.

The Mediterranean is likely to become less attractive for health reasons in the summer. Apart from the dangers increasingly associated with skin cancer, many Mediterranean beach resorts may simply become too hot for comfort in the peak season, with a much higher frequency of severe heat waves (Perry 1987). Carter (1991) has used an approximate index of climatic favourability to investigate changes of seasonal climate in Europe under possible future climate change. Results suggested that a climate warming in Europe of 4°C would lead to a shift in the optimal summertime climate from the traditional southern coastal resorts northwards to currently less fashionable regions. In the ACACIA report (2000) it was shown that under a high emission scenario summer temperatures in southern Europe could increase by 6–7°C by 2080. The attractiveness of the southern coastal zone in spring and autumn would be enhanced relative to the present. It is in the months of October–November that the lingering warmth and sunshine of the Mediterranean provides the biggest contrast with the weather in Northern Europe. At this season maximum temperatures are 8–10°C higher than in London, while in April this difference is only 5–7°C. Rotmans et al. (1994) suggest that the area suitable for sun-related tourism will decline in much of Italy and Greece as summer temperatures make beach tourism too uncomfortable. A few destinations (e.g. Cyprus and Corsica) offer the potential for commuting from hot beaches to cooler mountains, but the Mediterranean is likely to face other climate-related problems such as marine water pollution and the scarcity of fresh water supplies. The availability of water supply could become a major constraint and the quantity and quality of the water may not be sufficient to satisfy future tourist demands. Large-scale expenditure on desalinisation plants will be needed, especially in some island resorts if water supplies are to be guaranteed.

Drought

The Spanish drought of the early 1990s showed how island resorts like Majorca could become dependent on water being transported from the mainland with attendant political tensions (Wheeler 1995). In the last three decades there has been a decrease in spring rainfall in southern Spain and Portugal, with the rainy season ending earlier and the dry season onset also occurring earlier. Small islands, for example in the Aegean, could be particularly affected if tourism is allowed to continue to grow. Nicholls and Hoozemans (1996) have shown that in the Mediterranean there are 162 islands exceeding 10 square km in size. Most have a low resource base but significant tourist development. A decline in rainfall and water supply availability, together with beach erosion, could undermine their tourist industries and hence their local economies. It has been suggested (Karas 1997) that Crete could experience serious water shortages in five years out of six by 2010. There is likely to be an increase in friction, with a conflict of interest between local people and tourist authorities, on the use of scarce water. It has been calculated that a luxury hotel consumes around 600 litres of fresh water per night. Water-hungry land uses like golf courses and water parks will be seen as water-stealers by local people. Projected decreases in runoff will exacerbate the problem of salinisation of water resources. Increased degradation of the environment and spreading desertification is likely to make some areas less scenically attractive to tourists.

Heatwaves

Extended heatwaves, defined as ten days or more, appear to be becoming more frequent in the Mediterranean. In the 15 years to 1994, Italy endured eight such heatwaves. In addition short-duration heatwaves of three to five days with temperatures 7°C or more above normal occurred on 33 occasions in the Central Mediterranean between 1950 and 1995. Individual heatwave days have increased from 52 days in the decade 1950–59 to 230 in the decade 1980–89 (Conte et al. 1999). Heat waves cause rises in the death rate, especially in urban areas. In one episode from 13 July to 2 August 1983 in Rome, 450 deaths above the normal average occurred. In 1987 more than 1100 residents died in Greece between 20 and 31 July (Katsouyanni et al. 1988) with a combination of temperatures above 40°C and poor air quality. In 1998 in Cyprus 45 deaths attributable to heat were noted when the maximum temperature exceeded 40°C on eight successive days. In Athens the National Weather Service of Greece forecasts of heat wave emergencies and warnings are disseminated to the public. Extreme heatwaves and the deaths that they cause frequently get reported in the media of foreign countries and give a negative image to potential holiday-makers. While the worst effects of such heatwaves are inevitably experienced in cities rather than at the beach, the European Climate Assessment web site has shown that at a number of tourist resorts (e.g. Corfu) there has been a rise in the frequency of both very hot days and nights over the last 30 years. It has to be remembered that holiday-makers from northern Europe will be unused to temperatures as high as 40°C and they may be more at risk than local people who are used to long hot summers. Gawith et al. (1999) have shown that at Thessaloniki in northern Greece the temperature–humidity index (THI), which assesses the impact of high temperature and humidity, will rise above a value of 84 (when nearly everyone feels uncomfortable) for more than twice as long as at present by 2050. In addition there will be significant increases in the shoulder warm periods, suggesting a potential for lengthening of the summer season. Forest fires, such as were very widespread in August 1994 in Tuscany, Corsica, Sardinia and France can lead to evacuation from tourist facilities such as camp sites. Pinol et al. (1998) found that in coastal eastern Spain there has been increased fire activity and the number of days of very high fire risk are likely to increase further since there is a correlation between summer heat and fire occurrence.

The tourist industry is very vulnerable to natural disasters. The publicity given to heatwave deaths in Greece in summer 1984, if repeated regularly, could act as a deterrent to tourism. In that year there were stories in the UK press of holiday-makers staying in their hotel rooms to escape the intense heat on the beaches. Queues of Britons were reported at hospitals and pharmacies suffering from heatstroke and burns while others cut short their holidays and returned home early. Rising mean summer temperatures will inevitably be accompanied by more occasions of extreme maximum temperatures.

Sea Temperatures

Because of the concentration on beach holidays in the Mediterranean, sea surface temperatures (SST) and the way they may change in the future is an important consideration. There is a general increase in SST from west to east as well as from north to south (Fig 13.1).

At present SSTs in winter are too cold for swimming, except in the extreme east, around Cyprus and the Near East coast, where they rarely fall below 17–18°C. Given that for comfortable water activities SST should be 20–21°C there is no prospect that, even with warming of 2–3°C, this figure will be met over most of the Mediterranean where winter SSTs are 14–16°C. By May, SST ranges from about 21°C in the Eastern Mediterranean to about 15–18°C in the west. A rise of 2–3°C would allow swimming to begin earlier in the Central Mediterranean. The greatest benefit for sea swimming of warming of SST would come late in the season in October–November, particularly in the central and eastern part of the Basin.

Note: Based on data for 11 years of August data collected from AVHRR sensors. Temperatures range between 23 and 26°C, with the dark coloured areas having the highest temperatures.

Figure 13.1   Mediterranean Sea temperatures in high summer

ADAPTIVE RESPONSES

Background

Before we can consider adaptive responses to the projected climate changes we need to consider the socio-economic environment that will also play a major role in influencing Mediterranean tourism in the future.

Perhaps the most influential factor will be the increased proportion of older people in the European population. By 2001, one in four Europeans, were over the age of 55 and the average age of retirement is also getting earlier. Many of these older people were the mass travellers of the 1960s and 1970s, and are today's discerning and sophisticated travellers with the means and the will to travel. Increasingly they are looking at long-haul destinations, one of the fastest segments of the travel trade, since they are already familiar with many European resorts and cities. At the same time they are taking second, third and even fourth holidays, or short breaks, often with cultural or health interests paramount. Holidays will increasingly be about slimming bodies and broadening minds. In addition these sophisticated, discerning travellers will be alive to 'green issues', will expect clean attractive environments and will be familiar with the information technology to enable them to search for value for money. There will be a growing reluctance to buy holidays to destinations where beaches are polluted or where there are hazards of other types. Unfortunately on the Mediterranean coast there is a shortage of destinations perceived by consumers as green (Davidson 1998). Tourists looking for a superior holiday experience, of which clean beaches are but one aspect, will also demand other changes to the physical environment such as improved security, and better air quality and traffic management. Initiatives such as the legislation in the Balearic Islands to improve the tourist environment and infrastructure will be copied elsewhere.

As it becomes less fashionable to have a golden tan and the small decline in beach holidays in the Mediterranean that has already been noticed becomes more marked, the traditional sea and sun beach holiday will decline at the expense of cultural tours, cruising and activity- and skill-based holidays. Probably the best chance of extending the season will be to capitalise on art and archaeological treasures and historic cities such as Florence and Athens that will be avoided in the heat of summer (Jenner and Smith 1993). More concern with self-improvement and self-expression will be reflected in holiday needs, especially of these older people. Elderly and retired people are more likely to take long-stay winter holidays. This market has been concentrated in a relatively small number of resorts, noticeably on the Costa Blanca in Spain and in Cyprus. This market is likely to grow and there is scope to extend to other more southerly resorts, for example in Crete. A destination like Malta, with its rich historical, colonial and military legacy and its poor beach resources has already managed to increase the number of winter tourists to 40–45 per cent of the annual total. However the Mediterranean is likely to continue to be at a disadvantage to the Canary Islands and to long-haul destinations that offer less winter rainfall, even though winter temperatures in the Mediterranean are expected to increase. Harlfinger (1991) in a study of the holiday bioclimatology of Majorca, Spain found that in winter 86 per cent of older German holiday-makers claimed that the change of climate benefited their health. He suggested a bioclimatological calendar for the alleviation of particular complaints. Respiratory and skin diseases were most alleviated in winter and psoriasis and muscle-joint rheumatism in summer.

Business and incentive travel, conferences, trade-fairs and conventions are likely to grow in importance, even allowing for the growth of video-conferences. Further growth in low-cost airlines will promote short breaks and weekend 'ad-ons' to such events.

Adaptive Capacities

Tourism is a continuously adapting industry, responding to changing demographic and economic conditions as well as to new demands and technologies. Climate change will present new challenges but also lead to new opportunities for tourist investment to capitalise on the new environmental conditions. Work has only just begun on 'translating' the suggested future climate scenarios into their impacts on tourism but already some interesting adaptations are emerging:

1. Higher air and sea temperatures are likely to encourage a longer tourist season. If the summer becomes widely perceived as too hot, the season could become 'doughnut shaped', with peaks in spring and autumn months and a hole in high summer. This would be rather akin to present day conditions at a resort like Dubai in the UAE. Resorts need to discourage a closing-down attitude at the end of summer. Higher temperatures will allow a prolongation of the season and, if possible, added cultural and sporting attractions should be encouraged to help this process. Breaking the traditional seasonal pattern has as much to do with changing consumer attitudes as with developing new attractions, and more targeted advertising could help in this respect. A longer tourist season would allow quicker returns on investment with more intensive utilisation of facilities over a longer period.

2. The larger numbers of older people in the population will still wish to escape the dark, dreary winters of northern Europe. More are likely to consider moving permanently to, or buying a second home in, Mediterranean areas. King et al. (1998) have shown that in several retirement destinations including the Costa del Sol and Malta, the most important reason given for moving to the chosen destination was climate. Thus the climate of the receiving region for these migrants has been considered to be the most important pull factor. There are considerable planning implications if the growth of new apartments, villas and bungalows is not to cause environmental blight in some of these coastal areas

3. Tourists will increasingly expect holiday accommodation to be air-conditioned. Such accommodation will attract a premium price, whilst poorer quality self-catering apartments and rooms without air-conditioning will be much less attractive in summer. At present only a fifth of rooms in hotels in Mediterranean countries are in the 4 and 5 star categories. Increased pressure will be put on electricity supplies from the demand for additional cooling systems.

4. There will be a higher risk of epidemics of cholera and typhoid as well as infectious diseases such as malaria, dengue fever, and so on. Adverse publicity would follow such public health scares and frighten tourists away as happened at Salou, Spain a few years ago. More care will be needed on hygiene matters, particularly in hotel and restaurant food preparation if the incidence of dysentry and E. coli is not to dramatically increase. Adverse publicity for tourism would also accompany an increase in illegal refugees from North Africa, fleeing environmental degradation in their home countries.

5. The beaches that are the principal assets of coastal tourism will be at considerable threat from erosion as sea levels rise (Nicholls and Hoozemans 1996). This will also apply in many cases where coastlines are flat, with tourist accommodation and other infrastructure immediately behind the beaches. New tourist resorts should locate all long-life infrastructure inland from the coast and only place easily removed structures near the beach. Expensive beach nourishment schemes may be appropriate in some places where there is a shortage of sandy beaches and their erosion or removal will severely disadvantage tourism. Additional costs would be incurred by escalating costs of coastal defence protection and repairs. Nautical tourism has stimulated the building of large numbers of marinas and berths which could be affected by sea level rise. Management efforts need to be expanded to consider the implications of climate change and to conduct vulnerability surveys.

CONCLUSIONS

The Mediterranean has long been familiar to tourists because of its per-ceived good climate. The Mediterranean region can justifiably claim to have been the focus of the modern tourism industry and yet in recent years it has begun to lose some of its gloss. The tourist industry is by its very nature fragile and susceptible to political, economic and social changes and the probability of climate change adds another element of uncer-tainty to planning future developments. More research is needed to quan-tify the climatic well-being of tourists by developing tourism climatic indices and beach comfort indices, which can be calibrated to include the effects of climate change. Past growth and attractiveness are not necessar-ily a guide to the future, and the Mediterranean tourist industry cannot assume an untroubled and guaranteed future. The primary resources of sun, sea and beaches are likely to be re-evaluated in the light of climate change.

REFERENCES

ACACIA (2000) *Assessment of Potential Effects and Adaptations for Climate Change in Europe.* Jackson Environment Institute, University of East Anglia.

Carter T.R. (1991) *The Hatch Index of Climatic Favourability.* Finnish Meteorological Institute, Helsinki.

Conte R., Sorani R. and Piervitali E. (1999) 'Extreme climatic events over the Mediterranean'. In J. Brandt (ed.) *Mediterranean Desertification, Vol. 1 Thematic Issues*, Wiley, London.

Davidson R. (1998) *Travel and Tourism in Europe*, 2nd edition. Longmans, London.

Gawith M.K., Downing T. and Karacostas T.S. (1999) 'Heatwaves in a changing climate'. In *Climate Change and Risk*, ed. T. Downing, A. Oissthoorn and R. Toll (eds). Routledge, London, pp. 279–307.

Giles A.R. and Perry A.H. (1998) 'The use of a temporal analogue to investigate the possible impact of projected global warming on the UK tourist industry', *Tourist Management* **19**, 75–80.

Harlfinger O. (1991) 'Holiday bioclimatology: a study of Palma de Majorca Spain'. *Geojournal* **25**, 377–81.

Hoolihan C. (1989) 'Health and travel in 19th century Rome'. *J. Hist. Med. Allied sci.* **44**, 462–86.

Howarth P. (1977) *When the Riviera was Ours.* Routledge and Kegan Paul, London.

Jenner P. and Smith C. (1993) *Tourism in the Mediterranean.* Economic Intelligence Unit Research Report, London.

Karas S. (1997) *Climate Change and the Mediterranean.* Web site: www.greenpeace.org.

Katsouyanni K. et al. (1988) 'The 1987 Athens heat-wave'. *Lancet* **3**, 573.

Kevan S. (1993) 'Quests for cures: a history of tourism for climate and health'. *International Journal of Biometeorology* **37**, 113–24.

King R., Warnes A.M. and Williams A.M. (1998) 'International retirement migration in Europe'. *International Journal of Population Geography* **4**, 91–111.

Nicholls R.J. and Hoozemans F.M. (1996) 'The Mediterranean vulnerability to coastal implications of climate change'. *Ocean and Coastal Management* **31**, 105–32.

Perry A.H. (1987) 'Why Greece melted'. *Geographical Magazine* **59**, 199–203.

Pinol J., Terrada S. and Lloret F. (1998) 'Climate warming, wildlife hazard and wildfire occurrence in coastal eastern Spain'. *Climate Change* **38**, 345–57.

Rotmans J., Hulme, M. and Downing T.E. (1994) 'Climate change implications for Europe'. *Global Environmental Change* **4**, 97–124.

Wheeler D. (1995) 'Majorca's water shortages arouse Spanish passions'. *Geography* **80**, 283–6.

Yeo B. (1882) *Climate and Health Resorts.* Chapman and Hall, London.

14. Sensitivity of tourist destination choice to climate

Wietze Lise and Richard S.J. Tol

INTRODUCTION

Tourism has become the biggest industry in the world, and it is even more important in the Mediterranean. Many tourists find it important to have a high chance of sunny and warm weather at their holiday destination, in order to relax by swimming, sunbathing and sightseeing in foreign places; however, tourists are also deterred by hot and humid conditions. Yet, it is not known just how important climate is for the destination choice of tourists, let alone how tourism behaviour would change with climate. One would expect that currently popular holiday destinations in the Mediterranean would face increased competition from more northerly destinations – as England and Germany, for example, would become more pleasant – and a shift from summer to spring and autumn holidays – as Greek and Spanish summers grow unbearably hot. This chapter is one of the first attempts to quantify the strength of these shifts.

The larger part of the literature on tourist demand (see Crouch, 1995; Lim, 1997; and Witt and Witt, 1995 for surveys) takes the climate of tourists' homes and destinations for granted, focusing on factors such as prices and expenditures, and sociological and psychological considerations. In addition, these studies have a short time horizon, assuming that the climate at the tourist destinations is constant. In the longer term, however, climate is not constant. Climate is expected to change at an accelerating pace due to human activities, particularly fossil fuel combustion (Houghton *et al.*, 1996). The tourism industry is accustomed to rapid change, due to, among other things, political stability, price changes, fashion and social trends. Nevertheless, climate change could have major implications for the tourist industry – for instance by making currently popular areas less attractive and bringing new competitors to the market. This chapter investigates the sensitivity of tourist demand for vacation destinations with respect to climate in order to draw conclusions for the possible impact of climate change in the long term. First, a general picture is obtained of the link between tourist demand and temperature. Next, this general picture is unravelled with a case study of Dutch tourists to study the link between the demand for tourist activities during holiday trips and temperature. Finally, we briefly discuss adaptation of tourist suppliers.

The analysis of this chapter is based on datasets at two levels. At the macro level, time-series on tourist numbers, destinations, and expenditures at the aggregate, national level are readily available from sources such as the OECD (World Bank, the Organization for Economic Cooperation and Development), WDI (World Development Indicators) CD-ROM and national statistical services. Climate data are obtained from various sources, including Cramer and Leemans' and Schlesinger and Williams' global climate data as well as data from tourist guides. In addition, at the micro level, data were purchased from the CVO (Foundation for Continuous Vacation Surveying). The micro-data consist of over 6000 trips by Dutch tourists who were asked for their tourist destination and about their activities during their visit. The data include characteristics such as age, income, total holiday expenditure, departure date, destination-code, travel group-size and duration of stay. These micro-data cover only two years, 1988 and 1992. Because of research budget constraints, we could neither obtain more data nor more recent data. This micro dataset is extended by travel distance and travel cost from the World Wide Web. This chapter assumes that tourists have complete information about the climatic conditions at the travel destination. This assumption is intuitive as tourists are becoming better informed through use of the Internet, and shared experience with friends who have visited their intended travel destination.

The chapter is organized as follows. The second section briefly reviews the literature on tourist demand, and the few studies that look into the relationship between climate and tourism. The chapter then continues with a statistical analysis at two levels. More specifically, the third section analyses international tourist flows, to explore the sensitivity of tourism to climate in general. First, all tourist arrivals are pooled country-wise to study a general global trend. Secondly, eight individual countries of tourist origin and their travel destination are considered to verify the extent to which tourist demand is country-specific. Finally, a more detailed analysis is performed to explore whether the demands of Dutch tourists differ from those of British tourists. The CVO data are studied at the individual level with a factor and regression analysis in the fourth section to study the demand for tourist activities. This section also studies the link between the demand for activities by Dutch tourists and climate change. The fifth section concludes by highlighting the main findings from both the macro and the micro analysis and placing these in the context of global climate change.

292 Climate change and Mediterranean coastal areas

LITERATURE SURVEY

Tourist Demand

The number of studies devoted to tourist demand is vast (Lim, 1997; Martin and Witt, 1989; Smeral and Witt, 1996; and Witt and Witt, 1995) with both a general focus (Bakkal and Scaperlanda, 1991; Divisekera, 1995; Eymann and Ronning, 1997; Hannigan, 1994; Melenberg and Van Soest, 1996; Opperman, 1994; Pack *et al.*, 1995) and with a regional focus, but the impact of climate and climatic change on tourism has received remarkably limited attention. This section focuses on tourist demand alone, to point out which factors other than climate affect the tourist demand.

Witt and Witt (1995) made a survey of empirical research on tourism demand, to conclude that 'it is not possible to build a single model which is appropriate for all origin destination pairs' (Witt and Witt, 1995, p. 469). Their finding is confirmed by Crouch (1995) who concludes from his meta-analysis that tourism demand is indeed situation-specific. The analysis of this chapter confirms this conclusion although, at the same time, some remarkable generalities are found.

Lim (1997) reviewed existing studies on tourism demand which use regression techniques. Most models are linear or log-linear, based on annual time-series data, and mainly include economic variables. The lack of sufficient data is seen as a clear limitation of these models. Usage of yearly data does not capture the volatile character of the tourism sector; even the length of the time-series cannot compensate for this. Alternatively, cross-section data could be used to focus on linkages between tourist choices and economic and climate data, which is the approach taken in the fourth section of this chapter. Ryan (1991) argued that time-series on tourism are susceptible to variations in macroeconomic growth which may lead to heteroscedasticity: in times of recession tourism appears to be income inelastic, while in times of growth tourism becomes income elastic. Ryan (1991) provided a qualitative approach to tourist demand. The choice of a travel destination is a complex process. Tourism is a fast changing industry, which has developed recently and is now globally the biggest industry. Within tourism there are many interlinked processes, such as economic demand and social demand. Psychological factors, such as time availability and the need to escape from the daily routine in an organized versus adventurous manner, also play an important role. Psychological considerations can explain a great deal of recent changes in tourist considerations and are, according to Ryan, the most important aspect for explaining tourism demand. Quantitatively, a factor analysis, which reduces a large set of decision variables into a few distinctive and meaningful variables, can be used to analyse datasets on psychological responses for tourist actions at holiday destinations (see the pooled travel cost model, later).

Climate and Tourism

Within studies on tourist demand, some authors have stressed the need to incorporate climate factors in their analysis. Barry and O'Hagan (1972) studied British tourist expenditure in Ireland and included a weather index in the descriptive variable list, which turns out to be always insignificant.

Syriopoulos and Sinclair (1993) studied the choice of British, German, American, French and Swedish tourists for a destination in a Mediterranean country: Greece, Spain, Portugal, Italy and Turkey, using the AIDS (almost ideal demand system) model. They use time-series for 1960–87 and consider several types of costs. Climate is considered in their model by studying price elasticities between tourists from 'cold' countries to 'warm' countries.

Various authors have looked at the potential impact of climate change on the tourism and recreational industry: UKCCIRG (1991, 1996) qualitatively discussed the impact of climate change on tourism in Great Britain; Mendelsohn and Markowski (1999) and Loomis and Crespi (1999) investigated the impact of climate change on outdoor recreation in the USA; Agnew (1997) looked at the quantitative impacts of weather variability on tourism in the UK; Wall (1988) looked at the impact of climate change on skiing in Canada; and Gable (1997) looked at the implication of climate change and sea level rise for tourism supply in the Caribbean.

To our knowledge, Maddison (2001) is the only quantitative study that looks at tourist demand in the context of climate change. Using a pooled travel-cost model (PTCM), Maddison estimated the importance to British tourists of climate at the holiday destination, and also calculated the change in consumer surplus for certain climate changes. This model is adapted for Dutch tourists in the next section and is compared with his results.

SENSITIVITY OF INTERNATIONAL TOURIST DEMAND TO CLIMATE

This section discusses the sensitivity of destination choices by international tourists to climate. We investigate this relationship using three datasets. The first is crude but covers almost the whole world; the third is very detailed but covers only Dutch tourists; and the second dataset is somewhere in between, covering selected OECD countries in some detail. Our analyses of the three different datasets are necessarily mutually inconsistent; we simply cannot include the same explanatory variables in all regressions. Nonetheless, the analyses are constructed such that climate parts are comparable.

Global Perspective

To study the sensitivity of tourist demand to climate at international level, data from the World Development Indicators CD-ROM (World Bank, 1998) on the total numbers of tourist arrivals and departures per country are used. The origins and destinations of these tourists are, however, not provided. As a result, travel distances and costs are unknown. Nevertheless, these data can be used to estimate which factors are decisive for making a country of destination popular in terms of number of visitors. Climate is represented by temperature and precipitation. We use the average temperature of the warmest month over the last 30 years, using the IIASA database for mean monthly values of temperature on a global terrestrial grid by Leemans and Cramer (1991): the temperature of the capital of a country is assumed to be representative for the entire country. Precipitation is taken from Schlesinger and Williams (1999), who report monthly total rainfall for whole countries; we use the total rainfall over June, July and August – the main OECD tourist season.[1] The crudeness of the analysis is compensated by the fact that there are data for 17 years (1980–96) for 210 countries. All data are pooled together and treated as cross-section data, which gives 1730 observations. The model is estimated with Ordinary Least Squares.[2] The estimated model is:

$$LNARRIVALS = \beta_0 + \beta_1 YEAR + \beta_2 AREA +$$
$$\beta_4 POPDEN + \beta_5 COAST + \beta_6 GDPPC + \beta_7 TW + \quad (14.1)$$
$$\beta_8 TW^2 + \beta_9 PS + \beta_{10} PS^2 + error$$

Table 14.1 defines the variables. The two main climate variables are temperature and precipitation, both in the main tourist season.

The natural logarithm of the number of tourist arrivals is used throughout the chapter, which leads to a considerably higher statistical significance for the explanatory variables than in the case where the number of tourist arrivals is used as an independent variable. The variable *YEAR* is included to filter out all unexplained trends. The variable *AREA* accounts for the possibility that bigger countries can receive more tourists. This is only true in a limited sense, as a lot of tourists can be accommodated in a small place. The variable *COAST* captures the potential for beach holidays. The variable *GDPPC* captures destination price levels as well as tourists' dislike for poverty. *TW* is the climate. Table 14.2 presents the results.

Obviously, we could have added other explanatory variables, such as exchange rates and crime rates. However, such data are hard to interpret. What matters, probably, is the exchange rate at the (unknown) time of booking, and the crime noticed by tourists – for which data are hard to get – rather than the annual average exchange rate or general crime rates – for which data can be obtained. The main interest of this chapter is the estimated climate sensitivity of tourist destination choice, and sensitivity analyses around model (14.1) suggest that we can estimate that with sufficient confidence (see later). Not surprisingly, the explanatory value of the model is low (an R^2 of 0.50). The results are convincing because the (statistically significant) estimates of the parameters of major interest (temperature) are plausible, stable over the sample, and robust to variations in the model specification.

The inclusion of both temperature and temperature-squared implies that there is an optimal summer temperature for tourism. The optimal temperature (T^{opt}) follows from:

$$T^{opt} = \frac{-\beta_7}{2\beta_8} \tag{14.2}$$

Its standard deviation ($\sigma_{T_{opt}}$) is approximated with its first-order Taylor expansion:

$$\sigma^2_{T_{opt}} \approx \frac{1}{4\beta_8^2}\sigma^2_{\beta_7} + \frac{\beta_7^2}{4\beta_8^4}\sigma^2_{\beta_8} - \frac{\beta_7}{2\beta_8^3}\sigma_{\beta_7,\beta_8} \tag{14.3}$$

It turns out that the optimal temperature is about 21°C, with a standard deviation of 3°C; see Table 14.2. This is reasonable given that this is the average over day and night temperatures in the warmest month (TW). The optimal temperature corresponds to the present temperatures found in northern Spain, southern France, northern Italy, the former Yugoslavia and Uganda. The first three are well-known tourist resorts, the former Yugoslavia used to be, and Uganda may become one. Using different climate indices, Maddison's (2001) temperature optimum (for the British) is also found in the European part of the Mediterranean. Tourists prefer dry places over wet ones, but there is no clear optimum amount of rainfall.

The optimal temperature occurs in countries with many beaches. It may be that tourists care more about the presence of the beach than about the climate. The implications of climatic change would then be dramatically different. To test this, we excluded the explanatory variable *COAST* from the regression. The variable *AREA* then becomes significant – there is a high correlation (0.56) between *AREA* and *COAST* – so we also ran regressions with neither *AREA* nor *COAST* and with only *COAST*. Table 14.3 displays the results. It shows that the estimated influence of temperature on international tourist arrivals is independent of whether *AREA* or *COAST*

Table 14.1 Definition of the variables used

Variable	Description	Source
AGE	Average age of the interviewed tourists (years)	*CVO*
AREA	Land surface area per country (km²)	WDI
COAST	Total length of the coast of a destination country (km)	www.wri.org
DIST	Distance (as the crow flies) between capitals (km)	www.indo.com/distance
DUR	Number of days spent on holiday (number)	CVO
GDPPC	Country-wise PPP-based per capita income (US$ per year)	WDI
INCOME	Average income of the interviewed tourists (Dutch guilders per year)	CVO
LN *ARRIVALS*	Natural logarithm of the number of international tourist arrivals per country per year	WDI, OECD, CBS
LNVISITS	Natural logarithm of the number visits to a destination country by a Dutch tourist	CVO
PDAY	Average daily expenditure per person (Dutch guilders per day)	CVO, www.airfair.nl
PERSON	Number of persons travelling	CVO
POP	Total population (number)	WDI
POPDEN	Population density (number per square km)	WDI
Q1	Dummy for the first quarter (winter)	CVO
Q2	Dummy for the second quarter (spring)	CVO
Q3	Dummy for the third quarter (summer)	CVO
PRECIP	Total precipitation in the quarter of travelling (inches per month)	http://traveleshop.com/ menus/weather.shtml
TQ	Average day and night temperature in the quarter of travelling (°C)	Cramer and Leemans
TW	Average day and night temperature of the warmest month (°C)	Schlesinger and Williams
PS	Average cumulative precipitation in June, July and August (cm/summer)	CVO, WDI, IIASA
YEAR	Year of observation	

Table 14.2 Regression results for the global and national tourist destination models[a]

	World	Canada	France	Germany	Italy	Japan	Netherlands	Neth (CVO)	UK	USA
Constant	-1	24*	-18	-117***	-91***	-124***	-70***	11	-90**	28*
	(1)	(22)	(28)	(24)	(25)	(27)	(11)	(101)	(34)	(21)
$YEAR$ 10^{-2}	0.4***	-1.6*	-0.1	5.4***	3.7***	5.7***	2.8***	-0.5	3.9**	-1.5*
	(0.1)	(1.1)	(1.4)	(1.2)	(1.2)	(1.3)	(0.6)	(5.1)	(1.7)	(1.1)
$DIST$ 10^{-4}		-1.3***	-2.5***	-1.5***	-1.5***	-2.4***	-12.1***	-1.5***	-1.4***	-1.9***
		(0.1)	(0.1)	(0.1)	(0.1)	(0.6)	(0.9)	(0.5)	(0.1)	(0.1)
$AREA$ 10^{-7}	0.3*	0.3*	-4.4***	-3.6***	-3.6***	-0.1	4.8***	-0.1	-3.4***	1.6***
	(0.2)	(0.3)	(0.4)	(0.3)	(0.3)	(0.3)	(0.6)	(0.5)	(0.4)	(0.2)
$POPDEN$ 10^{-3}	0.3***	5.0***	-2.8*	-0.4	-0.7	3.4***	3.9***	-0.2	-11.6***	3.2***
	(0.1)	(0.8)	(1.3)	(1.0)	(1.3)	(1.1)	(0.7)	(0.6)	(1.7)	(0.8)
$COAST$ 10^{-5}	7.9***	10.4***	5.7***	4.0***	-1.7*	4.5***	1.5*	-0.2	0.9	5.5***
	(0.8)	(1.1)	(1.1)	(1.1)	(1.2)	(1.5)	(0.9)	(0.7)	(1.5)	(1.6)
$GDPPC$ 10^{-4}	2.1***	67.3***	2.9***	1.6***	2.3***	1.6***	0.8***	1.3***	1.5***	0.4***
	(0.1)	(12.2)	(0.2)	(0.1)	(0.2)	(0.2)	(0.1)	(0.2)	(0.2)	(0.1)
TW	0.44***	1.58***	2.99***	2.01***	2.33***	1.87***	1.93***	0.04	2.28***	1.15***
	(0.04)	(0.10)	(0.16)	(0.10)	(0.09)	(0.10)	(0.21)	(0.05)	(0.14)	(0.09)
TW^2 10^{-2}	-1.04***	-3.44***	-6.84***	-4.36***	-4.81***	-3.98***	-4.0***	0.06	-4.90***	-2.42***
	(0.09)	(0.24)	(0.39)	(0.25)	(0.23)	(0.26)	(0.5)	(0.15)	(0.33)	(0.24)
PS 10^{-1}	-0.08**	1.67***	41.3*	1.26***	2.92***	0.68*	-1.91***		1.03**	2.23***
	(0.03)	(0.02)	(30.9)	(0.28)	(0.32)	(0.56)	(0.39)		(0.37)	(0.23)
PS^2 10^{-3}	0.04*	-3.76***	-2.57***	-4.06***	-7.50***	0.04	4.79***		-2.01***	-3.95***
	(0.03)	(0.39)	(0.55)	(0.50)	(0.59)	(1.63)	(0.86)		(0.66)	(0.40)

(continued overleaf)

Table 14.2 (continued)

	World	Canada	France	Germany	Italy	Japan	Netherlands	Neth (CVO)	UK	USA
# Observations	1686	158	156	170	140	145	376	187	157	159
R^2	0.50	0.95	0.94	0.93	0.96	0.93	0.67	0.54	0.84	0.91

Notes:
[a] Regression of the natural logarithm of the number of arrivals in a country, either from all other countries (world) or from a particular country (Canada to USA).
* P<0.05
** P<0.01
*** P<0.001
Asterisks refer to statistically significant estimates.
Standard deviations are given in brackets.

is used as an explanatory variable. The optimal holiday temperature varies between 20.6°C and 21.1°C, a difference that is not statistically significant. In fact, the correlation between coastal length and temperature is quite low (0.03). Both beaches and a nice climate attract tourists (see Table 14.2).

Table 14.3 Important correlation coefficients in the aggregated dataset

Variables	1988	1992
GDP & *POP*	0.603	0.709
DIST & travel cost	0.777	0.831
TQ & *TQ²*	0.961	0.950

Besides climate, tourists' choices are determined by other factors. The number of arrivals increased significantly over time. Larger countries attract more tourists, but this effect is only barely significant. More densely populated countries attract significantly more tourists; tourists prefer a certain level of provision of services (transport, hotels, museums, etc.) that cannot be found in lightly populated regions. Countries with long coastlines attract significantly more tourists, as do countries with a higher per capita income; the explanation for the latter is that poverty apparently deters tourists, even though holidays in poor countries may be cheap.

Different Countries of Origin

The model described gives a general picture about the sensitivity of tourist demand to climate at the international level for tourists of all origins. It may be, however, that tourists from different nationalities have different tastes for the climate of and the distance to their holiday destination, as is indeed found by Crouch (1995) and Witt and Witt (1995). For verifying the difference in tastes among tourists from different nations, appropriate data are a real constraint. The OECD publishes data on tourist destinations and origins for selected countries. Their 1997 report (OECD, 1997) is used, which has data for the period 1984–95, for destination countries in the OECD from the countries of origin listed in Table 14.4. For the Netherlands, the more detailed Internet database of the Central Bureau of Statistics is used (http://www.cbs.nl), covering 1970 to 1995 and more European countries (the destinations Canada and Japan are added from the OECD data). The data are the total, annual number of, for example, Germans or Italians arriving in, for example, France or the Netherlands. There are many missing observations; some countries report on the basis of residence, others on nationality; and some countries only count visitors whereas others count tourists separately. Such crude data only allow for a simple model to be estimated. As before, the purpose is to test whether there is an optimal temperature by treating the time-series as cross-section data. The estimated model per origin country is:

$$LNARRIVALS = \beta_0 + \beta_1 YEAR + \beta_2 AREA +$$
$$\beta_4 POPDEN + \beta_5 COAST + \beta_6 GDPPC + \beta_7 TW + \qquad (14.4)$$
$$\beta_8 TW^2 + \beta_9 PS + \beta_{10} PS^2 + \beta_{11} DIST + error$$

As before, Table 14.1 defines the variables and Table 14.2 presents the estimated parameters and a summary of the results. The estimated optimal temperatures for the individual countries do not deviate significantly from the world estimate of 21.0°C. The optimal temperature varies between the French who prefer 21.8°C and Italians who prefer 24.2°C at their country of holiday destination. This difference, however, is not significantly different from zero. Standard deviations vary between 2°C and 4°C.

Table 14.4   The countries included in the analysis

Both in 1988 and 1992	Australia, Austria, Belgium, Cyprus, Denmark, Finland, France, Germany, Greece, Indonesia, Ireland, Israel, Italy, Luxembourg, Malta, Morocco, Netherlands, Norway, Poland, Portugal, Romania, Russian Federation, Spain, Sweden, Switzerland, Tunisia, Turkey, United Kingdom
Only in 1988	Bulgaria
Only in 1992	Iceland, New Zealand, Slovenia

If the number of arrivals (rather than its natural logarithm) is used as a dependent variable, the estimated temperature optimum is somewhat different, but not significantly so. In the linear model, however, the temperature optimum for tourists from Canada and Japan cannot be estimated with any accuracy, as the t-statistics of the temperature variables become too low.

Opinions on precipitation are more diverse on precipitation than on temperature. No clearly optimal rainfall can be found for all tourists and those from France, the UK and, particularly, Japan. Dutch tourists apparently prefer rather wet or rather dry conditions: a minimum number of Dutch tourists are found where this is around 20 cm of rain per summer. Tourists of other nationalities have a clear optimum precipitation, ranging from 15 cm/summer for Germans to 28 cm/summer for US citizens. These differences are significant. An optimum amount of rainfall is intuitively plausible, as tourists prefer both sunny weather and a lush vegetation.

The other explanatory variables tell a more diverse story. Tourist numbers significantly increased over time, except for France, where the number of international trips remained constant, and for Canada and the USA, where numbers may have fallen. Distance, or perhaps travel cost, deters tourists. Dutch and US tourists prefer to travel to large countries, Canadians have the same tendency but are largely indifferent, whereas other Europeans prefer to travel to small countries. The Japanese are indifferent. All other things being equal, small countries may attract proportionally more OECD tourists because frequent international travellers prefer to visit as many countries as possible in their life. The findings for North America may be explained by the distance factor; Canadians take holidays in the US, while US Americans travel to Canada. Many Dutch people spend their holidays in nearby Germany. The Japanese are again indifferent. UK and, to a lesser extent, French tourists prefer lightly populated countries (recall that this dataset contains travel within the OECD only), whereas Canadian, Dutch, US and, to a lesser extent, Japanese tourists would rather visit densely populated places. Germans and Italians are indifferent. Tourists of all nationalities prefer to travel to countries with long coastlines, except for the British, who are largely indifferent. The Italians seem to prefer countries with little coast. Tourists of all nationalities prefer to travel to richer countries; this is surprising, as there is little absolute poverty in the OECD; apparently relative poverty deters too, and is stronger than the cost of living effect.

The other explanatory variables do not influence the estimated temperature preferences. Table 14.2 shows the estimated optimum temperature for the full model (14.4) as well as for reduced versions of that. The estimated optima are not significantly different. Table 14.3 shows the results of a further sensitivity analysis, for all tourists only, focusing on area, coastline and precipitation. Also in this case, the estimated optimum temperature is insensitive to the specification of the model.

Since the results of the macro analysis are quite crude, it is useful to undertake a more detailed analysis with micro-data. Therefore, aggregated Dutch micro-data are the basis of the analysis in the next section.

SENSITIVITY OF DUTCH TOURIST ACTIVITIES TO CLIMATE

A Pooled Travel Cost Model (PTCM)

In order to refine the analysis of tourist demand, a PTCM is estimated for the particular case of Dutch tourists. This type of model was chosen to allow a comparison of our results with an earlier study (Maddison, 2001) on tourism demands of British tourists, and to show the difference in tastes of tourists from two different countries for a destination climate. This comparison is made possible by aggregating the CVO dataset into quarterly data per destination. After deleting all destination countries with missing data, excluding the trips from within the country of origin to other parts of the same country (the Netherlands), and by considering four seasons and two years (1988 and 1992), 177 valid observations remain. Table 14.4 gives an exhaustive list of included destination countries. Business trips are excluded from the dataset.

Each destination has a number of climatic characteristics, such as temperature, rainfall and hours of sunshine. Climate data (average daily maximum temperature and precipitation) were obtained from http://traveleshop.com/menus/weather.shtml, a standard source of such data for tourists and tourist operators, comprising 30 year averages over major cities in the world. Climate data are quarterly (January–February–March, April–May–June, July–August–September, October–November–December).

Each destination also has a number of non-climatic characteristics, such as distance and airfare to reach that destination. Following Maddison (2001), the distance between Amsterdam and the capital of the country of destination is based on the great circles distance (see http://www.indo.com/distance/). The CVO data only contain a variable on the total travel expenditure, which are travel costs plus expenditures at the holiday destination. Expenditure at destination is approximated by subtracting the travel cost. The cheapest airfare to a destination is taken as a proxy for the travel cost (see http://www.airfair.nl). We assumed that each person, either travelling in a group or alone, pays the same (minimum) airfare, ignoring travellers who are prepared to pay more for travelling. It also ignores the fact that tourist destinations can also be reached by other modes of transport. Due to the crude fix of the travel costs, it is possible that it can exceed the total expenditure on a holiday. Thereupon, by assumption, the travel cost is calculated in such a way that it never exceeds 80 per cent of the total expenditure on a holiday.

As before, Table 14.4 shows the countries that are included in the analysis, and Table 14.1 defines the variables that are used. The following tourist demand equation is then estimated to find which variables contribute most to the number of tourists a certain country attracts. This model is also known as PTCM. The main limitation of PTCM is that it assumes that all the included descriptive variables are constant over all visited tourist sites:

$$\text{LN}VISITS = \beta_0 + \beta_1 FARE + \beta_2 GDP + \beta_3 POP +$$
$$\beta_4 POPDEN + \beta_5 COAST + \beta_6 PDAY + \beta_7 DIST + \beta_8 TQ + \quad (14.5)$$
$$\beta_9 TQ^2 + \beta_{10} PRECIP + \beta_{11} Q1 + \beta_{12} Q2 + \beta_{13} Q3 + \text{error}$$

Table 14.5   Log-linear regression of climate on the number of visitors in a country: a comparison between Dutch and British tourists

	British tourists (Maddison), 1994	Dutch tourists (CVO), 1988 and 1992
Constant	−8.3	4.1***
	(0.5)	(0.5)
FARE	−5.6***	−0.30**
10^{-2}	(1.0)	(0.12)
GDP	7.3***	0.022***
10^{-4}	(1.5)	(0.004)
POP	1.4**	7.1
10^{-6}	(0.6)	(4.7)
POPDEN	2.0***	1.2
10^{-4}	(0.6)	(6.5)
COAST	1.4***	−0.025***
10^{-3}	(0.3)	(0.007)
PDAY	1.3**	0.85***
10^{-2}	(0.5)	(0.22)
DIST	7.6	19*
10^{-5}	(5.9)	(11)
TQ	0.17***	−0.007
	(0.04)	(0.065)
TQ^2	−3.0***	0.066
10^{-2}	(1.0)	(0.184)
PRECIP	−0.11	11.1
10^{-3}	(0.13)	(9.4)
Q1	0.11	−0.17
	(0.25)	(0.34)
Q2	−0.28	0.17
	(0.24)	(0.37)
Q3	−0.13	0.67
	(0.24)	(0.41)
Optimal TQ	29.3***	
# Observations	305	177
R^2	0.50	0.47

This model is the same as that of Maddison and differs from our previous model (14.4) in the sense that *FARE* and *PRECIP* are not yet included, while *GDP* and *POP* are substituted for *GDPPC*. Tourists are expected to prefer destinations which can be reached at a low travel cost, and where the amount of rain is relatively low. For a further explanation of the included variables in PCTM, we refer to Maddison (2001). Table 14.5 summarizes the main statistics of the estimated equation.

Comparing our results with Maddison (2001), population, population density and temperature have become insignificant, while distance has become positively significant. This indicates that the population, population density and the temperature do not matter for Dutch tourists, while they do matter for British tourists. Further, the regression result indicates that Dutch tourists prefer a longer distance to the holiday destination, while British tourists do not have such a preference. The signs of FARE(−) GDP(+) and PDAY(−) are significant and the same for Dutch and British tourists, while the coastal length is positively correlated for British and negatively correlated for Dutch tourists; a result we also found in the previous subsection. This indicates that Dutch and British tourists prefer to spend their holidays in richer and cheaper countries at a relatively low travel cost.

Behaviour of Dutch Winter and Summer Tourists in 1988 and 1992

The behaviour of Dutch tourists in the summer and winter seasons is examined using a factor analysis on the set of 25 dummy variables concerning the choice of activity during a holiday, to reduce this set into independent activity choices and to indicate the priorities. Factor loadings greater than or equal to 0.5 in absolute terms, are called dominating factors; these factors symbolize the main considerations within a decision (Harman, 1967). When the dominating factor loading is negative the indicator works the other way around. For example, a negative factor loading for using a car means that not using a car is an important consideration. Tables 14.6 and 14.7, respectively, show the dominating factors of each principal component for summer tourists (from May until September) and for winter tourists (from October until April) in 1988 and 1992. The rotated factor matrix is used here to maximize the factor loadings, so that the most likely distinct choice patterns are obtained in each case. A factor analysis helps in determining the main and independent considerations for going on holiday, while comparing a normal winter (1992) with a mild winter (1988) and a normal summer (1988) with a hot summer (1992) gives an indication of the possible impact of climate change. Table 14.8 shows the weather characteristics for these specific years. Table 14.9 shows that the dataset consists of two-thirds of summer tourists. Business trips are excluded from the dataset.

There is great similarity in the behaviour of Dutch summer tourists in 1988 and 1992 – factors 1, 2, 6 and 9 are the same. Hence, in both years the most important activity for Dutch summer tourists is sunbathing. After that, sightseeing has the highest priority. Water sports gets sixth priority, while walking gets ninth priority. There is also great similarity between factors 3, 4 and 7. The third priority is given to leaving the car at home and travelling by another means of transport; in 1988 this is accompanied by a

Table 14.6 Component matrix: choice of Dutch summer tourists

Factor	1988									1992									
	1	2	3	4	5	6	7	8	9	1	2	3	4	5	6	7	8	9	10
1. Touring by car			-x		x							-x							
2. Touring by bicycle					-x														
3. Touring by bus or train			x									x							
4. Touring by excursion steamer																			
5. Going for a walk									x									x	
6. Visiting an amusement or recreation park				x									x						
7. Visiting the zoo or safari park				x									x						
8. Visiting a folkloristic event		x									x								
9. Visiting a monument, old cities or churches		x									x								
10. Visiting a museum		x									x								
11. Eating in a restaurant or bistro																			
12. Visiting a theatre, concert hall or cinema																			x
13. Outing to a café or dancing			x													x			
14. Sunbathing	x									x									
15. Visiting a beach	x									x									
16. Visiting a sauna								x											x
17. Swimming	x									x									
18. Sailing, rowing, canoeing						x									x				
19. Windsurfing						x									x				

(continued overleaf)

Table 14.6 (continued)

Factor	1988									1992									
	1	2	3	4	5	6	7	8	9	1	2	3	4	5	6	7	8	9	10
20. Fishing																			
21. Playing tennis or squash							x							x					
22. Playing miniature golf														x					
23. Playing golf								x											x
24. Horse or pony riding				x													x		
25. Skiing or cross-country skiing							x									x			
Percentage of variance explained:	9.0	7.5	6.0	5.3	4.7	4.5	4.3	4.2	4.1	8.5	7.4	5.9	5.5	4.7	4.5	4.4	4.1	4.1	4.1

Note: Extraction method: principal component analysis. Rotation method: varimax with Kaiser normalization. Dominating factors are displayed as 'x', negative dominance is displayed as '–x'.

Table 14.7 Component matrix: choice of Dutch winter tourists and some factors for all tourists

Factor	1988										1992										All tourists		
	1	2	3	4	5	6	7	8	9	10	1	2	3	4	5	6	7	8	9	10	2	4	7
1. Touring by car						x							x										
2. Touring by bicycle								x											−x				
3. Touring by bus or train	x										x												
4. Touring by excursion steamer																							
5. Going for a walk						−x														x			
6. Visiting an amusement or recreation park										x												x	
7. Visiting the zoo or safari park																						x	
8. Visiting a folkloristic event																						x	
9. Visiting a monument, old cities or churches		x									x	x											
10. Visiting a museum		x									x	x											
11. Eating in a restaurant or bistro				x														x					
12. Visiting a theatre, concert hall or cinema											x												
13. Outing to a café or dancing				x														x					

(continued overleaf)

Table 14.7 (continued)

Factor	1988										1992										All tourists 1992		
	1	2	3	4	5	6	7	8	9	10	1	2	3	4	5	6	7	8	9	10	2	4	7
14. Sunbathing		x									x												
15. Visiting a beach		x									x												
16. Visiting a sauna			x												x								x
17. Swimming			x												x								
18. Sailing, rowing, canoeing							x							x									
19. Windsurfing							x							x									
20. Fishing									x														
21. Playing tennis or squash					x												x						x
22. Playing miniature golf					x																		
23. Playing golf					x												x						
24. Horse or pony riding										x						x							
25. Skiing or cross-country skiing																			x		−x		
Percentage of variance explained	9.7	7.1	5.9	5.2	4.8	4.8	4.7	4.6	4.4	4.0	9.6	8.2	5.8	5.4	5.0	4.8	4.5	4.4	4.3	4.1	7.8	5.2	4.3

Note:
Extraction method: principal component analysis. Rotation method: varimax with Kaiser normalization. Dominating factors are displayed as 'x', negative dominance is displayed as '−x'.

Table 14.8   Weather characteristics in the Netherlands

	Winter	Summer	Year
Sunshine (hours, cumulative)			
1987	143	444	1312
1988	113	447	1293
1991	192	587	1566
1992	172	620	1599
Precipitation (mm, cumulative)			
1987	161	325	927
1988	283	226	887
1991	144	228	716
1992	137	294	957
Temperature (°C, average)			
1987	1.5	15.6	8.9
1988	5.0	15.8	10.3
1991	2.2	16.6	9.5
1992	3.9	17.8	10.5

Table 14.9   Number of observations for winter and summer tourists

Year	Summer tourists	Winter tourists	All tourists	Total dataset
1988	3504 (68%)	1622 (32%)	5126	6659
1992	3763 (67%)	1839 (33%)	5602	6757

café visit. The fourth priority is given to visiting an attraction; in 1988 this is combined with horse riding. The seventh priority is given to skiing; in 1988 this is combined with tennis and in 1992 it is combined with a café visit. The main change in behaviour from 1988 is factor 5 on travelling by car without cycling, which has disappeared in 1992. Instead, tennis and mini-golf are given fifth priority in 1992. Finally, the combination of factor 8 in 1988 (golf and sauna) resembles factor 10 in 1992 (with visits of theatres added). Hence, the behaviour of summer tourists does not change much between a hot summer (1992) and a normal summer (1988). This indicates for both years that sunbathing, sightseeing and travelling are the three most important activities during a holiday for Dutch tourists. That the effect of Dutch summer weather on tourists is limited can also be demonstrated by data on total tourist numbers (domestic and abroad) for the period 1969–95. These data suggest that a summer which is 1°C warmer than average increases the number of domestic holidays in the same year by 4.7 per cent (standard deviation 2.2 per cent), and increases the number of foreign holidays in the following year by 3.1 per cent (standard deviation 1.5 per cent) (Tol *et al.*, 1999). There are two possible explanations for this. First, Dutch tourists may expect a bad summer to follow a good one. This mistrust is unwarranted, as the correlation coefficient between successive summers is positive at 0.52. CBS (1993) finds that snowfall in popular ski-resorts in this season is a good predictor for next season's visitor numbers. An alternative explanation is that the money saved on a cheap domestic holiday for this year is spent on a more expensive foreign trip next year.

While tourist activities in summer are not very sensitive to weather conditions, activities of winter tourists are. They have just one factor that fully corresponds in both years: tourists who go for warmer weather during the winter season (factor 2 on sunbathing). A striking result is the change in the first factor. In 1988, this is dominated by visiting a monument or a museum, but in 1992, the first factor contains the same indicators, but with the addition of travelling by public transport and visiting a theatre. This means that travelling in winter is becoming more packed, combining more and more activities into a holiday. From Table 14.7 it can be seen that a number of factors appear in both 1988 and 1992, but with different priorities, for instance:

- Factor 3 in 1988 resembles factor 5 in 1992 (visiting a sauna, swimming).
- Factor 4 in 1988 resembles factor 8 in 1992 (out in the city: visiting a restaurant or café).
- Factor 5 in 1988 (tennis, mini-golf, golf) almost resembles factor 7 in 1992 (tennis, golf).
- Factor 7 in 1988 resembles factor 4 in 1992 (sailing, windsurfing).

Finally, factor 6 (driving the car and no walking), factor 8 (cycling), factor 9 (fishing) and factor 10 (visiting an amusement or recreation park, horse riding) in 1988 have been interchanged by factor 3 (car driving), factor 6 (horse riding), factor 9 (no cycling, skiing) and factor 10 (walking).

Sensitivity of Dutch Tourist Activities to Other Factors

To obtain the sensitivity of the choice of activity during a holiday to climate variability and other variables, the calculated factors of the last subsection can be used for a regression analysis on the total dataset. As a first step in a regression analysis, an appropriate dependent variable needs to be chosen. There are many possibilities for that (Hsieh and O'Leary, 1997; Mendelsohn and Markowski, 1999):

- activities during a holiday;
- destination (home/abroad, hot/warm/medium/cold);
- duration of the holiday;
- number of visits; or
- cost of stay.

In order to establish a logical link with the last subsection, the first variable is most meaningful. This dependent variable gives the driving factors behind tourist activities during a holiday, where the sensitivity to climate variability can be studied as well.

As a second step in a regression analysis, consider the descriptive variables to be included. As before, the CVO dataset is used, altered by information from other sources in order to study the sensitivity of tourist activities to climate. Thereupon, the square of temperature is included in the variable list to find a significant estimate for both coefficients, so that the optimal temperature can be derived.

Given the available data it is possible to estimate the following ordinary linear regression model:

$$\text{Factor } i = \beta_0 + \beta_1 TQ + \beta_2 TQ^2 + \beta_3 PRECIP + \beta_4 SUN +$$
$$\beta_5 PDAY + \beta_6 DIST + \beta_7 DUR + \beta_8 PERSON + \qquad (14.4a)$$
$$\beta_9 INCOME + \beta_{10} AGE + \text{error}$$

Initially, this equation is estimated for nine to ten different factors, for summer, winter and all tourists, and for 1988 and 1992; in total, 57 regressions (Lise and Tol, 1999). In order to have a manageable number of regressions, only those cases where β_1 and β_2 are statistically significant are presented. Table 14.10 shows the results, where the adjusted R^2 is quite low in each case. However, when the t-statistics are significant, the result can still be treated meaningfully.

Equation (14.4a) contains three climatic variables and six socio-economic variables. Let us first interpret the signs of the socio-economic variables. The coefficient for *AGE* is generally negative, except for sightseeing. This indicates that all considered activities are preferred by younger people except for sightseeing. While this pattern holds for the 57 regressions, mentioned, it is also confirmed by Table 14.10. The positive signs for *DIST* and *DUR* indicate that tourists who go further away for a longer time undertake more activities. The significant estimates for *PDAY* indicate that the daily expenditure is low for car-travellers and high for travellers who go out in the city and play tennis/use the sauna.

While the optimal temperatures are almost constant for the country-wise tourists flows, more variation is found when tourist activities are considered; see Table 14.10. Clearly, sporting activities (sailing, windsurfing, horse riding

Table 14.10 Regression results for the micro model for choice of holiday activity in 1992[a]

	Winter tourists					All tourists	
Meaning of factor	Factor 3: Car driving	Factor 4: Sailing, surfing	Factor 6: Horse riding	Factor 8: Outing in city	Factor 2: Sight-seeing, no skiing	Factor 4: Visit attraction	Factor 7: Tennis, sauna
Constant	-3.3 (0.6)	-2.1 (0.6)	-1.8 (0.7)	-1.4 (0.7)	-5.7 (0.4)	-1.4 (0.4)	0.60 (0.36)
TQ	0.12 (0.02)	0.059 (0.018)	0.058 (0.020)	0.042 (0.020)	0.19 (0.01)	0.035 (0.011)	0.023 (0.010)
TQ^2	-0.0025 (0.0007)	-0.0028 (0.0008)	-0.0028 (0.0009)	-0.0025 (0.0009)	-0.0037 (0.0004)	-0.00088 (0.00036)	-0.0011 (0.0003)
PRECIP			-0.057 (0.032)	-0.10 (0.03)	-0.12 (0.02)	0.10 (0.01)	
SUN	-0.12 (0.02)				-0.17 (0.02)		
PDAY	-0.0014 (0.0004)			0.0026 (0.0004)			0.00085 (0.00024)
DIST		0.00028 (0.00002)	0.00017 (0.00003)	9.6E-05 (2.7E-05)	5.60E-05 (1.7E-05)		
DUR					0.021 (0.002)	0.014 (0.002)	0.0077 (0.0024)
PERSON	-0.016 (0.003)				-0.013 (0.002)		0.0073 (0.0025)
INCOME	4.3E-06 (1.8E-06)				4.2E-06 (1.0E-06)		-2.2E-06 (1.1E-06)

AGE		−0.0050 (0.0013)	−0.0058 (0.0014)	−0.0040 (0.0014)	0.0079 (0.0007)	−0.0081 (0.0008)	−0.0075 (0.0008)
Optimal TQ	24.1 (4.4)	10.5 (4.3)	10.4 (0.9)	8.6 (1.4)	24.8 (1.3)	20.1 (2.8)	10.2 (1.7)
# Observations	1310	1310	1310	1310	4301	4301	4301
Adjusted R^2	0.08	0.12	0.04	0.04	0.13	0.06	0.03

Note: [a] Regression on holiday activity as expressed by a factor. Standard deviations are given in brackets.

and tennis) are preferably undertaken in cold weather ($TQ^{opt} \approx 10°C$). There is a great difference in optimal temperatures between similar activities, namely an outing in the city (9°C), visiting an attraction park (20°C) and sightseeing (25°C). This low temperature for outing in the city is clearly caused by a sole focus on winter tourists. An optimal temperature of 24°C for winter tourists is more difficult to explain, but it indicates that car driving is preferred under as high as possible a temperature, as there are only two tourist destinations with temperatures above 24°C, namely Australia (25°C) and Indonesia (31°C). Most activities are more likely to take place with lower amounts of rain, except for indoor activities such as visiting a monument or a museum. The negative sign for the number of sun hours for car driving and sightseeing shows that these activities are preferred in milder climates.

DISCUSSION AND CONCLUSIONS

This chapter concludes that climate is an important consideration for tourists' choice of destination. This should not surprise anyone. However, it also finds that climate matters in a *regular* way that can be *quantified*. We find that an average temperature of about 21°C is the ideal for the large bulk of international tourists, and this preference is largely independent of the tourists' origin.

However, only the broad patterns are regular, not the details. We find small differences in behaviour of Dutch tourists from 1988 to 1992. These may be random, shifts in preferences, or due to differences in weather in these two years. Age and income are important explanatory variables, suggestive of significant trends in the behaviour of Dutch tourists. However, the limitations of the data do not allow further exploration. The factor and regression analyses show that different dominant holiday activities imply different preferences for holiday climates (or, perhaps, vice versa). Younger and richer people do different things during their vacations than do older and poorer tourists. This suggests that preferences for climates at tourist destinations differ between particular age and income groups. It also suggests that, however regular the macro preferences may be at present, there is little reason to assume that future aggregate preferences will resemble current aggregate preferences. One cannot substitute the spatial climate gradient with a temporal climate gradient.

Assessing future aggregate preferences would require quite detailed projections. Obviously, the micro study reported here would need to be replicated for more years and many more countries. In that process, other relevant climate indicators should be included as well to get a more complete picture of the sensitivity of tourist demand to climate change.

This study suggests that people's preferred vacation activities are largely independent of climate. Instead, people select a climate that suits their holiday plans. A gradual warming would thus induce tourists to seek different holiday destinations, or travel at different times during the year. Climate change is likely to lead to drastic changes in tourist behaviour.

However, the tourists probably do not care much – they substitute one destination for another, or one travel date for another. This substitution would keep holiday budget and holiday pleasure largely unchanged, that is, as long as they were otherwise unconstrained.

Some people have the freedom to take a holiday whenever they want, but others do not, and the ratio between the two will be different in the future. Vacation periods are often tied to seasons of the home climate, national and school holidays, and agreements at work. Changes in economic structure, demography, and air-conditioning could loosen these ties. Because of this, and the reasons indicated, it is very hard to predict changes in tourist behaviour due to climate change.

Whereas tourists can readily change their behaviour if the climate changes, suppliers of tourism services cannot always do so. Tour operators can rapidly change their product. It does not matter much whether they sell a ticket to A or to B. The competition in the tourist sector is such that the profit margins are low anyway. Competition also guarantees that novel consumer preferences, because of climate change or otherwise, are rapidly catered for. Owners of hotels and resorts are less flexible. However, the tourist industry changes so fast that most investments have a very short pay-back period. Currently, the tourist industry consists of many small and medium-size players. However, consolidation is ongoing, including vertical integration (e.g. travel agencies operating aircraft and hotels). This would reduce the flexibility of the sector as a whole, but would probably lead to an increase in professionalism. The impact on vulnerability is unclear (Agnew and Palutikof, 1999).

Although tourists and tourist operators are adaptable enough to cope with climate change, the same cannot be said of local providers of tourist services and local economies dependent on tourism revenues. They would see the attractiveness of their region to tourists change beyond their control. Some would benefit and some would lose, but local losses may be dramatic, particularly in regions with few alternatives and a culture of immobility. The tourism peak may shift away from the peak in the supply of temporary workers.

In sum, climate change will alter tourism, but predictability is limited. For tourists and tourist operators, the changes are changes in behaviour rather than in welfare or profits. For local tourism suppliers, the impact of climate change is distributional, with large winners but large losers as well.

NOTES

With kind permission of Kluwer Academic Publishers, authors republish in this book a part of their article, impact of climate on tourist demand, appearing in *Climatic Change* **55**(4): 429–449, © 2002 Kluwer Academic Publishers. Printed in the Netherlands. Financial support by the European Commission, Directorate-General XII (ENV4-CT97-0448) and the National Science Foundation through the Center for Integrated Study of the Human Dimensions of Global Change (SBR-9521914) is gratefully acknowledged. Comments of Peter Mulder, Xander Olsthoorn, Kees Dorland and attendants during presentations at Delhi School of Economics, University of Delhi, India, 5 August 1999, at the European Course in Advanced Statistics, Garpenberg, Sweden, 5–10 September 1999, and the EMF Climate Change Impact and Integrated Assessment Workshop, Snowmass, CO, USA, 26 July–4 August 2000, helped to improve the chapter. Remaining errors are the authors'.

1. Climate variables for other periods (e.g. annual average temperature or precipitation, temperature of the coldest month) do not explain tourism behaviour as well. Tourists can be expected to care only about the climate of their destination during their holidays.
2. The data could also, perhaps should be treated as panel data. It may be that, in addition to the explanatory variables, there are country-specific random effects. However, the model is already richly specified, particularly compared with the number of observations in the next subsection. Using standard OLS in lieu of panel data technique implies efficiency loss, but no bias. The standard errors of the estimated parameters are small enough with OLS to interpret the results. The standard errors are corrected for heteroskedasticity using the method of White (1980).

REFERENCES

Agnew, M.D. (1997), 'Tourism', in J.P. Palutikof, S. Subak and M.D. Agnew (eds), *Economic Impacts of the Hot Summer and Unusually Warm Year of 1995*, pp. 139–148, University of East Anglia, Norwich.

Agnew, M.D. and Palutikof, J.P. (1999), *Workshop on Economic and Social Impacts of Climate Extremes: Risks and Benefits*, Climate Research Unit, University of East Anglia.

Bakkal, I. and Scaperlanda, A. (1991), 'Characteristics of US Demand for European Tourism: A Translog Approach', *Weltwirtschaftliches Archiv*, **127**(1): 119–137.

Barry, K. and O'Hagan, J. (1972), 'An econometric study of British tourist expenditure in Ireland', *Economics and Social Review*, **3**(2): 143–161.

CBS (1993), *Nederlanders op Wintersport 1978–1992*, 1993–20, Central Bureau of Statistics (CBS), The Hague.

Crouch, G.I. (1995), 'A meta-analysis of tourism demand', *Annals of Tourism Research*, **22**(1): 103–118.

Divisekera, S. (1995), 'An econometric model of international visitor flows to Australia', *Australian Economic Papers*, **34**(65): 291–308.

Eymann, A. and Ronning, G. (1997), 'Microeconometric models of tourists' destination choice', *Regional Science and Urban Economics*, **27**: 735–761.

Gable, F.J. (1997), 'Climate change impacts on Caribbean coastal areas and tourism', *Journal of Coastal Research*, **27**: 49–70.

Hannigan, K. (1994), 'A regional analysis of tourism growth in Ireland', *Regional Studies*, **28**(2): 208–214.

Harman, H.H. (1967), *Modern Factor Analysis*, University of Chicago Press, Chicago.

Houghton, J.T., Meiro Filho, L.G., Callander, B.A., Harris, N., Kattenberg, A. and Maskell, K. (eds) (1996), *Climate Change 1995: The Science of Climate Change – Contribution of Working Group I to the Second Assessment Report of the Intergovernmenal Panel on Climate Change*, Cambridge University Press, Cambridge.

Hsieh, S. and O'Leary, J.T. (1997), 'An investigation of factors influencing the decision to travel', in E. Laws, B. Faulkner and G. Moscardo (eds), *Embracing and Managing Change in Tourism – International Case Studies*, pp. 398–414, Routledge, London.

Leemans, R. and Cramer, W.P. (1991), *The IIASA Database for Mean Monthly Values of Temperature, Precipitation and Cloudiness on a Global Terrestrial Grid*, RR-91-18, International Institute for Applied Systems Analysis, Laxenburg.

Lim, C. (1997), 'Review of international tourism demand models', *Annals of Tourism Research*, **24**(4): 835–849.

Lise, W. and Tol, R.S.J. (1999), *On the Impact of Climate on Tourist Destination Choice*, Working Paper W-99/30, Institute for Environmental Studies, Amsterdam.

Loomis, J.B. and Crespi, J. (1999), 'Estimated effects of climate change on use and benefits of selected outdoor recreation activities in the United States', in R.O. Mendelsohn and J.E. Neumann (eds), *The Impact of Climate Change on the United States Economy*, pp. 289–314, Cambridge University Press, Cambridge.

Maddison, D.J. (2001), 'In search of warmer climates: the impact of climate change on flows of British tourists', in D.J. Maddison, *The Amenity Value of Global Climate*, Earthscan, London.

Martin, C.A. and Witt, S.F. (1989), 'Forecasting tourism demand: a comparison of the accuracy of several quantitative methods', *International Journal of Forecasting*, **5**: 7–19.

Melenberg, B. and Van Soest, A. (1996), 'Parametric and semi-parametric modelling of vacation expenditures', *Journal of Applied Econometrics*, **11**: 59–76.

Mendelsohn, R.O. and Markowski, M. (1999), 'The impact of climate change on outdoor recreation', in R.O. Mendelsohn and J.E. Neumann (eds), *The Impact of Climate Change on the United States Economy*, pp. 267–288, Cambridge University Press, Cambridge.

OECD (1997), *Tourism Policy and International Tourism in OECD Countries*, OCDE/GD(97)173, Organisation for Economic Cooperation and Development, Paris.

Opperman, M. (1994), 'Regional aspects of tourism in New Zealand', *Regional Studies*, **28**(2): 155–167.

Pack, A., Clewer, A. and Sinclair, M.T. (1995), 'Regional concentration and dispersal of tourism demand in the UK', *Regional Studies*, **29**(6): 570–576.

Ryan, C. (1991), *Recreational Tourism: A Social Science Perspective*, International Thomson Business Press, London.

Schlesinger, M.E. and L.J. Williams (1999), COSMIC – COuntry Specific Model for Intertemporal Climate (CD), Electric Power Research Institute, Palo Alto.

Smeral, E. and Witt, S.F. (1996), 'Econometric forecasts of tourism demand to 2005', *Annals of Tourism Research*, **23**(4): 891–907.

Syriopoulos, T.C. and Sinclair, M.T. (1993), 'An econometric study of tourism demand: the AIDS model of US and European tourism in Mediterranean countries', *Applied Economics*, **25**: 1541–1552.

Tol, R.S.J., Dorland, C., Lise, W., Olsthoorn, A.A. and Spaninks, F.A. (1999),

Weather Impacts on Natural, Social and Economic Systems in the Netherlands, Institute for Environmental Studies, Vrije Universiteit, Amsterdam.

UKCCIRG (1991), *The Potential Effects of Climate Change in the United Kingdom*, United Kingdom Climate Change Impacts Review Group (UKCCIRG), First Report, prepared at the request of the Department of Environment, HMSO, London.

UKCCIRG (1996), *Review of the Potential Effects of Climate Change in the United Kingdom*, United Kingdom Climate Change Impacts Review Group (UKCCIRG), Second Report, prepared at the request of the Department of Environment, HMSO, London.

Wall, G. (1988), *Implications of Climate Change for Tourism and Recreation in Ontario*, CCD 88-05, Environment Canada, Downsview.

White, H. (1980), 'A heteroskedasticity-consistent covariance matrix estimator and a direct test for heteroskedasticity', *Econometrica* **48**: 817–838.

Witt, S.F. and Witt, C.A. (1995), 'Forecasting tourism demand: a review of empirical research', *International Journal of Forecasting*, **11**: 447–475.

World Bank (1998), *World Bank Development Indicators CD-ROM*, World Bank, Washington, DC.

Index